Poverty and Shame

Global Experiences

Edited by
Elaine Chase and Grace Bantebya-Kyomuhendo

OXFORD
UNIVERSITY PRESS

OXFORD
UNIVERSITY PRESS

Great Clarendon Street, Oxford, OX2 6DP,
United Kingdom

Oxford University Press is a department of the University of Oxford.
It furthers the University's objective of excellence in research, scholarship,
and education by publishing worldwide. Oxford is a registered trade mark of
Oxford University Press in the UK and in certain other countries

Published in the United States of America by Oxford University Press
198 Madison Avenue, New York, NY 10016, United States of America

British Library Cataloguing in Publication Data
Data available

Library of Congress Control Number: 2014939951

ISBN 978–0–19–968672–8

Printed in Great Britain by
CPI Group (UK) Ltd, Croydon, CR0 4YY

Acknowledgements

This book was very much a collaborative effort. The detailed evidence presented derives from research funded by the United Kingdom Economic and Social Research Council and the Department for International Development under the ESRC-DFID Joint Fund for Poverty Alleviation Research (grant number RES-167-25-0557). This research was intensely collaborative involving a group of scholars who worked together to secure funding and then to collect and analyse the many kinds of information that make this book possible: Sohail Choudhry, Erika Gubrium, Ivar Lødemel, JO Yongmie (Nicola), Leemamol Mathew, Amon Mwiine, Sony Pellissery, YAN Ming with Frederick Golooba-Mutebi, Sattwick Dey Biswas, and Monimala Sengupta.

Above all we want to thank the people with direct experience of poverty and others living in the same communities in China, India, Norway, Pakistan, South Korean, Uganda, and Britain who gave of their time to be interviewed and to share experiences that provide the core content of this collective work. Others whose thoughts have been invaluable and influential as the work developed include members of the project advisory group chaired by Lutz Leisering: Jimi Adesina, Jo Boyden, Charlotte Heath, June Tangney, and Timo Voipio; participants in a seminar held in Oxford in 2012 to reflect on the early findings: David Campbell, Mike Daly, Amelia Gentleman, Joanne Green, Krzysztof Hagemejer, Sophia Ireland, Sian Jones, Dann Kenningham, Kornelia Kozovzka, Helen Longworth, Gareth Matthews, Kate Lloyd Morgan, Maeve Regan, Ehtasham Sarwar, Magdalena Sepulveda, Deborah Shipley, Bedreldin Shutta, Yasmin Sidhwa, Diana Skelton, Nicola Smith, Jane Stephenson, Brian Woods, and Ruslan Yemstov; policymakers and practitioners who engaged with the study in Oslo (in 2010 and 2011), Anand (in 2011), Beijing (in 2012), and Kampala (in 2012) who are too numerous to mention by name but no less important for that.

We also wish to thank students and colleagues within and outside of our respective universities who have supported and encouraged the project throughout. In particular: Rosemary Akinyi, Nick Bailey, Fabrizio Barca, Ben Baumberg, Christina Behrendt, Fran Bennett, James Cateridge, Guillaume Charvon, CHEN Yanyan, Michael Cichon, Brendan Coyne, Mary Daly, Susie Devins, Cristina Diez, Paul Dornan, Eldin Fahmy, Donna Friedman, Declan

Gaffney, Xavier Godinot David Gordon, Chris Goulden, Julia Griggs, HAN Xiao, Mary Hardwick, Dann Kenningham, Kate Legge, Sophie Lendon, David Levy, Ruth Lister, Mattias Lundberg, Carol Matiko, Simon Pembleton, Maria Ogando Portela, Kei Takahashi, Katherine Trebeck, Thierry Viard, and YAN Haiying. Finally, it goes without saying that our huge thanks go to Robert Walker who led this project from the outset and steered it to its fruition.

Contents

Contents

Preface

Poverty is not just a lack of income, wealth, and assets. Rather it is the multiple consequences of this lack that are experienced simultaneously by people in poverty. Moreover, some of these consequences in later times serve to prolong poverty and thus become the causes, if not of poverty per se, then of its perpetuation.

One such consequence of poverty is shame. The Nobel Laureate, Amartya Sen, has argued that shame lies at the absolutist core of poverty; by implication it is an attribute of poverty that is experienced by individuals, families, and communities everywhere. While the research presented in this book does not provide definitive proof of Sen's universalistic assertion, it offers strong evidence that is consistent with it. Shame is shown to be part of the lived experience of poverty, albeit culturally nuanced, in settings as different in terms of economic development and cultural legacy as rural Uganda and India; urban China, Pakistan, South Korea, and the United Kingdom; and small-town and urban Norway. And the suggestion is that this may long have been so. Oral traditions in Uganda and India reveal traces of shame that are similarly reflected in the classic literatures of each country and more recently in the medium of film. It is also possible that the shame associated with poverty is increasingly intensifying as cultures worldwide become more individualistic, and conspicuous consumerism comes to be the dominant expression of social status.

But why is shame important? First, because it is painful and persistent. Everybody has felt ashamed on occasion and knows how hurtful it can be. Psychologists have talked of a psychic scar that refuses to heal. Imagine what shame must be like if it is experienced every day and is caused by something over which one has little or no control. In this, shame differs profoundly from guilt. Guilt arises from things one has done and can be assuaged by a change of behaviour. Shame, on the other hand, appertains to who one is and to what one has become. Moreover, shame, while internally felt, is externally imposed by others: by the people one knows; the officials that one encounters; and by the politicians one hears who help to shape public opinion.

Shame is important because of its medium- and longer-term consequences. Individuals respond to the shame associated with poverty in various ways.

They keep up appearances and pretend that everything is normal, which means living with the fear of being found out or shown up; it risks, too, overextending on finances and incurring bad debts. People in poverty typically reduce social contact to avoid experiencing situations in which they are exposed to shame, but as a result lose the protection borne from the potential for reciprocity when times are particularly harsh. Sometimes shame drives people into clinical depression, to substance abuse, and even to suicide. Shame divides society, the public rhetoric of deserving and undeserving reinforcing the gaps between rich and poor and causing people in poverty to suspect their equals of dishonesty and depravity. Shame saps self-esteem, erodes social capital, and diminishes personal efficacy, raising the possibility that it serves also to perpetuate poverty by reducing individuals' ability to help themselves.

This volume demonstrates that the same experiences of shame are associated with poverty in very disparate settings, despite using diverse local definitions of poverty with different material consequences. This observation points to the validity of relative notions of poverty in which poverty lines are set in relation to local living standards. It also offers the prospect of engaging in a meaningful global debate about poverty that simultaneously embraces people affected by poverty in the rich global North and in much less prosperous countries clustered in the global South. Poverty feels the same to people experiencing it irrespective of its material manifestations. Moreover, the shame associated with poverty brings with it many of the same deleterious consequences.

Yet the shame experienced as a result of being in poverty is not solely an individual problem. It is imposed by society, with overwhelmingly detrimental personal and social consequences. But, importantly, given the political will, it can also be readily addressed by society at minimal expense. The third section of this volume establishes the validity of reports by people in poverty that they are made to feel ashamed by those who are more affluent. This happens because individuals who are more prosperous dismiss people in poverty as being worthless and lazy. The latter are casually exploited as cheap labour and consistently blamed for the failures of the state and the weakness of the economy. The affluent have a vested interest in perpetuating poverty to the extent that it reduces living costs, while a strong attachment to the work ethic and the value of meritocracy, often echoed by popular press and politicians, provides apparent justification for their own material success.

Shame is evident in the framing, structure, and delivery of anti-poverty programmes in each of the seven study countries, albeit manifest in a variety of ways. (The evidence for this is provided by Gubrium, Pellissery and Lødemel, 2013.) Sometimes the imposition of shame in the form of stigma is justified by policymakers and supported by popular opinion. Both naming and shaming, and blaming and shaming are commonly thought to be effective ways of policing access to welfare benefits and changing and regulating anti-social and self-destructive behaviour. However, such beliefs are based on two false assumptions, as is discussed in the companion volume *The Poverty of Shame*, also published by Oxford University Press. Firstly, poverty is overwhelmingly a structural phenomenon caused by factors beyond individual control relating to the workings of the economy, the mix of factors of production, and the outcome of primary and secondary resource allocation. It is not primarily the result of individual inadequacy or personal failings. Secondly, the scientific evidence powerfully demonstrates that shaming generally does not lead to constructive behavioural change even in situations where change would be possible. Rather, shame merely imposes personal pain that triggers the counterproductive individual and social consequences noted above and explained in detail in this groundbreaking volume.

So why has so little attention been paid to shame associated with poverty if it is so important? One possible reason is that shame is itself elusive. It masquerades under different names: embarrassment; loss of face; feeling flustered; stigma; humiliation; and, even, guilt. To admit to feeling ashamed is often itself shameful. Furthermore, various academic disciplines have prioritized different names and expressions of shame, and few scholars, even in psychology and sociology, have sought to provide a comprehensive overview. Albeit focused on poverty-related shame, an important contribution of the current volume is that it systematically documents the expression and personal and social consequences of shame in contrasting cultural settings.

Another reason why poverty-related shame has been neglected is that global scientific and policy attention has been focused elsewhere. The Millennium Development Goals drew attention to the importance of tackling poverty globally and to the importance of being able to measure progress. Measures based on income and expenditure were comparatively simple to implement and only latterly has the multidimensional nature of poverty come to be appreciated and the importance of the so-called 'subjective' dimensions been recognized. While this volume does not offer direct measures of poverty-related shame, it provides the strongest possible case for developing them and, indeed, such measures have already been developed based on the research and used effectively to demonstrate its prevalence in the United Kingdom (Bailey et al., 2013).

But while policymakers and researchers may hitherto have underplayed the salience of shame, people with direct experience of poverty have repeatedly underlined its importance when given the opportunity to do so. ATD Fourth World is an international, non-governmental organization committed to facilitating the voices of people in poverty being heard. Global participation by people with direct experience of poverty caused the organization to recognize poverty as violence (ATD Fourth World, 2013a). One participant, a mother from Peru, spoke for many when she said that 'the worst thing about living in extreme poverty is the contempt...experienced...every day; it hurts us, humiliates us and makes us live in fear and shame' (ATD Fourth World, 2013b, p. 6). Another, Jose Nuñez (2014), a father living with his wife and two children in a homeless hostel in New York, speaking before the United Nations' Commission for Social Development in February 2014, first illustrated the stigmatizing nature of welfare policies in the United States: obtaining shelter is 'literally like you are walking into prison'. He then outlined an appropriate policy response:

> Good programs need to treat people like human beings. They need to treat people with empathy. The offices and the staff should put themselves in other people's shoes. They should take the time to ask how you are, to build a personal relationship, and treat you with kindness. We don't need to be babied or carried, much less demeaned. We just need a push and some support. Somebody persistent and committed, who's going to remember your name and pick up your calls. People need meaning in their lives. That's part of the problem in communities of poverty—people feel like they don't matter, that they don't have a voice. We have to find ways to build meaning for people if they are going to have success in life. (Nuñez, 2014)

This volume systemically demonstrates that such experiences and views are not exceptional but, largely irrespective of culture, constitute what it means to live in poverty. It illustrates, too, how even small changes in policy could result in disproportionate improvements in people's lives. This is not to say that treating people with respect is all that needs to be done. Rather it is the very least that should be done.

Research is a collective venture. The contributors to this volume are members of a research team that it has been my privilege to lead. They have, in turn, drawn on the work of hundreds of scholars and, as importantly, listened to the voices of hundreds of adults and children with direct experience of poverty and others prepared to give of their time to share their views on the nature and causes of poverty. The resultant findings, skilfully assembled by the editors, previewed above and synthesized in the companion volume *The Shame of Poverty*, take the reader into the lives of real people and expose poverty for what it is, a shameful and festering wound that scars lives and entire societies. Moreover, it is a wound that each of us deepens day by day with careless and cruel words and through thoughtless and self-serving behaviour.

Robert Walker
New York
February 2014

List of Figures

List of Tables

List of Contributors

Bantebya-Kyomuhendo, Grace, Professor, School of Women and Gender Studies, Makerere University, Kampala, Uganda

Chase, Elaine, Research Fellow, Department of Social Policy and Intervention and Green Templeton College, University of Oxford

Choudhry, Sohail Anwar, Lead Researcher, Pakistan, for global Poverty and Shame Project, University of Oxford

Gubrium, Erika, Assistant Professor, Oslo, and Akershus University College, Norway

Lødemel, Ivar, Professor of Social Sciences, Oslo, and Akershus University College, Norway

Mathew, Leemamol, Consultant Psychologist, Department of Psychology, Bangalore University

Mwiine, Amon Ashaba, Assistant Lecturer, School of Women and Gender Studies, Makerere University, Kampala, Uganda

Nicola Jo, Yongmie, Research Assistant and DPhil Student, Department of Social Policy and Intervention, University of Oxford

Pellissery, Sony, Associate Professor of Public Policy, National Law School of India University, Bangalore, India

Walker, Robert, Professor of Social Policy, Department of Social Policy and Intervention, University of Oxford

Yan, Ming, Professor, Institute of Sociology and Center for Social Policy Studies, *Chinese Academy of Social Sciences, Beijing*

References

ATD Fourth World (2013a) *Ending the violence of extreme poverty—a must for sustainable societies*; Pierrelaye: International Movement ATD Fourth World; <http://www.atd-fourthworld.org/IMG/pdf/rio_updated_proposals.pdf>.

ATD Fourth World (2013b) *Towards Sustainable Development that Leave No One Behind: The challenge of the post-2015 agenda*, New York: International ATD Fourth World Movement.

Bailey, N., Besemer, K., Bramley, G. and Livingston, M. (2013) *How Neighbourhood Context Shapes Poverty: some results from the Poverty and Social Exclusion UK Survey 2012*, Paper presented to the 'Poverty Neighbourhoods' workshop, European Network for Housing Research conference, Tarragona, 19–22 June.

Gubrium, E., Pellissery, S., and Lødemel, I. (2013) *The Shame of It: Global perspectives on anti-poverty policies*, Bristol: Policy Press.

Nuñez, J. (2014) *Statement to the Civil Society Forum*, Fifty Second Session of the United Nations Commission for Social Development, New York, 10 February 2014.

1

Introduction

Elaine Chase and Grace Bantebya-Kyomuhendo

Poverty and Shame: Global Experiences draws on substantive empirical evidence to demonstrate how paying greater attention to the psychological and social consequences of poverty provides new insights into how poverty is perpetuated. It reveals how, irrespective of whether people live above or below a designated poverty line, in cultures as diverse as rural India and Uganda and Pakistan, urban/suburban UK, Pakistan, China, and South Korea, or small-town Norway, the ability to participate in society as a full and recognized citizen is largely contingent on having the material resources deemed normal for that society. When such means are not available, the common response is to save face by withdrawing from society, thus limiting opportunities to exit poverty and helping to perpetuate its cycle. Yet society in turn plays its role in persistently evaluating others against dominant norms and expectations and prioritizing certain explanations of poverty over others. Hence shame in relation to poverty is co-constructed (Chase and Walker, 2013), a dynamic interaction of internally felt inadequacies and externally inflicted judgements.

Collectively, the volume offers the building blocks for the analysis presented in *The Shame of Poverty,* the sister volume to the current one in which Robert Walker (2014) maps the cultural, historical, political, and spiritual pathways over several millennia which have fundamentally shaped modern day conceptualizations and experiences of poverty across the globe. *Poverty and Shame: Global Experiences*, while briefly scoping out the conceptual bases of poverty and shame, is more concerned with examining the by-products of such trajectories; the emergent poverty discourses and debates which occupy much social, political, rhetorical, and media space in contemporary societies and which directly impact on the day-to-day lives of those living in poverty. The chapters in this volume provide rich evidence of how the poverty–shame nexus has emerged and is maintained in vastly different cultural contexts, and of the intricate web which binds poverty and shame with other complex social constructions such as class, caste, gender, and ethnicity.

Four contrasts which tend to drive and often polarize poverty debates lie at the heart of the poverty–shame nexus. They include: the distinction between absolute and relative poverty; its uni- or multidimensionality (and the subsidiary question concerning what should make up the constituent parts of such multidimensionality); the persistent notion of the deserving and undeserving 'poor'—typically played out through practices of conditionality and public scrutiny; and whether poverty is perceived as being the result of individual failings and inadequacies or of wider structural inequalities. These same themes, in their various guises, frame responses to poverty at community, national, and global levels and repeatedly surface in each of the different contexts within which research took place.

Poverty and Shame Conceptually

Poverty

The matter of defining and measuring poverty is a science that has been evolving over the past hundred or more years. Measures provide a baseline, a sense of how 'bad' things are for people in certain circumstances compared to others. Thresholds and imaginary lines punctuate academic and political debates on poverty across the globe—the numbers of people with resources below or above such lines at successive points in time providing some proxy measure of economic or social 'development' in relative terms. In introducing the countries of the current study to the reader of this volume, such measures are equally applied (Table 1.1), offering important points of comparison between the various contexts within which the research took place.

Discourses and debates about poverty are replete with concepts such as 'absolute' and 'relative'. These are not detailed here but can be read in the accompanying volume to this one (see Walker, 2014) and the important works of Peter Townsend (1979) and Amartya Sen (1983) and many others. More generally, the presence or absence of poverty tends to be defined by local standards and protocols at any given point in time. These are not considered in any depth in the current volume since they are somewhat tangential to the argument. Suffice here to emphasize that throughout the volume, poverty is understood not solely in terms of whether there is enough food to eat or clothes to wear, but whether people have the resources to adequately function within a society, to play the roles of mother, father, community member, and citizen. It is within the vacuum created by the lack of such resources that the fecundity for shame and shaming is likely to emerge.

Shame

Shame, along with embarrassment, pride, and guilt, is widely understood as a 'self-conscious' rather than a basic emotion such as anger or fear. Essentially it entails a negative assessment of the self, made with reference to one's own aspirations and the perceived expectations of others (Tangney et al., 2007). While the literature on human psychology has engaged extensively with shame as a social emotion (Tangney and Fischer, 1995; Gilbert, 1997; Tracy and Robbins, 2007), it has tended to explore its dynamics outside of the social matrix (Scheff, 2000; 2003; Chase and Walker, 2013). And while the literature generally characterizes shame as inherently negative, having damaging effects, it has also been argued that it can play an important role in binding communities and societies and ensuring that its members remain integrated and valued (Mencious as cited in Wong and Tsai, 2007).

Overwhelmingly, however, the social psychological literature strongly suggests that shame causes a painfully negative self-evaluation (Tangney et al., 1992) leading to a sense of being exposed and an urge to withdraw from the social environment (Lewis, 1992). Its effects can be debilitating since it can limit people's ability to take action (Lynd, 1961) and may lead to their alienation from the broader society (Oravecz, Hárdi, and Lajtai, 2004). Importantly however, shame in any social context is co-constructed, it combines an internal sense of inadequacy and an imposed or imagined external judgement by others (Cooley, 1922; Mead, 1934; Goffman, 1967). Shame has multiple manifestations across cultures and time and carries with it its own taboo (Scheff, 2000; 2003) meaning that its existence is silenced or disguised under a cloak of euphemisms or what have been described elsewhere as the 'colloquialisms' of shame (Chase and Walker, 2013).

Important distinctions have been made between shame and guilt (Lewis, 1971; Lindsay-Hertz, 1984; Tangney et al., 2007; Tracy and Robbins, 2007), the most fundamental being that concerning the locus of control. While shame is attributed to a negative evaluation of the global self, or sense of failure, over which one has little or no control; guilt, on the other hand, is associated with an internal negative assessment of behaviour which is controllable or could have been avoided. Guilt implies that such behaviour was executed as a result of free will—conscience dictating that it was wrong or inappropriate, that one feels the need to take restorative action and that they have the power, opportunity, and choice as to whether or not to make amends for what they have done or failed to do. Shame on the other hand is an emotion stemming from a sense of acute inadequacy and inability to have been able to do things differently—it is indicative of a lack of power, control, or choice to behave differently or to change anything. While at the individual level these may be unarticulated differences, for instance, people are shown to use the words 'guilt' and 'shame' interchangeably (Scheff, 2000; 2002; Chase and Walker, 2013); they are nonetheless important and here the focus is on the emotion of 'shame' and not that of 'guilt', even if the former is vocally disguised by the latter. The real difference, it is argued, is context bound; emerging from the circumstances within which shame (or guilt) is insinuated or communicated.

A further important semantic distinction which is important to clarify early on in this text and one that is rarely made (see Walker, 2014) is between shame and stigma. The basis of such a distinction is evident in its intention. While, as noted earlier, shaming may have a laudable goal in certain circumstances (guiding others, for example, or bringing them back into the societal or cultural fold); stigma and the active process of stigmatizing has no such redeeming features—it is tantamount to discrimination, labelling, and psychologically branding individuals or communities in ways which dehumanize, and as such it never has a worthy objective. When shaming is carried out with these same intentions, then it is indistinguishable from such stigmatization. Moreover, when it is carried out at the level of the establishment, it is transformed into systemic institutionalized discrimination—perhaps most notably evidenced in the framing, shaping, and delivery of policies (see Gubrium et al., 2013).

Poverty and Shame Together

In an attempt to question the material deprivation-based conception of poverty and to distinguish between absolute and relative definitions, Amartya Sen (1983) delineates between capabilities, the potential individuals possess to lead satisfying lives; and functionings, the material resources available to facilitate individuals to attain their capabilities (Sen, 1999; 2005). Whereas capabilities are universally invariant across cultures, functionings are socioculturally determined and mainly influenced by the availability of resources. According to (Sen, 1999) individuals fall into poverty when they do not have the means to attain their capabilities, or attain what is socially and/or economically expected of them in their society.

Sen (1983) and Alkire (2002) identified the 'ability to go about without shame' as a fundamentally important capability which was situated at the 'irreducible absolutist core in the construction of poverty'. Sen argues that whereas the material resources needed to prevent one from feeling ashamed vary across cultures and level of socio-economic development, the actual experience of poverty-induced shame and its impacts are universal and invariant. Although some previous work has strengthened the circumstantial evidence of the shame associated with poverty (Schwarz, 1997; Clasen et al., 1998; Beresford et al., 1999; Edin et al., 2000; Narayan et al., 2000; Castell and

Thompson, 2007), this has never previously been systematically examined and the universality of the association has remained empirically untested.

Drawing from the above context, the international, cross cultural, and comparative study, on which this volume is based, sought to examine the theoretical proposition that shame is universally associated with poverty. Nonetheless, the approach adopted was investigative, or inductive, as not much is known about the poverty–shame nexus across cultures. The analysis utilized a maximum difference framework arguing that, if shame and poverty are intimately connected, albeit culturally nuanced, in the diverse milieux selected, the relationship is likely to be robust. If it is, then it may provide a sound basis for re-thinking both how poverty is understood and how policy might be best framed, structured and delivered in order to take account of this association and its psycho- social consequences (Gubrium et al., 2013).

The Contexts

The countries examined here are not those which routinely lend themselves to international comparisons. The maximum difference framework purposefully engaged countries with highly different historical, social, economic, and developmental trajectories. Table 1.1 (below) illustrates these differences according to the United Nations Human Development Index (UNDP, 2013). The underlying premise was that the greater differences between the contexts included in the research, the stronger the emerging evidence would be if a close association was drawn between poverty and shame in each of them. The seven countries include Christian, Islamic, and Confucian traditions; profoundly individualistic cultures and those adhering more to familial and collectivist beliefs; established parliamentary democracies, fragile political systems, and communist regimes; and advanced and highly developed market economies, former command regimes, and others committed to state-led developmentalist strategies together with largely rural economies with

Table 1.1. Human Development Index of study countries

Country	HDI Ranking (187) 2012	Life expectancy at birth	Mean years of schooling	Gender inequality Index ranking (148)	Poverty index (MPI)
Uganda	161	54.5	4.7	110	0.367
Pakistan	146	65.7	4.9	123	0.264
India	136	65.8	4.4	132	0.283
China	101	73.7	7.5	35	0.056
UK	26	80.3	9.4	34	N/A
South Korea	12	80.7	11.6	27	N/A
Norway	1	81.3	12.6	5	N/A

Source: (UNDP, 2013)

5

extreme levels of abject poverty. The following section sketches out the political, social, and economic landscape with respect to poverty in each of the seven countries (covered in order of ascending overall HDI) to provide some context to the subsequent country chapters in each section.

Uganda

Uganda has a population of some 30.7 million people, half of whom are aged under 15 years. Eighty five per cent of households reside in rural areas and 24.5 per cent of Ugandans are estimated to be living in poverty, corresponding to nearly 7.5 million persons in 1.2 million households. The incidence of poverty remains higher in rural areas than in urban areas (Republic of Uganda, 2010b).

Approaches to addressing poverty in Uganda have shifted substantially over time, influenced by both national and international agendas. The mixed economy approach which largely characterized Uganda's economic development from 1962 to 1971 was ended in the 1970s by Idi Amin's so called 'economic war' campaign. After his demise (in 1979) International Monetary Fund (IMF) Structural Adjustment Programmes (SAPs) were pursued until the instigation of the *Economic Recovery Programme* (ERP) of 1987. Since 1997, the *Poverty Eradication Action Plan* (PEAP) has provided a strategic framework under which coordinated actions are taken to ensure that Uganda, in line with the Millennium Development Goals (MDGs), reduces poverty by 2014. Currently, Uganda's development agenda is guided by the *National Development Plan* (Republic of Uganda, 2010a).

Key strategies to address poverty have included: the introduction of *Universal Primary Education* (UPE) in 1996 which has had mixed results (Kasaija, 2008); *Universal Secondary Education* (USE) in 2007 which increased secondary school enrolment by 25 per cent (UBOS, 2007; Republic of Uganda, 2010a); the *Plan for Modernisation of Agriculture* (PMA)—a multi-sectoral policy framework for agriculture and rural development with a vision for poverty eradication; and *Prosperity for All* (PFA), a rural development strategy established in 2005 and its subsequent wider version of holistic life improvement for all Ugandans in 2006. The *Expanding Social Protection Programme*, which to date has been piloted in three districts, will eventually target 600,000 people via a combination of non-contributory social assistance cash transfers; contributory social insurance schemes; social equity provisions which protect against discrimination of vulnerable groups in the workplace; and social welfare services providing care for people unable to provide for themselves.

As elsewhere, defining and measuring poverty in Uganda has posed a challenge to policymakers. However, since 2004, the PEAP has increasingly recognized its multidimensionality, settling on a broadly inclusive definition which recognizes lack of 'voice', social exclusion, and lack of information as important components of the experience of poverty. This perhaps signals a policy agenda which is becoming sensitized to some of the psychosocial impacts of poverty. Equally, however, with respect to the poverty–shame nexus, there have been some notable unintended consequences of anti-poverty policies which are described elsewhere (see Bantebya-Kyomuhendo and Mwiine 2013). The chapters in this volume provide depth and nuance to the experience of poverty and its associated shame in Uganda.

Pakistan

Despite having the sixth largest population and twenty-seventh largest GDP in the world (IMF, 2012), Pakistan's multidimensional poverty headcount stands at 49.4 per cent and it ranks 146th on the Human Development Index (OPHI, 2011; UNDP, 2013). The traditional systemic response to poverty has been to rely upon macroeconomic development and structural adjustment, approaches regularly conceived of and implemented with the financial and technical assistance of international monetary and development organizations. The last two decades have seen the execution of the World Bank assisted *Social Action Programme* of the 1990s, set up to improve access to education, health, water, and sanitation and, more recently, the ongoing *Benazir Income Support Programme* (BISP) started in 2008 which, recognizing the specific economic difficulties faced by women (PBS, 2013), provides several forms of social assistance to low-income female-headed households.

The BISP began in the aftermath of the global economic recession and was originally intended to mitigate the effects of high inflation by providing unconditional cash assistance. Since then, with improvements in design, identification, and delivery mechanisms, it has gradually evolved to include co-responsibility cash transfer schemes, micro-financing, vocational training, and conditional cash transfers (CCTs) in health and education. Despite its relatively large scale, this programme only covers an estimated 40 per cent of the population below the poverty line and 18 per cent of the total population (BISP, 2013).

Alongside other governmental social assistance provisions, *Zakat*, which started in the 1980s, has remained one of the most important programmes of social protection over the last three decades. Originally, a private charity in Pakistan, the *Zakat and Ushr Ordinance* of 1980 made *Zakat* one of the official safety nets of the country through introducing at-source deductions from the incomes of wealthy Muslims. Gradually, a shrinking resource base on account of ideological and structural impediments, has meant that the official *Zakat* programme, along with its sister programme *Bait-ul-Maal,* have been unable to keep up with the new social protection demands of twenty-first century Pakistan, thus necessitating the inception of BISP.

Pakistan's social protection policy lacks an over-arching welfare philosophy, identity, and structure and instead is made up of a number of ad hoc and often uncoordinated initiatives which have been criticized for not always providing support and assistance where they are most needed (Pasha et al., 2000). Usually area specific, these tend to comprise a mix of cash and in-kind provisions for the short-term and rehabilitation assistance for the long-term. Such initiatives are supplemented by a large-scale emergency assistance programme which is activated in times of natural and human calamities. The extent to which poverty and state responses to it in Pakistan alleviate or exacerbate the psychosocial impacts of economic adversity is explored in detail throughout the relevant chapters.

India

Home to more than 1.2 billion people, India is a complex and vastly diverse nation, comprising twenty-eight federal states and seven union territories and made up of people speaking 1500 different languages. Some 27.8 per cent of the total population is estimated to live below the income-based poverty line set by the Indian government (Planning Commission, 2012). The day-to-day reality of poverty is evidenced by the fact than 50 per cent of the population has no access to sanitation facilities; many live in poor housing, are malnourished, and have limited access to education and other public services.

Rapid economic growth in India in recent years has been unequal across different federal states, largely confined to urban centres and not mirrored in rural areas where some 68 per cent of the population live and work. Rural development is hampered by limited mechanization and resultant poor agricultural productivity (accounting for only 15 per cent GDP) and restricted access to education. Urban poverty, on the other hand, arguably runs deeper and is rapidly increasing, affecting some 81 million people living in urban informal settlements with little or no access to basic services such as water and sanitation (Ministry of Housing and Urban Poverty Alleviation and UNDP, 2009). Moreover, a total of 40 per cent of the workforce in India in both urban and rural areas is confined to the vagaries of casual and insecure daily wage labour in the informal sector, only 10 per cent of the population having access to full social security coverage guaranteed under formal contractual work arrangements (Pellissery and Walker, 2007).

Indian society is also characterized by its complex social stratification and imposed hierarchies according to caste, gender, and geographical areas which interact in complex ways with poverty and social exclusion. Four states in particular—Bihar, Madhya Pradesh, Rajasthan, and Uttar Pradesh—face persistently high levels of poverty and people from these areas are known to experience discrimination on the basis of their origins when they move to cities to seek work (CSP, 2001). Most profoundly stigmatizing, however, is the caste system in India which, despite widespread legislative and policy changes, remains a major contributor towards the disproportionately high poverty rates among people classified as *outcasts* (or formerly untouchables) and tribes people.

Combined, these groups constitute 24 per cent of the total population 'scheduled' within the Indian constitution for affirmative action and special protective measures; measures which seem, in effect, to have limited impact and are thought to be in and of themselves highly stigmatizing. The extent of the feminization of poverty in India is profound and stems from a combination of deep-set patriarchal and cultural traditions and unequal distribution of wealth and status among men and women across household, informal, and formal economies. The preference for male children is strong, female infanticide is common, and ostracizing of widows widespread. More broadly, the concept of *Izzat* ('honour') provides a powerful mechanism of social control of women. *Izzat* is easily compromised by poverty, frequently exposing women facing the worst economic hardships to the full brunt of poverty-related shame. The chapters throughout the volume illustrate the ways in which poverty and shame interact within an innately stratified modern-day India.

China

The conceptualization of poverty in China, as in other countries, has had its own unique history and development. Following the rise of communism after 1949, poverty was touted as the malicious face of capitalism. Abolishing private ownership and establishing a new classless socialist society became political imperatives, ultimately 'liberating' those in poverty to live happy and dignified lives. Full employment and comprehensive welfare provision were made possible under state socialism and the planned economy. Although the general living standard was low, poverty did not appear in public discourse and there was relatively little economic disparity between people's circumstances, at least in urban China.

The mid-1950s to the late 1980s saw the emergence of the idea of 'households in difficulty', although 'poverty' was still not part of the political discourse (Guan, 1999: 137–9). Such households were perceived as those families where adults were working but had too many dependents; or were defined within the category of the 'three nos' (those who had no reliable source of income, no ability to work, and no family support). By the end of the 1970s, China's ideological position had fundamentally shifted towards economic development and, in its pursuit, the compromise of 'allowing some to get rich first'.

The early economic reform period (1979–1980s) saw the ending of the commune and permission for private entrepreneurship accompanied by widespread poverty alleviation programmes in rural areas, implemented throughout the 1980s. While these measures led to a drastic reduction in rural poverty, urban poverty became increasingly severe following the urban economic reform in 1984 and especially from the mid-1990s onwards when marketization really took hold. The policy direction shifted from state security to social security and the gradual retreat of government from the provision of health care, education, and housing. It saw the steady closure of state-owned enterprises (SOEs) and the emergence of labour contracts, tax and wage reforms, and private insurances for old-age and unemployment. During this time, many enterprises closed down or became bankrupt, resulting in massive numbers of 'redundant' labourers who became the bulk of the 'urban poor', reaching an estimated 10 million in 1998 and rising to some 28 million by the early 2000s (Liu, 2004: 218; He and Hua, 2006: 5). It has been estimated that urban poverty in China affects anywhere between 14 and 37 million people (Zhu, 1997; Hussain 2003, Tang, 2003). This 'new urban poverty' has emerged in tandem with rising inequality in urban areas, the contrast between the 'haves' and 'have-nots' being starker than ever before in the history of the People's Republic of China.

The policy response in China to rapidly rising poverty from unemployment has been a new institutional mechanism, the Minimum Standard of Living Scheme (MSLS), intended to provide security while people search for work (Yan, 2013). The circumstances of people accessing MSLS however are confounded by access to few, insecure, and poorly paid work opportunities and the difficulties they face in adapting to a fall from the high social standing they enjoyed within SOEs prior to the economic reforms to becoming recipients of social assistance. Overall, these significant ideological, political, and economic transformations in China have created conditions of inequality which may be ripe for the poverty–shame nexus to emerge. Whether and in what ways this has been the case are themes covered throughout the chapters from China in this volume.

Britain

In 2011/2012 an estimated 13 million people in Britain (21 per cent) were living in poverty, defined as having incomes less than 60 per cent of the median, and more than half of them resided in households in which at least one adult was employed (MacInnes et al., 2013). Moreover, since average incomes in Britain have fallen by 8 per cent since 2008, an estimated further

2 million people have incomes in real terms which are below the 2008 poverty line but are not currently counted as being in poverty. Despite some indication of slow recovery in the economy following the 2007 recession, youth unemployment has continued to rise and the number of people in low-paid insecure jobs has reached an unprecedented 5 million (MacInnes et al., 2013). There also remain considerable regional differences in how well people fair with respect to health, education, and life expectancy in Britain, which are strongly correlated with levels of deprivation (ONS, 2013), and evidence that inequalities in wealth and income continue to rise.

Hence, despite its relative wealth by the standards of most of the other countries in our comparative frame, Britain has arguably created a surprisingly large space for the enactment of poverty-related shame. Since the inception of the Elizabethan Poor Laws, Britain has sustained a regimented history of categorizing people requiring welfare provisions and support into 'deserving' and 'undeserving' camps (Walker and Chase, 2013). Successive governments spanning the political spectrum have, with only slight shifts in tone, repeatedly claimed that social protection constitutes a burden on the state and 'tax payers' and that 'rolling back the state' is a political imperative. Policies have been underpinned by the assumption that welfare provisions create dependency, that those in receipt of them would, if left to their own devices, choose not to work, abuse the system, and require carefully metered 'tough love' to get them back on the right track towards economic activity. As will be recognized in the chapters relating to Britain, these assumptions bear little resemblance to the actualities of living in poverty in the British context, but play a profoundly important role in defining the day-to-day experience of economic hardship.

South Korea

The Republic of Korea currently has a population of 48.9 million people, with around 25 per cent of the population residing in the capital city of Seoul which has been at the forefront of the country's economic and social development since the 1960s. The Korean peninsula was colonized by Japan for a period of 35 years until 1945 and soon after experienced a devastating war between North and South Korea (1950–53) by the end of which an estimated 60 to 70 per cent of the population of South Korea was living in abject poverty (PSPD/UNDP, 2000). South Korea's separation from North Korea was accompanied by political claims to democracy, although in practice the country entered forty years of dictatorship until around the late 1990s.

During that time South Korea experienced extraordinarily rapid economic growth, a period from the 1960s to the 1990s referred to as 'the Miracle of the Han River' (the name of the river running through the heart of Seoul) and during which the country experienced annual growth rates exceeding 10 per cent (Kim et al., 2007: 52). The state-directed, export-oriented industrialization, accompanied by high economic growth, resulted in low levels of unemployment and a notable decrease in abject poverty. For many years until the Asian financial crisis hit South Korea in 1997, economic growth was the principal government strategy for addressing poverty. The crisis resulted in bankruptcies, a dramatic growth in unemployment, and, in the absence of a secure social security safety net, considerable increases in poverty and personal indebtedness. In 2000, the government responded by introducing a universal social assistance programme for poverty relief, the National Basic Living Security Scheme (NBLSS), which remains the main social assistance programme.

South Korea currently confronts what has come to be known as the 'New Poverty', affecting different groups of the population and the product of disparate causes including growing inequality, low wages, a growth in insecure employment, high youth unemployment, a rapidly aging population, and increasing numbers of single-parents and single-headed households who lack any familial support (Kim et al., 2007; 2009). These new manifestations of poverty are yet to be adequately addressed by policy, not least because the dominant discourse surrounding poverty forged during the era of industrialization tends to consider people to be poor for reasons of their own making. Policies designed according to this premise, as we will see in the following chapters covering South Korea, can lead to people becoming trapped in systems of provision that exacerbate the social stigma and shame that they frequently experience as a result of their economic circumstances.

Norway

With a population of just over 5 million, Norway is one of the richest countries in the world, rated first out of 187 countries in the globally comparative Human Development Index (UNDP, 2013). However, Norway has had a chequered past before gaining its status as a modern bastion of equality and social justice. Industrialization in Norway surged at the end of the nineteenth century, forcing massive demographic and social changes, beginning with significant population drift towards increasingly large urban areas. Although slow to take off and not really coming into its own until the mid-1960s (Kangas and Palme, 2009) the system of welfare provision in Norway has gradually become world renowned for being founded on the principles of universalism and 'citizenship' (Gubrium and Lødemel, 2013). Norway's welfare system was designed to promote equal opportunities and to mitigate the effects of social inequalities through the provision of benefits including free health care and welfare transfers, as well as universal and free access to education (Esping-Andersen, 1990; Wiborg and Hansen, 2009).

Given its principles of (near) universalism and its de-commodifying policies, this social democratic model of welfare (Esping-Andersen, 1990) offers generous social insurance-based benefits to the majority of its citizens. Yet ironically, Norway has also been implicated in what has come to be termed a 'Welfare paradox' (Lødemel, 1997), in that the gradual extension of non-contributory social assistance to specific and identifiable groups of people has meant that such recipients have become increasingly marginalized and stigmatized—the residuum unable to 'function' in what is heralded as a largely inclusive and enabling social and economic environment. Today, those individuals living in poverty and those on social assistance tend to be one and the same (Halvorsen and Stjernø 2008).

Somewhat counterintuitively therefore, rather than being models of inclusiveness, Norway's strong economic and welfare systems are potent sources of a categorical 'other'—those in poverty—who are relegated to the bottom rung of the social hierarchy (Gubrium and Lødemel, 2013) and whose circumstances receive accentuated attention, judgement, and surveillance. The 'groups' associated with poverty in affluent Norway, including the homeless, long-term drug and alcohol users, immigrants, and the 'Roma', are therefore likely to experience considerable levels of poverty-related shame.

The Study

The study comprised four main components, the fourth of which, an analysis of a selection of anti-poverty policies in each country, provides the basis for landscaping the universal implications for anti-poverty policies which are detailed in *The Shame of It: Global Perspectives on Anti-Poverty Policies* (Gubrium et al., 2013). The three other components of the research provide the substantive material for the current volume. First of all, an analysis of cultural representations of poverty and shame and their intersection were investigated using samples of popular media. These were purposefully selected in each of the different contexts to variably include films, novels, poetry, and proverbs. This preliminary phase of the work served as a process of sensitization to how poverty and shame were culturally conceptualized on their own and in combination and the sorts of arenas and social interactions within which the coincidence of the two were likely to emerge. Secondly, in-depth interviews were conducted with an average of thirty or so adults and (where possible) additional children living in poverty in each of the countries. Interviews provided insights into the daily experience of poverty while focusing on the social and psychological impacts of living with inadequate resources and the individual and collective consequences of such hardship. Thirdly, focus group discussions with people not living in poverty to ascertain their understandings, views, and attitudes about poverty were combined with an analysis of newspaper reporting on issues of poverty in each country. This phase of the work tested out the contention concerning the co-construction of shame in relation to poverty, the side to shame which is externally imposed most notably by society and the media. Findings from the various components of the research were further contextualized using the World Value Survey (see Walker, 2014).

The empirical research was essentially qualitative and conducted in each context in such a way that it generated comparable data. However, it was also grounded in its approach—both in terms of the openness of questions and in the flexibility to allow the detail of the research interaction to be guided by the cultural context and milieu within which each research team was working. Grounded theory (see Glaser and Strauss, 1967; Corbin and Strauss, 2008) informed the methodology since it facilitates the generation of empirical insights which are not overly constrained by a priori theory but enable theory to emerge inductively throughout the course of the investigation.

The study design incorporated methodological innovation, drawing on disciplines across the social sciences as diverse as anthropology, sociology, psychology, economics, political philosophy, social policy, film, and literary studies. Each component of the research was developed collectively by all members of the research team during six-monthly scheduled meetings and then adapted accordingly to meet the practical constraints of each of the contexts within which the fieldwork took place. In the same way, the comparative analysis carried out at the end of each phase of the research was completed communally, using a process of constant comparison (Merriam, 2002), before the subsequent phase of the work began.

Section I of this volume illustrates how dominant cultural norms and values surrounding poverty and shame are reflected within a range of popular media such as film, literary works, and oral traditions. Section II then illustrates the poverty–shame nexus via the lived experiences of people in poverty in each of these contexts as they engage with the range of structures, institutions, and social arenas which make up contemporary society. Finally, Section III combines the views and perceptions of those currently not living in poverty with an analysis of recent media coverage of poverty in each of these same countries. Together, these illustrative case studies detail the similarities of the social construction of poverty-related shame across vastly different contexts, providing compelling evidence for the possibility of its universal existence and hence for the need to consider more closely its social and political implications.

References

Alkire, S. (2002) *Valuing Freedoms: Sen's Capability Approach and Poverty Reduction*, Oxford: Oxford University Press.

Bantebya-Kyomuhendo, G. and Mwiine, A. (2013) ' "Food that cannot be eaten": The shame of Uganda's anti-poverty policies', in Gubrium, E., Pellissery, S. and Lødemel, I. (ed.) *The Shame of It: Global perspectives on anti-poverty policies*, Bristol: Policy Press.

Beresford, P., Green, D., Lister, R. and Woodward, K. (1999) *Poverty First Hand: Poor People Speak for Themselves*, London: CPAG.

BISP (2013) At a Glance, Website Material of Benazir Income Support Programme, accessed 11 December 2013, <http://www.bisp.gov.pk/>.

Castell, S. and Thompson, J. (2007) *Understanding Attitudes to Poverty in Britain: Getting the public's attention*, York: Joseph Rowntree Foundation.

Chase, E. and Walker, R. (2013) 'The Co-construction of shame in the context of poverty: Beyond a threat to the social bond', *Sociology*, 47(4): 739–54.

Clasen, J., Gould, A. and Vincent, J. (1998) *Voices Within and Without: Responses to long-term unemployment in Germany, Sweden and Britain*, Bristol: The Policy Press.

Cooley, C. H. (1922) *Human Nature and the Social Order*, New York: Scribner's.

Corbin, J. and Strauss, A. (2008) *Basics of Qualitative Research: Techniques and procedures for developing grounded theory*. 3e, London: Sage Publications.

Crisis State Programme (CSP) (2001) Collaborative Research States of Crisis in South Asia. Crisis State Programme Working Paper No. 3 of the London School of Economics.

Edin, K., Lein, L., Nelson, T. and Clampet-Lundquest, S. (2000) *Talking to Low-income Fathers*, University of Chicago, Joint Center for Poverty Research Newsletter 4: 2.

Esping-Andersen, G. (1990) *The Three Worlds of Welfare Capitalism*, Cambridge: Polity.

Gilbert, P. (1997) 'The evolution of social attractiveness and its role in shame, humiliation, guilt and therapy', *British Journal of Medical Psychology*, 70(2): 113–47.

Glaser, B. and Strauss, A. (1967) *The Discovery of Grounded Theory: Strategies for Qualitative Research*, Chicago: Aldine Publishing Company.

Goffman, E. (1967) *Interaction Ritual*, New York: Anchor.

Guan, X. (1999) *Study on Urban Poverty Problem in China*, Changsha: Hunan People's Publishing House.

Gubrium, E. and Lødemel, I. (2013) 'Towards Global Principles for Dignity-based Anti-poverty Policies', in Gubrium, E., Pellissery, S. and Lødemel, I. (ed.) *The Shame of It: Global perspectives on anti-poverty policies*, Bristol: Policy Press.

Gubrium, E., Pellissery, S. and Lødemel, I. (2013) *The Shame of It: Global perspectives on anti-poverty policies*, Bristol: Policy Press.

Halvorsen, K. and Stjernø, S. (2008) *Work, Oil and Welfare*, Oslo: Universitetsforlaget.

He, P. and Hua, Y. F. (2006) *Study on the Social Security Policy and Implementation Measures of the Urban Poor Groups*, Beijing: Chinese Labor and Social Security Press.

Hussain, A. (2003) 'Urban Poverty in China: Measurement, Patterns and Policies', International Labour Office, Geneva.

IMF (2012) World Economic Outlook Database, International Monetary Fund, accessed November 2012.

Kangas, O. and Palme, J. (2009) 'Making social policy work for economic development: the Nordic experience', *International Journal of Social Welfare*, 18: S62–S72.

Kasaija, S. (2008) *Uganda's experience with social exclusion,* Paper Presentation to the Ad Hoc Group Meeting on Developing supplementary targets and indicators to strengthen social inclusion, gender equality and health promotion in the millennium Development Goals, Addis Ababa, 7–9 May.

Kim, Y., Kim, K., Kim, J., Jang, K., and Jung, K. (2007) *Social Welfare in Korea,* Yang-Seo-Won.

Kim, S., Lee, H. and Son, B. (2009) *Korea's Poverty—New Poverty Old Problem*, South Korea: Han-Wool Academy.

Lewis, H. B. (1971) 'Shame and Guilt in Neurosis', New York: International Universities Press.

Lewis, M. (1992) 'Shame: The Exposed Self', New York: The Free Press.

Liu, G. X. (2004) *A Brief History of Labor Security in the New China 1949–2003*, Beijing: Chinese Labor and Social Security Press.

Lindsay-Hertz, J. (1984) 'Contrasting experiences of shame and guilt', *American Behavioral Scientist*, 27: 689–704.

Lødemel, I. (1997) *The Welfare Paradox,* Oslo: Scandinavian University Press.

Lynd, H. M. (1961) 'On Shame and the Search for Identity', New York: Science Editions.

MacInnes, T., Aldridge, H., Bushe, S., Kenway, P. and Tinson, A. (2013) *Monitoring Poverty and Social Exclusion 2013,* York, Joseph Rowntree Foundation. Available at: <http://www.jrf.org.uk/publications/monitoring-poverty-and-social-exclusion-2013>. Accessed 20 January 2014.

Mead, G. H. (1934) *The Mind, Self and Society, From the Standpoint of a Social Behaviorist,* Chicago: Chicago University Press.

Merriam, S. B. (2002) *Assessing and Evaluating Qualitative Research*, in Merriam, S. B. Merriam (ed.) *Qualitative Research in Practice: Examples for Discussion and Analysis,* San Francisco: Jossey-Bass.

Ministry of Housing and Urban Poverty Alleviation and UNDP (2009) *India Urban Poverty Report*, Oxford: Oxford University Press.

Narayan, D. with Patel, R., Schafft, K., Rademacehr, A. and Koch-Schulte, S. (2000) *Voices of the Poor: Can anyone hear us*? New York: Published for the World Bank, Oxford University Press.

ONS (2013) *Life expectancy at birth and at age 65 for local areas in England and Wales, 2010–2012*. Statistical Bulletin, London: ONS. Available at: <http://www.ons.gov.uk/ons/dcp171778_332904.pdf>. Accessed 20 January 2014.

OPHI (2011) Oxford Poverty and Human Development Initiative, Country briefing Pakistan. Available at: <http://www.ophi.org.uk/wp-content/uploads/Pakistan2.pdf?cda6c1>.

Oravecz, R., Hárdi, L., and Lajtai, L. (2004) 'Social transition, exclusion, shame and humiliation', *Torture*, 14(1): 3–15.

Pasha, H., Jafarey, S. and Lohano, H. (2000) 'Evaluation of Social Safety Nets in Pakistan'; Research Report No. 32, Karachi: Social Policy and Development Centre, Pakistan.

PBS (2013) 'Labour Force Survey 2012–13' (Thirty First Issue), Pakistan Bureau of Statistics, Government of Pakistan, Statistics Division.

Pellissery, S. and Walker, R. (2007) 'Social security options for informal sector workers in emergent economies and the Asia and Pacific region', *Social Policy and Administration*, 41(4): 401–9.

Planning Commission (2012) 'Approach paper for 12th five-year plan', New Delhi: Planning Commission.

PSPD/UNDP (2000) *Poverty Status and Monitoring of Korea in the Aftermath of the Financial Crisis*, People's Solidarity for Participatory Democracy and the United Nations Development Programme, PSPD/UNDP.

Republic of Uganda (2010a) *Uganda National Development Plan: Growth, Employment and Socioeconomic Transformation for Prosperity*. National Planning Authority, Kampala, Uganda.

Republic of Uganda (2010b) *Uganda National Household Survey Report*, Kampala, Uganda.

Scheff, T. (2000) *Shame and the Social Bond: A Sociological Theory*, Santa Barbara: University of California at Santa Barbara.

Scheff, T. (2003) 'Shame in self and society', *Symbolic Interaction*, 26(2): 239–62.

Schwarz, J. (1997) *Illusions of Opportunity: The American dream in question*, New York: W. W. Norton and Company.

Sen, A. (1983) 'Poor, Relatively Speaking', *Oxford Economic Papers* 35: 153–69.

Sen, A. (1999) *Commodities and Capabilities*, Delhi: Oxford University Press.

Sen, A. (2005) 'Human Rights and Capabilities', *Journal of Human Development*, 6(2): 151–66.

Tang, J. (2003) *Report on Poverty and Anti-Poverty in Urban China*, Beijing: Huaxia Publishing House.

Tangney, J. P., Wagner, P., and Gramzow, R. (1992) 'Proneness to shame, proneness to guilt, and psychopathology', *Journal of Abnormal Psychology*, 101: 469–78.

Tangney, J. P. and Fischer, K. W. (eds) (1995) *The Self-conscious Emotions: The Psychology of Shame, Guilt, Embarrassment and Pride*, New York: Guilford Press.

Tangney, J., Stuewig, J. and Mashek, D. (2007) 'What's Moral about the Self-conscious Emotions?', in Tracy, J., Robins, R. and Tangney, J. (eds) *The Self-Conscious Emotions*, New York: Guilford Press, pp. 21–37.

Townsend, P. (1979) *Poverty in the United Kingdom*, London: Allen Lane/Penguin Books.

Tracy, J. and Robins, R. (2007) *The Self-conscious Emotions: A cognitive appraisal approach*, in Tracy, J., Robins, R. and Tangney, J. (eds) *The Self-Conscious Emotions*, New York: Guilford Press, 3–20.

UBOS, Uganda Bureau of Statistics (2007) Statistical Abstract, Kampala, Uganda.

UNDP (2013) The Human Development Index. Available at: <http://hdr.undp.org/en/data>. Accessed 5 March 2014.

Walker, R. and Chase, E. (2013) 'Separating the sheep from the goats: Tackling poverty in Britain for over four centuries', in E. Gubrium., S. Pellissery., and I. Lodemel. *The Shame of It: Global perspectives on anti-poverty policies*. Bristol: Policy Press.

Walker, R. (2014) *The Shame of Poverty*, Oxford: Oxford University Press.

Wiborg, Ø. N. and Hansen, M. N. (2009) 'Change over time in the intergenerational transmission of social disadvantage', *European Sociological Review*, 25: 379–94.

Wong, Y. and Tsai, J. (2007) 'Cultural Models of Shame and Guilt', Chapter 12 in Tracy, J., Robins, R. and Tangney, J. (eds) *The Self-Conscious Emotions*, New York: Guilford Press.

Yan, M. (2013) 'New Urban Poverty and New Welfare Provision: China's Dibao system', in Gubrium, E., Pellissery, S. and Lødemel, I. (eds) *The Shame of It: Global perspectives on anti-poverty policies*, Bristol: Policy Press.

Zhu, Q. (1997) '1996-1997 People's living conditions', in Jiang L. et al. (eds) *1996–1997 China's Society: Analysis and Forecast*, Beijing: China Social Science Press.

Section I
Cultural Conceptions of Poverty and Shame

Preface

This first section brings together a series of chapters detailing how conceptions of 'poverty' and 'shame' and the ways in which they interact are culturally constructed in each of the participating countries. Popular cultural media were selected for each country which variably included novels, films, poetry, and proverbs. The rationale for selection of materials is specified in each of the chapters and the method of analysis was broadly similar in each case, informed by the 'New Historicism' approach (Gallagher and Greenblatt, 2000). Such an approach allows the prevailing social context, the intended audience of the time, along with other contemporary historical, cultural, and political factors to be acknowledged and embedded in the analysis.

Each chapter demonstrates how selected media in each country and their associated language and symbols engage with the concepts of poverty and shame and whether and under what circumstances these phenomena are perceived to coincide. These mainly fictional portrayals are not, in and of themselves, presented as accurate accounts of individual experiences of poverty and shame. Instead the analysis uses 'poverty' and 'shame' as sensitizing concepts (Blumer, 1969), exploring how they are collectively represented and understood within different societies. The analysis follows the tradition of social scientists who view cultural media as lenses through which to glimpse social meanings (Coser, 1963; Lewis et al., 2008; Sutherland and Felty, 2010). In each case, the materials were subjected to two forms of analysis. Firstly, the analysis of the narrative content focused on the concepts of poverty and shame, their synonyms and antonyms, the situations in which they interacted, and the discourses surrounding them. The second involved targeted semiotic analysis which examined visual and contextual references (signs) to explore how shame and poverty and related concepts are connoted and ascribed meaning (Chandler, 2004).

This phase of work included analysis of seminal fictional works from China, India, Norway, Uganda, and Britain; films of different genres from India, South Korea, and Britain; and oral traditions including poetry and proverbs from India, Pakistan, and Uganda. In each case the analysis of cultural material has a temporal component since it spans significant time periods, allowing for shifts in cultural perceptions and understandings of these key concepts to be simultaneously captured. In some contexts, most notably in Britain, we see a clear path dependency in terms of the rather stolid ways in which poverty, its effects, causes, and impacts, have been conceived of over time. In others, such as China and South Korea, cultural media provide striking examples of how rapid economic and social transformations have increasingly prioritized economic growth and development at the same time fundamentally changing the cultural and sociological parameters around poverty and arguably generating greater collective space for the emergence of poverty-related shame. The analysis of different cultural media provided rich insights into the poverty–shame nexus, creating a substantive body of sociological investigation in its own right, while at the same time laying the basis for subsequent empirical research into the lived experiences of poverty and shame in each of the same contexts.

References

Blumer, H. (1969) *Symbolic Interactionism: Perspective and Method*, London: University of California Press.

Chandler, D. (2004) *Semiotics: The Basics*, London: Routledge.

Coser, L. (1963) *Sociology through Literature*, Englewood Cliffs: Prentice-Hall International.

Gallagher, C., and Greenblatt, S. (2000) *Practicing New Historicism*, Chicago: Chicago University Press.

Lewis, D., Rodgers, D., and Woolcock, M. (2008) 'The Fiction of Development: Literary Representation as a Source of Authoritative Knowledge', *Journal of Development Studies*, 44(2): 198–216.

Sutherland, J. A., and Felty, K. (2010) *Cinematic Sociology: Social Life in Film*, California: Sage Publications.

2

Oral Tradition and Literary Portrayals of Poverty; the Evolution of Poverty Shame in Uganda

Grace Bantebya-Kyomuhendo

Introduction

Drawing on analysis of traditional proverbs and selected books and plays from Uganda, this chapter examines cultural perceptions of the causes and experiences of poverty and poverty-induced shame. The analysis is premised on the understanding that oral tradition and literary works provide means of accessing and analysing dominant cultural values that shape our social understanding of how poverty is experienced; and shed light on how the stultifying effects of poverty, especially shame, have evolved over time.

Given its persistence in both ancient traditional and contemporary Ugandan societies, poverty is assumed to have taken on a type of subculture. In order to understand this culture it is essential to learn the language of poverty and its related indignities. This was achieved via an analysis of material which incorporated ninety Luganda and Runyakitara proverbs; two plays and two novels, spanning pre-modern, colonial, and postcolonial eras. The rationale for using traditional proverbs (*engero, enfumu, enfumo*) from Buganda, Bunyoro, and Ankole respectively, is not only that they are fairly well documented, but also that they are so integral to the dominant Bantu institutions which mirror the ethos and cultural values of their respective indigenous peoples. Although the use of proverbs in everyday speak has declined over time in both rural and urban Uganda, they still promote social cohesion especially in rural areas where social and cultural institutions are relatively strong, and individuals proficient in the use of languages rich in proverbs are, much respected. The specific timing and use of the proverbs is not certain, but what is indisputable is that their genesis and use is rooted in the ancient pre-modern era where use of proverbs was the rule rather than the exception; and that such use has been shaped by progressive socio-economic changes that have characterized the transition from the pre-modern to modern period.

Analysis of the proverbs and literature sought to elicit dominant social and cultural values, norms, and mores, and identify the dynamics which have shaped the social construction of poverty-related shame and shaming in Uganda over time. The underlying presumption of this approach is that poverty and poverty-induced shame are not recent phenomena, but are historically grounded in ancient pre-modern communities from which contemporary Ugandan society has evolved.

The pre-modern period covers the time before the advent of British colonial rule in 1894 that started in Buganda and later spread to the kingdoms of Bunyoro-Kitara, Toro, Ankole, and other chiefdoms in the rest of Uganda. The modern era, on the other hand, represents the colonial (1894–1962) and the postcolonial (1963–2012) periods. The transition from the pre-colonial, through the colonial to the postcolonial period was characterized by unique socio-economic and political changes, opportunities, and challenges that had a profound impact on the living conditions, behaviours, and aspirations of indigenous peoples. The ways in which people experienced and responded to poverty, or relative wealth, changed irreversibly over these respective periods.

The themes explored throughout the analysis include everyday experiences of poverty and relative wealth; attitudes towards those living in poverty and the relatively rich, including perceptions about how they are expected to coexist; and the extent, if at all, to which shame was or is seen as a consequence of poverty or relative wealth. Both oral tradition and literary texts in synergy provide rich sources for tracing the evolutionary origins of poverty-induced shame in Uganda.

The Pre-Modern Period: Poverty without Shame

Conceptions of Poverty and Its Causes

Evidence from traditional proverbs that represent the dominant Bantu (Ganda, Nyoro, and Nkore) cultural ethos in the pre-modern period portrays poverty in a broad perspective. Poverty (*enaku, obunaku, obwavu, obworo*) was not only seen in terms of deprivation of material and social resources required for decent living per se, but was generically used to describe unpleasant situations or phenomena like suffering, orphanhood, lack of immediate family or extended kith and kin, failure by men to marry (*obuhuuru*) and start a family, and gender-specific physiological defects like male impotence (*kufirwa*) and female infertility (*obugumba*). The latter types of poverty were frequently referred to as male poverty (*enakuy'ekisaja*) and female poverty (*enakuy'ekikazi*), respectively.

The poverty of material deprivation in the ancient indigenous communities is portrayed as endemic, severe, and painful. The proverbs portray it as sinister, a trap which is difficult to avoid or to extricate oneself from once caught:

Bwaavumpologoma, bw'otobulwanisa ofa.[1]
Poverty is like a lion. If you do not fight it, you will be killed instead.
Poverty is a formidable force that is difficult to resist.

Ekubaomunakutekya, esigalakumutwe.
The rain which falls on a poor person never stops, his head remains permanently wet.
The woes of a poor person never end, he lives with them constantly.

Tezikubamisinde (ennaku), ssingaomuntuaziwuliran'adduka.
Poverty has no footsteps; otherwise one would hear it coming and run away.
Poverty is unpredictable and inescapable.

Orwitaomunakurumuntambira.
What kills a poor person, is a blessing in disguise, it saves him/her from chronic suffering.
Poverty is worse than death.

In pre-modern Uganda poverty was attributed not to structural causes, lack of social capital or individual failure, but fate. Fate, defined primarily in terms of divine spirits (*bachwezi*), family curses (*emikyeno*), and malevolence (*amarogo*), was believed to determine who became rich or poor.

Ayakuhaireniweyanyimire.
The spirits that blessed you with wealth are the same that deprived me.

Omukisampewo, ne bw'oggalawoguyingira.
Luck is like the air, even when you close the door it still enters the house.
Good fortune is unstoppable, whatever the obstacles.

This broad definition of poverty, and its attribution to fate rather than individual failings, had the effect of downplaying its negative social effects, including shame. Further, poverty as commonly understood was widespread and considered normal in society, thus attracting little or no shame. Likewise since nobody had control over fate, the underlying determinant of poverty, material deprivation though painful and endemic was not stigmatized or seen as overtly shameful. The dearth of traditional proverbs about poverty-induced shame, and an abundance of those that define poverty and its everyday experience lend credence to the above argument.

---

[1] Each proverb cited in the vernacular is followed firstly by its literal translation and then by its cultural interpretation.

The Language of Poverty; Trivializing Shame

Numerous traditional proverbs not only highlight the ubiquity of poverty, but also point to the existence and legitimization of a poverty subculture complete with its ethos and language in the pre-modern era. In this language everyday experiences of poverty which might otherwise evoke feelings of shame are trivialized or portrayed with humour, in the process downplaying their potentially damaging effects. Further the language of poverty is portrayed as part and parcel of everyday dialogue.

> **Ennyanjay'omukopi, ebeerakulusebenju.**
> The lake of a poor person is by his house.
> A poor person's lake is the vegetable patch in his backyard. The poor cannot afford fish.
> **Kyewalyanga, bw'olabaennakuolekayo.**
> When you experience poverty, you stop eating delicacies.
> When poverty strikes you abandon former luxuries.
> **Omukoomwavu, akanyamagulu.**
> A poor son-in-law must persist with his legs.
> Since a poor man cannot afford to buy presents for his parents-in-law, the only way of maintaining a good relationship is to visit them frequently.

Evidence from the proverbs, apart from being suggestive of the existence of poverty without or with only limited shame, further indicates that the dominant Bantu cultures established social institutions that accommodated social inequality. In the interests of social cohesion, these institutions did not only encourage those in poverty to accept their station in life as a consequence of fate, but went further to offer them social protection. There is an abundance of proverbs in the oral tradition which empathize with those facing hardship, intimating that poverty can be reversed by a mix of fate and hard work, or individual resilience and that poverty was not a license for others to be exploitative.

> **Kola ng' omuddu, olye ng, omwami.**
> Work like a slave/poor person and eat like a chief.
> Comfort is a product of hardship and individual sacrifice.
> **Mukaomwavutalondwa.**
> A poor man's wife is not a prostitute.
> Poverty does not entitle a poor man's wife to be enticed or married by a wealthy man.

These proverbs reflect the extent to which pre-modern society went to accommodate, protect, and instil those experiencing poverty with a sense of self-worth. The rich knew that it was a taboo to exploit their poorer neighbours by, for example, enticing and marrying their wives. Likewise women in poverty knew that abandoning their husbands, committing adultery, or practising prostitution to escape poverty, were forms of deviant behaviour punishable by social ostracism. Arguably, therefore the institutionalization of the 'rights' of those in poverty, and the imposition of social sanctions equally on those with wealth and those without, ultimately minimized the damaging effects of poverty, including shame, and helped maintain social cohesion.

Imposing Limits on Those in Poverty and Maintaining the Status Quo

Yet while traditional proverbs indicate that pre-modern society accommodated and shielded to some extent those in poverty, encouraging them to accept and even take pride in their station in life, the same society ironically used proverbs to discourage interaction between people of different social and economic statuses. In this way the relatively rich maintained the status quo, and the fact that such limitations were accepted by those experiencing poverty testifies to their fatalistic view about their circumstances.

> **Akajjaobunakukeemanya, ejjanziterigendananzige; eriisolijjan'obukwinobwalyo.**
> A grasshopper does not fly with locusts; an eye is contented with its lashes.
> A poor individual should know his limitations.
> **Nnabyewanga, ng'akaligaakaliira mu nte (oba mu nyana).**
> A poor person who imposes himself onto a different group, like a lamb which grazes among cattle or calves is a disgrace.
> **Kagulumule, ng'omukazialyan'abaddu.**
> A puzzling individual, like a respectable married woman, who eats with the servants. It is not proper for a person of high status to interact with people of a low status like the poor.

Recognizing the Importance of Fate

> **Ayakuhaireniweyanyimire.**
> (You are) rich, but take caution, you may lose it all.

As noted earlier, poverty in the pre-modern era, though endemic and severe, was not universal. Clusters of relatively rich individuals coexisted with those in poverty, and poverty and wealth were both attributed to fate over which nobody had control. Those who were relatively rich were always reminded that the spirits (*Bacwezi*) that blessed them with wealth are the same that deprived those who were poor. The above proverb and others below typify this understanding and probably serve to explain why the relatively rich felt obliged, to some extent, to accommodate and respect those living in poverty. Both poverty and wealth were seen as transitory situations. The poor were encouraged to be hopeful, and the relatively rich not to brag about their wealth or behave shamefully lest they lose it all.

> **Abasajjamivule; giwaatula ne giggumiza.**
> Men are mivule trees; they shed off their leaves and later regenerate. In the same way, a rich person may become poor but regain wealth.
> Poverty and wealth respectively are not permanent situations.
> **Bw'ofunatoduulanga.**
> When you become wealthy, do not become snobbish.
> Wealth and poverty are not permanent situations; someday you may be in the same situation as the people you despise for being poor.

Similarly, proverbs played a role in reminding those with wealth of some of its drawbacks, for example that they were not genuinely liked and that they were always at risk of losing, not only their wealth but friends and relatives when the whims of fate deserted them and they were reduced to poverty and its potentially shaming effects.

> **Bw'ogwaawabi, ng'eyalimunnoakwerabira.**
> When you get poor, an old friend will forget you.
> Nobody likes associating with the poor.
> **Ddibalikaze, enyomozikolonge.**
> The hide/skin has dried. Let the brown sugar ants roll it.
> When poverty strikes, one is abandoned even by friends who used to depend on him.
> **Omunyarugandaakundaotungire.**
> A relative likes you when you are wealthy.
> The rich are not genuinely liked, even by relatives.

In the context where both wealth and poverty were largely attributed to fate rather than structural factors and individual failings, society expected the rich to share their wealth or to be generous to their underprivileged poor neighbours, even if they kept a social distance from them. The rich who did not conform to this expectation were seen as heartless, greedy, immoral, and potential victims of the destructive power of their greed. Their behaviour was considered deviant and shameful and a threat to social cohesion. Thus for the relatively rich, giving became a conscience cleansing ritual and those in need were expected to appreciate these selfless acts. Evidence from the traditional proverbs suggests that the poor readily appreciated whatever was given to them, heaping praises on the rich or even equating them with war heroes.

> **Gw'awaekinuamwebazanti, 'Yoga yogaSsalongo'.**
> Because when he gives something to someone, he is thanked like 'welcome back Ssalongo' (this has a hidden meaning implying welcome back from war, or hard task).

Omugagga g' waekintuobaebintuamwebazanti, 'Ompaddemwanawange'.
When a rich man donates something to a poor person, he is thanked thus; 'you have given me my child'.

Modern Times: The Emergence of Poverty-Induced Shame and Wealth Shamelessness

The Growing Importance of Money

The colonial (1894–1962) and the postcolonial (1963–2013) eras that broadly represent modern society in Uganda ushered in fundamental changes that impacted differently on the definition and experience of poverty and relative wealth. The changes in question include the establishment of colonial administrative structures; the introduction of currency as a medium of commercial exchange; the establishment of public service employment and taxation; the introduction of formal education and health services; the introduction of the cash crop economy (coffee, cotton, tea, tobacco, sugarcane); physical infrastructure development (roads, rail and marine transport); and the subsequent growth of both formal and informal commerce.

The combined effects of these changes were the gradual demise of communalism, the hitherto main ingredient for maintaining social cohesion; and the increasing emergence of a subculture of individualism and consumerism. Similarly, this period saw the diminishing role of fate as an explanatory distinction between those living in poverty and those enjoying relative wealth. Increasing emphasis was placed on the ability of the self to acquire, accumulate, and retain wealth. Shame to the self or family that had hitherto been attributed to individual transgressions or deviant behaviour per se; and regulated by social sanctions or pressures to conform, became increasingly seen in terms of individual ineptness to achieve, especially in regard to accumulation of material wealth and its associated social capital.

Probably the most significant of these changes was the introduction of legal tender (*ensimbi*) as a medium of commercial exchange. The subsequent cash economy did not only lead to economic transformation, but also created a new set of social values where the causes and perpetuation of poverty were seen differently. Individual ability to accumulate money was glorified and the belief that the spirits largely determined who became rich or fell into poverty gradually waned. Increasingly, any inability to accumulate money and material wealth was attributed to individual shortcomings and thus subject to criticism. Money became a form of deity to be worshiped, and those who did not have it became seen as objects of social ridicule.

Ennsimbiziwoome.
Money is sweet.
Ensimbiky'eremwaow'enkatatazinga.
Money is a solution to everything.
Omuntualinaensimbiennyingiasobolaokukolaekinuekizibuatazirinaky'
atasobolakukola.
One who is wealthy can solve difficult issues, which one without money cannot.
Ekiremeresente, naga.
What money cannot accomplish, throw it away.
Money is the solution to every challenge.

The diminishing role of the spirits (*Bachwezi*) in achieving both economically and socially, coupled with the heightened emphasis on individual capabilities and/or vulnerabilities saw the gradual emergence and entrenchment of poverty-induced shame and wealth shamelessness. Society became increasingly polarized, shaped by social and economic inequality where those who were seen as innovative, enterprising, creative, or shrewd were placed at one end of the spectrum and others who lacked these qualities, at the other. Those considered rich did not only enjoy a life of material comfort and elevated social status, but went about without guilt or shame.

The respective behaviours of the characters in the reviewed literature attest to the above changes. Arguably, the social and economic disparities between individuals which characterize the modern literary period are a reflection of the wider socio-economic changes which, on the one hand, created financial incentives to achieve and, on the other, created challenges which constrained individual ability to accumulate wealth or attain social capital. Poverty which is endemic, severe, and painful is synonymous with underachieving, while material achievement, even when acquired shamefully, is glorified.

Wealth Shamelessness and Poverty-Induced Shame

While previously those who were ungenerous with their wealth were viewed negatively by society, increasingly the shameless rich rationalized their material acquisition and enhanced social capital as glorious and poverty as tantamount to personal mediocrity, laziness, and lack of initiative. Proverbs like '*Bona tibaingana*' (All people are not equal); '*Enkumuzoonatizingana*' (All fingers on the same hand are not of equal size), reflect the attitudes of the 'shameless' rich at the time.

The language of poverty through which the poor were respected and encouraged to take pride in their hardship transformed into the language of wealth, where the poor were blamed for their plight and became legitimate targets of ridicule and criticism. Poverty became increasingly attributed to social vices such as laziness, sexual promiscuity, and financial indiscipline. Those facing hardship were identified with socially deviant behaviours, a factor that did not augur well for the maintenance of their dignity in society.

> **Ensimbiabula', asiibawaka.**
> The poor can't find the money because they stay at home.
> Money is earned for doing work not just sitting at home. Laziness/lack of initiative causes poverty.
> **Ensimbizenfunasimanyigyezida, awasebanobye.**
> The money they get just disappears. The poor marry divorced women.
> Adultery and promiscuity cause poverty.

The evidence from modern literary texts indicates that time and spatial differences have not had much effect on representations of the incidence and severity of poverty in Ugandan society. The poverty described is largely the subsistence type characterized by inability of individuals to afford basic consumer commodities, a lack of decent shelter, inadequate personal effects including clothing, and the inability to access basic health care. A common cause of these deprivations is chronic cash shortfalls, and the consequences for the affected individuals include ill-being, emotional pain, and shame. In the play, *The Burdens* (Ruganda, 1972), the poverty that is experienced by Wamala and his family is described as an 'omnipresent cancer in society—a cancer that has to be endured'.

The characters in the plays and novels of this modern era are afflicted by deprivation, typified as urban misery and rural poverty, respectively. While urban poverty is a new phenomenon, a feature of modernity, both are shown to evoke feelings of inadequacy, shame, despair, and lack of agency which were not evident to the same extent in the pre-modern era. The literary texts portray, on the one hand, shame that is self-inflicted and, on the other, shame inflicted by others. In both cases, their overarching causes are rooted in the social, economic, and political transformations that have characterized the transition from the pre-modern to the modern period.

Self-Inflicted Shame

This type of shame is embedded in the psyche of the self, and characterized by self-criticism following from the inability to live up to one's own expectations and those of society in terms of material and social capital. Once fate was no longer seen as the underlying cause of poverty, the space for such self-inflicted shame began to grow. And while there is some evidence in the literature to suggest that this fatalistic explanation of poverty spilled over from the pre-modern into the modern era—characters like Nabirye (Ssebanga, 2010), Berewa (Ruganda, 1973), and (Kyomuhendo, 1996), for example, variously attribute their extreme ill-being to God's providence or family curses—this perception is residual in the literature and suggests that fate no longer provides the main explanatory factor for poverty in modern society.

The acute poverty experienced by the protagonists and other characters in the plays and novels is seen to create in their respective inner selves seemingly irreversible feelings of inadequacy. Since such shame is not characterized by failure to conform to cultural norms, values, or morals; it cannot be prevented or moderated by the imposition of social sanctions. It is presented as taking the form of self-pity, suggesting an internalization of poverty as an identity and failure to cope with social demands and expectations. Further, it is the type of shame that is crippling to the inner self as it cannot be physically avoided.

Shaming and Being Shamed by Others

The reviewed literature suggests strongly that the rapid social, economic, and political changes accompanying the start of the modern era in Uganda created social hierarchies in which those in poverty, the non-achievers, were assigned to the bottom of the social pyramid, while the rich, the achievers, were placed at the top. This stratification determines individual opportunity with respect to access to material resources and attainment of social capital. Further it has implications for poverty-induced shaming, as those at the bottom are seen as the most at risk of falling into poverty and experiencing its negative effects, such as shame.

In sharp contrast to the pre-modern era, modern literary works provide ample examples of relatively rich characters shaming those in poverty. Such behaviour is typified in the play *Black Mamba* (Ruganda, 1973). Despite the racial and socio-economic divide between them, the short-lived relationship between the young woman Namuddu and the professor clearly illustrates the disposition of those with wealth towards those who have nothing. The professor despises Namuddu. Her naivety and disorderliness in the house disgust him. He regards her as a prostitute, and at best his attitude towards her is patronizing. He is ashamed of her presence in his residence and orders her to hide so that she is not seen by visitors. The professor advises her not to develop expensive tastes, and to remain a simple 'poor girl', satisfied with the handouts she receives from him. He assertively rules out socializing with her in public, as this would shame him, assertions which make Namuddu in turn feel ashamed.

Similar depictions of people being shamed by others are abundant in the novels and plays and such derision takes places in multiple spaces, making it difficult for those in poverty to evade public derision. Hence the home, the school, bars, the office, the village well, the village court and the neighbourhood, all became spaces of ridicule. These different arenas may determine the incidence and severity of the shame that is directly inflicted or internally felt.

For instance, in the play *The Burdens* (Ruganda, 1972), at home, the protagonist Wamala is incessantly reminded by his wife, Tinka, of his inability to provide for his family. Outside the home Wamala is then shamed by the secretary when he visits the Associated Matches factory and is thrown off the premises on account of his tattered attire and unsightly appearance. The only space where Wamala is not subjected to such shame is the Republic Bar where he spends most of his time consorting with fellow drunks.

In the novel *The First Daughter* (Kyomuhendo, 1996), the protagonist Kasemire is bullied on her first day at secondary school by her richer peers on account of her extreme poverty. While she has endured the material privations within the home over many years, home has not been a space in which she has experienced shame. It is only when the stark material and social differences between her and the other 'richer' students emerge, that school becomes the locus for shaming and emotional pain that she has to bear.

Likewise, the play *Wrinkled Faces* (Ssebanga, 2010) sees the entire Isabirye family ridiculed by the community because of their crippling poverty. They are compelled to rely on the mercy of neighbours for basics like salt or a pounding mortar, but are publicly mocked for doing so. When Isabirye is released from jail and returns home penniless, his home becomes a potent source of shame, where he is unable to provide even the most basic commodities. Like Wamala, he tries to evade shame by avoiding his home.

Discussion and Conclusions

Though increasingly more is being written about the lived experiences and consequences of poverty globally (Beresford et al., 1999; Narayan et al., 2000) and about the various causes of shame and its behavioural consequences in different cultures (Shaver et al., 1992; Menton and Shweder, 1994; Kitayama et al., 1997; Romney et al., 1997; Stipek, 1998; Fischer, Manstead, and Mosquera, 1999; Crystal et al., 2001; Li et al., 2004; Tangney and Stuewig, 2004; Tsai, 2006), most mainstream poverty research has ignored not only the poverty–shame nexus, but also how poverty-induced shame has evolved over time. This research, which has combined an analysis of oral tradition through proverbs with novels and plays spanning the pre-modern and modern periods in Uganda, suggests that poverty-related shame is a relatively recent phenomenon that began in the late pre-modern era, and has continued to evolve throughout the modern era.

Analysis of the traditional proverbs that largely represent the ancient pre-modern period indicates that during this time, though poverty was endemic and severe, those experiencing it, the majority, went about without its associated shame. The few relatively rich also went about without the guilt that is often associated with being rich where others are experiencing extreme poverty. Instead, shame in this era is presented throughout the cultural media as a consequence of sociocultural transgressions which were regulated by an articulate framework of sanctions. Both the rich and those in poverty were thus equally prone to shame since the social sanctions targeted all transgressors irrespective of economic or social status. Shame as a feeling of being negatively evaluated by others (Lewis, 1987) was arguably at that time primarily a moral emotion (Tangney and Stuewig, 2004), principally affecting the transgressor, although in some cases also the transgressor's family.

In pre-modern times, poverty was defined not just in terms of lack of resources but included all forms of suffering; orphanhood, prolonged bachelorhood, gender-specific physiological conditions such as male erectile dysfunction, female infertility, and lack of biological relatives or extended kith and kin. In this broad context, it was possible for one to be both rich in material terms and at the same time be considered 'poor' as a result of being, for example, sexually impotent or unmarried. Fate explained the fortunes of those experiencing poverty (in this widest sense) or relative wealth. Consequently, wealth was not celebrated, nor poverty stigmatized, since everyone was equally vulnerable to its whims.

Evidence from the novels and texts analysed suggests that residual aspects of this thinking spilled over into the modern era, some of the characters attributing their hardship to family curses or divine providence. More generally however, the modern period, characterized by fundamental social, economic, and political transformation, has had the overall effect of creating new and dominant values. The social and economic disparities between those in poverty and the rich became increasingly represented as a product of individual failings leading to poverty and its associated shame, or personal motivation leading to wealth and self-glorification. The cultural media imply that the growth in consumerism and individualism in modern society has progressively equated poverty with dysfunctional behaviour. In reality, however, those who have attained social or economic success are few. The divide between those living in poverty and the rich has increased, and living without shame is seen as an uphill struggle for those who are trapped in poverty.

In Chapter 9 we focus our attention on men, women, and children living in extreme poverty in a rural Ugandan setting with the aim of ascertaining the extent, if at all, to which poverty and shame are linked in real life. As will be appreciated, the literary representations of poverty and poverty-related shame, delineated in this chapter, closely resemble the everyday lives of people experiencing economic hardship in contemporary Uganda.

References

Beresford, P., Green, D., Lister, R., and Anderwood, K. (1999) *Poverty First Hand; Poor People Speak for Themselves*, London: CPAG.

Crystal, D.S., Parrott, W.G., Okazaki, Y., and Watanabe, H. (2001) 'Examining relations between shame and personality among university students in the United States and Japan; A developmental perspective', *International Journal of Behavioral Development*, 25: 113–23.

Fischer, A. H., Manstead, A. S. R., and Mosquera, P. M. R (1999)'The role of honour related vs. individualistic values in conceptualizing pride, shame, and anger; Spanish and Dutch cultural prototypes', *Cognition and Emotion*, 13: 149–79.

Kitayama, S., Markus, H. R., Matsumoto, H., and Norasakkunkit, V. (1997) 'Individual and collective processes in the construction of the self: Self enhancement in the United States and self-criticism in Japan', *Journal of Personality and Social Psychology*, 72: 1245–67.

Kyomuhendo, G. (1996) *The First Daughter*, Kampala: Fountain Publishers.

Lewis, H. B. (1987) 'The role of shame in depression over the lifespan', in Lewis, H. B. (ed.) *The Role of Shame in Symptom Formation*, Hillside, NJ: Erlbaum.

Li, J., Wang, L., and Fischer, K.W. (2004) 'The organisation of Chinese shame concepts', *Cognition and Emotion*, 18: 767–97.

Lule, J. and Namboze, J. (2006) *The Hidden Wisdom of the Baganda. Amagezig'Omugan-daAmakusike*, Arlington, Virginia: Humbolt and Hartman.

Menton, U., and Shweder, R. A. (1994) 'Kali's tongue: Cultural psychology and the power of shame in Orissa, India', in Kitayama, S. and Markus, H. R. (eds) *Emotion and Culture: Empirical studies of mutual influence*, Washington, DC: American Psychological Association, 241–82.

Narayan, D., Patel, R., Schaft, Rademacher, K., and Koch-Schuite, S. (2000) *Voices of the poor; Can anyone hear us?*, New York; Published for the World Bank, Oxford University Press.

Nsimbi Bazzebulala, M. (2004) *Siwa Muto Lugero*, Kampala: Crown Books Ltd.

Romney, A. K., Moore, C. C., and Rusch, C. D. (1997) 'Cultural universals: measuring the semantic structure of emotion terms in English and Japanese', *Proceedings of the National Academy of Science*, 94: 5489–94.

Ruganda, J. (1972) *The Burdens*, Kenya: Oxford University Press, East Africa Ltd.

Ruganda, J. (1973) *Black Mamba*, Nairobi: East African Educational Publishers Ltd.

Sentongo, K., Sentoogo, W., and Kirembeka, B. (2006) *Entanday'Omwogeziw'Olulimi-Oluganda*, Kampala: Fountain Publishers.

Shaver, P., Wu, S., and Schwartz, J. (1992) 'Cross-cultural similarities and differences in emotion and its representation: a prototype approach', in Clark, M. S. (ed.) *Review of Personality and Social Psychology*, Newbury Park, CA: Sage, 175–212.

Ssebanga Masembe, C. (2010) *Wrinkled Faces*, Kampala: Fountain Publishers.

Stipek, D. (1998) 'Differences between Americans and Chinese in the circumstances evoking pride, shame, and guilt', *Journal of Cross-Cultural Psychology*, 79: 616–29.

Tsai, J. (2006) 'Cultural differences in the valuation of shame and other complex emotions', cited in 'Cultural Models of Shame and Guilt', in Tracy, J., Robins, R., and Tangney, J. (eds) *The Self Conscious Emotions*, New York: Guildford Press.

Tangney, J. P. and Stuewig, J. (2004) 'A moral emotional perspective on evil persons and evil deeds', in Miller, A. G. (ed.) *The Social Psychology of Good and Evil*, New York: Guilford Press.

Tumusiime, J. R. (2007) *Entanda, y'Omugambiw'OrunyakoreRukiga*, Kampala: Fountain Publishers.

3

The Wealth of Poverty-Induced Shame in Urdu Literature

Sohail Anwar Choudhry

> Away from my native place; in bringing me death abroad
> How God averted my shame of helplessness going exposed[1]

Introduction

Ghalib,[2] the poet who wrote the verses above, is certainly not the only person seeking to hide the shame of inadequacy in the nineteenth-century Indian subcontinent. However, he is among the very few people of the time who eloquently portrays the bitterness of the experience of helplessness; exposure to which, he thinks, is worse than dying in a foreign land. For Ghalib, such helplessness is not merely poetic illusion but an account of his survival of a turbulent time of Indian history, which witnessed the decline of Moghal power and the ultimate subjugation of India as a British colony (Hyder, 2006).

Ghalib bears witness to his own poverty-related helplessness in his diary of 1857–58, in which he narrates his abject economic condition, and that of others around him, and the emotional distress it causes; 'A few poor, reclusive men, who received their bread and salt by the grace of the British, lived scattered . . . these humble peaceful people . . . I was one of these helpless, stricken men' (Quoted in Raja, 2009: 46). Dependent on someone else's grace

---

[1] Self-translation of poem 78(1), p. 31 of the Bodleian Library digitized copy of Dīvān-i-Ghālib-iUrdū (1883) Lakhna'uMunshi Naval Kishor, accessed 27 February 2013 at <http://solo.bodleian.ox.ac.uk/primo_library/libweb/action/dlDisplay.do?vid=OXVU1&docId=oxfaleph016995792>.

[2] Asad Ullah Khan Ghalib (1796–1869) Urdu and Persian poet included in the sample.

for food, the greatest poet of his time neatly illustrates the power of words to portray the social and emotional circumstances of an entire era.

This chapter traces how the connection between poverty and shame is portrayed in samples of poetry and short stories from the last three centuries of Urdu literature and investigates whether or not shame is a core attribute of the cultural conception of poverty in Pakistan. The rationale behind investigating literature as a potentially valuable source of information is the widely held belief that literature mirrors a society's values, norms, and social mores (Daiches, 1938; Trilling, 1970). Over 425 short stories and 3,650 poetic compositions by ten of the most respected Urdu writers have been examined to explore and understand the historical and literary expressions of and associations between poverty and shame. A discourse analysis was carried out on extracts of texts, within the 'new Historicism approach' (Gallagher and Greenblatt, 2000). This enabled in-depth investigation of the themes of poverty and shame within the texts, taking account of their prevailing socio-economic and political contexts.

The findings of this analysis suggest a lasting interaction between poverty and shame within Urdu literature, despite political, intellectual, and social changes over time. The remainder of the chapter discusses this connection, with particular focus on the literary perceptions of poverty and shame, their mutual interaction, and the arenas in which they coincide. The chapter ends with a discussion of the perceived consequences of shame resulting from poverty and the sorts of coping strategies used to mitigate its impact.

Representations of Poverty

The evolution of the Urdu language can be traced to the eleventh-century blending of the languages of the Persian and Turkish invaders with native languages such as Punjabi, Sindhi, and Sanskrit (Sadiq, 1964; Bailey, 2008). Pre-nineteenth century Urdu literature shows a relatively stronger tradition of fictional prose and poetry, especially 'ghazal'[3] which is structurally suited to communicating philosophical, spiritual, and romantic ideas. However, with major political upheavals in the mid-nineteenth century culminating in the end of Muslim rule in India, the literature of the post-1860s placed a new emphasis on society, social circumstances, and people. This change is vividly reflected in the new poetry recital gatherings of 'munazima'; a progressive twentieth-century movement which required poets of the time to focus their

---

[3] A poetic composition of couplets that follow a certain meter and rhyme scheme yet are thematically autonomous of each other.

literary intellect towards delivering poems on pre-assigned topics of human interest, everyday life, and its realities (Kanda, 1998).

However, what has not changed over the centuries is how writers have continuously portrayed the harshness of the experience of poverty; from hunger and material deprivation to feelings of social inadequacy and emotional distress, they have used various literary techniques to capture the negative nature and associations of poverty. For instance; in one of the verses of classical eighteenth-century Urdu poetry, Meer[4] (1723–1810) uses the symbolism of poverty to evoke a sense of deep unhappiness:

> My heart stays extinguished in the evening
> Just like the lantern of a poor fellow[5]

In this verse, although the object of distress appears to be in the poet's heart, the most potent reference he finds to compare his emotional distress is the material deprivation of someone in poverty. The imagery subtly combines emotional and material inadequacy. This contrasts sharply with another eighteenth-century poet, Nazeer,[6] who boldly presents poverty as sheer degradation:

> A destitute person cannot keep his honour in view
> He strives to death for each 'Naan' he sees
> He readily falls for a loaf of bread day or night
> Much the way dogs fight over a piece of bone
> Is how poverty makes the poor fight each other[7]

Two hundred years later, the literature of the second half of the twentieth century shows few signs of conformity in terms of how poverty is described. Faiz[8] artistically equates the overwhelming grief of his life to the cloak of a beggar, 'Life is like a beggar's tunic that picks on/Patches of pain each moment';[9] just as the protagonist of Chander's short story *Julie Kaseran* (Chander, 1984) equates poverty with a 'water level of circumstance' where to survive, one has to stay above this level (Chander, 2009).[10] However, alongside these more symbolic descriptions still run the vivid portrayals of misery and exploitation. Qasmi (2002), for example, shows the poor peasants of his short story, 'Lawrence of Thalabia', subjected to physical punishment from their feudal

---

[4] Meer Taqi Meer (1723–1810) Urdu poet included in the sample.

[5] Self-translation of Meer's couplet from Meer, T. M. (2008).

[6] Nazeer Akbar-Abadi (1740–1830), Urdu poet included in the sample.

[7] Self-translation of sixth Quintain of Nazeer's poem 'Muflisi ki Philosopy', from Akbar-Abadi (2010: 791).

[8] Faiz Ahmed Faiz, twentieth-century Urdu poet included in the sample.

[9] Verses 8 to 9 of Faiz's poem 'Chand Roz Aur Meri Jan', trans. 'A Few Days More My Love' from Kumar, S. K. (2001) 'The Best of Faiz', New Delhi: UBS Publishers, p. 34.

[10] Krishan Chander (1914–1977) Urdu short-story writer included in the sample.

lord; and the protagonist of the short story *Ab Aur Kehnay Ki Zarurat Nahin* (Manto, 1990),[11] routinely goes to jail for owning up to the illegal actions of the rich in exchange for money. These various representations of the experience of poverty are designed to fit within their respective fictional situations, thus reaffirming the complexity of poverty and the diversity of its experience.

Poverty and Agency

Urdu literature offers many illustrations of how poverty can limit people's choices and make them behave in certain undesirable ways. This diminished human agency is shown to make such people defenceless and further vulnerable to other external pressures. For instance, Fika, the protagonist of Qasmi's[12] short story *Safarish*, does not dare question the false promises and lies told to him by the narrator, because of his acute sense of poverty (Qasmi, 2002). Similarly, in Ashfaq's[13] *Bandrabin Ki Qunj Gali Mein* (Ahmed, 1963), the protagonist is unable to pay off and retain a library book which has great sentimental value for him.

The same diminished agency has long been recognized in Urdu love poetry, where the crucial role of material prosperity in maintaining amorous relationships is well-understood. Meer (2008) expresses it vividly in a monologue couplet, 'Devoid of power and of riches, On what assumption did you nourish this affinity?';[14] just as Ghalib (2005) acknowledges the need for it a century later; 'Beloved is rumored today to visit, Pity, no perquisite for visitation'.[15] Regardless of time and era, this diminished agency as a consequence of poverty is repeatedly shown to make it harder for people to benefit from social and emotional opportunities, exercise rational choices, or express their true emotions. Feelings of diminished agency can equally inculcate feelings of inferiority in an individual and lead to a 'confrontation between the self and socialization' (Fox, 1994: 10), a conflict that represents the contemporary psychoanalytical understanding of shame.

Urdu Literature and the Concept of Shame

While the conventional psychosocial understanding of shame is that of a painful negative view of 'self', Urdu literature also has a strong tradition

---

[11] Saadat Hasan Manto (1912–1955) Urdu short-story writer included in the sample.
[12] Ahmed Nadeem Qasmi (1916–2006), Urdu poet and short-story writer included in the sample.
[13] Ashfaq Ahmed (1925–2004), an Urdu novelist and short-story writer of the twentieth century.
[14] Self-translation of a couplet in Meer (2008: 141).
[15] 58:5 from Ghalib (2005).

of 'positive shame', related to attributes such as shyness, modesty, conscience, and appropriateness. In fact, the most prevalent translation of the word shame appears to be 'sharm' which captures these positive associations more accurately than the negative self-review. Ghalib (2005) tells his shy beloved, 'You make everyone swoon, your face full waxing moon; Why keep yourself from public immune, you are beauty incarnate', just as Iqbal[16] and Faiz are keen to celebrate this trait in their loved ones:

> You are like a reddened flower! Do not be shy so much;
> For I am nothing but a soft morning breeze[17]
>
> Rid this grace of innocence, my love!
> My sinful gaze is put to shame[18]

While such shame is presented as a positive attribute, literature considers lack of modesty, or behaving in an undignified or a socially unacceptable manner, as shamelessness. For instance; in *Do Haath* (Chughtai, 1978) and *Bachni* (Manto, 1990), it is not so much the fact that low-income female workers are extending sexual favours to others that is presented as shamelessness but the responses of others around them. For example, the behaviour of the husband and mother-in-law of Gori, the main protagonist in *Do Haath*, is seen as shameless in being prepared to ignore her indiscretions, as long as she is employable. In a different, slightly humorous incident, Ghalib indulges in a socially unacceptable behaviour when, penniless, he beseeches the bartender to allow him the leftover wine from the used glasses:

> To Saqi, 'tis hard to explain, that I don't disdain
> Content I remain, with remnants of wine to be treated[19]

While Ghalib's description of shamelessness is somewhat nuanced, literature has many examples of its extreme manifestation in relation to poverty. For instance, Nazeer (2010) describes the want for money in the following words:

> (People) sustain abuse and beating for money
> (And) let go of their shame and modesty for money
> Several of us are so intoxicated by money
> That they will lift it from filth through their teeth[20]

---

[16] Dr Muhammad Iqbal (1877–1938) Urdu and Persian poet included in the sample.
[17] Self-translation of couplet (Iqbal, 2000: 480).
[18] Self-translation of Faiz's couplet from Faiz, A. F. (2005).
[19] 110:2 from Ghalib (2005).
[20] Self-translation of lines 31, 32, 37, and 38 of Nazeer's poem 'Kori ki Philosophy', in Akbar-Abadi (2010: 780).

Poverty-Induced Shame

While the examples above identify the need or want of money as the cause of individual shameless behaviour, the real shame of poverty as understood in the psychosocial literature is presented entirely differently. With poverty-induced shame, the individual may not dare to come to the bar in the first place, let alone find the courage to look at the bartender eye-to-eye and make such a daring request as Ghalib's. Although the shame of poverty is sometimes induced by temporary hardship, it more often stems from long-term socio-economic failure, which can impose a permanent identity on those who are unable to overcome their economic circumstances.

The literature suggests that shame that arises from poverty leads to a complex process in which such shame feeds off the negative sense of self and thus becomes perpetuated and accentuated. This is well illustrated by the depiction of Meer narrating his efforts to seek administrative support:

> Such was I fed up with the hardship of poverty
> That I went to Sheikh's house hundreds of times
> There wasn't one friend of mine in the royal army
> Who did not testify of my plight to him
> So extremely desperate was I from my adversity[21]

Here the desperation of material deprivation makes Meer engage in a process whose outcome is beyond his control. While undergoing this process, he becomes apprehensive and uncertain, as is evident from the desperation of his narration. It appears that Meer's behaviour and social life are compromised by his pursuit of assistance from an official who is unavailable or uninterested. He has also undergone the shame of involving his 'friends in the royal army' to testify to his eligibility for assistance, and yet nothing has resulted in his favour. Having exhausted all the apparent options, what Meer does subsequently is even more sinister; he indulges in unnatural flattery and adulation of the 'Sheikh' to achieve his purpose:

> When nothing else worked for me
> I resorted to endless flattery of the Sheikh
> I went on and on about his princely lineage
> But as it is, he never gratified my supplication
> In the end, I lost honour and got all blemished[22]

---

[21] Self-translation of the twentieth stanza of poem 'The Other Quintain', in Meer, T. M. (2008: 956).

[22] Self-translation of the twenty-first stanza of poem 'The Other Quintain', in Meer, T. M. (2008: 957).

This above sequence of events suggests that while someone in need is likely to experience shame, other external factors often trigger, exacerbate, or perpetuate such shame. In this case, the inaction of 'Sheikh' induces in Meer a degree of humiliation that could otherwise have been avoided. In the end, the external shaming evokes in him an internal feeling of shame due to lost honour. Similarly Ghalib, in an almost identical situation, feels an acute sense of internalized shame even before presenting to the King his request to have his six-monthly allowance converted into a monthly one:

> Though for the shame of no ability
> I am so low in my own eyes
> That if I call myself made of clay
> I know the clay would feel ashamed of that (comparison). . . .
> (And yet) There does not exist in the world today
> A poet as fine and pleasant-wit as me. . . .
> Grant my salary on a month to month
> So that life is not so tough on me[23]

It is evident here that a perceived sense of personal failure has made Ghalib ashamed of his condition and that vicarious shaming can arise from mere self-comparison of one's inadequacy in relation to others. A previous experience (probably at the point of asking for a six-monthly allowance) has already humbled Ghalib, overshadowing his pride of being the greatest poet of his time.

Arenas for Shame and Shaming

The literature shows that as well as causing shame to individuals, economic failure can isolate and shame communities, castes, and tribes by placing them at the bottom of the social hierarchy. According to a note by the superintendent of the 1901 census in Bengal, demographic and economic factors had divided the Muslims of Bengal into two social divisions;

> (1) Ashraf or Sharaf and (2) Ajlaf. Ashraf means 'noble' and includes all undoubted descendants of foreigners and converts from high caste Hindus. By contrast, converts of lower ranks are known by the contemptuous term, 'Ajlaf', 'wretches', or 'mean people'. In some places a third class, called Arzal or 'lowest of all', is

---

[23] Self-translation of verses 5, 6, 23, and 28 of Ghalib's poem 'Guzarish Musanif Bahazoor-e-Shah' (Ghalib's supplication before the King) at page 99/100 of the Bodleian Library digitized copy of Dīvān-iG̱ẖālib-iUrdū (1883) Lakhna'uMunshi Naval Kishor, accessed 27 February 2014 at <http://solo.bodleian.ox.ac.uk/primo_library/libweb/action/dlDisplay.do?vid=OXVU1&docId=oxfaleph016995792>.

added. With them no other Mahomedan would associate, and they are forbidden to enter the mosque or to use the public burial ground.[24]

These observations provide a social backdrop against which many works of the writers can be better understood. For instance, in the short story 'Fashion', Najma convinces her maid to act as a secret go-between for herself and her prospective boyfriend, saying; 'being a daughter of a respectable man, it will be unbecoming of me to sneak into the house of a man I have no social connection with' (Qasmi, 2002: 31). On the one hand, this request illustrates the assertion of high-income people that they are of higher moral standing and, on the other, exhibits the little space that is available for low-income people, like the maid, to resist such insults. Since her economic circumstances and status mean that she has no choice, she indulges in an activity even though she may find it demeaning.

The literary analysis suggests that both high-income and low-income people adhere to a division of respect and respectability on the basis of money and social class. Although one of its most obvious sources remains the lack of income, poverty-related shame may equally arise from material deprivation, social class, profession, family lineage, and friends. Want of money and association with a lower social class carry a stigma that has endured the intellectual evolution of the past three centuries. Yet the cultural streak of shame of inadequacy goes even beyond money and social class. For instance, while Chander's Tai *Iesri* (Chander, 2009) is a motherly figure for her entire village, she still takes a purging bath if her hands ever come in contact with a low-caste person. And the shame of lineage becomes even worse for children in poverty born out of wedlock; as evident in *Ishq Pur Zor Nahin* (Chughtai, 1978).[25]

A highly enduring theme related to the issue of lineage is the preservation of the social status quo. In the short story *Jota* (Qasmi, 1995), a village headman goes to great lengths to buy an expensive jacket from a low-caste person, Karmo, so as to preserve the social decorum of the village, as he cannot tolerate a 'two penny low caste poor' person seen in public wearing a respectable garment. In *The last Salute* (Manto, 1990), Rab Nawaz (Sergeant) carries the stigma of being the son of a potter just as in *Bandrabin Ki Qunj Gali Mein* (Ahmed, 1963), the protagonist is faced with the dilemma of being the son of a fisherman.

Within the cultural context of the subcontinent, the shame of poverty further intensifies when it comes to dealing with certain social obligations such as matters of marriage and relationships. In the short story 'Chothi

---

[24] Quoted from Chapter X of the electronic version of B. R. Ambedkar's book *Pakistan or the Partition of India*, 1945 available at <http://www.columbia.edu/itc/mealac/pritchett/00ambedkar/ambedkar_partition/index.html>, accessed 27 February 2014.

[25] Ismat Chughtai (1911–1991); Urdu short-story writer in the sample.

Ka Jora' (Chughtai, 1978), there is an acute sense of shame on the part of an entire family to admit to their humble economic status before their future son-in-law. Often this attitude makes people spend and borrow beyond their means, something that results in further hardship for them and their families. Here Ghalib once again shows up in his imaginary bar, disclosing that the money he occasionally spent on wine was all borrowed:

> We were drinking on borrowed cash, knowing all the time
> That living beyond our means will mean dispassion one day[26]

Responses to Shame

Urdu literature supports the presence of an instinctive attempt on the part of shamed individuals to redress the weakness that is causing them shame. The young cigarette addict of Ahmed's short story *Pachtawa* quickly seizes the opportunity to end his shame of riding an old bike by agreeing to give up smoking in return for a 'respectable' new bike. Regarded as 'restore' or 'approach' behaviour by some social psychologists (Tangney, 1996; De Hooge et al., 2008), the shamed individual attempts to undo the damage caused to his threatened self. However, behavioural theory also indicates that 'approach' and 'withdrawal' behaviour, in most cases, occur in quick succession (Frijda et al., 1989; De Hooge et al., 2010). So while a person experiencing or feeling threatened by the risk of shame initially attempts to restore their sense of self dignity or status, if unsuccessful, they may quickly retreat from that social scenario to avoid any further ignominy and distress.

Understandably, when such shame is triggered by socio-economic conditions, it is often unlikely that it can be easily assuaged. Failing to restore the self from such feelings of shame, therefore, may lead to further negative consequences for physical, mental, and emotional well-being; despair and fatalism among the most common:

> There is not a ray of hope
> We do not see any scope[27]
>
> Life's deadlock who can break other than death, Asad
> A candle burns right till dawn, in every hue and aspect[28]

In the face of despair and fatalism, characters tend to withdraw from active participation, which over time results in their social exclusion. The analysis suggests that this exclusion jeopardizes an individual's further prospects of

---

[26] 60:3 from Ghalib (2005).   [27] 79:1 from Ghalib (2005).
[28] 'Ghalib; Rhymed Translations of Selected Ghazals' by Khawaja Tariq Mahmood, published by Ferozsons (Pvt). Ltd in 2005.

accessing economic, social, emotional, intellectual, and political benefits. Over time, many such characters become vulnerable to a disintegration of the 'self'. In some short stories as well as poetry, there is a vivid portrayal of the physical and mental disintegration of the characters bearing poverty-related shame for extended periods of time. In the first place, there seems to be a gradual decline in the socio-economic condition of the characters. This decline normally shows in the lifestyle, habits, and characters' qualities falling short of people's expectations, and gradually sets in motion a deterioration of the physical, psychological, emotional, and spiritual health of the characters.

Often a condition of loss of identity or an acute identity crisis also precedes or accompanies the disintegration of the self. In Ismat's Short story *Baikar* (Chughtai, 1978), the protagonist gradually becomes psychotic and finally succumbs to death because of the poverty and unemployment which forces his wife to work all day to feed their family. Some characters manifest an acute conflict between personal and social identities on their way to an ultimate emotional and psychological downfall. For some, this condition results in an intense desire to perish, along with their troubles:

> Ghalib is through with all the blights
> One blighted death is just another test[29]

However, as well as depicting the extreme horrors of poverty and shame, literature also acknowledges the presence of a sense of resistance to the shaming that is executed by those with economic and political control. At its most philosophical level, the idea of such a world of dominance is challenged altogether by writers such as Iqbal:

> Omnipotent, Righteous, Thou; but bitter the hours,
> Bitter the labourer's chained hours, in Thy world!
> When shall this galley of gold's dominion founder?
> Thy world, Thy day of wrath, Lord, stands and waits.[30]

In another poem, Iqbal goes even further in his craving to change the world by carving out an imaginary set of commands from God to the angels

> Rise, and from their slumber wake the poor ones of My world
> Shake the walls and windows of the mansions of the great!
> Find the field whose harvest is no peasant's daily bread—
> Garner in the furnace every ripening ear of wheat![31]

---

[29] 80:6 from Ghalib (2005).

[30] Verses 42 to 45 of poem 'Lenin before God', in *Gabriel's Wing* English translation p. 116 of Kiernan, V. G. (2004) *Poems from Iqbal; Renderings in English Verse with Comparative Urdu Text*, Oxford: Oxford University Press (rev. edn.).

[31] Verse 1–2 and 7–8 of poem 'God's Command to His Angels', p. 118 of Kiernan, V. G. (2004) *Poems from Iqbal; Renderings in English Verse with Comparative Urdu Text*, Oxford: Oxford University Press (rev. edn.).

At the individual level, such resistance is exhibited through traits of pride dignity and self-respect, in themselves important counters to feelings of poverty-induced shame. For instance; the protagonist of *Datan Walay* (Chander, 1984), refuses to accept a loan from a wealthy acquaintance to pay for the treatment of his wife. His wife ultimately dies of the illness with the result that he too commits suicide. Not much different is the story of Zaman in *Mystery King* (Ahmed, 2004), who, despite, a temporary spell of poverty, is reluctant to accept financial help from his friend to buy medicine for his son, who too subsequently dies.

The literature also suggests contentment as one of the counter-indicators of poverty-related shame. Nazir's long poem 'Contentment' highlights the happiness of a contented heart no matter how materially deprived. In Qasmi (1991) 'Mamta', the mother is prepared to starve to death rather than to recruit her son into the army in order to sustain her livelihood. Similarly, taking pride in work is presented as another counter-indicator to poverty-related shame, aptly portrayed by Iqbal in the following lines:

> Thy world is the world
> Thou dost create thyself.
> And not the world of bricks and mortar
> Before thy outward eyes.[32]

Conclusion

The analysis of Urdu poetry and short stories indicates a strong association between the experience of poverty and shame, an association that has lasting behavioural, social, and economic consequences for those experiencing economic hardship. The literary representations of poverty and shame suggest a process whereby poverty plays a significant role in undermining individual agency and enhancing vulnerability to feelings of shame. Shame, in turn, can lead to a poor self-image and a sense of inadequacy to participate fully in social and economic activities. This lack of participation may result in social exclusion, hence further aggravating the condition of poverty.

This analysis suggests that certain factors may trigger the processes of feeling shame. These include the established societal and cultural notions of respect and, based on them, the perception of the rich being superior to those living in poverty. This sense of superiority combines with the power to inflict shame on others and to bring the shaming process into effect. The capacity to shame, in individual situations, may involve a variable

---

[32] Verses from p. 506 of Iqbal (2000), translation from Iqbal Academy site at <www.allamaiqbal .com/>.

mix of money, social standing, and political privilege. Yet the other key contributor to the shaming process is the inability of the shamed individual to avert it. The literature suggests that the affluent, using the powers of money and social position, may create situations that are humiliating for those in poverty. Hence the space for shame emerges from the gap in wealth, and is reinforced by the hierarchy of social classes. It appears that in an ideal world, the social classes would prefer to abide by a process of social segregation and maintain the traditional status quo. But since such segregation is not possible in an economic system which requires these different classes to interact, they do so in a way which emphasizes the differences between them. Hence such interaction accentuates the sense of inferiority and appears to evoke shame in the members of the relatively poor and disadvantaged classes.

The literature indicates that the shaming process is generally insulting and agonizing for those living in poverty, and most commonly produces feelings of unworthiness and loss of pride. After an unsuccessful attempt of restoring their self-image, such people generally tend to withdraw and reduce their participation in social and economic activities. Some, however, are shown to develop resentment and anger against the rich at the individual and collective level. Others, albeit a minority, appear to respond differently by resisting feelings of shame; maintaining a dignified manner, trying to preserve self-respect by taking pride in their work, or resigning themselves to their circumstances. Yet, in its extreme, shame is shown to have the potential to provoke the physical, mental, and spiritual disintegration of those experiencing it.

All in all, analysis of Urdu poetry and short stories suggests a robust relationship between poverty and shame. Although this shame manifests itself in various forms, from subtle hesitation in social situations to physical abuse and torment, its source is rooted in material and income inadequacy. This lack in turn leads to a sense of inferiority, which hampers confident interaction with perceived superiors. Lack of participation is shown not only to marginalize such individuals socially but also to create further disadvantages, such as reducing access to availing economic and social opportunities, thus perpetuating the cycle of poverty and disadvantage.

References

Ahmed, A. (1963) *Aik Muhabat Sou Afsanay*, Lahore: Maktaba-e-Jadeed Press.

Ahmed, A. (2004) *Ashfaq kay Afsanay*, compiled by Tahir Saleem, Lahore: Noor Kitaab Ghar, Urdu Bazar.

Akbar-Abadi, N. (2010) *Kulyat-e-Nazir*, Khan, M. A. (ed.) Lahore: Al-Faisal Publishers.

Bailey, T. (2008) *A History of Urdu Literature*, Karachi: Oxford University Press.

Chander, K. (1984) *Chander Kay Muntakhib Afsaanay*, Muktaba e Shouq, Lahore.

Chander, K. (2009) *Karishan Chandar Kay Sou Afsanay*, Lahore: Chaudhry Academy.

Chughtai, I. (1978) *Do Haath*, Lahore: Maktaba-e-Urdu Adab, Lohari Gate.

Daiches, D. (1938) *Literature and Society*, London: Gollancz.

De Hooge, I. E., Breugelmans, S. M., and Zeelenberg, M. (2008) 'Not so ugly after all: When shame acts as a commitment devise', *Journal of Personality and Social Psychology*, 95(4): 933–43.

De Hooge, I. E., Zeelenberg, M., and Breugelmans, S. M. (2010) 'Restore and protect motivations following shame', *Cognition & Emotion*, 24(1): 111–27.

Faiz, A. F. (2005) *Nuskha Hae Wafa*, Maktaba e KarwaaN, Lahore.

Fox, P. (1994) *Class Fictions: Shame and Resistance in the British Working-Class Novel, 1890–1945,* Durham NC: Duke University Press.

Frijda, N. H., Kuipers, P., and TerSchure, E. (1989) Relations among emotion, appraisal, and emotional action readiness', *Journal of Personality and Social Psychology*, 57: 212–28.

Gallagher, C. and Greenblatt, S. (2000) *Practicing New Historicism*, Chicago: Chicago University Press.

Ghalib, A. K. (2005) *Ghalib; Rhymed translations* by Khawaja T. Mahmood, Lahore: Ferozsons.

Hyder, S. A. (2006) 'Ghalib and his Interlocutors', *Comparative Studies of South Asia, Africa and the Middle East*, 26(3): 462–75.

Iqbal, M. (2000) *Kulyaat e Iqbal*, Islamabad: Alhamra Publishing.

Kanda, K. C. (1998) *Masterpieces of Modern Urdu Poetry*, New Delhi: Sterling Publishers (Pvt.) Ltd.

Kiernan, V. G. (2004) *Poems from Iqbal; Renderings in English Verse with Comparative Urdu Text*, Oxford, OUP (rev. editn.).

Kumar, S. K. (2001) 'The Best of Faiz', New Delhi: UBS Publishers.

Manto, S. H. (1990) *Manto Nama*, Lahore: Sang-e-Meel Publishers.

Meer, T. M. (2008) *Kulyaat-Meer*, Lahore: Sang-e-Meel Publishers.

Qasmi, A. N. (1991) *Sannata*, Lahore: Asateer.

Qasmi, A. N. (1995) *Nila Pathar*, Lahore: Maktaba-e-Asateer.

Qasmi, A. N. (2002) *Kapaas Ka Phool*, Lahore: Asateer.

Raja, M. A. (2009) 'The Indian Rebellion of 1857 and Mirza Ghalib's Narrative of Survival', *Prose Studies: History, Theory, Criticism*, 31(1): 40–54.

Sadiq, M. (1964) *A History of Urdu Literature*, London: Oxford University Press.

Tangney, J. P. (1996) 'Conceptual and methodological issues in the assessment of shame and guilt', *Behaviour Research and Therapy*, 34: 741–54.

Trilling, L. (1970) *The Liberal Imagination: essays on literature and society*, Harmondsworth: Penguin, in association with Secker & Warburg.

4

Film and Literature as Social Commentary in India

Leemamol Mathew and Sony Pellissery

Introduction

Despite many historical discontinuities, such as invasions by other kings and states, the essence of Indian civilization and culture has remained more or less in tact since 8000 BC and, with subtle variations, is broadly similar across the South Asian continent. This long cultural history has created many symbolic forms or 'codes of honour and dishonour' (Casimir, 2009: 307) which play important roles in regulating social processes. This chapter examines how these social codes interact with poverty in a selection of popular cultural media in India and the extent to which they are implicated in the emergence of poverty-related shame.

As an empirical foundation to study the place of shame in Indian culture, we have relied on films, short stories, and proverbs. These cultural artifacts are effective means to study shame, since 'emotions are discursive public forms whose special power does indeed draw on embodied experience, without implying any parsimoniously describable universal biological substrate' (Appadurai, 1990: 93). Of all the cultural media in India, cinema in particular has captured the spirit of the populace (Vasudevan, 2000). In total, the chapter presents findings from an analysis of 30 films in six languages, 23 short stories in five languages, and proverbs from eight languages. The selected films span a period of sixty years, from 1950 to 2010, enabling us to assess whether any significant shifts have taken place in how poverty and shame have been culturally represented over time. The strong connection between cinema and literature, which has seen stories being reworked as screenplays for films, has been crucial in popularizing these different media.

Literature from four different eras was analysed, beginning with modern Indian literature, dating from the first independence mutiny in 1857. This body of work is essentially nationalistic, aimed at enlightening the masses about colonial rule and provoking resistance to it. The fundamental themes during this era centre on the oppressed life of the downtrodden and those living in poverty. This work was followed by the progressive movement in Indian literature which began in the 1930s and is characterized by a commitment to socialist ideology and its attack on social injustice and backwardness. Its aim was to inspire people to develop a collective identity through works that reflected the reality of their lives and which revered the least privileged as heroes and heroines. The ultimate aim of these writers was the abolition of poverty and inequality. The third body of work examined was Dalit literature which, although closely linked with the progressive works, stands as a distinct genre because it introduced a new approach to literature as a means of self-representation by a set of communities that have always been considered outcasts. Themes of poverty and related shame are prominent in Dalit literature since the social status of those from lower castes is invariably associated with lower status occupations. The fourth and final category of selected writers belongs to a body of contemporary Indian literature. Both the films and stories were chosen after consulting with experts in film and literary studies.

Representations of Poverty and Wealth in Indian Culture

The debate about what constitutes poverty is ongoing and largely centres on what resources, such as food, housing, and clothing, are considered necessary for a decent life (Sen, 1979). Values and culture shape the way needs are conceptualized and expressed, and thus the cultural dimensions of poverty not only complicate the debate about what constitutes poverty, but also dictate the 'representation' of poverty. This is significant because such cultural constructions ultimately inform the discourses underpinning the ideational basis for anti-poverty policies.

At a philosophical level, within Indian culture, poverty has always played a specific role. The Hindu tradition, for example, views whole reality as *maya* (or momentary appearance) within which *dharmic,* the righteous way of life, is opposed to the accumulation of riches. This is a well-known fact and one which has been elaborated in Weber's work on why capitalism, at least until relatively recently, developed rapidly in Western countries and not in India and China (1905/2002). The Buddhist critique of the Hindu tradition also assigned an important social role to suffering and poverty. The essence of Buddhism is to follow an eight-fold path to end *dukkha* (ill-being or suffering) primarily through the non-attachment to material things. In other words, through discipline and suffering, one overcomes misery and ill-being. These philosophical underpinnings lie at the heart of the proverb recognized in most Indian languages: 'Do not be arrogant of your richness, do not be ashamed of your poverty'.

At the same time, however, these premises sit at odds with what we discover when we examine the lives of protagonists in the various art forms. The systematic analysis of films and literature identified the pattern of images and phrases used to represent poverty. Some of the most common images in the films were of thin human beings in tattered clothes juxtaposed with fat rich people in glittering, colourful garments with flashy jewellery, riding around in plush vehicles. The impoverished characters in both films and stories are usually shown to be living in rural areas or urban slums. And while they are typically characterized as lonely and hard-working, their rich counterparts are usually portrayed in the company of family, relatives, and friends. Thus, wealth and poverty are defined not only in relation to the presence or absence of resources such as food, housing, clothes, and access to health, but also in terms of the social capital and networks on which people can draw.

Representations of Shame

Among the two linguistic roots in India (Sanskrit—mostly spoken in North India, and Dravidian—mostly spoken in South India) two different types of words are used to indicate shame. In Sanskrit the terms used are *Lajja* or *Saram*. Variations of the same are used in the North Indian languages such as Hindi, Bengali, Gujarati, Maithili. In South India the terms generally used are *Avamanam*, *Nanam*, and *Siggu*,[1] words commonly expressed in ways such as 'are you not ashamed?' or 'I feel ashamed' or sometimes, 'you shameless person!'.

The storylines and images in the films are revealing of how shame is associated with poverty. Characters with wealth and those living in poverty are often represented in very different ways with respect to their moral values. Rich people, for instance, tend to be depicted as being engaged in underhand business transactions, illicit sexual relations, and often only valuing other human beings for their material wealth. Those in poverty, on the other hand, are presented as innocent, faithful, light-hearted and with natural laughter, and willing to fight to the end for the values they uphold.[2] However, when it comes to the concept of shame, things become more complex.

---

[1] All these words can also be used in a positive sense to indicate a modest woman or young children hesitating to come into the company of adults.

[2] This antagonistic frame helps create the clash in storylines between good and evil in films and novels. The spectators often take the side of the good, and hence the film director or writer through these different media achieves the goal of 'social' responsibility.

Shame Embroiled with Honour

Honour has always been a central theme around which the storylines of many films and novels in India (probably in Asia as a whole) are formulated. Particularly in stories in which two feudal groups fight, the ascendancy of one group over the other is established by restoring honour. When a leader achieves honour, he does so not just for himself but for the whole community, often enduring episodes of hardship and loss of material resources in the process. In many respects, therefore, the maintenance of honour in Indian society supersedes the significance of poverty. In the Malayalam film, *Manassinakkare* (Sathyan Anthikkad, 2003), Kochu Thresia is a rich widow unable to enjoy the luxuries of her wealth. She is representative of many elderly people in India who are prone to poverty-induced shame in spite of living in rich families. Some are mercilessly thrown out of their homes or banished to retirement homes. Kochu Thresia, having divided her entire assets among her children, then realizes that her children have never loved her but only ever valued her wealth. In order to save her honour and avoid the shame she is made to feel, she decides to leave the house and in so doing accepts poverty in order to save her honour. It is against this supreme importance attached to honour that the representation of the antithetical concept of shame is examined.

Honour and shame interact in complex ways with wealth, social standing, and power, generating norms and social mores which percolate through community, social groups, family, and finally to the individual. People are shown, with some exceptions, to largely accept without questioning the power of those of higher economic and social standing. And the sense of powerlessness that people in poverty appear to experience in relation to those who possess wealth within their immediate households and communities is replicated in their relationships with the state, represented in various guises in film and literature by ministers, bureaucrats, and policemen.

Shame, Shaming, Caste, and Class

One of the well-rehearsed themes connecting poverty and shame in films and literature, irrespective of the era considered, is that of caste. Within the hierarchical arrangements of Indian society, caste occupies a central place providing a system of social stratification based on the principles of purity and occupation (Ghurye, 1969; Dumont, 1981). Outcasts (Dalits—literally meaning oppressed), who are subjected to the practice of 'untouchability' have long been considered to suffer injustice. Dalit writing has been recognized as a distinct genre because of its importance within the poverty–shame nexus. It is widely accepted that poverty in India is intricately linked with the rigid caste system,[3] birth into a lower caste in and of itself considered to be a shameful thing in many parts of India, resulting in social exclusion and discrimination. This is partly because of the beliefs in karma[4] that birth into a lower caste results from sins committed in a previous life. More broadly, and irrespective of where one is placed in the hierarchical class and caste structure, the salience of accepting one's place and not having aspirations above one's social status emerge as recurrent themes in film and literature.

The principle of purity within a hierarchical society such as India affords the greatest honour and dignity to those who have higher social ranking, with the result that those on the lowest rungs of the social ladder are regarded on a par with animals. The films protagonists are frequently people from lower castes, such as women engaged in domestic work, men carrying out agricultural labour and unclean jobs (such as cleaning toilets or the burial of carcasses), or young people eloping in the context of inter-caste marriage and their families who invariably become entwined in the ensuing chaos. All are shown to be subjected to persistent humiliation, mortification, and alienation because of their caste status.

In the film, *Vidheyan* (Adoor Gopalakrishnan, 1993), Baskara Pattelar, the feudal landlord, humiliates Thommy, a worker with the status of a bonded labourer, by addressing him in the following ways:

Patellar: Hey Dog! Come here
(*Thommy goes near Pattelar covering the torn portion of his clothes with his hand*).
Pattelar: What is in your hand? Do you feel like shitting? Don't you know to respect big people? Take your hands away from your back
(*Patellar kicks Thommy down and spits on his face*)
Thommy: Kindly spare me. Please!

In this situation, Thommy accepts his treatment as something he expects from his membership of a lower caste. A further chilling example is presented in the story of *Poisoned Bread* (Dangle, 1992) in which a lower-caste labourer

---

[3] Although, the Constitution of India outlaws caste-based discrimination, the caste system exists in India because of a strong belief system and political factors (such as caste-based mobilization of votes in Indian democracy). The caste divisions of Hinduism—Brahmin, Kshatriya, Vaisya, and Sudra—provide the dominant classifications. Below these castes are the outcasts and the untouchables. People who work in ignominious and unclean jobs are seen as polluting people and therefore considered as untouchables. What is known as *jati* (subcaste) is also largely based on occupational divisions (Ghurye, 1969).

[4] Belief in the laws of karma is strong in Hinduism. 'Karma', literally means, 'deed' or 'act', and more broadly names the Universal principle of cause and effect. The doctrine of karma states that one's state in this life is the result of actions in past incarnations. At the same time, tribal groups not sharing the ethic of karma (Pellissery, 2001) are also extensively found trapped in poverty. Therefore, karma alone cannot be blamed for poverty.

picks up the crumbs of food thrown to the domestic animals as wage for the day's labour. He does so with gratitude to the landlord and seemingly without demonstrating any sense of shame since, as with Thommy, the caste norms justify such action, and he feels that it is normal to obey them. In the latter story, however, the labourer's behaviour is contested by his educated son who is subsequently chastised by the labourer for not respecting such norms.

Yet in some instances, film is also used to contest and question the norms that perpetuate the shamefulness associated with the serendipity of birth into a lower caste and its associated poverty. In the 1954 Malayalam film *Neelak-kuyi*l, for instance, the director contrasts the general perception of shame associated with being born into a lower caste with the unorthodox ideas of the film's protagonist Sankar. A high-caste progressive individual, Sankar is criticized by the whole community when he decides to adopt the son of Neeli, a lower-caste 'untouchable' woman:

Crowd: Why do you shame your caste/community by taking this child?
Sankar: Can't you see? Aren't you human? Is there none among you with eyes to see? Does God want this child to be reared by men or beasts?
Crowd: He is born to a 'Pulayichi' (untouchable woman). You should be ashamed to take him.
Sankar: Isn't he a human child? Doesn't he have a right to live? Doesn't he? ... How can you bear to throw this baby into the streets? Do you trust God? Do you love your fellow beings? Does only the rich man's child have a right to live? This child has the same rights as you have. Like you, he's a citizen of the world. I'm no devil. I'm a human being. I cannot throw away this child. If God was not ashamed to create him, why should I be ashamed to take him?

In the story, *Poor Trishanku* (Parsai, 2003), Trishanku, the lead character, resides in a slum where his neighbours constitute the lowest strata of society. Being a school teacher, Trishanku considers himself to be superior to them, and his greatest ambition is to move to a larger house in a 'decent' neighbour-hood. Eventually, he manages to secure a superior home in an area named *Swargapuri* where he ostentatiously greets Indradev the owner of the house who, in turn, hardly acknowledges him. Instead, Indradev reprimands Trishanku for even having thoughts of living somewhere like *Swargapuri*. The following scene beautifully captures how the aspirations of those in poverty are stifled not just by lack of resources, but by class boundaries:

Trishanku: Why can't I live in that house? Am I not a man?
Indradev: *Looking at him intently*. No one who is just a man can live in this neighbourhood.
Trishanku: What do you mean?
Indradev: Simply, that you're not fit to live here. I need only look at a man to know all about him.

Trishanku: So what are the prerequisites for living here?
Indradev: *Looking at him with annoyance.* Beggars, for one, can't live here...
Do you have a car? A radiogram? A refrigerator? A sofa set?

Yet in contrast to the views imposed by the rich on those living in poverty, a scene in the film, *Kanchivaram* (Priyadarshan, 2008) demonstrates how fatalistic principles embedded within community norms equally generate and perpetuate differences in class and status. Vengadam, the hero in the film, is a silk weaver who is humiliated and criticized by his own people for appearing to have aspirations above his station. All through his life, Vengadam has dreamt of becoming the first person from his class to marry a bride with a silk sari. Unable, due to a lack of money, to fulfil his dreams, Vengadam finds himself humiliated on his wedding day by an old woman in the community who derides him for having ambitions above his station:

Old lady: *(taunting)* Why is she in a cotton sari? Where is the silk sari? Since the age of five you've been singing to the whole village that when you marry, your bride will be in a silk sari. What happened? I thought you'd be marrying the lord's daughter.
Vengadam doesn't respond, but puts his head down in shame.
Old lady: A silk weaver can only weave silk, not wear it.

The Gendering of Poverty and Shame

Since gender is central to allocating roles, responsibilities, resources, and rights in any society, it is likely to exacerbate the poverty of women in patriarchal societies. Culture and symbolic values have significantly contributed to the status of women in India. On the one hand women have been accorded supreme importance (including the status of Goddesses), while on the other, women are treated as commodities. As the relevance of religious symbolism fades over time, the ideational frameworks which uphold the status of women deteriorate, and only the commodified entity of womanhood is available for discourse and practice.[5] This is evident from widespread practices of female infanticide, as well as the reduced status of widows in India.

---

[5] Similar experience also exists when we look at the symbolic value that some other social groups are experiencing in poverty such as 'beggars', eunuchs (third gender), the elderly, and sex workers. Previously, 'beggars' were considered as wandering saints who had rejected 'worldly material wealth'. Eunuchs were believed to have power to take away curses and were invited for dancing on certain occasions. Elderly people had traditional authority in joint family settings, which has since withered. Sex workers were a tax-paying respected social group, sometimes called *devdasis* (servants of God). With the emergence of modern India, the ritual significance these groups occupied has faded and their material deprivation has become instrumental in defining their social exclusion.

Analysis of films and short stories showed that the female protagonists invariably bear the brunt of poverty-induced shame more than their male counterparts. Two overriding themes are worth highlighting. The first relates to dowry and the second relates more broadly to the modesty of women.

Since dowries constitute a system of bargaining in India, significant shaming takes place for women in the name of the dowry settlement. In the Bengali novel *Deonapana* (Tagore, 2008[1928]), Nirupama's parents are unable to secure the dowry they had agreed for her marriage. Therefore, from the moment she steps into her in-laws house, Nirupama receives a tirade of insults and is constantly subjected to harsh treatment. She is ashamed and humiliated at every stride since her poor father cannot find the means to raise the dowry price. The atrocities she faces, however, make Nirupama adopt a different perspective towards the dowry system and the value placed on woman. Having endured enough mortification, she finally tells her father, 'I will be humiliated only if you pay the money. Your girl has a certain dignity. Am I only a bag of money, having value as long as it is full? No, you should not humiliate me by paying this money' (p. 225). In the end Nirupama's constant exposure to shame and dishonour evokes a sense of resistance to the shame imposed on her, arguably a resistance easier to achieve through the director's poetic license than in reality.

A number of films show how *izzat* (honour associated with sexuality) operates as a mechanism of social control of women. In patriarchal societies like India, where violence against women is a common reality (Menon-Sen and Kumar, 2001), it would be surprising if such a theme was not depicted on the screen. In the Malayalam film, *Kalli Chellamma* (Sobhana Parameswaran Nair, 1969), Chellamma, the heroine, is a destitute, orphaned young woman. Despite her bravery, many people from different walks of life try to abuse her and take advantage of her poverty and beauty. She successfully resists these advances until she is trapped into a false marriage with Jose, who takes advantage of her womanhood and hard-earned money, concealing the fact that he is already married with two children. When Chellamma realizes the truth, she feels so ashamed and devastated that she finally commits suicide. In this film, the director illustrates the extent of abuse that young women in poverty were likely to endure in Indian society in the 1960s. A different style of sexual abuse can be seen in Pillai's (1969) story, 'Velutha Kunju' (The White Baby) which captures how women in remote Indian villages were sexually abused by the colonial rulers. In the story, Parayichi (a lower-caste woman) is tempted by a British officer and bears his child, a white baby. The event is presented as a serious shame on Parayichi, and the entire community.

The Impact of Poverty-Related Shame

Out of the thirty films selected, the lead characters in seven of them[6] take their own lives towards the end of the film as a result of the shame they are subjected to. This type of ending leaves a dramatic impact on the viewers, though real life is much more complex (a point to which we will return in our next chapter).

While suicide is the ultimate withdrawal from life, other forms of self-exclusion, undertaken in an effort to avoid shame, are frequently depicted in a number of films and literary works. In the film *Katha Parayumbol* (Mohanan, 2007) Balan, a barber, refuses to meet his childhood friend Asok Raj, now a celebrity, who is visiting Balan's village for a public function. While giving a speech, Asok Raj reminisces about his childhood friend Balan. Though present during the public function, Balan sneaks out without speaking to Asok. The conversation between both of them, after Asok Raj finds out where Balan is living and comes to visit him, exemplifies the rationale for such self-exclusion:

Balan: I heard your speech. I thought when you became famous, you had forgotten our past. Now I realize that I'm at fault and I'm sorry for that. Now you've come to my small house (hut) also.

Asok Raj: I searched for you everywhere, but I couldn't find you. But, you could have found me. Did you never feel the need to meet me in all these years?

Balan: I left our hometown without anything (due to a love marriage) and was trying to stand on my own feet for a long time. You became so famous in a short period of time. Initially, I thought of meeting you . . . a number of times. But, when years passed, I lost the courage to come before you. I felt you shouldn't see me in such an impoverished condition. May be that was just my feeling of inferiority.

Balan admits his fear and anticipation of being rejected by his friend and hence the need to avoid meeting him again, indicative of the paralysing effects of shame (Kaufman, 1996) and how it can lead to self-imposed exclusion and perpetuate poverty and hardship.

A contrasting response to withdrawal was, however, also present in some of the films. With shame comes the loss of self-honour and, as noted earlier, in India sustaining or re-establishing lost honour is essential for one's social existence. In the selected films and stories, some of the characters approach experiences which are deeply shaming with this restorative frame of mind. The reaction of Gandhi, in the film *Challenge* (Kondandarami Reddy, 1984)

---

[6] *Neelakkuyil* (1954), *Subarna Rekha* (1965), *Thulabharam* (1967), *KalliChellamma* (1969), *Vidheyan* (1993), *Kasthooriman* (2003), and *Peepli Live* (2010).

provides a good illustration of this point. When Gandhi attends a job inter-view, he is ill-treated by Ram Mohan Rao, the interviewer. The reason behind this ill treatment is that Gandhi's application has arrived with no stamp on it since he could not afford to buy one. In this situation, rather than allowing himself to be humiliated, an ashamed Gandhi counter-attacks:

Ram Mohan Rao: If you are so intelligent, why don't you use this intelli-gence to earn money?

Gandhi: Sir, every person has his own aim in life. Earning money is not an aim for everybody. In any case, earning money is not at all difficult.

Ram Mohan Rao: Don't argue like a fool. Poor people like you always argue in this way to satisfy your ego. You are poor and you are destined to be poor.

Gandhi: If that is the case, I will show you how I can change my destiny. I will earn 50 Lakhs in five years. It's my *Challenge.*

In the above scene, the humiliation by the officer in turn provoked Gandhi's pride, leading him to contest Ram Mohan Rao's assertion that he was destined to poverty. In the film Gandhi goes on to work hard and does in fact earn the 50 Lakhs in five years. Though he feels ashamed of his poverty, the humili-ation appears to spur him on to realize his aspirations.

Conclusion

In this chapter we have seen how the rich cultural heritage of India, associated primarily with religious and philosophical traditions, has deeply shaped the orientations towards poverty-induced shame; that such shame in turn inter-acts in complex ways with caste, class, and gender; and that particular social groups generate and sustain certain norms and codes with respect to shame and honour.

At the same time, however, the selected films and literary works demon-strate how codes of honour and shame have ambivalent significance. As shown in the chapter, acceptance by those in the lower echelons of society of the shame imposed by upper-caste members and those with wealth is prevalent, often leading to social exclusion and suppression of individual agency. However, the film and literature corpuses equally show how modern values proffer opportunities and create expectations that individuals will rise above and conquer such oppressions, their failure to do so reflecting their own inadequacies and failings.

The willingness to endure shame in the short term with the hope of even-tually redeeming dignity and honour is prominent in literature and film. On many occasions, such sacrifice is made in order to fulfil wider family or community responsibilities rather than for individual gain. An important question emerges out of the analysis of literature and films as to whether the overriding source of shame is in fact the state of poverty itself or the ascribed identity of being a member of a lower social class or, indeed as is most likely the case, a combination of both of these factors. An answer to this question helps clarify the different spaces for policy intervention to address poverty and its related shame in India. If the cultural material studied is to be believed, then such interventions need not only address the wider economic disparities and inequalities that perpetuate poverty but must also respond to the strong and embedded cultural and philosophical traditions that transcend contemporary society and which accentuate the importance of class, caste, and gender differences in the poverty-shame nexus. Whether or not class, caste, and gender have the same salience in real life as they do in fiction is the subject of Chapter 11 in this volume.

References

Appadurai, A. (1990) 'Topographies of the self: Praise and emotion in Hindu India', in Lutz, C. A., and Abu-Lughod, L. (ed.), *Language and the Politics of Emotion*, Cambridge: Cambridge University Press, 92–112.

Casimir, M. R. (2009) 'Honor and dishonor and the quest for emotional equivalents', in Rottger-Rossler, B., and Markowitsch, H. J. (ed.) *Emotions as bio-cultural processes*, New York: Springer, 281–316.

Challenge (1984) Directed by A. Kondandarami Reddy [Film]. India: General Pictures.

Dangle, A. (ed.) (1992) *Poisoned Bread: Translations from Modern Dalit Literature*. Hyderabad, India: Sangam Books Ltd.

Dumont, L. (1981) *Homo Hierarchicus: The Caste System and Its Implications*, Chicago: University Of Chicago Press.

Ghurye, G. S. (1969) *Caste and Race in India*, Mumbai: Popular Prakashan.

KalliChellamma (1969) Directed by Sobhana Parameswaran Nair [Film]. India: General Picture.

Kanchivaram (2008) Directed by Priyadarshan [Film]. India: Percept Picture Company.

Katha Parayumbol (2007) Directed by M. Mohanan [Film]. India: Lumiere Film Company.

Kasthooriman (2003) Directed by A. K. Lohithadas [Film]. India: Lumiere Film Company.

Kaufman, G. (1996). *The Psychology of Shame: Theory and Treatment of Shame-Based Syndromes* (2nd edn.), New York: Springer.

Manassinakkare (2003) Directed by Sathyan Anthikkad [Film]. India: Subair.

Menon-Sen, K. and Kumar, A. K. (2001) *Women in India, How free? How equal?*, New Delhi: UNDP.

Neelakkuyil (1954) Directed by P. Bhaskaran and Ramu Kariat [Film]. India: Chandrathara Productions.

Parsai, H. (2003) *Inspector Matadeen on the Moon* (trans. C. Naim), Delhi: Katha.

Pellissery, S. (2001) 'Science-Religion Dialogue: A Tribal Perspective', *Journal of Tribal Studies* 6(3): 28–43.

Pillai, T. S. (1969) 'Velutha Kunju', in *Vellappokkathilum Mattu Pradhana Kathakalum*, India: DC Books/Current Books.

Peepli Live (2010) Directed by Anusha Rizvi [Film]. India: General Pictures.

Sen, A. (1979) 'Issues in the measurement of poverty', *Scandinavian Journal of Economics*, 81(2): 285–307.

Subarna Rekha (1965) Directed by Ritwik Ghatak [Film]. India: J.J. Films Corporation.

Tagore, R. (2008) *Collected Works of Tagore*, New Delhi: Seng Books.

Thulabharam (1968) Directed by A. Vincent [Film]. India: General Pictures.

Vasudevan, R. S. (2000) 'Shifting codes, dissolving identities: The Hindi social film of the 1950s as popular culture', in Vasudevan, R. S. (ed.) *Making Meaning in Indian Cinema*, New Delhi: Oxford University Press, 99–121.

Vidheyan (1993) Directed by Adoor Gopalakrishnan [Film]. India: General Pictures.

Weber, M. (1905/2002) *The Protestant Ethic and the Spirit of Capitalism: and Other Writings*, London: Penguin Classics.

5

Poverty and Shame in Chinese Literature

Ming Yan

Introduction

This chapter focuses on the cultural representations of poverty and shame in a selection of Chinese literature. A content analysis of the selected works was carried out through which the following were analysed: literary depictions of the experiences of poverty and poverty-related shame; whether and the extent to which the selected authors identify a link between poverty and shame; and how the characters in the selected texts are shown to generate or respond to the shame associated with poverty.

Given the large number of literary works published in China—at the publishing peak of the late 1990s about 1000 novels and between 3,000–4,000 short stories were published annually (Li, 2000; CSF, 2008)—strict criteria were applied so that the selection of novels and short stories included influential or popular works by the most distinguished Chinese writers which touched on the theme of poverty. The secondary school curriculum for Chinese language and literature (designed by experts in the field) provided the main corpus from which the novels were chosen. While for a few authors, the decision about which of their works to include was easy, as they produced only a single classic novel, for the more prolific writers, criteria for selection was based either on the relevance of the work to the themes of poverty and shame or on the prominence of the author's work. Other factors considered in the choice of works included whether or not they had won prestigious literary awards in China, such as the Maodun Literature Award, the Lu Xun Literature Award, or the National Short Stories Award; the diversity of topics explored; the coverage of various historical periods (traditional, Communist, and postreform eras); and ensuring representation of both urban and rural life. In total, thirty-four works (thirteen novels and twenty-one novellas or short stories) from twenty-eight authors were included in the analysis.

Representations of Poverty in Chinese Literature

Throughout China's history, poverty in absolute terms was severe and experienced by the majority of the population. Only in recent decades has there been a gradual shift towards relative poverty as the overall standard of living in China continues to rise. Thus poverty, characterized by a lack of basic necessities such as food, clothing, and shelter, was the predominant theme in many of the selected works. Hunger, for example, is described as so real that a poor man's main, and, at times, mere goal in life is to fill the stomach, or in Yu Hua's (1998) terms, 'to be alive'.

Poverty in both rural and urban settings prior to the post-reform era is portrayed in the extreme. The regular meal of poor peasants consisted of porridge mixed with small amounts of grains and vegetables. Times of drought posed the threat of starvation, compelling many people to become beggars, living primarily on the mercy of others. Equally, poor health was capable of crushing a peasant family (Zhou, 1948/1983). For those living in poverty in urban areas, such as the rickshaw pullers, life was no better. Their jobs are described as so arduous and the salaries such a pittance that they could hardly feed themselves or their families (Lao, 1936).

Hunger during the socialist era was largely the result of policy failures and was particularly prevalent during the 'three disaster years' (1959–1962). During this time, in order to feed themselves, some people are depicted as having to sell their household goods. In the novella *Sailing Away* by Cong (1982), for example, a highly educated man treasures his collection of world classics but is forced to accept that his mother sell these books off one by one in order to buy food. Those without assets are portrayed as using their own bodies as currency—selling blood to hospitals just so that the family can eat a bowl of noodles (Yu, 1998). The pursuit of other interests are shown as having to be suppressed in favour of 'having a full stomach', seen as the only route to happiness (A, 1999: 157).

A number of the selected works illustrate how acute the problem of affording adequate clothing is for their characters. Many are depicted in rags or whatever material they can find to wrap themselves in, such as paper or, in the case of coal mine workers, cement sacks (Chen, 1980/2001), while others are forced to stay in bed most of the day throughout the winter. In the novel *Violent Storm*, Zhao, an impoverished peasant forced from his home as a result of drought, arrives in the village as a beggar. Zhao's wife works in the field, largely naked, and will not return home until after dark when she cannot be seen. On one occasion, she is spotted by a fellow villager when she peeks out from the corn field and from then on 'Naked Zhao' becomes a popular nickname in the village (Zhou, 1948/1983).

Lack of decent shelter is portrayed in the literature as another dimension of subsistence poverty. Depending on the region in which they live, peasants are often described as living in straw or mud huts, while the rich live in brick houses. Those living in urban areas are commonly depicted living in cramped, overcrowded, one-room rented houses which constantly leak and run the risk of collapsing when it rains. Worse still, the residents are in constant fear of being evicted by the landlord for failing to pay the rent. For those characters who are beggars roaming urban areas, their situation is portrayed as so precarious that, to avoid freezing to death in the winter, they stay in 'rooming hotels' where dozens of people share a single bed in one room. Here, stealing is so common that none of the lodgers will even undress or take off their shoes (Liu, 1985). During the socialist period in China, and particularly in the 1970s and 1980s, the urban housing shortage became very severe as rapid population growth exceeded the stagnant housing supply, a situation clearly depicted through the Yin family in *Life Full of Chores* (Chi, 1989).

Literary Portrayals of Poverty-Related Shame and Shaming

While the main focus of this work is on the association between poverty and shame, it is important to first make a distinction between *shame* and *shaming*. Figure 5.1 provides a framework for illuminating the dynamics between *shame* and *shaming* in relation to poverty.

In the figure, *shame* refers to the feeling of shame, or the felt shame of those in poverty, while *shaming* means the imposition of shame through the attitudes or actions of others towards those in poverty. Thus, the presence or non-presence of shame and shaming intersect and result in four possible situations represented by the four quadrants. Quadrant I indicates that even though poverty is present, neither *shame* nor *shaming* is apparent; Quadrant II indicates that shame is internally felt by those in poverty but there is no

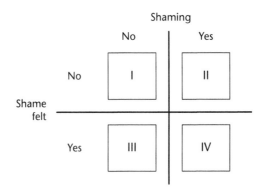

Figure 5.1. Depiction of poverty, shame, and shaming.

evidence of it being externally imposed; Quadrant III indicates that while shame is being imposed on those in poverty, i.e. bringing or causing shame, it does not seem to have the desired effect of provoking a sense of shame; Quadrant IV indicates that people in poverty both have an internal sense of shame and are shamed by others. The analysis of literature produced examples to illustrate each dimension of this framework.

Quadrant I: Poverty without Shame and Shaming

In the selected Chinese literature, poverty without shame or shaming occurs under three types of conditions. In extremely harsh circumstances, for instance, those in poverty are forced to engage in a constant struggle for survival, facing unimaginable challenges just to have enough to eat. In the novel *Damned Grains* (Liu, 1986/2001), for example, a woman collects mule dung from a passing team of luggage carriers, dries the dung in the sunshine, and then washes it in the river. As the waste is washed away, a pile of undigested corn grains are left, the makings of a 'good meal' for her family. In this story, there is no apparent shame since conditions of survival are so brutal that any such human feelings are suppressed. Instead the woman's ingenuity not only provides a means of sustenance, but also a sense of accomplishment.

The literature also provides evidence that certain characters experience poverty without shame due to a number of cultural and social factors. In cultural terms, the notions of fate and karma in Buddhism prevail in some literary works. Hence, differences in the amount of wealth possessed are attributable to differences in fate, such as 'good and lucky lot' or 'bitter lot', or 'your lot attracts poverty' (Zhou 1948/1983: 54, 57). The belief that poverty may continue into the afterlife, is demonstrated by expressions such as, 'when you are alive, you are a poor person; when dead, you are a poor ghost' (Xiao, 1941/1996: 646). Conversely, it is also believed that when a poor person dies, he or she may be reborn into a wealthy family (Han, 1985/1999), usually on the condition that they have done sufficient good deeds in their previous life. Those in poverty, therefore, accept their circumstances as normal since they cannot change them; and the wider structural conditions which limit social mobility tend to confirm this view.

Some literary works present characters from rich and poor backgrounds forming patronage systems in which those in poverty provide labour in exchange for financial or other kinds of support from the rich. In *The Memoirs of River Hulan,* for example, Feng is grateful that the landlord allows his family to stay in a storage room where there is nothing but straw to cover his newborn son (Xiao, 1941/1996). A more widely recognized character is Liu Laolao (Granny Liu) depicted in the classic *Dream of the Red Chamber* (Cao, 1784/1972) and known for her skills in handling those with wealth.

Drawing on an earlier-established connection between her son-in-law's fore-fathers and those of the wealthy family; she goes to ask them for financial help under the guise of visiting a relative. She praises their wealth and prestige in such a way that the rich feel good about themselves, her comic character and self-deprecation keeping them amused. In return, Liu is rewarded with large amounts of money and gifts. Later on, when the fortunes of the wealthy family take a turn for the worse, Liu courageously agrees to raise the daughter whose mother has died and who is about to be sold. Liu's story illustrates the strength of the patronage system in traditional China and how it enables the possibility of experiencing poverty without overt shame.

The second condition under which poverty appears to exist without shame is found among the old literati class who lived in poverty out of choice. Wang Mian, a character in *The Scholar* (Wu, c.1750/1981), for example, mainly teaches himself literacy and painting. He rejects several invitations to take official positions, a behaviour demonstrating the Confucius teaching that 'a gentleman can stay in poverty', the emphasis being on morals rather than worldly goods.

The third condition for the existence of poverty without shame is found after the 1949 Communist revolution which brought about fundamental changes to the social structure of Chinese society, and to how poverty was conceptualized. Around this time, poverty is understood from the perspective of class struggle, and the sufferings of those in poverty are seen as the result of exploitation by the wealthy. Thus, the inevitable solution was revolution to eradicate social class by seizing the assets of the rich and reallocating them to those facing poverty and disadvantage. In several novels addressing this theme, the rich are depicted as evil, typically using extreme cruelty to accumulate wealth at the expense of those who have nothing (Zhou, 1948/1983; Zhou, 1961/2004).

A crucial part of the Communist revolution was to urge those living in misery to 'wake up' to the fact that it was the exploitation by the rich, rather than their 'lot' that caused their poverty. In fact, throughout the revolution, those with no resources were encouraged to take pride in their identity: 'the poor of the whole world belongs to one family, and we all have the same last name "poor"'; 'mud stuck with mud makes the wall; the poor help the poor become the king' (Zhou, 1961/2004: 390, 103).

Quadrant II: Poverty and Feeling Shame but without Shaming

There is evidence in the literature to suggest that characters living in poverty can experience shame which is only felt internally, with no evidence of it being externally imposed. This is illustrated by the experience of Lin, the protagonist in the *Scattered Feathers* (Liu, 1991). In the 1980s, at the beginning of economic liberalization in China, a young educated couple, Lin and his wife, experience material deprivation as well as the social pressures to keep up with others in improving their living standards. Lin is offered a temporary evening job, selling ducks on the street. The pay is very attractive compared with his regular work in the office, so he accepts it. However, he dares not look up while selling the ducks and is terribly worried about being seen by his acquaintances. As soon as he gets home afterwards, he quickly takes a shower and changes his clothes to get rid of the smell. In this instance, the shame which Lin feels is not externally inflicted by others but is anticipated because of the demeaning job, even though Lin benefits from it financially.

Quadrant III: Poverty but Resisting Being Shamed

The literature further provides examples where, despite attempts by others to impose shame, those in poverty either reject it or fail to acknowledge it. Subculture theory in sociology has long argued that in the socially constructed reality, multiple sets of norms exist. For instance, where those living in poverty and those who inflict shame belong to two separate value systems, attempts at shaming those worse off may be fruitless since the targets of the shame do not subscribe to the underpinning values or expectations of the 'shamers'. The woman in *Dad Dad Dad* (Han, 1985), for example, manages to feed herself and her disabled son from the grains provided by the clan to feed the cats that catch mice in the shrine (and stop them eating the clan's precious genealogy books). Ignoring people's suspicious gossip, she angrily stares at them, apparently feeling no sense of shame despite the overt attempts to shame her, her only concern being to feed her child.

In some senses, this apparent resistance to external shaming may be equated with what is often termed as 'shamelessness'. However, it is important to draw some distinctions around this term. In its general usage, 'shamelessness' implies a value judgement from the standpoint of the shamer and tends to refer to behaviour that is deviant or even destructive for society. In the context of poverty, the 'shameless' can be those who become 'fallen' in the sense that they engage in criminal or deviant behaviour. Examples are Long-Neck Han and Donkey Li in *The Violent Storm* (Zhou, 1948/1983), two impoverished peasants who assist the rich in abusing the poor villagers. On the other hand, 'shamelessness' can be viewed from the standpoint of those in poverty who may act immorally but for justified causes, hence a situation of 'shaming without shame'. For example, Yang's wife in *Damned Grains* (Liu, 1986) steals on a number of occasions, but manages to win the reader's sympathy because she does so to feed her starving children. Similarly, while she dawdles when working in the communal field, she works exceptionally hard in the family field. Again, even though her conduct is viewed as shameful in the eyes of her fellow villagers, we as readers admire her for her agency in tackling hardship.

Quadrant IV: Poverty, Feeling Shame, and Being Shamed

Literary scenarios in which those in poverty experience both an internal sense of shame and the shame imposed by others are common. It is interesting to note that even though there are examples in the select literature where the rich attempt to shame those in poverty, shaming appears to occur more commonly within the immediate environment, imposed by family members, relatives, or neighbours. Characters are shown to react differently to such shaming, with some putting up with it while others resist it. At times, they are faced with the difficult decision as to whether to save face and avoid shame or endure the shame in exchange for material gains. In *A Pile of Wheat* (Tie, 1986) one man offers a fellow villager the opportunity to sleep with his wife in exchange for a pair of Japanese boots. Similarly, in order to save money to buy his own rickshaw, Xiangzi in *Rickshaw Boy* (Lao, 1936) switches from being a quiet, modest character to one who aggressively intercepts the business of other rickshaw pullers in order to get the trade. They curse him or stare at him with anger, and he stares back at them. Xiangzi marries Tiger Girl, who despite being much older, ugly, and of nasty temperament, as the daughter of a rickshaw shop owner she is in a position to buy him a rickshaw of his own.

Occasionally, however, those in poverty are able to manage a balance between saving 'face' and receiving benefits. The protagonists in both *Life Full of Chores* (Chi, 1989) and *Scattered Feathers* (Liu, 1991) go to great lengths to shop for gifts that look expensive but do not cost very much. In Liu's (1985: 348) *Bell and Drum Towers*, Hao and her husband adopt spending patterns which enable them to keep up appearances. So while they spend very little on food, they 'extracted savings from between the teeth', their clothing and household goods appear fairly decent. Likewise, they buy a 12-inch black-and-white television to display their financial capability but rarely turn it on in order to save electricity.

The Responses to Shame

Whether internally felt or externally imposed, the characters in the literary works are shown to respond in a number of different ways.

Valuing Other than Material Things

One way in which the characters are shown to cope with their deprivation and maintain a degree of dignity is through fully appreciating the things that they do have in life and the social relationships that they enjoy. Despite his daily material struggles, for example, Feng in *Memoirs of River Hulan* (Xiao,

1941/1996) leads a fulfilling life, and the birth of his son provides a major source of joy and meaning to his existence. Similarly, some characters are shown to draw dignity from their physical or moral actions through which they can feel superior to others. In the novel *Rickshaw Boy* (Lao, 1936), Xiangzi takes much pride in his physical strength, superb pulling skills, and being able to earn food by selling his labour. He sees the latter as honest work compared with those individuals in similar circumstances who engage in criminal conduct to survive. These feelings help cushion him from hardships in life.

Counter-Shaming

Counter-shaming can be seen as a proactive or sometimes aggressive response by those in poverty to mitigate the adverse effects of attempts to impose shame. In The *Bell and Drum Tower* (Liu, 1985), Guo, a young woman from the rural village, visits the family of an old friend of her father's where she meets Feng, a much more educated woman of similar age. During the conversation, Guo is furious when Feng talks down to her about scientific knowledge, computers, and the like. Guo responds by saying that rather than knowing about things such as computers which have no relevance to her, she does know a great deal about animals and plants, things which are crucial for her village life.

Similarly, professional beggars are represented in the same novel as a distinctively creative group with respect to counter-shaming. They are shown to organize themselves into guilds, divided territories, and to develop strategies including 'soft begging' (giving blessings in rhythm), 'tough begging' (saying wicked words), and 'miserable begging' (displaying scars or disabilities). Counter-shaming also takes on a radical form in some novels set in the context of the Communist revolution, where class and the asymmetrical power structure are such that the only way for those in poverty to become liberated is to overthrow the oppressors and deprive them of their assets and privileges.

Spiritual Victory

In comparison with the downtrodden empowered through the revolution, some characters with the least means are depicted as maintaining internal peace through a form of spiritual victory, a term coined by Lu Xun (1921/2005) in his famous novella *The True Story of Ah Q*. Spiritual victory is a euphemism for self-deception when faced with extreme defeat or humiliation. Ah Q, who is homeless, survives by doing various odd jobs. He is a bully to those less fortunate than himself but fearful of those who are above him in rank, strength, or power. He persuades himself mentally that he is spiritually 'superior' to his oppressors even as he succumbs to their tyranny and suppression. The story has a tragic and ironic ending when Ah Q is mistakenly arrested and told to sign a paper, something he is unable to do since he is illiterate. He is then asked to draw a circle instead and although he starts to feel ashamed when he is unable to draw it round enough, he soon tells himself that only stupid people can draw very round circles. The day when he is taken for execution, his last words exemplify his spiritual victory when he loudly declares, 'In twenty years, I'll come back '(Lu, 1921/2005: 551).

Withdrawal

Among the responses to shame portrayed in the literature is self-withdrawal from society, when characters appear to give up all hope. This seems to result from the consequences of long-term failure or from some traumatic events. In *Rickshaw Boy* (Lao, 1936), Xiangzi starts out as a young, strong, and proud rickshaw puller who wants to earn a decent living through his own sweat. However, he is repeatedly challenged by a series of misfortunes—he is robbed both of his hard-earned rickshaw and the money saved to buy a new one, his wife dies, and then so does the woman he loves. At the end of the novel, Xiangzi, although still young, lives a life which can best be described as 'existential hopelessness', simply waiting for his life to end. One response in the novels to hardship, adversity, and tragedy is to commit suicide, an act of terminal withdrawal (Lao, 1936).

Other Factors Exacerbating Poverty-Related Shame

While feelings of shame or experiences of being shamed in the various novels can be a result of the characters' poverty or disadvantage, other factors are also often shown to combine to accentuate their experiences of shame. Factors such as: deviant behaviour, like gambling or stealing; strained family relations or conflicts; or particular values and beliefs, mean that certain groups of people occupy even more disadvantaged positions in the poverty–shame nexus.

Older people and the young are frequently presented as being less or not at all productive and creating a burden within the family. When absolute poverty prevails, their dependency makes them even more vulnerable to being shamed by others. Children, for example, are depicted as being sold when parents cannot afford to feed them, forced to do heavy work to help the family survive, and subjected to beatings as their parents take out the frustrations of their own poverty on them.

As a result of the rural–urban divide in China, the city is viewed as representing modernity—the power centre, better life chances, and a higher standard of living. During the 1980s, as rural productivity began to increase, peasants travelled to the city, where they often encountered 'shame', a theme covered in a number of novels. When Chen has sufficient grain stored, he goes to the city, looking forward to the experience, but is looked down upon by the hotel receptionist (Gao, 1980/2001). Lin in *Scattered Feathers* (Liu, 1991) is made to feel inadequate in front of his wife who is a city girl. Interestingly, in addition to the shame imposed on him by his wife Lin experiences another type of shame when dealing with relatives from his hometown who travel to the city, as he has insufficient resources and networks to fulfil their expectations for tourism, medical care in a good hospital, or to buy goods in short supply. By contrast, those who have adopted urban lifestyles may equally be rejected when returning to the village, accused of putting on airs and graces, as is the case in *The Qin Opera* (Jia, 2005).

Women characters in the novels are frequently shown to bear the brunt of poverty and shame compared to men, mainly as a result of having very limited independent sources of income. Men are also routinely shown to vent their frustrations by beating their wives. Worse, cruelty is often imposed on women by other women, typically mother-in-laws mistreating daughter-in-laws. Women are most often depicted as having to depend on men to provide for them, and consequently being subjected to servitude or exploitation, as is the case of the women in *Na Wu* who are forced to become the concubines of an older man (Deng, 1981/1985). More generally, poverty is frequently shown to go hand in hand with prostitution when women have no other means of survival.

However, women's traditional subordination is shown to radically change in those novels depicting life after the revolution. Now, arranged marriages can be cancelled by women at their own will; wide participation of women in the labour force enables them to provide for the family and at the same time earns them status and respect. During the post-reform era, women seem to play an even more proactive role by both pushing their husbands to 'get ahead' and engaging in opening businesses themselves, for example during the time of the privatization of state-owned enterprises, when their husbands or they themselves were laid off (Xiao, 2002).

As well as the gendered dimensions of the poverty–shame nexus, ethnicity also appears as an important factor in certain literary works. Ethnic Manchurians, for example, emerge as a distinctive group within the literature depicting modern China. While they were initially a privileged group which conquered the Han Chinese and established the Qing Dynasty (1644–1911), they suffered rapid economic and social decline after the founding of the Republic (1911–1949) when the stipends they regularly received during Qing were terminated, and they lacked occupational or business skills to thrive economically. Yet the Manchurians are portrayed as making painstaking efforts to maintain their lifestyles as well as retain their dignity. Their humiliation at having to 'earn a living with ten fingers' (Deng, 1981/1985: 102) and the desperate struggles over material hardships and loss of status and dignity are vividly depicted in a number of literary works.

Conclusions

This chapter has focused on how the dynamics of shame and shaming in relation to poverty are portrayed in samples of Chinese literature. The analysis tends to lead to the conclusion that the relationship between poverty and shame is complex, and whether poverty induces shame has to do both with the prevailing cultural values in the given socio-historical period; and with the social-economic backgrounds of the protagonists.

The literature selected covering the mid-eighteenth century through to the present shows that Chinese society can roughly be divided into three broad periods in which the cultural values shape the poverty–shame dynamics around three paradigms: the traditional, Communist, and post-reform eras. Traditional Chinese society is characterized in the literature as a clan-based hierarchy in which the poor are the majority and their chances of upward mobility are slim. Poverty is accepted or endured through the integrative patronage between those with wealth and those without. The dominant cultural values in accordance with this social reality, represented by Confucianism, Daoism, and Buddhism, respectively emphasize virtue, no action, or fate and karma, all of which justify the existence of poverty without shame.

Literature framed by the Communist revolution furthers the idea of poverty without shame by rejecting the 'fate and karma' interpretation and attributing 'shame' to the asset class, who are blamed for exploitation of those in poverty, while those without wealth were instilled with much 'pride'. Yet the post-reform period signals a dramatic turn from the Communist paradigm. With the opening up to Western capitalism, the remnants of traditional and Communist values are exposed to a hybrid of multiple traditions or values, which take hold. In particular, the prevailing spirit is captured in popular sayings like 'getting rich is glorious', which determine the experience of poverty as shameful and serve to legitimize the growing socio-economic disparity.

While the literary works provide rich sources for analysis of the interaction between poverty and shame, it is important to recognize their limitations as representations of reality. It is imperative to take into consideration the authors' diverse backgrounds and perspectives of the worlds in which their works are created. We should be cautious of taking from the literature the idea that poverty without shame, until fairly recently, dominates in China. After all, literature is an art form that is normally produced by those who are relatively better educated and wealthier than their protagonists. Therefore, these works, no matter how insightful, should not become a substitute for social research which seeks to understand the direct experiences and perceptions of those living in poverty. Nonetheless, literature does provide us with important cultural clues and symbols concerning the poverty–shame nexus and, particularly in the case of China, it offers some essential insights into how prevailing cultural, social, and political norms at different points in history may have shaped this nexus.

References

A, C. (1999) 'The Chess King', in Wang, M. (ed.) *The People's Republic of China Literature Masterpieces Library Five Decades: The Novella Volume (II)*, Beijing: The Writers' Press, 147–74.

Cao, X. (1784/1972) *Dream of the Red Chamber*, Beijing: People's Literature Press.

Chen, J. (1980/2001) 'Upon Sealing the Coffin', in Cao, W. (ed.), *The End of the 20th Century Chinese Literature Selection: Novels*, Volume I. Beijing: Beijing University Press, 31–43.

Chi, L. (1989) 'Life Full of Chores', in Wang, M. (ed.) *The People's Republic of China Literature Masterpieces Library Five Decades: The Novella Volume (II)*, Beijing: The Writers' Press, 541–75.

Chinese Society of Fictions (CSF) (ed.) (2008) *1978–2008: Thirty Years of Chinese Fictions*, Tianjin: Tianjin People's Press.

Cong, W. (1982/1999) 'Sailing Away', in Wang, M. (ed.) *The People's Republic of China Literature Masterpieces Library Five Decades: The Novella Volume (II)*. Beijing: The Writers' Press, 1–67.

Deng, Y. (1981/1985) 'Na Wu', in Deng, Y. (ed.) *In and Out of the Capital*, Beijing: The Writers' Press.

Gao, X. (1980/2001) 'Chen Huansheng Going to the Town', in Cao, W. (ed.) *The End of the 20th Century Chinese Literature Selection: Novels*, Volume I, Beijing: Beijing University Press, 1–11.

Han, S. (1985/1999) 'Dad Dad Dad', in Wang, M. (ed.) *The People's Republic of China Literature Masterpieces Library Five Decades: The Novella Volume (II)*, Beijing: The Writers' Press, 350–78.

Jia, P. (2005) *The Qin Opera*, Beijing: The Writers' Press.

Lao, S. (1936/1993) 'Rickshaw Boy', in *Collected Works of Lao She*, Volume 3, Beijing: People's Literature Press.

Li, Y. (2000) *Fifty Years of Chinese Contemporary Fictions*, Guangzhou: Jinan University Press.

Liu, X. (1985) *The Bell and Drum Towers*, Beijing: People's Literature Press.

Liu, H. (1986/2001) 'Damned Grains', in Cao, W. (ed.) *The End of the 20th Century Chinese Literature Selection: Novel, Volume I*, Beijing: Beijing University Press, 231–42.

Liu, Z. (1991/2001). 'Scattered Feathers', in Cao, W. (ed.) *The End of the 20th Century Chinese Literature Selection: Novel, Volume II*, Beijing: Beijing University Press, 128–73.

Lu, X. (1921/2005) 'The True Story of Ah Q', in *Complete Works of Lu Xun*, Volume 1, Beijing: People's Literature Press, 512–52.

Tie, N. (1986/1999) 'A Pile of Wheat', in Wang, M. (ed.) *The People's Republic of China Literature Masterpieces Library Five Decades: The Novella Volume (II)*, Beijing: The Writers' Press, 435–83.

Wu, J. (*c*.1750/1981) *Scholars*, Beijing: People's Literature Press.

Xiao, H. (1941/1996) 'Memoirs of River Hulan', in Guo, J. and Wang, J. (ed.) *Complete Works of Xiao Hong (II)*, Changchun: Arts and Literature Times Press.

Xiao, K. (2002) 'The Last Worker', in *Selelcted Classical Works of Chinese Writers: The Volume by Xiao Kefan*, Beijing: Guangming Daily Press, 505–98.

Yu, H. (1998) *Alive*, Haikou: Nanhai Publishing.

Zhou, E. (1961/2004) 'Shanghai's Morning', in *Collected Works of Zhou Erfu*, Volume 6, Beijing: Culture and Arts Publishing House.

Zhou, L. (1948/1983) 'Violent Storm', in *Collected Works of Zhou Libo*, Volume 2, Changsha: Hunan People's Publishing House.

6

Poverty and Shame

Seeking Cultural Cues within British Literature and Film

Elaine Chase, Robert Walker, and Sohail Anwar Choudhry

> It got you slowly, with the slippered stealth of an unsuspected malignant disease... You fell into the habit of slouching, of putting your hands into your pockets and keeping them there; of glancing at people furtively, ashamed of your secret, until you fancied that everybody eyed you with suspicion. You knew that your shabbiness betrayed you: it was apparent for all to see. You prayed for the winter evenings and the kindly darkness. Darkness, poverty's cloak. Breeches backside patched and repatched: patches on knees, on elbows. Jesus! All bloody patches.
>
> (Walter Greenwood, *Love on the Dole*, 1933)

Introduction

Lewis Coser (1963: 2) claimed that 'Literature, though it may also be many other things, is social evidence and testimony', preserving 'the precious record of modes of response to peculiar social and cultural conditions'. Though still limited, there has been a growing recognition that cultural media offer reputable sources of data for social enquiry and a number of academics have extolled the unique contribution that such media can make to social science. Lewis et al. (2008), for instance, have argued that examining fictional representations of the nebulous concept of 'development' within a broader analysis, helps shed light on the less obvious contextual factors affecting the development process. Others have argued that a retrospective analysis of fictional works can help explain the evolution of contemporary phenomena once we become sensitized to them for the first time (McDowell, 2005; Perry,

2005). Increasingly, social scientists have engaged with contemporary films to examine sociological phenomena (Lay, 2002; Sutherland and Felty, 2010), while Connor (2012) has examined iconic works of art as political and ethical representations of poverty and 'the poor' over centuries.

Equally, cultural media provide rich material for examining important social phenomena in open-ended and inductive ways. Responding to what he saw as the constraints imposed on empirical research by predetermined social theory, Blumer (1954: 9) encouraged the use of 'sensitising concepts'. He saw these as a way of avoiding treating abstract ideas as fixed and definitive when they may only be 'vague stereotypes', and instead enabling an investigation of their multifarious properties through systematic research. Taken up and embedded within grounded theory (Glaser and Strauss, 1967; Corbin and Strauss, 2008) sensitizing concepts have been defined as 'ideas to pursue and sensitise you to ask particular kinds of questions about your topic' (Charmaz, 2006: 16).

In order to test out the hypothesis that shame was an attribute of poverty within the British context, we need to develop an understanding of the types of cultural signs and symbols of such shame, its causes, and the circumstances under which it was likely to emerge. Treating *'shame'* and *'poverty'* and their intersection as sensitizing concepts and systematically examining the phenomena within samples of British literature and film offers an unobtrusive, albeit somewhat proxy, entry point for such investigation.

With this sensitization objective in mind, a thematic analysis was carried out of the representations of poverty, shame, and their intersection within a sample of thirty British novels (selected from national 'A' level syllabuses) spanning 170 years of Victorian (1837–1901), modern (1902–1960), and contemporary (1960–) eras; and a film corpus of thirty social-realist films from the 1960s through to the late 2000s. A targeted semiotic analysis, a study of the cultural signs and symbols (Berger, 2012) of poverty and shame, their connotations and denotations within specific contexts (Chandler, 2004) enabled us to characterize dominant and subordinate ideologies that appear to have shaped the poverty–shame nexus over time.

Representations of Poverty

The Imagery of Poverty

Using different strategies towards the same objective, authors and film directors alike draw our attention to the existence of poverty; authors through the use of rich descriptions, directors through the camera lens as it shifts from the macro to the micro circumstances of the film's protagonists. Authors from the Victorian era conjure a broadly consistent image of spatial and contextual poverty in an era of urban industrialization. Wellingborough in *Redburn* (Melville, 1849: 186) conjures up the abject poverty he witnesses on Liverpool's Victorian docks: 'Every variety of want and suffering here'.

Eighty or so years later, Walter Greenwood's description of Hankey Park (*Love on the Dole*, 1930: 11), generates an image of similar hardship:

> Jungles of tiny houses cramped and huddled together. The cradles of generations of the future. Places where men and women are born, live, love, die and pay preposterous rents for the privilege of calling the grimy houses 'home'.

Similarly, in the opening scenes of many of the films, the symbolism of poverty is variously presented through a backcloth of industrial smoke, high-rise tenement blocks with graffiti-daubed walls, and back-to-back houses.

Zooming in on the lives of individual characters, the detail of hardship is magnified by the sharing of beds, the presence of large numbers of children in overcrowded conditions, the penury of the homes' interiors, the sparseness of the fare on the table, and the characters' clothes and appearances. Bill Douglas's work on the life of Jamie growing up in a poor working-class mining village in Scotland after the Second World War (*My Childhood*, 1972) captures the depth of poverty, with meal times reduced to porridge or bread soaked in milk and eaten by hand.

Evident in both corpuses is a gradual shift in representations of poverty over time. Novels of the Victorian era typically highlight the suffering, distress, and hardship of absolute poverty. John Barton in *Mary Barton* (Gaskell, 1848: 27) claims, 'his mother had died from absolute want of the necessaries of life'. By constrast, through the modern and contemporary literature, reflections on the relativity of poverty begin to emerge. Owen in *The Ragged Trousered Philanthropist* (Tressell, 1914: 427), comments on how poverty, more than merely a lack of money, was about 'being short of the necessaries and comforts of life'. Some eighty years later, Paula Spencer in *The Woman Who Walked into Doors* (Doyle, 1996) is preoccupied not so much with putting food on the table but with being able to afford a spare pair of shoes for her daughter, Leanne.

Likewise, the relativity of poverty emerges prominently in the social-realist films. Stevie in the film *Riff Raff* (Loach, 1991) similarly has enough to eat, for example, but homelessness, the precariousness of work arrangements for himself and colleagues, and the ill-fitting suit for his mother's funeral are clear signs of privation. And while Phil and his family in *All or Nothing* (Leigh, 2002) appear to live relatively comfortably in their high-rise tenement flat, the precariousness of their financial situation is brought to our attention when we see Phil scrabbling down the back of the sofa for loose change, in order to pay the rental on his taxi cab, his only source of income.

The Causes of Poverty

Through both film and literature we become sensitized to largely polarized discourses on the perceived causes of poverty; the result of individual or collective inadequacies on the one hand and the consequence of structural economic and political processes, such as industrialization, capitalism, and modernization, on the other. In *News from Nowhere*, (Morris, 1891), the old man, implicates the prime cause of poverty as 'the systematised robbery on which it (society) was founded'. Despite turning to suicide as a result of total deprivation, the worker's valedictory note in *The Ragged Trousered Philanthropist* (Tressell, 1914: 129) makes a declamatory statement about the injustices leading up to his own death, 'This is not my crime, but society's'.

The structural causes of hardship are often suggested in film and literature through the protestations of certain characters that assume the role of social reformers, even though they may sit at odds with dominant views about the 'lazy poor' and are largely ignored. In *Howard's End* (Forster, 1910: 155), Helen's assertion that the rich are partly responsible for the plight of those in poverty is quickly dismissed by Mr Wilcox, who later states, 'You do admit that, if wealth was divided up equally, in a few years there would be rich and poor again just the same. The hard-working man would come to the top, the wastrel sink to the bottom.'

The existence of the '*working poor*' is conjured in film and literature through the prominence of low paid, low-status, and often mind-numbing work, typically in mines or factories. Theresa, in the film *Letter to Brezhnev* (Bernard, 1985), comically describes her job in the chicken factory to her friend Elaine, '(I) take the innards out of chickens, put them into little plastic bags and stuff them back up again'. The opening scene of *Saturday Night and Sunday Morning* (Reisz, 1960) sees Arthur working in a factory making machinery parts. He comments on the thankless, lowly paid, and unrewarding work, 'Fourteen pounds, three and tuppence for a thousand of these a day. No wonder I've always got a bad back'.

While both media represent contrasting views as to whether a certain pride can be attributed to being in employment, they are broadly united on the impact of unemployment and the accentuated suffering which results. Accessing social assistance in whatever form frequently becomes the subject of social commentary in which unemployment and its association with personal failure is a well-rehearsed theme.

Responses to Poverty

Responses to economic adversity are played out in literature and film on a collective as well as individual basis. Hardship is mediated in a number of the films through mutual resistance and support. In *The Full Monty* (Cattaneo, 1997), Gerald's friends rally round to collectively resist the bailiffs when they come to repossess his goods. Conversely, we are sensitized through both film and literature that the harshness of poverty intensifies as a result of the breakdown of family and other social networks. In *Cathy Come Home* (Loach, 1996), it is the point when Cathy's mother throws the family out of her flat that the full impact of their circumstances really takes hold.

And despite instances of solidarity, there are also ample examples where those who are relatively better off exploit the circumstances of the worse off. In *Vera Drake* (Leigh, 2004), Lilly pockets two guineas from every woman she puts in contact with Vera who continues to 'help them out when they can't manage', through providing illegal abortions, unaware of the price that the women are paying.

The loan shark and pawnbroker are often depicted as practically living on the doorstep, featuring as persistent social predators over the different periods of time. Typically, spiralling debt intertwine with violence, as illustrated in Loach's *Raining Stones* (1993), in which Bob fails to repay the loan taken out to pay for his daughter's first Holy Communion dress.

In several novels, authors engage with the protracted experience of poverty and the consequent resignation and disintegration of the characters over time, a sense of giving up the ghost. Typically, following a fall in their socio-economic circumstances, a gradual decline in lifestyle and social status ensues, culminating in a physical, psychological, emotional, and spiritual deterioration, in combination with a loss of identity.

Representations of Shame

The literary descriptions of shame throughout the novels are particularly rich, with words such as 'coloured', 'flamed', 'sullen', and the 'flow' of humiliation used to evoke the emotion of the lived experience. Tressell, in *The Ragged Trousered Philanthropist* (1914: 247) describes the collective 'shamefaced' mannerisms of those without work, just as Greenwood in *Love on the Dole* (1933: 233) mentions Helen and Harry staring at each other outside the workhouse, with expressions of 'shame-faced self-consciousness'.

Cinematographic representations bring to life the demeanour, mannerisms, and body language of characters experiencing shame; their subtleties at times profoundly moving. Shame is shown to have multiple causes and be experienced across classes. It is associated with transgressions of social and cultural mores or the failure to live up to personal, familial, or societal expectations. Equally, shame is variably imposed by other individuals, groups, or at an institutional level. While Gaz In *The Full Monty* (Cattaneo, 1997) is derided by his ex-partner for his circumstances, 'unemployed, maintenance arrears of £700 and now you've been arrested for indecent exposure . . . still think you're a suitable father do you?' Cathy and Reg's children in *Cathy Come Home* (Loach, 1966) are finally taken into care because, according to the housing officer, they have 'failed to find a home for their children'.

Shame, Shaming, Class, Gender, and Ethnicity

Both literature and film also sensitize us to the intersection of poverty-related shame with other forms of social stratification such as gender, class, and ethnicity. Those of higher social class are commonly shown to be repulsed by people of lower status, often associating them with negative attributes such as want, squalor, bad manners, and a lack of credibility. The wealthy characters of *A Room with a View* (Forster, 1908: 66) epitomize these views with statements such as, 'It is dreadful to be entangled with low-class people'. Retaining power and maintaining social and physical distance from those who are socially inferior thus becomes a preoccupation of the rich. The narrator to the preface of *The Strange Case of Dr Jekyll and Mr Hyde* (Stevenson, 1886) comments on the social impact of the contemporary housing crisis and how the focus of middle-class anxiety was less overcrowding than the way in which the housing crisis was forcing the respectable working classes into proximity with the casual poor.

This social distancing is captured in the film corpus through the visual positioning and circumstances of characters in relation to each other. It is evident in *Billy Elliot* in the contrast between Billy's cramped back-to-back house in the Durham mining town and the suburban bungalow where Mrs Wilkinson his dancing teacher lives (Daldry, 2000); as well as in *Vera Drake*, with the close confines of Vera and her family's living quarters in the East End of London and the abject poverty of many of the women she 'helps', which contrast starkly with the large town houses of the middle classes that she cleans for a living (Leigh, 2004). Similarly, these social distances are reflected in the relationships between the characters: the deferential position Vera is shown in when on her knees cleaning the hearth of her wealthy employer; or the apprehension of Billy's dad as he approaches Mrs Wilkinson's house.

Irrespective of the era in which they were created, both literary works and films demonstrate how social respect and respectability are largely determined by a combination of material well-being and social position. Just as money gives the power to attract, assert authority, and own commodities, its absence provokes humiliation, or at least fear of it. The character of Bob in the film *Raining Stones* (Loach, 1993) insists, despite his wife's protestations, that his daughter Colleen has a brand new dress for her first Holy Communion, 'Fine . . . she walks up the aisle looking like a pauper and all her mates are clobbered up to the hilt.... She's gonna have a dress no matter how long it takes'. This potential for shame is as acutely felt by charity school children and low-paid clerks of the Victorian era as it is by the unemployed of the 1930s or people living on council estates or servicing menial, low-paid jobs in contemporary Britain.

Gender, shame, and poverty interact in complex ways throughout film and literature, with women and men equally struggling to fulfil the norms imposed on them by society. A recurrent theme equally pertinent in contemporary British film as it is in Victorian literature, is the dishonour of pregnancy outside of marriage and its coincidence with poverty. Tess in *Tess of the D'Urbervilles* (Hardy, 1891) is subjected to the excruciating public shame for herself and her family at having a child outside of marriage. The same theme is taken up in several films, including *Vera Drake* (Leigh, 2004), set in the 1950s, and *A Taste of Honey* (Richardson, 1966), in which Jo's mother, on learning about her pregnancy, comments, 'you know what they call you round 'ere...a silly little whore'. Donna in *All or Nothing* (Leigh, 2002) faces the wrath and violence of her boyfriend, who beats and humiliates her when she tells him about the pregnancy.

Male attitudes towards women, the social constructs and institutions that govern their experiences, and women's own responses to their 'lot' are all variably explored across both media. Class undoubtedly intersects in the typical portrayal of women, who tend to have a limited education, few employment options, and a high degree of dependency on men, all of which limit their choices and potentially make them more vulnerable to violence and abuse. Women are shown to frequently bear the brunt of public exposure to the shame of poverty, by queuing at the pawn shops, for example, or to receive social assistance. Yet they are also frequently depicted as resourceful and adaptable in the face of poverty, even when, as in the case of Jornia in *Brick Lane* (Ali, 2003), going out to work becomes a source of shame for her husband, who is criticized by the community for being unable to feed her.

Both genres shed light on notions of hegemonic masculinities and the psychosocial impact on men of not having the wherewithal to meet social norms and expectations of them as providers. Several works also demonstrate the intersection of disadvantage and racism. *This is England* (Meadows, 2006), for example, takes as its backdrop widespread unemployment and the resultant disenfranchised and disgruntled youth who look to project their frustrations on to minority communities through violent racist attacks.

Responses to Shame

Keeping Up Appearances, Pretence, and Withdrawal

Writers and directors alike address the multidimensionality of poverty and how its impact transcends material hardship and affects the core self. Ladislaw in *Middlemarch* (Eliot, 1871:434) equates the exclusionary impact of poverty with that of disease: 'poverty may be as bad as leprosy, if it divides us from what we most care for'. Without the necessary wherewithal to keep up appearances, those experiencing poverty are depicted as prone to self-exclusion and withdrawal, strategies which protect them from exposure to feelings of inferiority but which may impose a sense of unwanted solitude.

Collectively, the fiction presents many instances in which people from poor socio-economic backgrounds exclude themselves as a result of similar feelings. Jude in *Jude the Obscure* (Hardy, 1895: 89), avoids his cousin because, 'she seemed so dainty beside himself in his rough working-jacket and dusty trousers'; Pooter in *The Diary of a Nobody* (Grossmith, 1892), Leonard in *Howards End* (Forster, 1910), Joseph in *Nineteen Twenty-One* (Thorpe, 2001), and Gilbert in *Small Island* (Levy, 2004) all similarly choose to avoid social situations likely to expose their material and class inadequacies.

In order to avoid shame, it is important for the characters to create a respectable gap between their impoverished reality and their public image. Keeping up appearances to the cost of other necessities appears as important for characters in contemporary fiction as it is for those of Victorian times. While Wellingborough in *Redburn* (Melville, 1849) describes an embarrassing meeting with the ship's captain in which he tries, in vain, to hide his patched trousers with his jacket, Paula in *The Woman Who Walked into Doors* (Doyle, 1996: 87) talks of raising her son Jack and of how she has 'gone without food to make him look good'.

Novels in particular are peppered with references to characters feigning greater wealth or status than they in fact have. Virginia and Alice in *The Odd Women* (Gissing, 1893: 39) appear to enter a shared world of pretence in order to avoid engaging with the reality of their penury, 'they generally made a point of deceiving each other, and tried to delude themselves; professing that no diet could be better for their particular needs than this which poverty imposed'. In the *Full Monty* (Cattaneo, 1997) Gerald manages to maintain the illusion of going to work each day for a full six months before it is discovered by his wife Linda that he has in fact lost his job.

Anger, Powerlessness, and Fatalism

Anger arguably results from a sense of inadequacy and an inability to articulate feelings, or a demonstration of resistance against the circumstances and situations faced by the characters. A common storyline is that those in poverty blame the rich for their misery even if they do not always have the license to vocalize their resentment. Owen in *The Ragged Trousered Philanthropist* (Tressle, 1914: 35), on witnessing Hunter humiliate Jack Linden, speaks of how he wants to 'take him by the throat with one hand and smash his face with the other' but knows that the consequence would be the loss of his job and food for his family. John Barton in *Mary Barton* (Gaskell, 1848: 126) speaks openly about the inhumanity of the rich towards those in poverty, 'we pile up their fortunes by the sweat of our brows, and yet we are to live as separate as if we were in two worlds'. The rich being cruel, exploitative, or indifferent is a theme most prominent in Victorian literature.

More commonly, however, rather than showing resistance, people in poverty are presented as voiceless, powerless, and fatalistic. Like the isolated social reformers among the upper classes, the militant and rebellious protagonists of the lower classes are typically depicted as lone voices in a sea of listless inertia. In *Hard Times* (Dickens, 1854: 163) the leader of the worker's union calls on his 'fellow-countrymen' of Coketown, 'the slaves of an iron-handed and a grinding despotism', to defeat their exploitative 'oppressors'. Yet both literature and film suggest that on the whole, those in poverty fail to effectively engage in collective action to resist the exploitation that they are subjected to. Larry in *Love on the Dole* (Greenwood, 1933) strives, with limited success, to instil a sense of consciousness among his fellow workers of how they are being exploited; while his namesake in *Riff Raff* (Loach, 1991) attempts, with little success, to unionize the men on the building site to improve their pay and conditions.

Dignity, Aspirations, and Resistance

Yet responses to hardship are not always negative or fatalistic, neither are characters routinely rendered powerless through the adversity they face. The most uplifting scenes in the films are where the characters demonstrate even small-scale resistance against the oppression they feel. The main storyline of *The Full Monty* (Cattaneo, 1997) is of unemployed, downtrodden men like Gaz, Dave, Lomper, and Gerald organizing themselves to make some money and prove their worth—to the full admiration of their packed audience when they pull off a strip-tease show.

The selected literature too, provides examples of maintaining dignity in the face of adversity, offering important antidotes to emotions of mortification and humiliation. Contemplating his departure for London, Redburn (Melville, 1849: 212) considers the scarcity of his funds alongside the moral values that he has set for himself, above all that one must not 'disgrace your family in a foreign land; you must not turn pauper'. However, some novels also show how economic hardship may force people to pay a high price for preserving their dignity and find themselves having to '*swallow pride*' and accept charitable gifts from a better-off family or acquaintances, or present themselves before the '*relieving*' board, as in the case of Linden in *The Ragged Trousered Philanthropist* (Tressell, 2014: 27).

The literature equally suggests that many of the characters aspire to changing their impoverished circumstances. While in most cases this proves unrealistic, there are some characters who manage through the twists of fate to turn their lives around and enjoy relative prosperity and social standing. Similarly, in the film corpus, aspirations and the desire for change and social mobility expressed by some characters counter the sense of fatalism of others. In *Sweet Sixteen* (Loach, 2002) Liam makes plans to secure a caravan for his mother before she returns from prison, with the hope that it will distance her from her drug-dealing boyfriend. In *My Beautiful Laundrette* (Frears, 1985), Omar has a vision for the renovated launderette to become 'the jewel in the Jacksy of South London'.

Dysfunction, Deviance, and Shamelessness

Alcohol, drugs, and crime emerge as recurrent themes in both film and literature, typically used to accentuate squalor and to generate stereotypes of people who are out of control or of dubious moral character. Alcohol use is presented either as one of the few luxuries enjoyed by those with scarce resources, or a means of coping with hardship, alcoholism being synonymous perhaps with defeat. In *Secrets and Lies* (Leigh, 1996), Cynthia copes with her socially isolated life outside work in the paper-box factory by drinking alone. Sue's dad in *Rita, Sue and Bob Too!* (Clarke, 1986) typifies the dysfunctional alcoholic— unemployed, out of control, abusive, and pathetic—while Hussein, Omar's father in *My Beautiful Laundrette* (Frears, 1985), retains a degree of public dignity and respect despite his inability to get out of bed on most days or to hold down a job as a result of his drinking. Such depictions are mirrored in literature through the archetypal drunk in *The Ragged Trousered Philanthropist* (Tressell, 1914: 183)—'a shabbily dressed, bleary-eyed, degraded, beer sodden, trembling wretch'—and the notion of alcohol as a social panacea—'public houses by the score where forgetfulness lurks in a mug'—*in Love on the Dole* (Greenwood, 1933: 11). Similarly, the use of drugs as a coping mechanism is neatly described by Renton in the film *Trainspotting* (Boyle, 1996), 'When you're on junk you've only one worry, scoring. And when you're off it, you're suddenly obliged to worry about all sorts of other shite'.

The dependency on drugs is a theme that is addressed widely within the film corpus, which presents the degree of social control inflicted by drug use over whole communities, and its effect of rendering the characters powerless to resist them. *Sweet Sixteen* (Loach, 2002), *Nil By Mouth* (Oldman, 1997), *Trainspotting* (Boyle, 1996), *My Beautiful Laundrette* (Frears, 1985), and *Kidulthood* (Huda, 2006) all contain examples of drug dealing becoming the mainstay of social and economic activity in the absence of other alternatives.

Both film and literature offer up the concept of shamelessness, with characters seemingly oblivious to the expectation to feel shame, or resistant to the idea that it should ever be experienced. Contrary to the withdrawal which is typical of a sense of shame, shamelessness is manifested by characters actively pursuing actions that could become a source of shame. There are examples of poverty apparently leading to dishonourable behaviour, variably associated with brazenness, petty crime, working the system, or deceitfulness. Yet the association of shamelessness is not confined to those living in poverty; and there are protestations in literature and film alike of the blatant exploitation and degradation by the rich of those facing poverty and disadvantage.

Conclusions

This chapter is not the product of film studies or literary criticism analysis per se. Rather it describes how a particular lens of analysis can be applied to examine how certain forms of cultural media in Britain have represented the concepts of poverty and shame over time. The analysis served to sensitize the research team to possible configurations of the poverty–shame nexus in real life and real time.

Manifestations of poverty and shame in the select sample of literature and films were ample and, although often secondary to the central foci of their subject matter, provided important structures on which the plots of novels and social-realist films were built. The association between the two, however, is interwoven in complex ways with class, gender, ethnicity, wealth, and power. And while class distinctions are arguably less pronounced in contemporary rather than Victorian or modern literature, the importance of money and material well-being and their role in generating shame is more sustained, a conjecture supported by the contemporary film corpus.

When experienced, shame is shown to evoke a range of responses. The film and literature corpuses commonly indicate a poor self-image, an intrinsic sense of inferiority, or, where a sense of shame is prolonged, the disintegration of the core self over time. In order to mitigate the social consequences of such feelings, protagonists are typically shown to adopt strategies through which they strive to protect their social integrity. Hence, pretence, avoidance, and social withdrawal are all presented as rational responses to the social dilemmas imposed by poverty, processes which may in turn exacerbate and perpetuate poverty.

The representations of poverty and shame in both corpuses suggest that those with wealth and class commonly impose shame on those who have fewer resources and less status. This combines with a systemic process of shaming, underpinned by dominant understandings of the causes of poverty as largely attributable to individual inadequacies rather than economic and political structural constraints. This external shaming is often shown to coincide with a process of self-deprecation, producing a sense of unworthiness and further withdrawal.

Across both corpuses too, the close association made between poverty and an alleged 'under class' is at times unnerving, leaving an uncomfortable sense of collusion with the idea of the inevitable drift from hardship to harshness and depravity. The ubiquitous presence of alcohol, drugs, prostitution, and related crime, particularly within films, also generate dominant images of microcosms of society which are dysfunctional, have low moral standards, and if anything are devoid of shame.

Combined, the selected films and literature provide us with rich insights into the poverty–shame nexus, supporting the contention that they are important sources of social enquiry in their own right and offering a wealth of signals as to how best to examine poverty and shame as social phenomena in the real world.

References

A Taste of Honey (1961) Directed by Tony Richardson [Film]. UK: Woodfall Film Productions.
Ali, M. (2003) *Brick Lane*, London: Scribner.
All or Nothing (2002) Directed by Mike Leigh [Film]. UK: Thin Man Films.
Berger, A. (2012) *Media Analysis Techniques*. 4th edn. California: Sage Publications.
Billy Elliot (2000) Directed by Stephen Daldry [Film]. UK: Tiger Aspect Pictures.
Blumer, H. (1954) 'What is Wrong with Social Theory?', *American Sociological Review*, 18: 3–10.
Cathy Come Home (1996) Directed by Ken Loach [Film]. UK: BBC.
Chandler, D. (2004) *Semiotics: The Basics*, London: Routledge.
Charmaz, K. (2006) *Constructing Grounded Theory: A Practical Guide Through Qualitative Analysis*, London: Sage.
Connor, S. (2012) 'Who are the Poor? From Lady Poverty to Welfare Queens', paper presented to the Joint East Asian Social Policy Research Network (EASP) and United Kingdom Social Policy Association (SPA) Annual Conference 2012, 'Social Policy in an Unequal World', 16–18 July 2012, University of York, UK.
Corbin, J. and Strauss, A. (2008) *Basics of Qualitative Research* 3rd edn., California: Sage Publications.
Coser, L. (1963) *Sociology through Literature*, Englewood Cliffs: Prentice-Hall International.
Dickens, C. (1854) *Hard Times*, London: Chapman and Hall.
Doyle, R. (1996) *The Woman Who Walked into Doors*, London: Jonathan Cape.
Eliot, G. (1871) *Middlemarch*, London: William Blackwood and Sons.
Forster, E. M. (1908) *A Room with a View*, London: Edward Arnold.
Forster, E. M. (1910) *Howards End*, London: Edward Arnold.
Gaskell, E. (1848) *Mary Barton*, London: Chapman and Hall.

Gissing, G. (1893) *The Odd Woman*, London: Lawrence and Bullen.

Glaser, B. and Strauss, A. (1967) *The Discovery of Grounded Theory: Strategies for Qualitative Research*, Chicago: Aldine Publishing Company.

Greenwood, W. (1933) *Love on the Dole*, London: Cape.

Grossmith, G. (1892) *The Diary of a Nobody*, London: J.W. Arrowsmith.

Hardy, T. (1891) *Tess of the D'Urbervilles*, London: Osgood, McIlvaine & Co.

Hardy, T. (1895) *Jude the Obscure*, London: Osgood, McIlvaine & Co.

Kidulthood (2006) Directed by Menhaj Huda [Film]. UK: Revolver Entertainment.

Lay, S. (2002) *British Social Realism: From documentary to Brit-Grit*, London: Wallflower Press.

Letter to Brezhnev (1985) Directed by Chris Bernard [Film]. UK: Palace Pictures.

Levy, A. (2004) *Small Island*, London: Headline Book Publishing.

Lewis, D., Rodgers, D., and Woolcock, M. (2008) 'The Fiction of Development: Literary Representation as a Source of Authoritative Knowledge', *Journal of Development Studies*, 44(2): 198–216.

McDowell, P. (2005) 'Why Fanny Can't Read: Joseph Andrews and the (Ir)relevance of Literacy Fiction', in Backscheider, P. R and Ingrassia, C. (eds) *A Companion to the Eighteenth Century English Novel and Culture*, Oxford: Blackwell.

Melville, H. (1849) *Redburn*, USA: Harper and Bros.

Morris, W. (1891) *News from Nowhere*, London: Reeves and Turner.

My Beautiful Laundrette (1985) Directed by Stephen Frears [Film]. UK: Working Title Films.

My Childhood (1972) Directed by Bill Douglas [Film]. UK: British Film Institute Production Board.

Nil By Mouth (1997) Directed by Gary Oldman [Film]. UK: EuropaCorp.

Perry, R. (2005) 'Home Economics: Representations of Poverty in Eighteenth-Century Fiction', in Backscheider, P. R and Ingrassia, C. (eds) *A Companion to the Eighteenth Century English Novel and Culture*, Oxford: Blackwell.

Raining Stone (1993) Directed by Ken Loach [Film]. UK: Channel Four Films.

Riff Raff (1991) Directed by Ken Loach [Film]. UK: Parrallax Pictures.

Rita, Sue and Bob Too! (1986) Directed by Alan Clarke [Film]. UK: British Screen Productions.

Saturday Night and Sunday Morning (1960) Directed by Karel Reisz [Film]. UK: Woodfall Film Productions.

Secrets and Lies (1996) Directed by Mike Leigh [Film]. UK: Thin Man Films.

Stevenson, R. L. (1886) *The Strange Case of Dr Jekyll and Mr Hyde* London: Longmans, Green & Co.

Sutherland, J. A. and Felty, K. (2010) *Cinematic Sociology: Social Life in Film*, California: Sage Publications.

Sweet Sixteen (2002) Directed by Ken Loach [Film]. UK: Alta Films.

The Full Monty (1997) Directed by Peter Cattaneo [Film]. UK: Redwave Films.

This is England (2006) Directed by Shane Meadows [Film]. UK: Warp Films.

Thorpe, A. (2001) *Nineteen Twenty One*, London: Jonathan Cape.

Trainspotting (1996) Directed by Danny Boyle [Film]. UK: Channel Four Films.

Tressell, R. (1914) *The Ragged Trousered Philanthropist*, Dublin: Grant Richards.

Vera Drake (2004) Directed by Mike Leigh [Film]. UK: Thin Man Films.

7

Disclosing the Poverty–Shame Nexus within Popular Films in South Korea (1975–2010)

Yongmie Nicola Jo

Introduction

The South Korean film industry is over a century old, with film being one of the most widely enjoyed forms of commercial entertainment and a cultural institution through which social reality is reproduced and shaped. Hit films these days are seen by up to a quarter of the population, and the influence of film, in this 'era of 10 million audiences' (SportsSeoul, 2013), is very possibly far more wide-reaching than that of literary works and other art forms.

The aim in this chapter is to uncover how poverty, shame, and the relationship between them have been differentially portrayed in South Korean film over time, both as a reflection of developing cultural norms and as an influence upon them.[1] Amongst 1,600 synopses of films released between the mid-1970s and the 2010s, forty films were sampled according to two main criteria: priority given to films featuring poverty as a significant theme and those that gained most popularity measured according to the annual chart of the total number of audience that went to see the film in cinemas that year. Typically, between one and three films fitted the criteria each year, with one or two films being selected for detailed analysis. There were several years during the mid-1980s and mid-1990s when no suitable films were identified, which in itself may lead us to infer that during that time poverty had less salience within the discourse of popular film and possibly also on a broader social level.

---

[1] I would like to acknowledge the generous editorial help and support of Professor Robert Walker in the writing of this chapter, in particular the conclusion.

The period over which the films were selected mirrored an era of enormous economic and social change in South Korea. Per capita GDP rose ten-fold and inequality, high by South East Asian standards, increased markedly, but the rate of absolute poverty fell from around 25 per cent to negligible levels in the 1990s although relative poverty increased after the Asian financial crisis in 1997 (OECD, 2012). Life expectancy increased at a faster rate than any other Asian country and the fertility rate at the end of the period was one of the lowest in the world (Hirschman, 2011). Military dictatorships that had been in control since 1961 were formally replaced in 1987, although democracy argu-ably only became fairly operative in the late 1990s. Democratic governments continued the developmentalist policies of their authoritarian predecessors but faced a real societal-level need to respond to the demands for a better social security system following structural adjustment austerity measures imposed by the International Monetary Fund (IMF) in response to the financial crisis in 1997.

This chapter divides into two substantive sections. Conceptualizing the space for shame to be determined by the distance between understandings of poverty and not-poverty, the first charts the changing portrayal of the poverty–shame nexus in South Korean film. The second considers social and personal responses to poverty-related shame seen through the lens of film.

Tracing the Poverty–Shame Nexus on the Screen

Individuals living in underprivileged circumstances rarely speak of, or identify themselves as, being '[the] poor'. Rather, poverty is identified by more affluent others who determine and identify signifiers of poverty (Lister, 2004), typically detectable by sight, though sometimes through other senses, and then interpret them with respect to predisposed and often stereotypical notions of what poverty is. Likewise, for poverty to exist as a narrative element in a film, it needs to be represented on the screen so as to be recognized and understood by cinema viewers. Accordingly, screenwriters, photographers, and directors behind the camera choose various cues that to them signify poverty in the belief that they will be similarly identified by viewers, enabling them to distinguish characters who are living in poverty from those who are not. Sometimes they may convey messages about poverty of which they themselves are unaware.

Recognizing distinctions between people who are poor and others that are not and the degree of difference between them is crucial to understanding the connections between poverty and shame because shame is an emotion that arises from the perceived difference or separation of the self from others (Figure 7.1; also Fromm 1956). Only when a distinction is made on screen between poverty and what is not poverty is there a potential to present and perceive shame. Moreover, the way in which rich and poor are portrayed in

Distinctions are drawn between poverty and not-poverty on the screen
↓
Distance between the two opens up potential room for shame
↓
Portrayals of poverty and not-poverty are observed by the viewers, as are the relationships between them
↓
(Other significant factors shaping the nature of the relationships between poverty and not-poverty on the screen: Chosen sources of shame, social value judgements regarding money and wealth, definitions of success and happiness, dominant pursuits and aspirations of life)
↓
Poverty–shame nexus of varying degrees and nature is (consciously or subconsciously) communicated to the viewers

Figure 7.1. Tracing the construction of the poverty–shame nexus in South Korean film.

film, the nature of the relationships, and the distance between them will affect the level of shame that the viewer perceives to be attached to poverty. Also relevant are the sources of shame and the settings in which shame occurs, value judgments about money and wealth, definitions of social success and happiness, or the kinds of popular aspirations which symbolize the 'good life'. In the analysis of South Korean films, portrayal of the poverty–shame nexus varied much more over time than it did within any particular year. As such it may well be reflecting and arguably influencing secular changes in public opinion that have accompanied the massive changes in South Korean society over a period of transformational economic growth.

Portraying Poverty on Screen

South Korean film-makers rely heavily on visual cues to represent poverty and these have changed noticeably over time. From the mid-1970s until the early 1980s (1975–1982), poverty was usually signified by location and represented via homogenously deprived neighbourhoods. The neighbourhoods chosen were often the so-called Moon villages (*Dal-Dong-Nae*), as in the 1978 film *The Woman I Abandoned* (Jung). Moon villages were unauthorized settlements on top of the steep hillsides (thus 'nearer the moon') surrounding the city of Seoul in which new migrants to the area congregated on the only land that remained undeveloped and vacant. Accordingly, poverty during this time was portrayed as a collective, typically urban phenomenon that encapsulated the aspirations of migrant workers chasing the dream of a better life for their families back home in the rural hinterland, while they themselves were living in urban squalor. The Moon Village then largely disappeared from the film screen in the 1990s when poverty itself was neglected on screen, and, although it returned in the 2000s, it became merely the backdrop to a much more individualized experience of poverty.

Occupation was, during the late 1970s and early 1980s, a further clue to poverty and to the shame that accompanied it. People living in the same area often held similar kinds of occupations as, for example, most of the characters appearing in the 1975 film *Young-Ja's Heyday* (1975) who worked in manufacturing occupations or those in The *World without Mom* (Lee, 1977) who worked in the saltpans. Sometimes life trajectories were told in terms of occupation as, for example in the case of Young-Ja in *Young-Ja's Heyday* (Kim, 1975), whose decline is mapped out as a series of five jobs, all of which were symbolic of female poverty but differed in the degree of degradation associated with them: a housemaid in a rich household, a bus guide, then a sewing factory worker, a hostess in a bar, and finally a prostitute. These occupations also symbolized urban life as a main focus of the films and, again, they tended not to feature in films released after the early 1980s.

Juxtaposing Poverty with Wealth

Poverty on the screen is often juxtaposed against conspicuous wealth, sometimes symbolized by location and often personified in the characteristics of protagonists. Here again, portrayals of both poverty and affluence have changed markedly over time. In the 1970s through to the early 1980s, the poverty found in the Moon Village was frequently contrasted with the wealthy areas and bright lights of Seoul that showed the prosperity attained by a relatively small group of people through the fruits of national economic development. Yet, the city of Seoul was also presented as a place of opportunity and hope, embodying a sense of zeal and the heartfelt aspirations of people for a better future. Young-Ja may have found love in the city in *Young-Ja's Heyday* (Kim, 1975) but she migrated in search of wealth: 'I didn't come to Seoul searching for romance. I am here to earn money! [...] I came with a strong-willed heart. I have got to earn money'. Through film, Seoul was shown to bring together the stark distinctions between poverty and wealth, united in a single life. Abject poverty, portrayed as hunger, homelessness, unemployment, orphanhood, the inability to attend school, and the powerlessness to keep family together was, nevertheless, set very closely against a brighter future attainable through education and hard work: '[n]o matter how hard the environment is, you should never give in' thirteen-year-old Young-Chool is told by his teacher in *The World Without Mom* (Lee, 1977), 'You have to live with courage and faith. I also lost my parents when young, but I studied hard [and became established as a teacher]'.

When poverty and wealth were represented through protagonists during this time, the affluent were frequently shown to derive their riches from illegitimate and unjust activity, the pursuit of money driven by greed and achieved through selfishness, the abuse of power, and often the exploitation of people in poverty. In film, the wealthy frequent a world of their own characterized by comfort, luxury, and security, entirely disconnected from disadvantaged neighbourhoods and largely immune to the pressures found there. People in poverty, on the other hand, are depicted as representing the moral high ground. They are upright and hard-working, prioritizing the virtues of love, justice, family, and a sense of community. The injustice that is conveyed during this period is palpable: the virtuous poor are exploited by the amoral rich such that the finger of blame and shame are firmly pointed at the wealthy.

Yet, by the 2000s, the focus switched to the people in poverty, who were portrayed as economic and social failures in a society where others became prosperous and consumption-orientated (Jo and Walker, 2013). While the rich were often still portrayed as being cruel, perhaps even more so than in the 1970s, as in the film *The Game* (Yoon, 2008), they were also the undisputable victors, willing and able to exert power and authority over the dejected and disorganized losers languishing at the bottom of the economic ladder. In this modern era, persons in poverty portrayed on film seem to acknowledge this reversal in fortune and feel the need to hide their poverty from public display. Back in the 1970s, to take the film *The World without a Mother* (Lee, 1977) as an example, the main role featured a thirteen-year-old boy, Young-Chool, who readily acknowledged the family's state of impoverishment and the difficulty of coping. However, he described his dilapidated house as 'heaven', 'cosy', and 'home' in a genuinely self-believing tone. In contrast, protagonists in films made in the 2000s try to conceal their poverty. Moreover, they are presented as failures rather than confident people striving to improve their livelihoods, as in the case of Young-Chool. So, for example, Sung-Woo in *Waikiki Brothers* (Lim, 2001) and Tae-Shik in *Crying Fist* (Ryu, 2005) are depicted in visuals, actions, and words as being low in self-esteem, depressive, and cowed. Poverty takes its toll in leading to divorce, isolation, and loss of pride. Emotionally wounded, people in poverty are portrayed as hot-tempered and unstable and find that they are disliked and shamed by other people, even by those to whom they have previously been close. They end up frightened, angry, and bitter, placing all their hopes of rebuilding their lives, which seems possible only through winning prosperity and success, on one-off opportunities that carry a high risk of ultimate failure.

Relationships, Distance, and the Space for Shame

Once the distinction is established on film between who is in poverty and who is not, the relationship between the two is then shaped in various ways. In the late seventies to early eighties, the distinction was very clear between poverty and wealth, with reference to humble origins contrasted against established lineage, inherited wealth, and educational achievement. But despite these differences, films such as *The Woman I Abandoned* (Jung, 1978) and *Barefooted Youth* (1979) tended to establish a distinctively common bond—love or goodness—which could unite protagonists. For instance, Hae-Mee in *Barefooted Youth* (Kim, 1979), who comes from a wealthy background, meets the poverty-stricken Doo-Shik, a boxer, who was brought up in an orphanage and has a criminal record. They fall in love and, while Hae-Mee's father objects and belittles Doo-Shik's aspirations to become successful, Hae-Mee acknowledges goodness in Doo-Shik with genuine love, which is shown to be sufficient to overcome the economic gulf between them. Hence, love draws them together as equals in pursuit of mutual happiness, and with no emotional distance between them, there is no space for shame.

In the 1980s (until around 1987), distinctions between rich and poor became blurred as the result of a shifting focus towards rapid social mobility, which emphasized competition within socio-economic classes rather than between them. People in poverty were portrayed as themselves becoming rich (*Mrs Speculator,* Lim, 1980), through seemingly fair means (such as marrying the wealthy, even if without love [*Our Joyful Young Days*, Bae, 1987]) or by foul (hypocritically displaying illicit prosperity as in the case of *X* [Ha, 1983]). The prospect of higher incomes and the competition for prosperity emerged as a source of conflict during this period. Accordingly, jealousy became the motivation, and deceit and fakery became tools to climb the financial and social ladder, with shame being associated with both success and failure. While the distinctions between rich and poor became less clear-cut, with the advent of the notion of social mobility and the general pursuit of life becoming the acquisition of wealth, status comparisons and moral judgements between people of similar economic circumstances became unprecedentedly acute. The space for shame and shaming inevitably also opened up within families and close social milieu, driven by the emotional distance that grew between people with increasingly individualistic aspirations for economic advancement.

The quest for money and prosperity has continued as a popular theme in films to the present day, though with subtle differences in tone. Around the turn of the 1990s, the clear distinction between rich and poor briefly returned, although with harsher edges than in the 1970s and little prospect for reconciliation through love or any other emotion. Rich and poor were often presented as being in opposition, demarcated by differences in social interest and power. Employee was set against employer, property owner against tenant, with nothing to recommend poverty over wealth; instead everybody aspired to the latter and to the privileges that were denied to the underprivileged.

Thereafter, in the years until the Asian financial crisis and its aftermath in 1997, poverty itself became largely invisible on screen as the attention panned to the lower-middle class and their aspirations to become rich. Again their endeavours were treated with some disdain, for those intent on success were portrayed as being necessarily cut-throat or corrupt and yet, this time around, they were seldom juxtaposed with the 'virtuous poor' but usually only against the economically successful. Shame, therefore, became presented as a product of economic failure rather than as a result of avarice or corruption. Furthermore, no doubt echoing the reality of the financial crises that led to substantial numbers of bankruptcies and much unemployment, films in the 2000s were prone to use poverty as the symbolic manifestation of the loss of pride associated with economic failure and to present the fear of poverty as an important motivator in life. Rich and poor were presented as distinct and distant groups; while protagonists in poverty aspired to be rich, the rich feared the enormous shame of becoming poor. By the late 2000s, direct shaming of people in poverty was common, and the use of derogatory language and exploitative interactions were shaped by the power of wealth.

Common Features Across Time

While portrayal of the poverty–shame nexus in South Korean films has shifted dramatically in the last forty years or so, certain things have remained largely consistent. Poverty has always been seen as something unpleasant or a circumstance to be overcome. This was as true in the 1970s as it was in the 2000s, the difference is that in the earlier period poverty was typically portrayed as endemic, unavoidable, and an inevitable backdrop to the lives of the majority. Hence, the prevailing emotions evident in films of the time were those of struggle, distress, and sorrow rather than shame.

That said, even in the 1970s protagonists in poverty were likely to experience shame and shaming, but not so much owing to their state of poverty. The shame was sometimes a consequence of circumstances and characteristics that were shaming or stigmatizing themselves, for example, orphanhood, illegitimacy, or disability. Alternatively, the shame was a product of immoral behaviours, such as theft, sexual immorality, deceit, and betrayal; even when it was made necessary by the need to survive without adequate resources. Young-Ja in *Young-Ja's Heydays* (Kim, 1975), for instance, who loses her arm in an accident at work, is so ashamed of her physical disability that she is unable to ask her family for help and is eventually forced into prostitution. As another example, Jung-Hye in *The Woman I Abandoned* (Jung, 1978), who marries for love a rich husband 'when she was nothing but an orphan', is nevertheless abandoned by her husband when accusations are made concerning the legitimacy of her child.

Another constant in the cinematic portrayal of poverty is the assault that is imposed on masculinity. Traditional South Korean society built on Confucian principles of filial piety places precise and often onerous obligations on men to provide for the wider family and thereby to justify their status as the family head. Without wealth, experiencing poverty, or confronting the prospect of becoming poor, men are shown as vulnerable to losing face and self-pride, unable to fulfil the social expectations that society holds for them, a theme prominent in films across time including *Young-Ja's Heyday* (Kim, 1975), *A Little Ball Sent off by a Dwarf* (Lee, 1981), and *Crying Fist* (Ryu, 2005). Men in such circumstances are portrayed as losing wives and lovers, engaging in criminality, and gambling to restore wealth and respectability, expressing their self-loathing and participating in directed and gratuitous violence.

Violence emerges as a dominant theme in South Korean films dealing with poverty. Sometimes it is a by-product of dangerous occupations made necessary by poverty, such as pick-pocketing, robbery, illegal organ donation, hostess work, and prostitution, which leave the protagonists as likely to be victims of violence as they are perpetrators. In older films, violence was often a subtext, a necessary aspect of a life made hard by poverty but which, on screen, was largely manifest in fist fights and the like resulting from people being ripped off or betrayed. In the aftermath of the 1997 financial crisis, a new genre of film (often dubbed 'gangster movies') has emerged, characterized by extreme violence often triggered by a protagonist's experience of total financial loss and their desire both for societal revenge and recovery of their social status. *Crying Fist* (Ryu, 2005) is typical of many others, including *A Dirty Carnival* (Yoo, 2006), *The Game* (Yoon, 2008), and *Breathless* (Yang, 2009). In it, Tae-Shik, an ex-national champion boxer, loses everything when his business becomes bankrupt. His wife and child leave him and he is despised or ignored by his friends until he climbs back into the ring to fight to restore his pride and masculinity on which his life depends.

Responses to Shame and Shaming

While in earlier films, shame associated with poverty was often contingent on the presence of other stigmatizing characteristics such as physical disability and lack of basic education, or disreputable behaviours to do with immorality, shame portrayed in the period after the 1997 Asian financial crisis more often than not was attached to the state of living in poverty itself. Moreover, the impact of shame is shown to be invariably personally destructive. At a basic level, shame is captured on film as loss of face or as an assault on the pride that lies at the motivating heart of individuals. It is variously presented in films such as *Ulala Sisters* (Park, 2002), *Family* (Lee, 2004), *Crying Fist* (Ryu, 2005), and *A Dirty Carnival* (Yoo, 2006) as a loss of confidence in self, as the erosion of manhood, and as a decline in social standing, leading to the loss of self-respect and in turn to self-neglect, social isolation, and deep despair. In the *Waikiki Brothers* (Lim, 2001) and *Miracle on First Street* (Yoon, 2007), the consequences of poverty-related shame are even more severe, leading to depression and suicide. In *Crying Fist* (Ryu, 2005), *Family* (Lee 2004), and *A Dirty Carnival* (Yoo, 2006) the focus is on the breakdown of relationships, including divorce, leading to loneliness and the need to struggle single-handedly without help or support. In *The Game* (Yoon, 2008), *Ulala Sisters* (Park, 2002), and *Sympathy for Mr Vengeance* (Park, 2002) the isolated individual, alone and bereft, gambles everything on risky ventures in an effort to escape poverty and to regain respectability.

There are detectable differences over time in the ways that South Korean film portrays people responding to poverty and the associated shame. These reflect the evolving social conceptualizations of poverty from something inevitable to something structural, or at least outside of individual control, to poverty being a product mainly of personal failure. During the 1970s, film-makers portrayed positive and often highly romanticized, sometimes aspirational, responses to poverty. Both *Barefooted Youth* (Kim, 1979) and *A Little Ball Sent off by a Dwarf* (Lee, 1981), for example, emphasize that virtue can offset the pain of poverty and that a commitment to values such as love, family, justice, and truth lays the foundation for self-respect and social approval irrespective of any shame attaching to rags and missing school events due to them being unaffordable. Alternatively, films such as *Young-Ja's Heydey* (Kim, 1975) and *The World without a Mother* (Lee, 1977) recognize the hardship of poverty and its moral uncertainties but point to the role of family and community ties and solidity in supporting people to cope if not prosper. This perhaps reflects the traditional collectivist culture of Korean society and the importance of *'Jung'*—a Korean term describing warm affection shared with others extending beyond direct family ties to include, for example, neighbours and colleagues at work. *Barefooted Youth* (Kim, 1979) and *A Little Ball Sent off by a Dwarf* (Lee, 1981) in fact contain elements of both philosophies.

Films in the 1970s that adopted a more heroic take on poverty perhaps necessarily emphasized agency. Sometimes protagonists were rebellious, taking up the cudgels of a cause and challenging the status quo that held people down and kept them in their place. Elements of this can again be seen in the characterizations of the main female protagonists in *Young-Ja's Heydey* (Kim, 1975) and *The Woman I Abandoned* (Jung, 1978) in which the two both speak with no signs of shame or timid behaviour against the better-off. Furthermore, films of the time seem to preach the virtues of hard work and resilience, to dream the dream and to turn aspiration into reality through study and hard graft as is epitomized by Young-Chool in *The World without a Mother* (Lee, 1977). The contradiction inherent in these films is that while poverty is presented as endemic, the solutions proposed are individual, in effect echoing the political propaganda of the time, and also portending the more explicitly individualistic attitudes that were to become evident in film a couple of decades later.

Occasionally, even in the 1970s, films dwelt on the negative and destructive consequences of poverty and shame. *Young-Ja's Heydey* (Kim, 1975), for instance, documents the social isolation and mental breakdown that can follow poverty and the shame that attaches to various related states of being. Such negativity was much more evident, however, in the 1980s and 1990s when films such as *The Day a Pig Fell into the Well* (Hong, 1996) show protagonists hiding their poverty and becoming embroiled in a web of lies and deceit, and *Stairway to Heaven* (Bae, 1992) for example portraying the pursuit of money as futile and the product of greed, only attained by sacrificing morality and humility. But it was during this period, also, that the first films were produced that began to heap praise on protagonists who aspired to money and a good life defined in terms of material consumption for themselves. *Something to Die For* (Koo, 1999), is a case in point, in which wealth is pursued almost to death solely for the sake of attaining more money, not as a byproduct of the hero being virtuous or for any other meaningful purpose. Such films were to typify South Korean cinema in the 2000s much more so than films like *Ku-Ro Arirang* (Park, 1989) which sought to explore the structural causes of poverty and to promote the cause of labour movements seeking to shift the balance of power from state-supported industrial conglomerates (*chaebols*) to workers.

While the grim negativity attaching to poverty and shame continued into the 2000s with an emphasis on the consequential lying, deceit, fantasy, and self-pretence (*Family*, 2004; *Miracle on First Street*, 2007), personal breakdown (*Crying Fist*, Ryu, 2005), crime and violence (*The Sympathy for Mr Vengeance*, 2002; *Breathless*, Yang, 2009), a marked difference was the growing acceptance that it is fair to shame those in poverty as failures in society. Largely gone is any evidence of *Jung*, communal support. Instead, individuals are on their own, responsible for their own poverty and for its continuance. For the protagonist, salvation and social acceptability arrives when they acknowledge this new social truth and they are empowered, through their own effort, to become economically successful again. In films, such as *Ulala Sisters* (Park, 2002), *Miracle on First Street* (Yoon, 2007), and *Breathless* (Yang, 2009), it is as if the audience sits in judgement, metaphorically shaming protagonists until they accept the shame, at which point, feeling ashamed, they are motivated towards self-improvement and a pathway out of poverty.

Conclusion

The changing conception of poverty and shame in South Korean film is summarized in Table 7.1. Echoing fact and social changes occurring from the mid-1970s through to the 2000s, the portrayal of poverty in film has shifted from being endemic to being individualistic but the framing of causality and consequence is much less informed by statistical realities. While film reflects society, it has a social existence of its own and may in turn influence social perceptions and discourses.

In the 1970s, poverty provided a backdrop to social life that was held together by strong bonds of family and community. The rich were portrayed as greedy and corrupt and deserving of moral shame. This is not to say that no shame was attached to poverty in film. It was, but was associated with factors likely to cause poverty, for example lone parenthood, disability, and the

Table 7.1. Portrayals of poverty and shame in South Korean films, 1975–2010

	1975–1982	1983–1989	1990–1999	2001–2010
Values and pursuits	Love, genuineness, family, community	Prosperous, intellectual lifestyle, better life	Money, fame, sex above pure love	Self-pride associated with economic status
Money	Means to life but not an end in itself	Unavoidable reality that binds and separates people	Common object of pursuit and desire	The entire life and happiness at stake without it
Reason for poverty	Endemic, not being greedy or opportunistic enough	Belonging to a different social group	Unemployment, bankruptcy of business, social status	Individual inadequacy, structural factors, fate
Response to poverty–shame	Priority given to ethical values rather material circumstances, collective support from community ('*Jung*')	Pursuit of truth and genuine love, antithesis of structural blame for poverty	Concealment of poverty, deceit, violence, social isolation, pursuit of wealth	Acceptance of personal responsibility, violence, personal breakdown, social isolation
The rich	Greedy, corrupt, unjust wealth, despises poverty	Hypocritical, exploitative, no heart for genuine love or pursuing truth	Uses and pursues money as the power to attain anything they wish, oppressive	Relative-rich, evil employer, ultimate power-holder
Dominannt place of shame	Unjust rich	Exploitative rich	Immoral rich	Failed poor

shameless types of behaviour needed to survive without adequate resources. The cinematic response was to emphasize morality over desire and the importance of solace provided by the family or community.

Film charts the decline in collectivist values over the subsequent twenty years and responds to the societal decline in the levels of absolute poverty by making it often largely invisible until the 1997 financial crisis generated bankruptcies, unemployment, and a new social context for film. For much of the earlier period analysed here, the rich remained the principal targets of opprobrium, being variously seen as unjust or greedy in 1970s, structurally exploitative in the 1980s, and increasingly immoral in the 1990s. At the same time, with poverty becoming the exception not the rule, film-makers increasingly focused on its destructive components, social isolation, concealment, and personal disintegration, which are symptoms of the shame and stigma attributable to being different. By the 2000s, however, the compass of blame had entirely reversed direction. Poverty was now portrayed as a legitimate consequence of not succeeding against the new social expectation of prosperity. To be rich was to be successful and strong; to be poor was to be a failure. Moreover, the portrayal of the causes of poverty in the film narratives has become much more individualistic and less societal or structural. While poverty in contemporary film is still portrayed as cruel, hard, and violent as it was in the past, it is now presented as the result of individual misfortune or weakness, intended to be interpreted both as a reflection of character and a result of personal incompetence.

References

A Dirty Carnival (2006) Directed by YOO Ha [Film]. South Korea: SidusFNH.

A Family (2004) Directed by LEE Jung-Chul [Film]. South Korea: Tube Pictures.

A Little Ball Sent off by a Dwarf (1981) Directed by LEE Won-Sae [Film]. South Korea: Han-Jin Heung-Up.

Barefooted Youth (1979) Directed by KIM Soo-Hyung [Film]. South Korea: Hab-Dong Film.

Breathless (2009) Directed by YANG Ik-Joon [Film]. South Korea: Mole Film.

Crying Fist (2005) Directed by RYU Seung-Wan [Film]. South Korea: Sio Film.

Fromm, E. (1956) *The Art of Loving*, New York: Harper.

Hirschman, C. (2011) 'The Demographic Transition in Asia: 1950 to 2050', paper presented at the conference 'Population Dynamism of Asia', 11 July 2011, Kuala Lumpur.

Jo, Y. and Walker, R. (2013) 'Self-sufficiency, social assistance, and the shaming of poverty in South Korea', in Gubrium, E., Pellissery, S., Lodemel, I. (eds) *The Shame of It: Global perspectives on anti-poverty policies*, Bristol: Policy Press.

Ku-ro Arirang (1989) Directed by PARK Jong-Won [Film]. South Korea: Hwa-Chun Kong-Sa.

Lister, R. (2004) *Poverty*, Cambridge; Malden, Mass.: Polity Press.

Miracle on First Street (2007) Directed by YOON Jae-Kyoon [Film]. South Korea: Doo-Sa-Boo Film.

Mrs Speculator (1980) Directed by LIM Kwon-Taek [Film]. South Korea: Sae-Kyung Heung-Up.

OECD (2012) *OECD Economic Surveys Korea,* Paris: Organisation of Economic Cooperation and Development.

Our Joyful Young Days (1987) Directed by BAE Chang-Ho [Film]. South Korea: Tae-Heung Film.

Something to Die For (1999) Directed by KOO Im-Seo [Film]. South Korea: Tae-Won Entertainment.

SportsSeoul (2013) *Korean Cinema Ten-million Hit Era! What changed in 2013?*, <http://www.sportsseoul.com/?c=v&m=n&i=32253>.

Stairway to Heaven (1992) Directed by BAE Chang-Ho [Film]. South Korea: Dong-A Export.

Sympathy for Mr Vengeance (2002) Directed by PARK Chan-Wook [Film]. South Korea: Studio Box.

The Day a Pig Fell into the Well (1996) Directed by HONG Sang-Soo [Film]. South Korea: Dong-A Export.

The Game (2008) Directed by YOON In-Ho [Film]. South Korea: Prime Entertainment.

The Woman I Abandoned (1978) Directed by JUNG So-Young [Film]. South Korea: Woo-Sung-Sa.

The World without a Mother (1977) Directed by LEE Won-Sae [Film]. South Korea: Han-Jin Heung-Up.

Ulala Sisters (2002) Directed by PARK Jae-Hyun [Film]. South Korea: May Film.

Waikiki Brothers (2001) Directed by LIM Soon-Lae [Film]. South Korea: Myung Film.

X (1983) Directed by HA Myung-Joong [Film]. South Korea: Hab-Dong Film.

Young Ja's Heyday (1975) Directed by KIM Ho-Sun [Film]. South Korea: Tae-Chang-Heung-Up.

8

'Then' and 'Now'

Literary Representation of Shame, Poverty, and Social Exclusion in Norway

Erika Gubrium

Introduction

This chapter traces the discursive representations of poverty, shame, and social exclusion in a selected corpus of influential Norwegian novels and short stories. The guiding theme is that conditions of society percolate through its cultural material, providing a discernible channel for understanding the identities and selves in question (Holstein and Gubrium, 2000). The working question is in what ways, if at all, the identities, actions, and strategies represented in literary works resonate in the articulated experiences of people living in poverty in Norway.

The absence of the term 'poverty' from public discourse for more than half a century noted earlier (Hagen and Lødemel, 2010), was reflected in the preliminary search for relevant literature in Norway. Consequently, the search primarily yielded novels and short stories written before the Second World War and revealed a notable gap in literature concerning this topic in the period between 1939 and the mid-1970s. This is, however, understandable if we consider the fact that the number of individuals living in Norway considered to be 'poor' decreased drastically within these years and that those remaining in poverty became increasingly marginalized. Accounting for this shifting definition of poverty, selection of post-1945 literature employed search terms reflecting the groups who have largely made up Norway's social assistance population—single parents, unemployed non-Western immigrants, the long-term unemployed, drug users, those with long-term mental or physical health conditions (van der Wel et al., 2006; Naper et al., 2009), and also children, who gradually moved into the social assistance system via Norway's child welfare services (Backe-Hansen, 2004; Helgeland, 2008; Hjelmtveit, 2008).

Since the aim was to examine *how* the selected texts portrayed the concepts of poverty, social exclusion, and shame, a second criterion was applied which focused on selecting those texts that directly discuss or describe shame, embarrassment, humiliation, stigma, and social exclusion within the context of poverty. In the absence of a Norwegian 'canon', the search yielded eleven texts seen as influential by professionals and scholars in the field of Norwegian literature.[1] The texts generally cover three key periods: before, during, and after the development of the welfare state, with some works spanning two or three of these periods.

The literary works were analysed using content and discourse analyses, employing methods associated with the New Historicism approach, described earlier in this volume. Discourse analysis is concerned with how social, historical, and political meaning is created and represented through language (van Dijk, 1997); in this case how words are used by the respective authors to describe poverty and shame. In particular, we explored how each text linked social and personal identities to varying systems of power. This emphasis proved especially useful for understanding how poverty and those experiencing it in Norway are defined in literature as being attached within dominant Norwegian discourses to various social hierarchies and normative systems which create the social space for shaming and stigmatization.

Representations of Poverty, Social Exclusion, and Shame

The texts portray differential experiences of poverty, social exclusion, and shame, depending on the protagonists' social and demographic characteristics such as age, class identity, and gender, as well as geographical location (urban, small town, or rural). Further, many of the texts describe the changing experiences of poverty and social exclusion over the life course. Moreover, these shifts in how the poverty–shame nexus is represented in literature over a period of 100 years provide insights into how social, political, and demographic changes in Norway have brought with them changes in conceptions of poverty and social exclusion over that same era.

---

[1] Experts and professionals in the field of Norwegian literature were consulted. Sources for refinement of the list included the literature and children's literature reference desks at the Deichmanske National Library, Oslo and Ellen Rebecca Rees at the University of Oslo Institute for Linguistic and Nordic Studies.

Several texts portray an older conception of poverty, wherein shame is not necessarily attached to poverty per se, but rather to deviance from social or economic norms. The protagonist in Roy Jacobsen's (1991) *The Conquerors* lives in 1930s coastal northern Norway, where the class lines are distinct and secure: the farmers and fishermen struggle to make ends meet, but do so with a pride in their identity as 'producers'. Poverty is portrayed as a structural reality for the protagonist, Johan, a fact of life in pre-industrial, pre-urban society and not a mark of personal failure. Johan's hardscrabble existence is presented as the normal course of things, tempered only by the assurance of having the means to independently provide for his family.

Impoverished and homeless Knut, Hamsun's unnamed protagonist in *Hunger* (1890), on the other hand, lives in the harsh circumstances of an industrial, pre-welfare-state Oslo of the 1890s. Jobless and with no access to welfare benefits, he becomes a wandering vagrant and feels shame for having to beg for money. His social exclusion is, in large part, due to the insecurity connected to his severe living circumstances. The character is not only materially impoverished, but has minimal access to social networks. In the novel he spends much of his time searching for a friend to provide a meal or a warm place to sleep, simultaneously dependent upon the kindness and generosity of his few friends and acquaintances yet alienating them by his constant demands for assistance. Similarly, Ambjørnsen's (1986) *White Niggers* depicts the shame and stigma connected to dependency on others within a pre-welfare state context, albeit from a modern vantage point. He describes the humility of two older women (ostensibly brought up during pre-welfare state Poor Law years) sitting in a modern (1970s era) social assistance office. Both 'remember the poor house', and are 'meek'.

In a more modern Norwegian welfare state setting, the emotional impact of poverty, social exclusion, and shame are shown to be increasingly contingent upon one's identity within a complex hierarchy of culture and privilege. The discourse of equality, enabled by the securities of the welfare state, results in more individualized shame being cast or felt by those who have done socially and financially better or worse than their peers. This notion of relative poverty and privilege also makes shame a more relational phenomenon. Jacobsen (1991), for example, describes this experience of relative poverty in *The Conquerors* via a bridging protagonist, Marta (Johan's daughter), who moves to the city during World War II. Happy with having had few resources during her youth, her improved material circumstances do not necessarily result in improved self-esteem. Workers are no longer independently able to provide for themselves and their families and, as she reflects, 'the city has its own way of making an individual poor right after receiving one's wages. . . . standards change all the time and must to a certain degree be followed' (166).

The literature implies that the arrival of a strong welfare state creates a greater potential space for shame arising from the dissonance between an expectation of socio-economic mobility and the reality of constrained options. Rather than pride in what one *does* and what one *produces*, shame becomes attached to the expectation of social mobility and agency. Jacobsen's (1991) most modern protagonist, Rogern, represents a newer poverty experience in 1960s compared to 1990s Norway. Rogern explains: 'Shame is, as Kundera says, not tied to something we *do*, but to what we *are*' (365). One is shamed for being unable to find one's way within the newly imposed, somewhat subtle expectations and pressures of the social and cultural hierarchy. The modern welfare state is thus shown to create the new possibility of being categorized as falling into the 'the invisible' (335), belonging to a 'little strange outsider group, silent people who don't strive for favour in either circle, people who know they don't have a chance in either of the places' (333). In contemporary society, therefore, socio-economic poverty is more likely to be perceived as the result of family dysfunction, poorly made life choices, or a general lack of motivation to fit in. As the economy strengthened and the welfare state provided protection from poverty for the majority of those not working, individually focused shame is shown to be increasingly targeted at those who have not fared so well.

The presence of the welfare state is not, however, always linked in literary terms to the heightened possibility of shame. Ambjørnsen (1986) and Jacobsen (1991) both offer a cynical view of the welfare state's impact, not necessarily only in terms of limiting social mobility, but also as providing a space for 'bonding social capital' on the margins of society (Putnam 2000). Ambjørnsen's protagonist, Erling (*White Niggers*, 1986), for example, feels a threatened sense of identity when his network is weakened: 'I was well used to being a deviant and an outcast, but I was also well used to surrounding myself with deviants and outcasts' (257). Ironically, it is Erling's need for a stable social network of 'outcasts' in order to minimize the chance of real social exclusion that ultimately encourages him to cast away his educational ambitions.

Women and Children's Experiences of Poverty and Related Shame

Several texts address women's enhanced risk of experiencing poverty, social exclusion, and shame. Sandel's novel (1945), *Krane's Café*, describes the 'difficult economics of being a woman, especially a mother' (in Wilson, 1985: v), as well as the unequal power relations between men and women before the full development of the welfare state. The female protagonist, Katinka, is shamed and stigmatized by her small-town peers, largely as a result of her resistance against the norms of what it is to be a good wife and mother. She and her two children have been abandoned by her husband. She must fend for her family without the help of modern-day childcare and housing benefits. 'Freedom' from marriage means that she is forced to 'stand outside in the bitter wind' (121). Her vulnerability as a woman is demonstrated through the town's expectations that she will be the sole carer of her children, despite the fact that her ex-husband has been the primary earner.

Yet neither does the heightened pressure for women to adhere to social norms end with the establishment of the welfare state. While the male protagonists in Ambjørnsen's (1986) novel *White Niggers* do not feel any shame in following their free-spirited lifestyle, their close female friend, Rita, experiences intense social stigma for her decision not to conform to the social norms of motherhood and companionship. She earns patronizing derision from her childhood peers for her decision to break free of the normal pattern of small-town life in Norway: 'She wanted to trample her own way, that wayward little goat' (75).

Women are also constantly shown to face public scrutiny concerning their physical appearance. How one appears becomes more important than what one *does*. For example, in the short story, *Shit Katrine*, the shame that is publicly attached to prostitution in a small town is lessened for those women who both know how to 'assert' themselves and who are able to present a neat and self-possessed image (Sandel, 1927a). The pressure women feel to keep up appearances in order to avoid shame and the negative emotional impact of one's poverty becomes a repeated theme in the literature (Skram, 1888; Sandel, 1932, 1945; Jacobsen, 1991; Haff, 1999).

While a number of female protagonists feel the shame of being unable to adequately provide for their children, such as the woman in Sandel's (1945) *Krane's Cafe*, these feelings are further exaggerated by the special burden that poverty places on children. The texts by Sandel (1927b; 1945) and Larsen (2006) describe these difficulties. In *The Mother*, a child of a so-called 'deviant' mother runs into the woods and disappears, his face 'swollen from crying' (Sandel, 1927b: 23). The boy's shame and urge to hide is heightened by his desire to remain loyal to his mother. Dag Larsen's (2006) short novel, *Beautiful Outlaw*, focuses as much on the loneliness that the protagonist, Naud, experiences as on the material deprivation that she withstands (she has a warm apartment to sleep in, but no regular food available). The author emphasizes that the social aspects of poverty matter as much as the economic ones. Naud and her mother are continually on the move, and the impermanence of her location translates into added insecurity: 'What about the school? The teachers must easily see how it was for her? That she was hungry. That she did all she could to be almost invisible? No, they hadn't begun to see it.... there wasn't anyone to notice her, and no one who missed her' (9).

Arenas for Shaming

Since shaming always occurs in a social context, it is understandable that the process of shaming within fiction is typically located within public spaces and institutions likely to magnify its impact.

A number of texts illustrate how school can provide a place for learning about shame early on in life and from which a cycle of shame can subsequently emerge. Schools are known to reproduce existing social divisions based on wealth, privilege, social markers, and power (Bourdieu and Passeron, 1977; Bourdieu, 1984). The novels of Ambjørnsen (1986) and Jacobsen (1991/2009) suggest that institutional cultures which impose systems of reward and punishment create spaces for fictional characters to be shamed and to shame others. Indeed, it is suggested that one first learns of one's (relatively low) social position within the hierarchy of the school setting. School-based shaming is represented in the form of teachers who drill social norms into the heads of their students and who punish students who do not fit these norms (Ambjørnsen, 1986; Jacobsen, 1991). The institutionalized practice of teaching selected students to feel shame and others to act as the 'shamers' works to break social solidarity among the students: what Ambjørnsen (1986: 121) refers to as, 'Divide and conquer. The old rule'. Students from struggling families are hampered in learning to read by the harsh feedback they receive from their teachers (Jacobsen, 1991). Internalizing this shame, Marta, for example, develops a temporary reading disability, describing her letters as 'looking like animals and people... resembling her teacher... and making her scared' (58).

Other individuals struggling to make ends meet are shown to experience shame when asking for assistance, either from the state or from private sources. The themes of dependence, patronage, worthlessness, and punishment running through texts written in pre-welfare state years are, surprisingly, remarkably similar to those described in more contemporary texts. Sandel's (1945) Katinka must depend on the kindness of community and the individuals around her in order to stay above subsistence level. Her work is exploitative and her 'benefactors' patronizingly suggest that they are doing 'what's best' for her by hiring her (25). Her peers offer the talk of tough love: if she is unwilling to 'learn to swim' she 'must go to the bottom'. After all 'if all the rest of us who can swim are going to have to tow those who can't, the whole caboodle will end up at the bottom' (42). She is made to 'feel like a pauper' (26). Her questionable morals are used to defend the social shaming and exclusion that she experiences.

Sandel's novel suggests that the cycle of overblown private patronage, social disciplining, and shaming translates into poor self-esteem and the loss of self-respect for those on the receiving end of assistance, while those on the delivering end are socially bolstered. Rigid demands on people in poverty concerning the exchange of work for dignity and subsistence pay, along with a protocol of social punishment, internal shame, and scant incentives are so punitive that Katinka gives up: 'You haven't the courage to do the work you want to do. And you haven't the time to do the things you ought to do.... You know there's only one solution: to get through it.... But you get so tired, so tired' (161).

In more modern literary settings, shaming occurs at the point of collecting public social assistance benefits. The punitive and tough love demeanour that Ambjørnsen's (1986) protagonist Erling faces is strikingly similar to Sandel's descriptions of private patronage. Social workers in Norway have always had the discretionary parallel tasks of cancelling and awarding aid. These texts portray the dilemma that follows, as professionals must carefully weigh social costs and personal benefits to determine their treatment of clients. Here is the modern parallel to the heightened sense of dependency, shame, and stigma that Hamsun's protagonist experiences when the assistance gets personal (Pinker, 1971). Ambjørnsen describes the shame that results from this asymmetrical relationship generated at the point of receiving social assistance thus; 'we were all too broke to make such an uproar so near to the money purse. We had come to beg.... This is what it is to be a poor shit: honour and conscience are lost' (17).

Refusing to overtly humble himself to his caseworker, Ambjørnsen is, nonetheless shamed at having to take part in this pretence in the first place: 'The whole thing was a disgusting affair that definitely had reduced my self-esteem significantly, even if it hadn't been so damn high before' (307).

Thus, within both the private and public contexts portrayed in the texts, the recipient of aid understands that there is a dilemma on the part of those on the delivering end. Aid must be generous enough so the recipient is able to subsist, hence reducing the level of abject poverty. Yet it must not be so generous that the recipient loses motivation and becomes dependent. The recipient, sensing the tension generated by such a calculation, experiences the shame of dependence, of failing to contribute appropriately to society or community and possibly being judged as 'undeserving'.

Responses to Poverty-Induced Shame

The selected authors commonly describe the types of behavioural responses to poverty-induced shame by those experiencing or at risk of experiencing it. The shame arising from poverty and the ways in which different characters react to it, are invariably bound by the context within which it occurs.

Displacing Shame

As 'looking glass selves' we cast and feel shame about our identities through the eyes of others (Cooley, 1922; Goffman, 1963). The literary representations of shame examined likewise suggested that the phenomenon of shame is both externally generated and internally felt. One evident strategy adopted by characters to minimize feelings of shame is to reflect shame back to the 'shamer'. Hamsun (1890) and Haff (1999) both illustrate this strategy of 'shaming upward'. Hamsun's protagonist turns his feelings of shame into disdain for the good fortunes and easy lives of those surrounding him: 'To take comfort and make it up to myself, I began to see all sorts of faults in these happy people who were gliding by . . . I lifted my head and felt deep down how blessed I was to be able to follow the straight and narrow' (105).

Similarly, Idun, Haff's (1999) protagonist in the novel *Shame*, uses her sister and brother—who share her shameful past and yet lead seemingly 'successful' lives—as foils to suggest that they are hiding behind a façade of respectability and are leading 'false' and corrupt lives. She, however, has done 'nothing to hide' her sense of stigma (362). Sandel (1927a) and Jacobsen (1991) describe the flip side of this strategy in which the response is to shame 'downward', targeting a less fortunate discreditable scapegoat. The target is shamed by the local community and serves as 'a brick in the wall . . . that in turn held up the others, an institution' (Sandel, 1927a: 43) or is a school peer of Rogern's who 'has it even worse' and is targeted to 'ease the pressure a little' (Jacobsen, 1991: 325).

A further strategy to project, rather than internalize, shame is described by Hamsun (1890). His protagonist deliberately helps those he deems more disadvantaged than himself and thus asserts his own position as relatively better off. More specifically, the protagonist reclaims a sense of dignity by taking on the identity of provider and not recipient of aid. While these strategies may enable the characters to effectively divert shame and its negative impact on the self, they simultaneously engage in a process of 'othering'; creating a social distance between themselves and those who might otherwise be included in their peer group.

Succumbing to Existential Hopelessness

Existential hopelessness emerges in the literature at times when the protagonists constantly fail to mitigate the shame they experience as a result of their chronic poverty, and hence conclude that death is the only way out. Haff (1999), Ambjørnsen (1986), and Skram (1888) all suggest that, though seemingly irrational, such an extreme response may in fact signify an assertion of agency. For example, Ambjørnsen (1986) and Skram (1888) present the suicides of two characters as final acts of agency. In both cases, since the characters have lost the ability to choose their path, suicide appears to be the only remaining option. Rita, the close friend of Ambjørnsen's protagonist Erling, states: 'I have not thought that anyone will choose for me . . . I *will* go to hell' (42 and 45; Ambjørnsen's emphasis). Skram's (1888) protagonist in the novel *Lucie* chooses death in response to her complete social exclusion and existential hopelessness. Implying the agency that only suicide can offer, she says, 'What if she had gone out and done away with herself. People *could* take their own lives' (118). It is noteworthy that only the female protagonists in our texts employ this strategy, yet this perhaps substantiates the idea that they are more likely to be subjected to critical public scrutiny (Lacan, 1978) than men.

Resisting Shame

Limiting the analytical focus to only those strategies that reflect reactions to and negotiations of shame, once experienced, fails to acknowledge many of the alternate strategies that characters in poverty are shown to employ when threatened with the shame of their circumstances. Indeed, four texts (Hamsun, 1890; Ambjørnsen, 1986; Jacobsen, 1991; Stranger, 2006) suggest that their impoverished protagonists, notably all male, actively refuse to take on shame, either through direct avoidance strategies or through more covert strategies of pretence that are attempts to save face. Contrary to the burdensome public scrutiny that is imposed on women, it is perhaps the enhanced social capital that comes from masculinity that enables these actions.

Two texts, for example, illustrate how class solidarity can directly thwart the process of shame and shaming. The pre-industrial era protagonist, Johan, in Jacobsen's (1991) novel relies upon the promise of class rebellion to refuse the shame he may experience from being exploited for his work. A class revolution will ultimately enable the working class to 'inherit the earth'. The working class will ultimately be 'history's conquerors' (41). While not counting on a full-blown class revolution, the more modern Erling in Ambjørnsen's (1986) novel describes the social solidarity he and his co-workers establish while working low-level jobs: 'it was a bottomless solidarity, completely without limits. You fought for the lazy shit sacks tooth and nail, and they fought for you' (209). In a similar way to the social networks on the margins that Erling uses to maintain his self-image, the system of solidarity that he builds with his co-workers acts as a bulwark against the tedium and depression that might be associated with his status as part of the 'lumpen proletariat'.

Similarly, some texts demonstrate how certain characters do not necessarily passively assume a sense of self inscribed by society, but engage in a dialogical process in which they actively play a part in determining their own identities (Hermans et al. 1992), thus saving face. Simon Stranger's (2006) and Hamsun's

(1890) protagonists, for instance, create framing devices to rationalize their actions and to refuse the more shameful identities that would otherwise be thrust upon them. This activity takes the form of storytelling.

In his children's novel, *The Ghosts*, Stranger's (2006) protagonist, a statue of Henrik Ibsen, comes to life and uses his recollections of a better past and his earlier identity as a successful playwright to avoid facing the shame of his present circumstances. The protagonist in Hamsun's (1890:) novel is able to avoid acknowledging the depressing particularities of his circumstances through the creation of stories about his identity. At various points throughout the novel he presents himself as a highly-esteemed professional journalist, on the way to writing his next breakthrough story.

These acts of solidarity-building or face-saving storytelling are, however, often met with the cold reality of the characters' situations, at which points they are faced with the hopelessness of being unable to surpass their material circumstances. This constant uncertainty is what preoccupies the protagonists. The risks associated with refusing shame may be contingent upon the character's relationships with others, on their current or past identities or their relative positions of strength on the social and economic hierarchies by which they are constrained.

Conclusions

Our findings are drawn from an analysis of a sample of influential literature and thus can be said to represent some of the dominant ideas concerning poverty and shame expressed through cultural media over the past 100 years in Norway. The analysis suggests that demographic particularities, such as age, class identity, and gender, in fact, change the way that individuals living in poverty experience shame in connection with their economic and social circumstances. The selected texts thus sensitized us to the many variations in the experience of poverty and its related shame, which as a research team we needed to be mindful of in subsequent interviews with people facing economic hardship.

For example, the literature suggests that women may experience heightened stigma and shame attached to their poverty compared to men, due to the expectations attached to their roles as caregivers and because of the increased emphasis placed on how they should present themselves in public. Consequently, in our later analysis of interview material, we focus on gender differences concerning social and caregiving expectations, exploring whether or not the burden of the public gaze has been a significant part of the shame that women living in poverty have experienced.

Similarly, given our findings concerning a continuum of social exclusion and the possibility for social bonding within the setting of a welfare state, our study of interviews with individuals living in poverty has applied a more nuanced analysis of what it means to be socially mobile. For example, the literature indicates that the possibilities promised by the equalizing aims of the welfare state may in fact shape the ways individuals experience shame within the context of their economic and social difficulties. We have likewise considered how individuals living in poverty characterize their social networks and how these networks may (or may not) be useful in displacing or refusing shame.

So too did the literature provide insights into the social spaces within which characters were most likely to experience poverty-related shame. School and institutions providing aid in Norway are indicated in the literature as locations in which poverty-related shaming may be particularly noticeable. Interview data, described in the following section of this volume, add depth and variability to this picture, for example through demonstrating how the norms, rights, and expectations that are attached to the public provision of minimum income assistance heighten the experience of shame. The texts also point to the shame that is experienced as a result of how characters are categorized as 'poor', 'needy', or 'dependent'. As noted later in this volume, the same 'shame of categorization' emerges as a strong theme within our analysis of interviews with people living in poverty.

Finally, the literature suggests that individuals facing poverty may employ multiple strategies in attempts to diffuse or minimize shame. Individuals do not passively accept the identities that society assigns them, but instead play an active role in determining their identities and social roles. In our interviews with individuals living in poverty (described in Chapter 15), we explore these themes further, examining the differing contexts and relationships, which define the experiences of feeling shame and being shamed, and exploring how the language of passivity and agency are used. The samples of literature, therefore, have provided important insights into the varied nuances of the poverty experience and how we might begin to investigate the real-life experiences of those living it day-to-day.

References

Ambjørnsen, I. (1986) *HviteNiggere* [*White Niggers*], Oslo: CappelenDamm AS.
Backe-Hansen, E. (2004) 'Barn ogungeshåndteringavvanskeligelivsvilkår [Children and youth's handling of difficult living conditions]', NOVA Rapport 12/04, Oslo.
Bourdieu, P. and Passeron, J-C. (1977) *Reproduction in Education, Society and Culture*, London: Sage.
Bourdieu, P. (1984) *Distinction: A Social Critique of the Judgment of Taste*, Cambridge, MA: Harvard University Press.
Cooley, C.H. (1922) *Human Nature and the Social Order*, New York: Scribners.

Goffman, E. (1963), *Stigma: Notes on the Management of Spoiled Identity*, New York: Simon & Schuster.

Haff, B. H. (1999) *Shame*, London: The Harvill Press.

Hagen, K. and Lødemel, I. (2010) 'Fattigdomstiåret 2000–10: Parentes eller ny kurs for velferdsstaten?', in Frønes, I. and Kjølsrød, L. (eds) *Det Norske Samfunn*, Oslo: Gyldendal, Ch. 12.

Hamsun, K. (1890) *Hunger*, London: Penguin Books.

Helgeland, I. M. (2008) '"Det handler ikke bare om penger." Barnevernsbarnogfattigdom ["It's not just about money." Children in child welfare services and poverty'], in Harsløf, I. and Seim, S. (eds) *FattigdommensDynamikk* [*Poverty's Dynamic*], Oslo: Universitetsforlaget, 171–85.

Hermans, H. J. M., Kempen, H. J. G., and Van Loon, R. J. P. (1992) 'The dialogical self: Beyond individualism and rationalism', *American Psychologist*, 47: 23–33.

Hjelmtveit (2008) 'Langvarig økonomisk sosialhjelp i barnefamilier: fattigdomsfelle for foreldre og barn? [Long-term economic social assistance in families with children: poverty trap for parents and children?]' in Harsløf, I. and Seim, S. (eds) *FattigdommensDynamikk* [*Poverty's Dynamic*], Oslo: Universitetsforlaget, 148–70.

Holstein, J. A. and Gubrium, J. F. (2000) *The Self We Live By*, Oxford: Oxford University Press.

Jacobsen, R. (1991) *Seierherrene* [The *Conquerors*], Oslo: CappelenDamm AS.

Lacan, J. (1978) *Seminar XI: The Four Fundamental Concepts of Psychoanalysis*, London: W.W. Norton and Co.

Larsen, D. (2006) *Fagerfredløs* [*Beautiful Outlaw*], Oslo: Omnipax.

Naper, S. O., Wel, K. van der, and Halvorsen, K. (2009) 'Arbeidsmarginalisering og fattigdom blant langtidsmottakere av sosialhjelp i 1990 og 2005', in Harsløf, I. and Seim, S. (eds) *Fattigdoms dynamik: Perspektiver på marginalisering i det norske samfunnet*, Oslo: Universitetsforlaget, 80–110.

Pinker, R. (1971) *Social Theory & Social Policy*, London: Heinemann Educational Books.

Putnam, R. (2000) *Bowling Alone: The Collapse and Revival of American Community*, New York: Simon & Schuster.

Sandel, C. (1927a) 'Shit Katrine', in *Cora Sandel: Selected Short Stories*, Seattle, WA: The Seal Press, 45–54.

Sandel, C. (1927b) 'Mother', in *Cora Sandel: Selected Short Stories*, Seattle, WA: The Seal Press, 22–7.

Sandel, C. (1932) 'A mystery', in *Cora Sandel: Selected Short Stories*, Seattle, WA: The Seal Press, 114–29.

Sandel, C. (1945) *Krane's Café*, London: Peter Owen Ltd.

Skram, A. (1888) *Lucie*, Norwich: Norvik Press.

Stranger, S. (2006) *Gjengangeren* [*The Ghosts*], Oslo: N. W. Damm & Son.

Van der Wel, K., van der, Dahl, E., Lødemel, I., Løyland, B., Naper, S.O., and Slagsvoldet, M. (2006) *Funksjonsevne blant langtidsmottakere av sosialhjelp*, Oslo, HiO Report.

Van Dijk, T.A. (1997) *Discourse as Structure and Process*, London: Sage.

Wilson, B. (1985) 'Introduction', in *Cora Sandel: Selected Short Stories*, Seattle, WA: The Seal Press, pp. v–viii.

Section II
Experiences of Poverty and Shame in Seven Countries

Preface

Section I of this volume considered the different ways in which poverty and shame were conceived of within a range of different cultural media including films, novels, poetry, and proverbs from seven countries. Despite the cultural nuances found, collectively and comparatively the analysis established a strong association between poverty and shame and illustrated the numerous arenas within which they were likely to emerge and interact, at least in fictional worlds.

Section II builds on the analysis drawn from the samples of cultural material, bearing in mind the growing body of literature that supports the idea that representations of social phenomena captured in the arts are, in and of themselves, bona fide testaments of social reality (Coser, 1963; Perry, 2005; Lewis et al., 2008; Sutherland and Felty, 2010). Here we make the shift into real time to consider the narratives of people living in poverty in the contemporary societies of the same seven countries and investigate how far the messages carried in oral traditions and in works of imagination are replicated in their day-to-day lived experiences.

The evidence for this section is drawn from a mix of ethnography and in-depth interviews with adults and sometimes children in each of the study countries (details of samples or participants are found in each of the following chapters). In selecting people for interview, a careful balance was sought between the need to facilitate some comparison across countries without doing damage to the veracity of lives lived within particular cultures. Interviews were conducted in rural areas in India, Uganda, and Pakistan; urban settings in China (Beijing), South Korea (Seoul), Britain (two areas of high deprivation in the South Midlands), and Pakistan (Lahore); and in three small towns in Norway. For the most part, the adults interviewed had dependent children, although in Beijing respondents belonged to a new class of poverty, former workers of now dissolved state-owned enterprises who tended to be older than persons interviewed elsewhere. Children themselves were interviewed in Britain, India, Pakistan, and Uganda.

Despite the differences in material deprivation across the different contexts, as a whole, this section reveals the uncanny similarities between the psychological and social impacts of poverty across the seven countries. Shame in relation to poverty undeniably emerges as a vital component in the actual realities of poverty, just as it did in its various guises in the fictional portrayals of the poverty experience. The following chapters detail the often subtle nuances of how poverty and shame intertwine across the different contexts, at the same time illuminating the distinct roles of wider social constructs, such as gender, ethnicity, class, and caste; the prevailing cultural norms and standards in each country; as well as the structural and institutional frameworks and systems which scope out the social, cultural, political, and economic landscape within which people on the economic margins of society are expected to sustain themselves as successful social citizens.

References

Coser, L. (1963) *Sociology through Literature*, Englewood Cliffs: Prentice-Hall International.

Lewis, D., Rodgers, D., and Woolcock, M. (2008) 'The Fiction of Development: Literary Representation as a Source of Authoritative Knowledge', *Journal of Development Studies*, 44(2): 198–216.

Perry, R. (2005) 'Home Economics: Representations of Poverty in Eighteenth-Century Fiction', in Backscheider, P. R., and Ingrassia, C. (eds) *A Companion to the Eighteenth Century English Novel and Culture*, Oxford: Blackwell.

Sutherland, J. A., and Felty, K. (2010) *Cinematic Sociology: Social Life in Film*, California: Sage Publications.

9

'Needy and Vulnerable, but Poverty Is Not My Identity'

Experiences of People in Poverty in Rural Uganda

Grace Bantebya-Kyomuhendo

Introduction

Although Uganda has made steady progress in alleviating poverty, reducing the countrywide incidence from 58 per cent of the population in 1992 to 24.5 per cent in 2009, poverty remains entrenched in the country's rural areas, home to more than 87 per cent of Ugandans. About 30 per cent of all rural people, some 10 million men, women, and children, still live below the national rural poverty line (Republic of Uganda, 2010). With a per capita income of US $170, Uganda today is one of the poorest countries in the world (Republic of Uganda Ministry of Local Government and World Bank, 2009; UNDP, 2013). This chapter, while drawing on the above context, is not immediately concerned with poverty levels in Uganda per se, but with the psychological and social impacts of penury and how these are experienced at individual and family levels (Republic of Uganda, 2005; Uganda NGO Forum, 2009). More precisely, in keeping with the objectives of the wider cross-cultural and comparative study, it examines whether and in what ways poverty and shame are associated in the context of rural Uganda, the circumstances within which the poverty–shame nexus is likely to occur, and what its likely consequences are.

The study sites were purposively selected as areas of high deprivation in two parishes in one district of Central West Uganda. In-depth interviews were carried out with thirty adults, most of them household heads, and thirty children and young people aged 10 to 18 years experiencing extreme poverty and disadvantage. Young people interviewed were at the time of the research living in the same homes as adult interviewees and were enrolled in school.

Interviews aimed to elicit respondents' views and perspectives on the nature and experience of hardship, the causes of poverty, and the feelings and/or behaviour evoked in them as a result of dealing with disadvantage at an individual as well as family level.

Poverty was approached as a complex multifaceted phenomenon, in recognition of the fact that human beings are individuals each of whom is affected differently by factors such as level of income, access to productive resources, voice in the community, access to opportunity, and perceived evaluation of the self by others with respect to meeting the community social norms and expectations. Children and young people interviewed were asked about their experiences of hardship both at home and at school, and the research tools were adapted to include topics tailored to their age cohort. Interviews with children and young people were conducted in the homestead after those with adults had been completed. Care was taken to ensure that discussions with children took place out of earshot of the parents or other family members. Informed consent to interview children and young people was sought and obtained from parents and from children and young people themselves, and all participants were assured about the confidentiality of the gathered data and anonymity with respect to reporting of research findings.

Poverty and the Emergence of Shame from Within

All adult respondents described themselves as subsistence cultivators, a livelihood option synonymous with production of foodstuffs for basic family consumption. Subsistence cultivation, it was noted, was pursued as a last resort rather than as a deliberate occupation and, in most cases, levels of production proved too meagre to meet the family's basic needs. As a result, people spoke of how they were invariably compelled to engage in other income-generating activities to make ends meet, such as providing casual labour or engaging in the production and selling of petty merchandise. Being forced by economic circumstances to take up casual labour, which usually involving digging in other people's fields, was described by both adults and children as being both financially unrewarding and extremely degrading.

Participants in all of the thirty families talked of facing chronic income shortfalls and living on the edge. In most of the households residential accommodation consisted of makeshift temporary or semi-permanent structures, without cooking or basic sanitation facilities. Commodities such as food and safe water were in chronically short supply and other services such as health care, education, and recreational facilities were severely limited. On the whole, respondents were openly bitter about the daily hardships they had to tolerate, attributing them to lack of opportunity and circumstances outside their control, rather than to any individual failings. A few, however, referred to fate, divine providence, or family curses as the causes of their plight, and consequently appeared to be resigned to lives that providence had dealt them.

Most people interviewed spoke of how they entertained certain economic and social aspirations. For the most part, such ambitions centred on reversing their adverse economic circumstances by accumulating material wealth and with it the related elevation of social status. There was unanimity in people's narratives that achieving in material terms, no matter by what means, was the catalyst for attainment of social capital and recognition.

In reality though, it emerged throughout the course of the research that most participants alluded to how they had given up hope of extricating themselves from the poverty trap, and believed it unlikely that such aspirations would amount to anything more than wishful thinking. They had, they said, become despondent, disillusioned, and overall tended to evaluate themselves negatively in comparison with their relatively better-off neighbours. People made repeated references to the fact that they felt ashamed of being materially and socially deprived. Such shame tended to have its locus in the psyche or the inner self, a factor that rendered it difficult for them to go about without some degree of embarrassment or discomfort within their local communities. Such feelings were said to persist irrespective of whether or not others said anything or acted in ways likely to provoke such emotions. Nonetheless, such pervasive feelings of inadequacy became further accentuated and even more devastating when others acted or spoke in ways which reinforced this sense of failure.

Being Shamed by Others

Chapter 2 of this volume presented evidence from oral traditions indicating that in pre-modern Ugandan society poverty was largely attributed to fate and, consequently, shame directly associated with poverty was not felt or inflicted in quite the same ways as it is in present times. Shame was instead the result of social transgressions, and regulated by clearly spelled out sanctions that were socially binding. In contemporary society there appears to have been a fundamental shift in perceptions and understandings about the causes of poverty, with the result that shame directly associated with reduced economic circumstances has displaced that previously stemming from the contravention of societal norms and mores. This paradigm shift has, according to the accounts of people interviewed, inevitably widened the scope and space for denigrating and criticizing those who have failed to thrive economically, making it socially acceptable for them to be held solely responsible for their lot.

A number of different loci were described by participants as spaces within which shame was regularly inflicted on them. For adult respondents these included their homes, their immediate communities, trading centres, bars, the village well, the local church, and the public market. Moreover, shaming also commonly took place in public forums such as local council and other meetings, or at feasts or burial gatherings. These multiple public arenas, typically found in any local community, rendered it difficult for both adults and children to avoid exposure to poverty-induced shame and regularly forced them to publicly bear the full brunt of it.

For the most part, people taking part in the research did not hold a positive view of those within their communities who were relatively better-off. They intimated that, as a result of the social and economic divide between themselves and their richer neighbours, the latter often treated them with undisguised contempt. There was agreement among those experiencing poverty that their wealthier peers saw them as directly responsible for their circumstances and blamed them for their plight. And even though participants were acutely aware of the sorts of inequalities and lack of opportunities that made it so hard for them to improve their situations, they believed that such factors were ignored by the relatively rich, who largely attributed poverty to negative behavioural traits including laziness, dishonesty and promiscuity, lack of financial discipline, drunkenness, and lack of ambition in life. Since these assumptions were so widely held, participants often portrayed scenarios in which their material deprivation automatically led to them becoming at once social pariahs and legitimate targets of shaming within the community.

Interviews conducted with children and young people demonstrated their acute awareness of their family poverty and how feelings of poverty-induced shame develop early in life. Children and young people articulately depicted the extent of material deprivation frequently experienced in their homes. Although many of them claimed to be proud of their homes and the efforts of their parents, the privations therein notwithstanding, others openly expressed contempt for their circumstances. These young people not only spoke openly about regretting being born into their families but also despised the means by which their parents earned a living, deriding subsistence farming as unproductive and shameful. They especially resented being compelled to engage in what they considered to be degrading casual labour in order to help sustain their family incomes.

For children and young people, the shame they described emerged primarily from a constant negative self-evaluation with respect to their peers, which seemed to be most intense at school. At home too, however, young people spoke about a similar sense of shame, which tended to be triggered by the constant comparisons they were prone to make between their own circumstances and those of other economically better-off families. Children gave accounts of situations where they avoided inviting their friends home to visit for fear of the ramifications of others seeing the full extent of their poverty, which they believed was obvious from the poor quality of their homes. Yet, despite being sorely felt, the shame described by children and young people for the most part appeared to be self-inflicted and, unlike the case of their parents, there was limited evidence of it being directly imposed on them by others. So, while at home children described feeling profound internal shame and at school they tended to devalue themselves compared to their wealthier peers, incidents of direct shaming either by the teachers, fellow pupils, or significant others were not directly referred to during the course of interviews.

Responses to Poverty-Induced Shame

In order to cope with the daily experiences of poverty-induced shame, adult respondents indicated that they had adopted diverse strategies to avoid, camouflage, or merely help them deal with its damaging effects. It is worthwhile to note that whether the shame was self-inflicted or directly inflicted by others, the strategies adopted to cope with it were more or less similar.

Withdrawal

A number of adult participants reasoned that since they had no possibility of being able to escape poverty in their lifetime, they felt compelled to avoid its shaming effects by confining themselves to the home environment as much as possible. In practice, this meant discouraging visitors or, when they arrived unannounced, restricting them to the courtyard so that they could not witness the deprivations inside their houses. Moreover, all family members, irrespective of their age, were urged to be tight-lipped about what went on in the family and especially not to mention any circumstances likely to predispose them to ridicule as a result of their poverty. The respondents in such households were adamant that they had no option but to deliberately opt for this apparently socially deviant behaviour, since the alternative would be to endure the pain and discomfort of being harangued and stigmatized by others because of their circumstances. Whenever any family member ventured out of the home, the cardinal rule was reportedly to avoid unnecessary dialogue with outsiders apart from exchanging greetings, which is a customary norm. One old man described how he had been driven to the extreme of living like a hermit, a lifestyle that had so well shielded him from the risk of being derided and criticized that he had no intention of ever returning to mainstream society.

It should be noted that this behavioural strategy, one which was commonly referred to by people participating in the research, is tantamount to transgression of the social and cultural ethos and mores in the study communities, where social interaction is a cultural expectation, and indispensable for maintaining social cohesion. Hence, those facing daily hardship were forced to strike a trade-off between being visible and active in their communities, and in so doing risking exposure to poverty-induced shaming; or transgressing societal expectations by deliberately withdrawing from their community to avoid the shame of poverty, yet at the same time laying themselves open to disapproval for not adhering to communal norms and values. The research evidence clearly suggests that those in poverty were increasingly choosing the latter option, a response that does not augur well for maintenance of the social fabric, and the overall functioning of rural communities.

In a similar vein, a number of people spoke of how, even though they went out to socialize, they deliberately avoided the company of individuals whom they considered to be financially or socially better-off than themselves. Instead, they chose to only spend time with those seen either as equally poor or worse off and argued that socializing with the relatively rich was equivalent to inappropriately straying out of their social sphere. Several participants referred to the fact that those facing similar deprivation had much in common, including a shared language of poverty, several noting that 'abanakutwinaomulingotwetegerezangana', literally meaning, 'we who are living in poverty have a common bond which enables us to interact and understand each other'. One man disclosed that by mixing only with those who faced similar circumstances to his own or more especially those he considered worse off gave him an elevated sense of agency and effectively shielded him from the emotional pain associated with exposure to shame outside of his immediate circle.

Some people interviewed recounted behavioural responses to their crippling circumstances that were akin to total withdrawal from society. One man of advanced age explained how, feeling overwhelmed by his persistent deprivation, he had completely abandoned his family. At the time of the research he was homeless and living in a neighbour's disused storage shed, surviving by procuring occasional casual work. He lived, he said, from hand to mouth, spending his meagre earnings on food, alcohol, and tobacco. At the same time, however, he asserted that he had no regrets about this lifestyle and claimed not to be at all concerned about how he was viewed by those around him or society in general. Such declarations appear, on the surface at least, to indicate the possibility of transcending the shame associated with subsistence poverty and the shame linked to the often inevitable transgression of social mores which poverty obliges. Such behaviour, irrespective of how it was rationalized, could perhaps also be interpreted as a means of self-immunization from the persistent indignities and the stultifying social effects of living a life of deprivation; complete withdrawal and its acceptance is therefore synonymous with social suicide.

Keeping Up Appearances

Some adult respondents admitted to how, in a bid to conceal their poverty, they strived hard to maintain public appearances of being able to cope and relatively satisfied with their lot. They pretended to be content with their hardship, rationalizing it as normal since it was unrealistic to expect everybody to be successful in terms of both material acquisitions and social capital. They took pride in the fact that they had at least not stooped to the level of begging for household basics from their neighbours, although this often meant doing without essentials like salt. Whenever members of such households stepped out in public, they made sure, they said, that they or their children were smartly dressed, even if it meant being attired in their Sunday best. When their circumstances were temporarily eased and they were in a position to buy 'luxuries' like beef, sugar, or cooking oil using cash, they made sure that such transactions were undertaken in full view of the public.

Women and men recounted how they endeavoured to camouflage their poverty by sacrificing everything else to dress smartly, style their hair, don jewellery, and apply make-up so as to appear presentable in public and avoid the shame of appearing shabby or unkempt. One impoverished young man, for example, narrated an incident in which he pledged to make a hefty financial contribution during a meeting in preparation for a wedding so as to avoid the shame of being considered too poor to make such a donation. Other relatively rich people were contributing or pledging large amounts of money, and, cash-strapped as he was, he followed suit, in order to salvage his 'status' that he felt was at stake. Although honouring the pledge had drained his meagre savings, he felt proud that he had at least proved his worth and avoided the public shame of not being able to live up to the promise.

In a similar vein, a further strategy which several participants implied they had used in order to mask often extreme hardship was to make public donations to those who were considered even worse off than themselves. All of the adult respondents had at one time or another, they said, engaged in acts of generosity, including donating foodstuffs or clothing to a neighbour in desperate need, offering free casual domestic or farm labour, or transporting a sick neighbour to hospital. Importantly, practically all those who engaged in such acts of kindness reported deriving extreme emotional satisfaction and/or spiritual fulfilment from them. Whether or not these actions were inherently altruistic or whether they in fact stemmed from a desire to find occasions to deflect poverty-induced shame to those who were even worse off than themselves is unclear. It is rational to argue that in light of the emotional benefits which the respondents reportedly derived from their unsolicited generosity that these acts of kindness may have had an ulterior motive of mitigating the insidious and persistent effects of poverty and its associated shame.

Deflecting Shame

Actively deflecting or at least verbally denying feelings of shame associated with poverty were strategies most commonly insinuated by women taking part in the research, irrespective of whether they were married and cohabiting with their husbands or unmarried and living with male relatives. They asserted the fact that issues of family welfare and social status were outside their domain and hence they had no control over them. They argued that since their husbands or male relatives were the de facto household heads and providers, they were likewise the legitimate targets of any public criticism for failing to live up to their socially ascribed roles such as providing for the family.

One young woman living with her uncle, for example, acknowledged the hardship the family was experiencing and the public criticism they were prone to because of it. Yet she was quick to point out that it was her uncle who bore the brunt of such shaming by virtue of the fact that he was the household head. In reference to the dilapidated residential structure in which they lived, she defensively asserted that in her culture she as a woman was not expected to build a house and that it was her uncle who, as a result of failing to provide adequate shelter for his family, faced the most damaging type of shame (*okuhemuka*).

One woman, in spite of her obvious life of extreme hardship, was adamant that she had not experienced shame as a result. Her strategy, she said, was to consciously block out any emotional pain and feelings of inadequacy as a result of her poverty. These emotions, she asserted, were relegated to her inner subconscious self. She likened her mind to a suitcase, a sort of Pandora's box, in which all her life challenges, including vulnerability to poverty-induced shame, were securely locked up, '*omutimasanduko, gwahurabyona, ebirungin'ebibi*'. As a result she refused to acknowledge her poverty and low social status and felt, she said, able to go about the community without shame, interacting freely with all community members irrespective of their social or economic status. She described constantly striving to exude an aura of warmth, good heartedness, open mindedness, good neighbourliness, and self-confidence. This tactic, she claimed, had served her well, enabling her to simultaneously live in poverty without resentment and to forestall any related shame.

Three other adult respondents directly attributed their poverty to fate or powers beyond their control. Their hardship emanated, they said, from the actions of ancestral spirits or was the result of family curses, malevolence by others, or divine providence. In all cases they initially spoke of how they consequently felt shielded from any shame associated with their poverty since as mere human beings they had no say in the workings of the divine or the supernatural. However, their coping strategy notwithstanding, these respondents were unable to hide their true social disposition for long and went on to divulge how they were nonetheless prone to negative self-evaluation and feelings of inadequacy and failure. In effect, their beliefs about the causes of their poverty and its inevitability did not guard them from the shame that such poverty evoked, something which all three described as a constant challenge.

Defensiveness and Anger

Some of the men participating in the study spoke of how, as a result of having always experienced hardship they were inclined to displaying seemingly irrational responses to events and circumstances they came across, such responses often perceived as counts of unprovoked hostility. These men alluded to always being primed to respond aggressively to incidences of real or imagined attempts at public criticism or ridicule. They narrated scenarios in which they had angrily stormed out of village meetings or local drinking joints, claiming that they had been shamed.

This same behavioural response to poverty was also evident in the narratives of some young people interviewed. Several recounted how their experiences of feeling inadequate as a result of their poverty often evoked in them feelings of frustration and anger. One 13-year-old boy, for example, commented,

> Unlike me, my friends dress well. They dress smartly in good uniform, shoes, and belts. They carry school bags. They have mathematical sets and enough pens. They come to school with pocket money for lunch. I stay hungry at school. Sometimes I feel angry and humiliated ('*harohoobumpurraobusungun'okuswara*').

A number of other young people alluded to the fact that, like their parents, their 'guard', was always up, ready to react aggressively to incidences of real or perceived shaming.

Resenting the Stigma of 'Poverty'

Irrespective of the extent and type of social stigma, ridicule, or criticism that people were subjected to, the majority of adults and young people interviewed uniformly resented the idea that poverty should become a label or an identity.

121

When this occurred it was considered as extremely degrading and shameful and adults and children frequently emphasized the fact that they believed nobody is born or destined to be poor, *'obunakutibuzarrwa'*. Instead, they stressed that they were forced to live in poverty as a result of the lack of opportunity presented by unfavourable institutional, structural, and other factors which were beyond their control. Participants were critical and resentful of how governmental anti-poverty programmes they had witnessed or been recipients of in their communities repeatedly enforced on them labels denoting their failure and inadequacies. Programmes that were specifically named included Universal Primary Education (UPE), the Plan for Modernisation of Agriculture/National Agricultural Advisory Services (PMA/NAADS), and Prosperity for All (PFA), all of which used in their respective modes of framing, structuring, and delivery the classification of people as 'poor', 'needy', or 'vulnerable' before they met the criteria to qualify for and subsequently access the benefits of such interventions.

As documented elsewhere (Bantebya-Kyomuhendo and Mwiine, 2013), the UPE programme in Uganda has in itself become a system of stigmatization. Those families with the necessary wherewithal tend to remove their children to the private sector, hence leaving UPE schools to cater almost exclusively for children from the poorest families. Consequently, for children and young people enrolled in government UPE schools taking part in the current research, the free tuition and other benefits notwithstanding, this type of education was seen as indisputable proof that they were 'needy'. The lives of children enrolled in private schools, where tuition and other fees were high and standards of education were considered infinitely superior, were openly coveted by children participating in the research. Wealth, it was believed, shielded these other children from the dreaded stigmatization of poverty, which they endured as a result of being associated with UPE schools. Similarly the parents of these children felt stigmatized for having no choice but to send their sons and daughters to schools considered within the community to be inferior and of generally poor quality.

Yet, while individually the adults and children who were interviewed repeatedly voiced their resentment of such stigmatization, there was little or no evidence of any collective active resistance to the sorts of treatment and interventions they described as degrading and belittling. Poverty-induced shame, although routinely experienced by people living in poverty who took part in the research, was endured largely in isolation and had not become a cause around which those living it on a daily basis had found any opportunity to rally.

Conclusions and Implications

Although the men and women who were interviewed were acutely aware that the realities of the poverty they experienced and its true causes were divergent to the views and understandings promulgated within society—that poverty is the result of laziness and lack of ambition—their lack of voice in society made it difficult to influence societal views and entrench their thinking; a fact that perpetuated their vulnerability to criticism and derision by their relatively better-off neighbours. Imposing shame on those living in persistent and long-term poverty appears to have become part of everyday life in contemporary Uganda; a psychological and emotional burden that those in hardship are forced to bear.

Our research has not only provided an opportunity to engage with people living in extreme poverty, but has also provided evidence of how shame is a regressive negative emotion that is sorely felt by those facing disadvantage. Shame, it was found, was commonly self-inflicted, requiring no external agent or space, instead having its locus in the inner psyche. All respondents, particularly children, indicated that they were prone to this type of shame and its effects, and that such feelings often rose out of a sense of anticipation that others would mock or criticize them because of their circumstances if they were given occasion to do so. Yet the experiences of the adult men and women who were interviewed bore witness to the fact that poverty-induced shame is most effective and damaging when there are external people and spaces to trigger it.

This research illustrated that shame was more often than not inflicted by relatively better-off neighbours with whom people in poverty routinely interacted. The contempt, disdain, and criticism meted out by others was referred to as deliberate and malicious, allegedly with the express aim of evoking damaging emotional pain and often requiring no provocation. Aside from their social interactions, however, those interviewed throughout the research equally reflected on how they resented the way various institutions and systems unjustifiably associated them with negative behavioural traits or attributed to them the dreaded labels of 'the poor' or 'needy', terms which they considered inherently stigmatizing.

Shame was portrayed by those interviewed as a negative emotion with potentially destructive effects, both at individual and family level. However it was provoked, those experiencing it described the pain of feeling continuously undermined and socially inferior within their communities, and recounted the diverse strategies that they adopted in attempts to avoid or find ways of tolerating these indignities. Whether shame was internally felt or externally inflicted, such strategies entailed deliberately avoiding certain individuals, groups, or locations that were felt to leave them susceptible or likely to be exposed to such shame. This inevitably meant self-withdrawal to various degrees from mainstream society; in the extreme it meant cutting off of all family and social ties and self-imposed total isolation.

Some of the coping strategies adopted by our respondents appeared to be positive, or at least harmless. Working hard, deliberately adopting morally appropriate conduct in society, increased participation in community life, avoiding begging or falling into debt, dressing self and the family well, and making every attempt to sustain pride in the face of adversity, all constituted attempts to counter the indignities of poverty and arguably helped mitigate the effects of its associated shame. More commonly, pretence and hiding poverty were behaviours employed to stave off anticipated negative social judgements. Other tactics employed by those living in poverty were potentially more hazardous, and included anger and deflecting shame to those worse off than themselves.

For children and young people, it emerged that feelings signalling the associated shame of poverty are experienced early in life, and the school is the space where they are most likely to first emerge as a result of negative self-evaluation in relation to their better-off peers. Importantly though, feelings of failure suffered by children and young people appeared largely self-inflicted. There was, in fact, no evidence throughout the research of peers or teachers deliberately stigmatizing or provoking any sense of inadequacy. Nonetheless, it should be noted that children and young people, unlike their parents, arguably have fewer options to evade school as the arena within which they painfully judge themselves in relation to others.

Research in Uganda has unequivocally shown that poverty and shame are inextricably linked. Poverty carries a dreaded stigma which compels those living with it to find mechanisms to cope with it as best they can. The multifaceted and dynamic nature of the poverty–shame nexus has evident implications for the formulation of anti-poverty policies which have hitherto, with few exceptions, tended to construe poverty in terms of measurable deprivation. Such implications are discussed in detail elsewhere (Bantebya-Kyomuhendo and Mwiine, 2013). Greater attention need also be paid, however, to the negative impacts of the poverty–shame nexus at societal level and in particular to how shame generated by public discourses, actions, and the media equally serves to cripple individual agency and in turn perpetuate the vicious cycle of poverty. These are themes we turn to and consider in further detail in Chapter 17 of this volume.

References

Bantebya-Kyomuhendo, G. and Mwiine, A. (2013) ' "Food that cannot be eaten": The shame of Uganda's anti-poverty policies', in Gubrium, E., Pellissery, S., and Lødemel, I. (eds) *The Shame of It: Global perspectives on anti-poverty policies*, Bristol: Policy Press.

Republic of Uganda (2005) *Uganda Participatory Poverty Assessment Process Report*, Kampala, Uganda.

Republic of Uganda (2010) *Uganda National Household Survey Report*, Kampala, Uganda.

Republic of Uganda, Ministry of Local Government AAMP and World Bank (2009) *Poverty Entrenched in Country's Rural Areas*, Kampala, Uganda.

Uganda NGO Forum (2009) *Unlocking Uganda's Development Potential. 8 Fundamentals for Success of the National Development Plan (NDP): A Civil Society Perspective*, Kampala, Uganda.

UNDP (2013) The Human Development Index. Available at: <http://hdr.undp.org/en/data> (accessed 5 March 2014).

10

Tales of Inadequacy from Pakistan

Sohail Anwar Choudhry

Introduction

The inviolable right to dignity for all citizens is enshrined in Pakistan's Constitution, which was promulgated in 1973. The brief Article (14) reads, 'The dignity of man and, subject to law, the privacy of home, shall be inviolable'.[1] The only other place where the word 'dignity' appears in the Constitution is in Article 11 of the chapter on fundamental rights, which states that any compulsory service that is incompatible with human dignity contravenes such rights. What constitutes 'dignity', however, is left to the imagination of policymakers responsible for the secondary legislation pertaining to the Constitution and, since the breach of this 'inviolable' right has not found its way into the provisions of the 'Pakistan Penal Code', no citizen deprived of dignity can register a police case against the violators. The only legal remedy in this case would be filing a writ petition in the High Court or filing a suit for compensation in a civil court, legal options which involve considerable cost.

Inevitably, therefore, Article 14 of the Constitution provides an added degree of security around the dignity of the affluent who, in the unlikely case of its breach, have the agency and resources to have their grievance redressed and recompensed. For someone without money, this clause may not only be of little use but counterproductive. With no economic resources to pursue expensive court proceedings, such a clause only serves to accentuate the inequalities experienced by people on low incomes in Pakistan. Ultimately, the policy structures exclude them from benefiting from a legally binding

---

[1] Article 14 of the Constitution entitled 'Inviolability of Dignity of Man, etc.' accessed 06 June 2014 at http://www.pakistani.org/pakistan/constitution/part2.ch1.html.

constitutional right which only their affluent counterparts can in effect enjoy. Interviews with people living in poverty in Pakistan suggested that, for the most part, they were ignorant of this structural inequality and its impact on their dignity, and instead spoke of several other more immediate inequalities which undermined their dignity and with which they were forced to contend on a daily basis.

Hence, the issue of dignity was central to the interviews with low-income people who participated in the Pakistani component of the research. The selected sample of forty-eight people comprised sixteen men, women, and children respectively. Half of the respondents were Christians, one of the largest religious minorities in Pakistan. The inclusion of women, children, and Christians in the sample was purposive since it enabled closer investigation of the specific vulnerabilities likely to be experienced by these demographic groups. The four research sites included urban Islamabad and Lahore, two of the most developed districts of the country, and rural Muzafargarh and Bahawalpur; two of the least developed districts. The recruitment of participants was carried out through a combination of random selection from lists of recipients of income support programmes and snowballing. The latter method was used to recruit children from the families of the selected adult participants in order to achieve the desired sample.

The respondents were first invited to engage in conversations about their economic life and working conditions and to share as much detail of their circumstances as they were comfortable with. Their perceptions of poverty and shame emerged within the broader narratives of these circumstances. Further questions were then asked, as necessary, which placed greater emphasis on their accounts of the psychological and social dimensions of their experience of poverty, such as its effects on self-esteem, relationships, and social life.

Perceptions and Experiences of Poverty

Respondents' individual perceptions and descriptions of poverty varied according to their demographic circumstances, current livelihood opportunities, degree of privation suffered at the time, and their perceptions about the causes and consequences of their social and economic challenges. One of the foremost observations of the analysis was how the language used by respondents to describe poverty reflected their own low opinion of it. For instance, one 15-year-old girl described her neighbourhood thus: 'some people (in our neighbourhood) are good, but the vast majority are impoverished'. This description implicitly equated 'good' to relative wealth, and, by association, 'bad' to impoverishment. Other respondents too, when describing the same context, frequently juxtaposed expressions such as 'decent' housing, 'agreeable' salary, and 'better' circumstances with phrases such as 'bad' conditions, 'lousy' salary, and 'rough' neighbourhood in ways which tended to downgrade poverty and exalt wealth and at the same time portray the adverse social and economic challenges which they were experiencing.

Participants almost exclusively and emphatically used the word 'equality' to describe economic and monetary situations. They viewed money as the real determinant and reference point for economic equality or inequality; and therefore found it impractical to compare themselves with those who possessed more money than themselves, as one man put it, 'How can we be equal with the rich?...there is no sense in this comparison...you cannot be equal without money'.

As for understandings of poverty, the majority of the respondents described it in terms of material deprivation rather than income deficit. It emerged that income was understood as a means to attain material assets. One woman disclosed that there were houses where up to 15 people shared a one-bedroom house in her Katchi Abadi,[2] while another described her life in such a dwelling as follows:

> We can't rent a house. We have no income...the only room of our Jhuggi[3] also serves as our kitchen, bathroom, and toilet. At night, we sleep on the ground... kids kick each other all night...everybody disturbs everyone.

Other respondents living in such neighbourhoods pointed to the lack of essential amenities such as portable water, sanitation, and basic health care as the epitome of their poverty. Nonetheless, among all their privations they assigned highest priority to their lack of immovable assets and the insecurity they felt as a result. This concern was typified by two representative remarks. A 64-year-old man remarked, 'If I have a ceiling over my head that I own...it is my little kingdom where I know I am safe, where no one can intrude forcibly'. Similarly, a 42-year-old woman stated, 'Everyone should have some space from where no one can evacuate them'. Almost all interviewees expressed this same strong desire to have their own home and other property. These sentiments are consistent with the Pakistan Social and Living Standards Measurement Survey 2010–11, which calculated that 86 per cent of households in Pakistan owned their houses. However, one low-income urban migrant explained this phenomenon saying, 'In villages, we simply set up a Jhuggi and call it a house. Nobody can afford any rents'.

---

[2] Unplanned and unregulated urban settlements (squatter camps), consisting of small makeshift houses often erected unlawfully on state land in the first place but later sanctioned for political and welfare considerations.

[3] A small dwelling made up of makeshift structures such as mud, wood, or canvas.

Besides poverty of space, respondents coped with other deprivations in their own ways; one woman spoke of how she 'ate lunches and skipped dinners'; another reported taking 'aspirin for all diseases'; while a man spoke of how he removed his children from school when they were only 9 or 10 years old as he could not afford their education any longer. Respondents frequently alluded to the fact that material well-being took precedence over the emotional aspects of life, a view reflected in the comment made by one man, 'those who have money; they say money can't buy happiness.... If the wall of my house collapses, do I need money or happiness to raise it again?'

Experiences of Poverty-Related Shame

The interviews suggested that people living in poverty not only experienced shame in a variety of everyday social settings, the family, and the community, but also at the personal level in non-social situations. Most respondents considered money as the basis of social respect and therefore saw little hope of ever achieving their aspiration of a respectable social life. At this internalized level of shame, respondents intimated that they were acutely self-conscious of their inadequacies in comparison with their affluent counterparts. While most of the respondents generally regarded poverty as an 'ordeal', a 'disease', or a 'hardship' which caused 'distress', some domestic workers employed in rich households thought that the comparison of their plight with the extravagance of the affluence around had the effect of subjecting them on a daily basis to a heightened sense of 'social exploitation', 'inferiority', and 'shame'.

It was disclosed however that beyond this internalized sense of shame from comparing oneself with others, interviewees were repeatedly subjected to active shaming, which occurred through segregation and verbal abuse directed at them by others. A Christian woman who worked as a domestic cleaner remarked, 'There is no question that if I drink water from my employers' glass, they would have it washed twice or would probably give it away to charity'.

The sorts of external shaming imposed varied according to the demographic and occupational statuses of the respondents. Participants living in rural areas described how considerations of caste, lineage, and occupation were more pronounced in rural areas than elsewhere and thus accentuated their shame of poverty. By contrast, people who had migrated to urban centres spoke of facing a shortage of assets, social networks, and security. The lack of house ownership which was typical in urban settings made several respondents vulnerable to humiliation at the hands of their landlords, one man commenting, 'I am mentally prepared to be verbally abused by him (the landlord) every month'. Other people interviewed spoke of how even where the actual humiliation did not take place, apprehension of it caused them acute anxiety and depression. One 18-year-old woman said, 'Towards the end of each month, the anxiety of rent takes our breath away'.

In several cases, the shaming experienced had taken the form of wage exploitation. One man spoke of how some employers simply refused to pay their maids' wages after an entire month of labour, while a woman domestic worker told of how she was falsely accused of theft by her employer when she asked for the wages owed to her. In other situations, shaming degenerated into physical abuse, typified by the remark made by a 48-year-old rural Muslim: 'why do you talk of the respect of poor people sir (to researcher)? One can beat them up with a shoe whenever one likes'. While this statement was in relation to a peasant–landlord relationship, a 15-year-old urban Christian respondent made a similar comment on his experience of working in an urban setting; 'As long as we are working fine, he (the employer) is good. When we make a mistake he beats us with anything that comes to hand'.

It became apparent that for most low-income people the choice they faced was between accepting humiliating conditions at work or giving up the job and being physically and mentally worse off. One woman commented, 'getting scolded by employers is easier than facing hunger'. However, another woman thought that not resisting this sort of oppression was not only 'cowardice' but counterproductive since it perpetuated the exploitation of 'the poor by the mean and cruel rich'. Although consistent with the social psychological literature that submission encourages exploitation and misery (Hill, 1995), this argument was not endorsed by most respondents who felt they had little agency to retaliate against the rich, especially in a non-egalitarian justice system. One man explained, 'you know our police... they will arrest a poor man for no reason. And they will take him away while slapping his face'.

It appeared that besides money, the nature of work greatly determined the place of low-income people in social hierarchies. In urban areas, most cleaning and sanitation jobs were done by either Christians or low-caste Muslims. One Christian man in the sample recalled, 'When I was young, I told my father I would not be a cleaner. I hated this work. I was so ashamed of my father who was a cleaner.... Now I am doing it myself.... This is where most of us find jobs.... I am doing it happily.' Such regression of aspirations bears testimony to the view that the self-esteem of disadvantaged groups suffers most from the negative psychological effects of discrimination and prejudice (Crocker and Blanton, 1999). Within the sample of people interviewed, the occupational identity of Christians as cleaners was so strong that even an impoverished Muslim woman engaged in domestic work remarked, 'look at our condition... we have to do jobs that are meant for Christians'.

This shaming between people on low-income themselves was not limited to religious factors. It was equally pronounced across Muslim castes. One woman who had migrated to urban Islamabad told how she was 'poor but . . . happy' in her village where she only mixed with women of her own caste. After migrating to the city, she was compelled to live in a slum where her next-door neighbour was a '*Musalie*' (a low-caste Muslim).

The Experiences of Children

While the sense of poverty-related shame was quite pronounced in the views of children who were engaged in child labour, many school-going children did not see a connection between money and respect. They thought that the latter was connected with moral attributes such as 'character and good deeds' or demographic ones, such as clan, family, or elders. Interestingly, the younger children in the sample were more convinced of these associations between respect and moral values than were the older ones. In comparison, only a minority of the adult respondents endorsed the 'moral' explanation of respect, while most stuck with the idea of social status linked to money.

This variation in views appears to be the result of the disinclination of many low-income parents to discuss their poverty with young children. However, as indicated by one respondent, this withholding of information could sometimes be counterproductive, as in their blissful ignorance, younger children demanded commodities that were beyond their parents' means, the denial of which could lead to other behavioural and emotional problems on the part of the children. A 14-year-old boy acknowledged that not having new clothes for 'Eid' made him unhappy, although he never outwardly made an issue of it with his parents despite his extreme disappointment. He did, however, stage his own silent protest, resorting to 'quietly skipping a meal or two'. It has long been recognized in social anthropology literature that while certain cultural norms repress the expression of emotions, they can also lead to acute depression (Boas, 1940). For other children, such protests were manifested through overt anger, directed against their parents or society at large.

The Intersection of Culture and Shame

The analysis suggests that some certain groups, notably women, children, and religious minorities, are culturally more prone to the shame of poverty than others. Some women in the sample thought that the culture of marrying within caste, tribe, or extended family created material and emotional hardships for them, as they were often obliged to accept matches incompatible with their intellectual, demographic, or economic circumstances.

A 44-year-old woman disclosed that she was the first wife of a 52-year-old polygamous husband, who had married a 26-year-old girl as a second wife. Although Pakistan's Muslim family Ordinance of 1962 does not allow a husband to enter into a second marriage without prior written consent of the first wife, she spoke of how she could not challenge this second marriage without risking her husband's wrath, which might be expressed in him divorcing or estranging her. Her husband's second marriage had not only resulted in the division of her husband's income but also brought social shame for both wives, as polygamy was widely frowned upon within the society.

However, the woman went on to imply that her emotional well-being was secondary to her immediate concern of securing food for herself and her children: 'at least he (my husband) gives us a meal two times a day; where else can we go?' This respondent's reference to priorities speaks to Maslow's (1954) hierarchy of human needs, which prioritizes the physiological needs of alleviating hunger and thirst over the intermediate needs of safety and social concerns before moving to the higher needs of self-esteem and self-actualization. Within this hierarchal framework, until the basic or lower needs are fulfilled, higher needs cannot become the focus of attention (Cofer and Appley, 1964). It emerged overall that women reported being so heavily reliant on their male family members for their immediate physiological survival that they paid little attention to their emotional and social needs.

Some of the working women in our sample felt that the prevalent cultural preference for large families obstructed their livelihood pursuits as they were constrained from allotting adequate time to their children, their work, household duties, and themselves. These pressures adversely affected their health and well-being. Large families also meant unhealthy competition among siblings for the scarce material resources, a factor which many children in the sample alluded to. It also promoted the culture of child labour, sometimes for children as young as five. Most children interviewed were involved in some form of work, mostly in the informal sectors of the economy, such as domestic work, collecting recyclable materials, and jobs or internships in informal businesses and small local shops. They were invariably exploited, one 14-year-old child describing how he had been working at a tailoring shop for over seven months but had still not been paid a salary. He was instead treated as an intern, supposedly learning the basics of the trade.

Some Christian respondents in the sample narrated how they suffered because of their exclusion from the official *Zakat*[4] programme. With widespread disagreement as to whether or not non-Muslims should be eligible for

---

[4] A charitable religious tax fixed at 2.5 per cent for those Muslims who have an accumulated annual wealth in excess of 87.48g (3oz) of gold, or its equivalent in cash.

this Islamic charity (Visser, 2009), the state as well as most of the cautious affluent people allegedly preferred Muslims to benefit from their *Zakat* contributions. A Christian respondent mentioned how this situation had resulted in 'double jeopardy' for the non-Muslim. On the one hand, they were deprived of *Zakat* assistance and, on the other, more generally the wealthy became less approachable and willing to help individuals since they believed they had already fulfilled their 'religious and moral obligation' through payment of their *Zakat* contributions.

Coping with Poverty and Its Related Shame

Certain specific responses emerged as being used by people facing financial hardship to deal with poverty and its related shame. At the most practical level, participants described carefully prioritizing their expenses to ensure that they lived within their means. Children used free recreational facilities and parks. Women tended to save as much money as they could—as a mother of three reported, 'We usually know (in advance) when we are going to need money. We start saving or arranging for it'. To cope with the demands of social events, many low-income people used savings, borrowed money, or skipped the event if possible. One boy remarked that he had only ever once been invited to a friend's birthday party, and could not attend because he had no money to buy a gift. Interviewees spoke of how when they were forced to avoid social events, they invented an excuse to save face. An old woman remarked, 'I can't go to see my married daughter because I cannot afford the fare and gifts to take . . . . I tell her that in our culture parents don't frequently visit the houses of their son-in-laws to avoid being a burden'.

Despite this resourcefulness, many respondents regretted the fact that they had to limit their social participation so as to avoid the shame of poverty. One woman remarked, 'When I get things from the store on credit, then I have to avoid passing through that road . . . until I am able to return the loan'. Many other interviewees similarly spoke of how fears about revealing their poverty constrained their well-being and often led to their social exclusion.

For most parents, their ability to send their children to school was seen as having the potential to mitigate the negative psychological impact of poverty. It instilled in them a sense of emotional fulfilment, and was seen as a positive achievement in regard to their current lives and aspirations for future. The idea of their children's brighter future gave many parents welcome relief from their daily anxieties. Within tightly knit family structures, interviewees assumed that their successful children would in the future not only support their own families but also their aging parents. Many felt that extended family systems generally offered financial, social, and emotional support to all members. Even when active monetary support was not possible, such family systems often provided emotional and mental strength. However, some respondents believed that with increasing corporate activity, more and more people relied on professional rather than family networks for support. Not having access to the support of employers, colleagues, or commercial borrowing opportunities therefore further exacerbated poverty.

A minority of research participants agreed that private, voluntary, and state assistance had in the past helped alleviate hardship. Interestingly, a number of them did not believe that income transfers caused them shame because they were, they believed, entitled to them. One woman, for example, who had recently been laid off from work, claimed that she had much more right over her country's resources than the 'corrupt politicians and government officers'. Similarly, a boy attending a school for children with special needs thought that all children at his school were immensely glad to receive charitable clothes, school bags, lunch boxes, and cash hand-outs during the end of year school ceremony.

In contrast, however, some able-bodied adult male respondents felt immensely ashamed of receiving free food twice a day from religious charities. Apparently, this dichotomy agrees with Nelson's (2002) argument that individuals are more likely to suffer low self-esteem if they feel they should have control over the cause of their stigma than if they feel they have no control over it (such as skin colour, disability, etc.). Hence, the sense of perceived control over their circumstances and how much they felt they deserved support may explain the varied nature and intensity of poverty-related shame experienced by the different individuals taking part in the study.

The Limits to Coping

The analysis suggests that despite resorting to a number of different coping mechanisms, most low-income people taking part in the research still suffered the adverse effects of poverty-induced shame. It is evident that the social identity of poverty bears heavily on the visage and countenance of people. Clothes, body language, personal grooming, confidence, manners, and conversation were all thought to be profoundly important for attaining social respect. While it is understandable that the respondents often appeared to be 'poverty personified', appearing unkempt, wearing poor clothing or no shoes, a shared observation of the researchers was that a number of them looked older than their age and carried an aura of physical and emotional exhaustion about them. They sometimes appeared to exude at once an awkward blend of despair and content; a world weariness and a resignation to their fate.

According to psychoanalytical theory, people make use of unconscious defence mechanisms to 'deal with feelings that are potentially destructive to the self, such as anxiety, fear, envy, hate and emptiness' (Lupton, 1998: 29). Through make-believe, people can substitute these painful inner feelings for better ones, and such strategies were evident in people's accounts of how they dealt with their circumstances. One girl, for example, knowing full well that she could not go to her first-choice private school because of poverty, claimed she sincerely believed that her current state school was much better than the private schools. Similarly, other adults seemed to take refuge in pretence and false pride.

A few respondents expressed their unblemished faith in the religious explanation that life on earth was merely a test of character and would be followed by an eternal life of bliss after death. Others however, were just waiting for some miracle to happen in their current lives. They all seemed to believe that elements beyond their control and comprehension had played a big role in shaping their lives; entities ranging from fate to state structures and institutions, and from elites to society in general. Such beliefs had diminished their agency, promoted inaction, and often reduced their social participation. Some of the respondents expressed an almost superficial compulsive gratitude for their lot, rather than grumbling about it. One woman, who initially used expressions such as, 'this is what is pre-destined for us' and 'we just remain thankful', by the end of the discussion frequently referred to the proverb: '*Mujbori ka naam shukriaya*' ('with no other choice, it's best to be thankful').

This same feeling of powerlessness was reflected in many of our respondents' narratives of their condition. They thought that because of their lack of material resources, they had surrendered the control of their lives to the rich and powerful. While commenting on the exploitation by the rich, one man remarked, 'It's not that they always treat you badly, it's just that it is always their choice how to behave on a given day'.

With the belief that control rests in the hands of others, many respondents appeared to be passive and silent spectators of the unfolding events in their daily lives. As acknowledged in the theory, failure and self-doubt may discourage people from attempting to achieve their objectives and targets (Rawls, 1995). Many participants appeared to recognize their limited agency, preferring instead to take refuge in the idea that one day their children would take control of and improve their circumstances. However, one man expressed the stark truth regarding any such aspirations he may once have had, saying, 'First we have hopes in our children. Then one day, they fall out of the school. Then they also become unemployed. Sometimes they take to drugs. Our whole life keeps falling apart as we go along'.

Conclusion

While dignity is acknowledged as a fundamental right in the Constitution of Pakistan, the interviews with low-income people suggested that in practice, money was the key factor in determining the thresholds of giving and receiving respect. The respondents repeatedly shared stories in which their sense of dignity was not only violated but they were also made to feel the acute shame of deficit and inadequacy, with little possibility of social or administrative relief. On many occasions it appeared that people in poverty had also accepted the code of respect based on relative wealth, and they faithfully adhered to it. Their language and vocabulary showed signs of inbuilt reverence for riches and its various associations. The experience of shame was both internalized and external.

The internalized shame was often triggered by comparisons between respondents' own material inadequacy and the wealth of affluent people with whom they were acquainted, often their employers. However, since individuals also tend to view themselves through the eyes of others (Cooley, 1922; Mead, 1934; Goffman, 1959), it appeared that even those respondents who did not have a reference point for such comparisons felt ashamed of their perceived shortcomings. Beyond these dimensions of internalized shame, there was the presence of active external shaming visible in the accounts of people and ranging from discrimination to verbal and physical abuse by the rich and powerful private individuals and state functionaries. Urban migrants taking part in the research particularly complained of their inhumane treatment at the hands of their landlords; a new emotional distress emerging to replace that of the shame of lineage and caste which they thought they had left behind in their villages.

It emerged that the nature and intensity of shame related by adults in the narratives differed from that of children, who often described a relatively uncontaminated understanding of the ideals of life, extolling the importance of morals and values over material gains. Nonetheless, the analysis suggests that it is women, children, and religious minorities who are more likely to bear the brunt of poverty-induced shame than others. Cultural vulnerabilities such as polygamy, large family sizes, the dominant male breadwinner model, and the constraints of having to marry within castes were some of the major factors exposing women to a higher risk of poverty and its related shame.

The analysis also suggests that people on low-incomes themselves mutually indulge in the categorization and shaming of each other, particularly on account of livelihood occupations, which accordingly determines, both the place of an individual in the social hierarchy and their social class (Argyle, 1992). Some menial professions were considered reserved only for the lowest social groups or religious minorities.

In their search for a sense of well-being in spite of their poverty, participants spoke of how they adopted a variety of coping methods to avoid, endure, or downplay the shame of poverty. These mechanisms included make-believe, saving money, the support of social networks where available, reduced participation to save on expenditure, and a focus on their children's future. However, as most of them acknowledged, these mechanisms provided them little, temporary, or no relief from the burden of their difficult material and emotional circumstances. In the end, they felt the pinch of shame and its anguish. Many of them appeared feeble, fatalistic, powerless, isolated, and prone to disintegration. The research with people on low incomes in Pakistan not only confirmed the common coincidence of shame with poverty but also reiterated the earlier findings emerging from the analysis of cultural conceptions of poverty and shame, explored through a lens of literary works and poetry (see Chapter 3). Although the respondents presented their experiences differently, the essence of what they lived through in poverty with respect to shame is best exemplified in the following comment made by one man:

> The thing is, one has to bow a little. One has to, you know. You have to lower your gaze a little. You don't have to; it lowers itself, when you ask for a favour. You cannot do but to remain a little humble.

References

Argyle, M. (1992) *The Social Psychology of Everyday Life*, London: Routledge.

Boas, F. (1940) *Race, Language and Culture*, New York: The Macmillan Company.

Cofer, C. N. and Appley, M. H. (1964) *Motivation; Theory and Research*, New York: Wiley.

Cooley, C. H. (1922) *Human Nature and the Social Order*, New York: Scribner's.

Crocker, J. and Blanton, H. (1999) 'Social Inequality and Self-Esteem: The Moderating Effects of Social Comparison, Legitimacy, and Contingencies of Self-Esteem', in *The Psychology of the Social Self*, New Jersey: Lawrence Erlbaum Associates. Inc.

Goffman, E. (1959) *Presentation of Self in Everyday Life*, New York: Anchor.

Hill, T. Jr. (1995) 'Servility and Self-Respect', in Dillion, R. S. (ed.) *Dignity, Character and Self-Respect*, New York/London: Routledge.

Lupton, D. (1998) *The Emotional Self; A Sociocultural Exploration*. London: Sage Publishers Ltd.

Maslow, A. H. (1954) *Motivation and Personality*, Harper: New York.

Mead, G. H. (1934) *Mind, Self, and Society*, Chicago: University of Chicago Press.

Nelson, T. D. (2002) *The Psychology of Prejudice*, Boston: Allyn & Bacon.

Rawls, J. (1995) 'Self-Resect, Excellences and Shame', in Dillion, R. S. (ed.) *Dignity, Character and Self-Respect*, London: Routledge.

Visser, H. (2009) *Islamic Finance: Principles and Practice*, London: Edward Elgar Publishing.

11

'I Am Not Alone'

Experiences of Poverty-Induced Shame in a Moral Economy

Sony Pellissery and Leemamol Mathew

Introduction

As we have seen in the earlier chapter on cultural conceptions of poverty-induced shame in India (Chapter 4), representations of poverty in literature and films have artistic aims, even though certain themes and messages may have emanated from people's actual experiences. For this reason, interacting with people living in poverty themselves becomes an important part of the process of ascertaining how far discourses identified through the analysis of literature and film have resonance in real life.

A central question that arises while trying to understand poverty and its impact through the eyes of those experiencing it in the Indian cultural context is as follows: Is poverty accepted as karma (a fatalist outcome justified on religious grounds)? Or do people living in poverty use their agency to try and escape from poverty? If poverty through karma is accepted by those living it day to day there is limited space to experience shame, since any sense of personal failure is arguably circumvented. In this chapter we examine the empirical data that emerge from rural India, returning in the concluding section of this chapter to the question of fatalism.

For this phase of the study, fieldwork was undertaken in rural areas in the two Indian states of Kerala and Gujarat and involved intense interaction with poor communities over a period of four months. Initially, the approach was ethnographic, combining key-informant interviews with participant observation. Through this approach we were able to identify poor households using community defined norms (rather than by using government lists which are

Table 11.1. Overview of research participants in India

Region	Adults		Children		Senior citizens
	Male	Female	Boys	Girls	
Gujarat	4	9	7	6	1
Kerala	8	8	7	8	2
Total	12	17	14	14	3

often faulty as a result of corrupt practices). In-depth interviews were then conducted with twenty-nine adults, twenty-eight children, and three senior citizens (Table 11.1). Each interview lasted between 40 and 50 minutes, and in many cases the same person was interviewed more than once to clarify a point that emerged through the ongoing data analysis. Fifteen per cent of interviews were audio-recorded. When recording was not possible, detailed field notes were taken and provided the data for analysis.

The analysis of data followed two approaches. Firstly, a thematic analysis generated common themes that emerged from different groups participating in the study, such as women, men, children, etc. Secondly, we compared these themes with the findings from our examination of cultural representations of poverty, the subject of Chapter 4. In the remainder of this chapter we report the key findings from this analysis.

Poverty: Everyday Fire-Fighting

Aside from people's accounts of their impoverished conditions, and the fact that the majority of them possessed a Below Poverty Line (BPL) ration card, the physical surroundings and the obvious deprivations within the homes of the participants also revealed the severity of their circumstances. Many of the participants lived in one-room houses which functioned as kitchen, living, and bedroom spaces. Sometimes, a torn cloth was used as a curtain to separate the kitchen and provide privacy to women as they carried out household chores. In most cases, there was hardly any ventilation in the houses and the floors were mainly made from dried cow dung or mud. The construction and the state of the houses gave the impression that people living in them were likely to be easily prone to illness. Only a few participants lived in houses with cement or tiled floors and most had no TV, radio, fridge, gas connection, fan, or any furniture at home, except the typical Indian cot (plastic or rope cradles with four legs) on which they slept. Similarly, it was rare to see any newspapers, magazines, or books, or indeed any material providing information about the outside world; especially in Gujarat. This said, mobile phones were an important source of connectivity for most people.

People taking part in the research frequently reported problems of poor-quality housing and overcrowding in the home, and the majority were not satisfied with their current housing. Some had received a partial grant from the government to build a house, but having little or no money to add to the subsidy, their houses usually ended up being structurally weak and inadequate. There were also those who were about to lose their house as a result of indebtedness. One woman, for example, had pledged her house to a money lender to raise cash for her daughter's marriage. Another woman, Rajamma[1] from Kerala, said, 'The other day also the bank manager called me and asked me to repay some of the money I owe ... This is the only thing I have. I can't afford to lose my house'.

Most of the respondents reported that their survival depended on the kindness of other neighbours, relatives, friends, shopkeepers, and so on, in order to borrow money or buy groceries on credit, for example. Without these types of assistance, they said that their families may starve. Jasubhai (from Gujarat) said, 'I earn Rs.1000 (approximately US$22) per month. It is not sufficient to run my family.... What to do? I borrow money ... and I have to pay interest.... Different persons take different interest ... 10 ... eight ... or ... five per cent'.

Almost everyone taking part in the study reported sporadic food shortages in the home, having to ask neighbours or friends for food, money, or having to secure groceries on credit from local stores. The difficulties in affording adequate food for the whole family were illustrated by Diwariben, a widow from Gujarat:

> Only I earn and sometimes my elder son goes to work, most of the time he doesn't. He is very small and he goes to play most of the days. We earn a total of Rs.1000 per month, but sometimes it is more and sometimes it is less [she reported that sometimes they earned up to Rs.2000]. It all depends on the availability of work. We don't get enough to run the family ... whatever we earn we spend ... if we don't earn there will be no money in the household. Such times are crucial and then we go to the grocery shop to borrow things to make food.... What to do? If I stay away [that is, not ask to borrow] my children will have to starve.

The Consequences of Enduring Poverty

A persistent lack of money took a serious toll on the physical and psychological health of the participants. Their physical appearance bore witness to the direct impact of poverty, many of them appearing very thin, an indication

---

[1] In order to ensure the anonymity of research participants, all the names included here have been changed.

of the scarcity of food. In general, young children and toddlers from these households and the surrounding neighbourhood appeared undernourished and wore very little, if any, clothing. One of the main reasons for this was that many of these children possessed only one set of clothes and when these went to be washed, they had to remain without clothes until they were dry again. Since priority for these families was food, the respondents spent a minimal amount of money on clothing, many of them wearing clothes which were torn and dirty. A clear geographical difference was observed in this respect, with respondents from Kerala generally appearing more presentable in how they dressed and carried themselves compared to those from Gujarat.

Equally, respondents were prone to poor health, often as a result of long and arduous working hours. Raiben from Gujarat said, 'We are dying by doing hard work...if we work hard we will get sick'. As a consequence, a considerable amount of people's hard-earned cash was spent on medicines to maintain their health, leaving too little to meet the needs of the rest of the family. The psychological impact of poverty was often expressed in terms of people's negative state of mind. They repeatedly used terms denoting sadness, helplessness, shame, and embarrassment; they described feeling small, worthless, rejected, dejected, hurt, or uncomfortable; and suggested states of mental turmoil, irritation, anger, and rage. One man, Jasubhai from Gujarat, said, 'We feel sad...if we had money then we could have a better life'.

Poverty and Intra-Household Expectations

In Indian society, family plays a key role in providing social security, and poverty often proves detrimental to family relations (Pellissery, 2005a). At the same time, the ability to stand together in times of hardship was said to strengthen family bonds. Feelings of embarrassment, sadness, and shame were noted among parents when they failed to meet the needs of their children. The inability to provide school fees, afford new clothes, buy good food or gifts for festivals and ceremonies, or pay for medical treatment were all cited as common difficulties. Moly (from Kerala), for example, said:

> Last year I bought two sets of uniform for my daughter, but one was torn within no time. She [her daughter] told me that she felt ashamed to wear the torn one. But, I couldn't get her a second set and it troubled me a lot. I was embarrassed inside, but told my daughter that I would get a uniform soon. I never told her about the tensions I was having inside...but I try to comfort myself thinking that there are many other students who do not even have a single set of uniform or dress.

Ramachandran (a parent from Kerala) said:

> I try my level best to meet the needs of my children. But at times, due to the shortage of money, I have to put off the purchase of goods for one or two days or even for a week. For example, during the last Onam festival,[2] I couldn't buy clothes for my children ... I was feeling a bit uncomfortable and mentally disturbed.

Often, the pressures felt by parents came from the expectations of their children, who were constantly comparing themselves with their peers. Some of the reported points of comparisons were clothes, ornaments, cosmetics, the number of pairs of shoes, the type of house they lived in, and whether or not they had other household goods and facilities such as access to electricity, a television, a fridge, and mobile phone. Shani, a 16-year-old girl from Kerala, described what she considered to be one of the most embarrassing situations in her life, 'I remember last year, I went out with a torn slipper. I was feeling so shy about myself. I was wondering what others would think about me'. Vysak from Gujarat, like the majority of other children participating in the study, reported feeling sad about not having a decent house with basic facilities.

Most of the children interviewed reported that they would not want their friends to visit their homes for fear that they would become aware of their deprived circumstances. The mother of Ambili (a 16-year-old girl from Kerala) said, 'This house was given to us from the Panchayath[3] in 2003. It was not so neat then. That's why Ambili doesn't like to invite her friends. She feels ashamed of the situation'. Some children also reported that since their house was so small, they had no space to study at home. The preoccupation of the children was clearly reflected in the parents' aspirations. One parent said, 'My first priority is to have a house of my own. I don't have many things here. But after building a small house of my own, I want to get a few electronic equipments [sic.] like a washing machine, a fridge, a grinder etc. which are found in every other house'.

Another important intra-household expectation was to provide adequate medical care to other family members, failing to do so leading to feelings of shame, sadness, and anger. In most of the situations, elderly people were described as suffering a great deal due to the lack of financial resources to seek medical help. Chandran (a man from Kerala) said that the saddest period in his life was his inability to provide enough medical care to his elderly mother in the last few years of her life. He explained,

> I was very sad that I couldn't look after my mother as much as I wanted. During her very last days, I was not able to give her good treatment. I too became sick and there was no money left. So I couldn't take her to a doctor. I asked my brother for

[2] An annual Hindu festival held in Kerala.   [3] Local government department.

help and he gave as much as he could. But there is a limit to what we could all do. When God decides something, there is no point going against it.

Jameela, a woman from Gujarat, similarly expressed shame along with sadness due to her inability to look after her elderly mother when she was seriously ill. She said,

Sometimes I fail. One such occasion was when my mother was very sick and I wanted to take her to hospital. I had no money with me. And when I tried to ask the hotel owner for help, she too had some urgent case. So I couldn't take my mother to a hospital. That is one instance which made me feel most ashamed of myself.

And Ramchandran, a man from Kerala, also recounted a similar situation when he was unable to afford treatment for his sick wife, and the impact this had on him:

Last year, I was not able to take my wife to hospital when she was down with fever . . . . The next morning I got some money and took her to hospital. I was most ashamed of myself when I think of that . . . I felt ashamed because it's my failure that I didn't have the money to take her.

Likewise, many other adults, both male and female, lamented that they felt sad, bad, and shameful at not being able to access good hospital treatment for children, parents, and other family members as a result of their poverty. Since medical treatment in government hospitals was considered to be substandard, many of these respondents were reluctant to access them, but they were unable to meet the high costs of private hospital treatment.

Poverty and Inter-Household Expectations

The struggle to meet the social obligations determined by significant cultural occasions such as death ceremonies, marriage ceremonies, house-warming parties, birth celebrations and other religious festivals was repeatedly cited as a difficulty for participants in the present study. What people were describing was essentially a struggle to have basic recognition (Honneth, 1995). If this is not achieved, then loss of face in front of one's 'own people' was said to occur. Raiben, from Gujarat, said, 'There are certain practices we have to do some-how. But most of the time we may not have money to perform them . . . . In the community, if our respect is at risk, everyone helps us. If we don't do it, we lose our respect and people will talk about us'. Consequently, respondents in the study repeatedly reported borrowing at times when they had no money to fulfil their social obligations, actions that put many families into further financial hardship. Ranajanben and her mother in-law, explained, 'even if there is no money we borrow it and do [carry out social obligations]'.

Some of the respondents spoke about the importance for those invited to an occasion to give a gift or money, and failure to do so resulted in loss of face. Subaida, from Kerala, said:

> We are not able to give the same amount of money that we have received. Usually the money is given by my husband and it is inside a cover.... Mostly I know how much he gives. Therefore, I feel a bit embarrassed when I meet those persons to whom we have given lesser money than we received. There are times when we are not able to give anything at all. At such functions usually we try not to go. And if we have to go at all, my husband goes alone.

Children and young people, however, frequently believed that most of the practices which placed such large financial pressures on families were unnecessary, though they understood the rationale behind them. Akhil, a child from Kerala, said,

> Even though poor people are affected, they too spend a lot of money for various functions and practices. This may be because of the prestige and pride associated with it. If they don't invite the relatives or friends for the religious ceremonies they organize, people stop talking to them and even helping them in times of need. They may start to speak ill of them. So to save their social reputation they try to spend a lot of money on such functions even it means borrowing it. This may cause them a lot of financial burden.

Institutional Settings of Shame

As was revealed in the analysis of films and literature (Chapter 4), caste emerged as an important institution of humiliation and shaming within respondents' accounts. Some described the workplace as a space where they were particularly likely to be subjected to discrimination, often forced to carry out 'dirty jobs' for very low wages. Yet most reported that rather than contest such treatment they tended to accept and tolerate it as customary practice, such avoidance of conflict being more pragmatic than ideational (Pellissery and Jalan, 2011). Identities such as being from an untouchable caste, a woman, or growing up in rural areas without being able to speak English, could all provide the basis for institutional shaming. In multiple arenas of social interaction, such as between bureaucrats and citizens, teachers and students, neighbours and residents, people interviewed spoke of how they were constantly categorized by their social identity and treated according to this identity and its associated status.

Children frequently gained their lessons of socialization in school and other social settings in which they experienced discrimination because of their identity. Anil, a boy of 16 years from a tribal community in Kerala, said, 'Many times in the school, especially in my previous school, students made fun of me by calling my caste name. Even my neighbours insult me by calling my caste name. In the school and in the neighbourhood, there are some types of partiality towards us. It is because of the caste difference and also because of the financial difference'. When further questioned as to whether he was ever ill-treated by the elderly people, he said, 'They usually make fun of us and insult us by making remarks such as "you caste people do like this... like that"'.

One child spoke of how such caste differences came to the fore even when children played sport together: 'while playing cricket, if a higher caste boy hits a sixer [sic.], we will have to respect it. But, if I hit a sixer, it is not accepted. If I demand it, they beat me up'. Hence children learned that achievements are still largely governed by a person's social identity rather than their own merit, which is only accorded if it meets with the approval of those in the upper caste.

Yet, though caste was undoubtedly an important aspect of shaming in some instances, we also met respondents who reported discrimination based solely on their economic status. Gracy, a 16-year-old girl from Kerala, said: 'I feel discriminated against since primarily the people there in church are only interested to talk to people who are rich and well-off. Since I am not from a rich background, I find I don't have friends there and I feel isolated'. Gracy went on to talk about her embarrassment about being sent to buy groceries on credit: 'when there are not many people I go quickly and come back home. But, sometimes, I wait for others to go away to avoid them seeing that I seek credit'. Children pointed to many instances in school which induced shame, such as being made to stand when given a wrong answer in the classroom, being unable to pay school fees, taking free midday meals, being seen using a charity school bag, notebook, or umbrella, or being categorized as poor or lower caste. These instances were, they felt, related to their family circumstances of poverty.

The class-based discrimination described by children and young people had wider implications. In 2009 the government of India passed the Right to Education Act, which required private schools to reserve a few places for children from low-income backgrounds. However, the implementation of this Act resulted in the children (and parents) from poorer families being subjected to profound degrees of shaming. The private school authorities (often made up of those from elite backgrounds) did not like their school premises being occupied by children from poorer families, and covertly tried to keep them away.

A range of institutional practices highlighted the highly gendered nature of poverty-related shame. At no time are women and their families more predisposed to shame than at the time of a marriage when a huge dowry payment is demanded by the groom from the bride's family. The inability to 'send off' one's daughter with a good dowry leads to public criticism by the whole society. Fear of such shame drives poor parents to incur debt in order to meet dowry demands and is often a reason for them to remain trapped in poverty. Where unmarried girls continue to live in the parental home as a result of being unable to meet the demands imposed by dowry, they become symbols of shame for the whole family. For those women that enter the bridegroom's house before a dowry is completely paid, they may be vulnerable to extreme forms of violence. Official statistics show that more than 6,000 women are killed every year in India over dowry-related disputes, and that 32.4 per cent of crimes against women are categorized as dowry-related violence. Equally, the increasing rate of abortion and female foeticide are indicative of gendered discrimination and have resulted in a marked decrease in the female to male birth sex ratio (941:1000 in the 2011 census).

Responses to Shame and Its Consequences

Our fieldwork revealed serious consequences arising out of feelings of poverty-induced shame. These consequences were, however, not uniform across social groups. Marked differences were noted in the attitude and behaviour of members of tribal groups and those of former untouchables (Dalits), even though both groups experience significant poverty. For instance, former Dalits who were interviewed, having experienced shame historically, appeared to have lower self-worth than interviewees from tribal groups who had been more isolated from mainstream society and seemed to have maintained a finer sense of honour. For example, when a former untouchable was asked to carry out a humiliating job, they rarely showed any resistance.[4] By contrast, people from tribal communities indicated that they would rather go hungry than carry out such degrading work. Despite these differences, we also identified common features in the experiences of and responses to poverty-induced shame.

One of the behaviours repeatedly described by participants was that of evading social situations in which they were likely to feel ashamed, which resulted in various degrees of social withdrawal. Some spoke of going home immediately after church rather than staying to socialize, or generally keeping a social distance so that awkward questions about their circumstances could not arise. In a strongly patriarchal society like India, we also noticed a gender dimension to this avoidance. Since men are usually responsible for financial matters, in situations of shame related to a lack of money, women family

---

[4] Exceptions are found in situations in which political emancipation has taken place (see for example, Breman, 2007).

members (usually the wife) were often more active in trying to resolve the situation, while men tended to withdraw from it. On the other hand, while women recounted how they avoided social functions because they lacked the appropriate clothing and jewellery to wear, men, they said, were able to attend since people paid less attention to what rural men wore than they did to how women presented themselves.

However, in situations where people had borrowed money from a relative or neighbour, it became increasingly impossible to avoid them, and some participants spoke of how they were regularly forced to endure the embarrassment of meeting people to whom they owed money but were not in a position to repay. It has been suggested that a significant proportion of those who have taken their own lives in rural India do so as a result of indebtedness to others, an indication perhaps of suicide as a permanent avoidance/escape from shame (Lester, 1997; Mathew, 2010).

Among children, such avoidance took on institutional forms. The midday meal (*Uchakkanji*) is provided for free to those students in school categorized as being most susceptible to poverty in India. In government-run schools, it is freely available for everyone. Generally, the students in the lower school tend to access the free meals, while students in higher secondary classes, on the whole, do not. Shani explained her own reasons for not attending the meals, 'Somehow I am not comfortable and I don't like to go for midday meal in the school because no one else in my class goes. Therefore, I feel shame thinking what others will think about me. If at least one student goes, I too will go for the lunch'. Most of the student respondents reported that they attended meals up to senior secondary school and then they stopped. Akhil reported that,

> No one goes for *Uchakkanji*, including me. This may be because of the self-esteem or ego.... Maybe thinking that going for Uchakkanji will reduce their self-esteem... I am willing to go for *Uchakkanji* and I have asked my friends to come. But no one else is willing to come. So I thought better not to go for it. How can I go alone? My friends will make fun of me. So I don't want to go for it'.[5]

Conclusions

We began this chapter by posing a question as to whether karma (a fatalist principle) plays a role in reducing poverty-induced shame by circumventing personal responsibility for poverty. Karmic acceptance of poverty could not be completely ruled out in the Indian rural context, especially since we have

---

[5] While avoidance at individual level affects take-up of welfare benefits by those in poverty, active discrimination based on group identity leads to poor targeting of the welfare programmes (Pellissery, 2005b).

noted that shame is inextricably associated with social identity. Being born into a certain social group increases the likelihood of leading a life of poverty due to different forms of social discrimination. This point was also made in the chapter on cultural representations of poverty in India (Chapter 4). A strong sense of social identity leads to group obligations to provide for others when adversity arises, as we have seen in the sections on intra-household and inter-household norms and expectations in this chapter. Thus, within the prevailing moral economy, there is a shared sense of responsibility, primarily among family and caste, for supporting those in poverty. However, this is not an indication that poverty is disconnected from shame. Rather, shared responsibility for poverty spreads shame across different members of the family and community rather than placing it on the individual. Thus, its impact is horizontal.

This diffused responsibility for poverty has implications for the societal response to its impacts. For instance, despite large numbers of farmer suicides evident in India, there has been no collective attempt on the part of those living in poverty to redress the faulty policies that have resulted in so many deaths. At the village level, the poorest segments of society remain dependent on the richest segments for their employment and livelihoods. Therefore, resistance by those on the economic margins of any community is largely constrained by those with wealth and status. In societies featuring such dependency relationships, structured around hierarchies of class and caste, shaming becomes an important mechanism of social control. Thus, shame is instrumental not only in perpetuating poverty but also in sustaining the inherent social structures of dependency and discrimination which exacerbates its impacts.

References

Breman, J. (2007) *The Poverty Regime in Village India: Half a Century of Work and Life at the Bottom of the Rural Economy in South Gujarat,* Delhi: Oxford University Press.

Honneth, A. (1995) *The Struggle for Recognition: The Moral Grammar of Social Conflicts,* Cambridge: Polity Press.

Lester, D. (1997) The role of shame in suicide, *Suicide and Life-Threatening Behvaiour,* 27: 352–61.

Mathew, L. (2010) 'Coping with shame of poverty: Analysis of farmers in distress', *Psychology Developing Societies,* 22(2): 385–407.

Pellissery, S. (2005a) 'Local determinants of exclusion and inclusion in rural public works programmes', *International Journal of Rural Management,* 1(2): 167–84.

Pellissery, S. (2005b) 'State-in-society approach and its implications for rural development policy', *Asia-Pacific Journal of Rural Development,* 15(1): 1–20.

Pellissery, S. and Jalan, S. (2011) 'Towards transformative social protection: A gendered analysis of the employment guarantee act of India', *Gender and Development* 19(2): 283–94.

12

Experiences of Poverty and Shame in Urban China

Ming Yan

Introduction

Prior to the 1990s, poverty in China was still primarily seen as a rural phenomenon. In the mid-1980s, the government initiated poverty alleviation programmes which targeted rural populations, had strong support from international organizations, and made noticeable progress in improving the circumstance of people living in poverty (World Bank, 2009). Since the mid-1990s, however, urban poverty has grown rapidly, becoming a phenomenon of great concern in both academic and policy arenas. This issue needs to be seen in the context of both the dramatic transition to marketization in China and state retreat from welfare provision. The transition from a planned economy to a market economy has meant that China has witnessed massive restructuring of state-owned enterprises (SOEs) and, as a result, the generation of large numbers of 'redundant' labourers. At the same time, social protection in urban China has shifted from enterprise provision to a social security system which emphasizes individual responsibility and which has seen the state gradually withdraw from the provision of social benefits in health care, education, and housing. A means-tested Minimum Standard of Living Scheme (MSLS), popularly known as *dibao*, introduced in urban areas in the late 1990s (and extended to rural areas in 2007), constitutes the main social assistance programme within China, providing a limited safety net for those facing economic hardships (Yan, 2013). It is within this context that there has been a resurgence in urban poverty in both absolute and relative terms.

To examine the first-hand experiences of poverty and its association with shame, in-depth interviews were conducted between March and June 2011, in an area in Beijing where SOEs had previously been concentrated. The sample consisted of thirty-three individuals (twenty men and thirteen women, aged 30 to 65) from twenty-eight families with school-age children. Interviewees were identified through local neighbourhood organizations, combined with introduction through research participants to other potential interviewees. The majority of them had previously been employed in government-owned industrial or service sectors and had been laid off as a result of the restructuring of SOEs. At the time of interview, fourteen worked full-time but only as contract workers with no employment security; five worked in the informal sector or part-time; three were retired; eleven were unemployed, three of whom had self-reported health problems or disabilities which prevented them from working. As *dibao* is the main social assistance programme in urban China and is means-tested, receipt of *dibao* is usually an indicator of low economic status. Among the interviewees, three-quarters (twenty-one out of twenty-eight) of the families were receiving *dibao*, three had previously received *dibao*, and four had never been recipients of *dibao*. In terms of marital status, sixteen were married, eight had remarried, two were divorced, and two were widowed. Interestingly, eighteen of the marriages were between 'Beijingers' and migrants from other parts of the country (sixteen Beijing men, two Beijing women). Such marital arrangements are indicative of disadvantaged socio-economic positions because this is considered 'marrying down' in China, since migrants are not eligible for a variety of 'benefits' (employment and public services).

The following sampling limitations should be noted: Firstly, the city of Beijing is among the most economically developed areas in the country and its residents enjoy a standard of living which is far higher than that typically found in other Chinese cities (Mei, 2010). Secondly, the fact that the selection of participants was largely made through neighbourhood organizations might have generated an atypical group of low-income people, more likely to demonstrate attitudes considered 'cooperative' and 'reasonable', from an official point of view.

Characteristics of Poverty

This low-income group had fallen into poverty primarily as a result of three factors. The first factor was unemployment or unstable employment; a number of respondents had been laid off as a result of the SOE restructuring, while others had left the SOE, as its decline became apparent, for better work or business opportunities, only subsequently to encounter unemployment or the failure of their own business ventures. At the time of interview, the majority of the respondents were working but were on the lowest wage, and most of them felt that their jobs were not stable and that they could be laid off at any time. It was these employment-related factors that had led to their poverty. The second common reason cited for poverty was related to the ill-health or disabilities that a number of interviewees, or their family members, had suffered, leaving them unable to work and/or burdened with high medical expenses. One woman commented on her husband's unexpected illness: 'It was like the sky suddenly fell off [*sic.*]'. The third identifiable cause of poverty was the effect of having a criminal record: two interviewees had previously spent time in prison and therefore experienced difficulty finding employment, as no employer would hire them.

The interviewees reported that life without financial security imposed significant challenges and they struggled to make ends meet. For almost all of them, the income from their wages or *dibao* was barely enough to get by. They reported that they were forced to cut their expenditure in all respects and only to focus on food, for which they had to consciously reduce their expenditure by, for example, trying to buy vegetables that were less fresh but cheaper. Some did not consume meat on a daily basis because it was considered expensive and several people said that they did not drink milk regularly as they could not afford it. As food was regarded as the top priority, spending on clothes became secondary; buying new clothes was rare, and receiving secondhand clothes from relatives and friends was common. The majority of respondents lived in poor housing, usually a one-room dwelling, although a few of the *dibao* claimants had received a governmental housing allowance in the form of cash in recent years, enabling them to rent more living space.

Two critical sources of financial stress came from the need for medical care and education. Many felt that they could get by as long as they, and their family members, were in good health, but that illness would quickly lead to them being 'crushed' by medical expenses, since they had insufficient or no medical insurance from their employment. Educational expenses were also seen as burdensome. Most of the families interviewed had young or school-aged children, and they reported that it was extremely challenging to meet the costs of their children's educational needs. Two kinds of educational expenses were identified: 'in-school' and 'out-of-school'. Tuition is free in China for those with children enrolled in compulsory education (First to Ninth Grade), but costs for kindergarten, high school, and college education are high. For example, day care expenses could amount to several times more than the monthly *dibao* allocation. In recent years, those receiving *dibao* have been eligible for a reduction in school fees, which has proven to be of help to low-income groups. Nevertheless, due to the intensity of competition and high expectations of parents, it has become common practice for children to be enrolled in afterschool or weekend classes in English, maths, arts, and sports, and low-income families reported finding it particularly difficult to cover the expenses of these activities. A lack of financial resources also meant that the recreational opportunities of the low-income families interviewed were very limited as they could not afford to go to restaurants or amusement parks, and they rarely participated in old classmate reunions,[1] as these events often took place in restaurants.

Poverty without Shame

There were many instances in which the interviewees reported that they had no time to think about being embarrassed or ashamed of their poverty because the constraints of having limited financial resources meant that the priority was to focus on strategies to survive. They took up whatever jobs were available; typically low-paid, unskilled, and dead-end jobs in the service sector. A number of them worked in the informal sector, as housekeepers, or in unregistered taxi services or recycling set ups. Such employment was obtained through three main sources: former employers (SOEs), the employment service office of the local government, and networks of family and friends. Many of them received subsidies from *dibao* as well. As income was limited, they did their best to minimize expenses, or 'keep the belt tight', viewing frugality or self-imposed restriction on spending as the way to survive. Some interviewees reported that that they felt that their clothes were adequate as long as they were neat and that they did not pay attention to style or fashion.

Many interviewees reported benefiting from significant material and emotional support provided by family, relatives, and friends, for which they felt enormously grateful and without which they believed they would not be able to get by or survive a crisis. Two respondents said that while they were unemployed they regularly ate meals at their mothers' home. Most of the interviewees' parents received pensions in retirement, which were often more favourable, in terms of the amount and stability, than the wages the interviewees received, making it quite common for the elderly to subsidize the expenses of their adult children and grandchildren. Occasional financial support offered by better-off siblings was also reported and considered to be acceptable, although recipients did not expect regular and major support from siblings since they had their own families to take care of. Such assistance included sporadic cash supplements to help finance special needs such as college tuition. They also welcomed relatives buying things for their children or taking them out for meals or entertainment. The assistance of the extended family was reported to be particularly necessary during serious illness, which often culminated in large medical bills, although some relatives not only

---

[1] Such reunions are important social events in China and take place on a regular basis.

shared treatment costs but also took turns to provide care for the ill in the hospital, which would otherwise have had to be provided by paid caregivers.

Since interviews were not conducted with children and young people within the current study, the limited insights concerning the impact of poverty on children are drawn from the responses of parents. Overall, parents believed that their sons and daughters were well aware of their family circumstances and reportedly coped admirably, parents frequently noting how 'mature' their children were for not demanding things that were unaffordable. Li,[2] for example, said that her son would not go to the supermarket with her and that they seldom ate out. The fast food franchises such as McDonald's and Kentucky Fried Chicken (KFC) are popular in Chinese cities, but unlike their American counterparts, which have the reputation of low price and low quality, they are relatively highly priced and perceived as fashionable by many Chinese young people. Sun spoke of how he only occasionally took his daughter to KFC because it was expensive and he considered it 'junk food'.

A number of interviewees commented that *dibao* really helped them, that they felt fortunate to be eligible for it and that there were five reasons why they did not associate *dibao* with shame. Firstly, *dibao* was crucial for their survival. Secondly, they believed it was their right to receive MSLS since they had paid their taxes and, after all, the state had been responsible for them being laid off; their *dibao* was a form of compensation. Thirdly, some interviewees said that they deserved *dibao* as they had disabilities or were too old to find work. Fourthly, and somewhat counterintuitively, some interviewees asserted that the publicity about the *dibao* application process was appropriate and they had no problem with their neighbours knowing about their situation[3] although, as noted below, other people found this public exposure upsetting. Finally, some parents spoke of how their children, as beneficiaries of *dibao,* were not treated as inferior at school, in fact they spoke of how certain teachers were especially sensitive to their circumstances and made sure not to let other students know about the reduction in tuition fees that they received.

Experiences of Poverty with Shame

The association of poverty and shame did, however, become clearly evident when interviewees described dealing with financial struggles which were seen

---

[2] All names used in this chapter have been changed to preserve the anonymity of respondents.

[3] This is in reference to the fact that recipients of MSLS are publically listed within a local area to demonstrate that the system is being appropriately administered, that is, supporting those most in need.

as imposing significant emotional strain on them. Stress or shame was reportedly experienced as a result of unemployment, underemployment, or insecure employment. Several interviewees shared their reactions to learning about the closure a few years previously of their former SOEs; they felt, they admitted, 'totally lost' or 'cheated'. They also knew of individuals who had committed suicide or had ended up being divorced as a result of losing their jobs. Once unemployed, most described having neither the financial resources nor the social contact to launch their own businesses and so had to try their luck on the service sector job market. The work they could acquire was mostly low-paid and insecure and, even though they did find work eventually, they still bore a strong sense of shame due to their experience of downward mobility.

Interviewees spoke of how the seniority they had acquired and the skills they had mastered at the SOE became obsolete and these 'assets' in fact became baggage as they moved forward. The former industrial workers faced tremendous disadvantages in terms of age, health, and motivation issues in the new labour market. One man, for example, spoke of how he had refused to take a job as an attendant in a parking lot as he perceived it as being too lowly compared to his former managerial position in a construction company. Several said that they had had to learn to be submissive to both their supervisors and customers in the service sector, and a few interviewees expressed their frustrations and even anger at being 'pushed around' by much younger supervisors or co-workers in their new jobs where they described losing their sense of identity. Ms Zhou, for example, compared her previous job in a state-owned factory with her new job as a salesperson in a gift shop. Although she was among the lucky minority in that her income had increased several times with the new job, she still missed, she said, the sense of security and the feeling of being a 'master' in the factory, where she had even felt able to confront the manager at times. In the gift shop, which was privately owned, she was always worried about her sales and her relationship with the supervisor and the customers and knew that she could be dismissed at any time.

Shame was also experienced when trying to make ends meet while having to cover such expenditure as paying rent, medical costs, or school expenses for children. Interviewees tried not to borrow money as this might lead to them being looked down upon. A mother reported feeling pain when she saw other children going on out-of-town trips which she could not afford for her son during the summer vacation; and another woman did not apply for the reduction in tuition fees at her daughter's school which she was entitled to as part of the *dibao* benefits, as it would make the girl feel ashamed.

Although many of the interviewees received much valuable help from family, relatives, and friends, they also reported experiencing shame in their interactions with friends and family. Mr Yang reported how his parents considered his better-off siblings more 'filial', as they were able to afford more and better gifts than him; as a result he felt quite embarrassed whenever he went to visit. A number of interviewees reported feeling extremely guilty that they could not give anything to their aging parents but instead had to receive monetary help from them. One man said that as 'a big man' he felt embarrassed to be accepting things from his younger brother, and one woman commented that although her sister offered tremendous help to her family, her brother-in-law refused to visit them because they were so poor.

Pressure on those in poverty was described as especially acute on special social occasions. For example, it is customary during the Chinese New Year for families and relatives to get together and for adults to give the children of relatives a little 'red package' containing money, which is symbolic of good luck. The amount to be given is flexible, and is related to the financial situation of the giver. Liu recalled that there were several times during his unemployment when he had the embarrassing experience of not being able to afford these New Year offerings but had to accept pre-prepared red packages from his mother to give to the children of his siblings and cousins. In addition, Liu was concerned about the gifts he had to bring when visiting relatives, as he could not afford expensive things, but thought that he might be frowned upon if he brought items which were considered 'too shabby'.

Those in poverty also reported finding it especially hard to have to meet the expectations arising from social events outside of the family. Mrs Wang cited her experience of taking her three-year-old daughter to a playground, where parents of children from better-off families prevented their children from playing with her daughter. Another woman never dared to invite the mothers of her daughter's friends to her home as she felt ashamed of her poor furniture. Several interviewees did not attend old classmates' reunions because they did not want their friends to know about their current circumstances.

Even though interviewees claimed not to be bothered about being publicly listed as recipients of *dibao,* the actual *dibao* application and its associated processes were said by some to evoke feelings of shame. A few interviewees expressed their reluctance to submit their *dibao* application until they had failed numerous times when applying for jobs or had exhausted all other possible means of support. Some reported that it had been the staff from the local neighbourhood organization that had approached them and urged them to submit an application when their predicament had become known about in the neighbourhood. Preparation of the required paperwork was tedious; in order to substantiate the various eligibility criteria, those who married women from out of town had to travel long distances to their wives' village (or city) of origin for certain documents (for example proof that they had no assets such as land), and it was necessary to go through the same tiresome procedure again every six months in order to renew the application. Those deemed to be of working age and physically able are obliged to show proof of having sought work prior to seeking *dibao*, and it is only granted if they can show that they have made at least three unsuccessful applications for a job. Xie said it was a humiliating experience for her to try to convince a prospective employer to provide a document specifying reasons why she was not fit for the position; 'the rich look down upon the poor', she remarked. In terms of the publicity requirement of the *dibao* application in the neighbourhood, even though quite a number of the interviewees felt this was a proper procedure, Liang felt that it undermined the privacy of applicants. Deng, spoke of how she felt too embarrassed to tell her family in the south-western part of China that she and her husband received *dibao* in Beijing.

A special group among the unemployed were men with criminal records who had served time in prison. Due to the common requirement of employers to carry out background checks prior to making an appointment, the chances of these men finding employment after release from prison were minimal. This group of men had to claim *dibao* for financial security and their sense of being discriminated against and institutionally shamed was quite strong.

Responses to Poverty and Shame

Responses to poverty and shame among those interviewed varied greatly. Some felt under tremendous pressure due to the financial struggles caused by their employment insecurity. Not surprisingly, many of the interviewees appeared resigned to their circumstances; Mr Lin, for example, had been coping with hardships for many years through sheer 'endurance' and continuously striving to 'overcome' them. Some commented: 'Really, there is nothing you can do about it', so they felt it was better 'to take it easy'. Zhang said that money was important but by no means the only focus in life. When asked about the importance of clothes, several women responded that they were not concerned about clothes, nor did they pay attention to fashion, jewellery, or make-up. Wang said it was crucial to think broadly and that there was no use getting upset or feeling frustrated by what you didn't have. Some tried to focus only on their own lives instead of comparing their lives with those of others. When they did make comparisons, they argued that although there were people who were much better off than themselves, there were probably even more people who were worse off, which led to them feeling content. On the whole, interviewees demonstrated varied responses to their poverty; some expressing strong gratitude towards parents and relatives who had helped them get through difficulties and even crises and, at the other extreme, others indicating that they had encountered unfair criticism and social ostracism as a result of their poverty.

Perceived Causes of Poverty-Defining Responses

The variation in interviewees' attitudes to their situation was closely related to what they perceived the causes of their poverty to be. These causes can be roughly grouped into individual and structural factors; with some interviewees referring to both factors. Among the individual factors, a few respondents said that they believed in fate, and that the reason for their poverty was that they had 'bad luck'. Some felt that one's economic situation was mainly determined by the level of an individual's abilities and efforts (or inability to work due to illness or disabilities). Many of the respondents had lost their employment security because of the SOE restructuring; this situation was perceived in two ways. Some thought that it was the former manager(s) who had done an awful job, or that it was their self-interestedness or corruption that had led to the closedown of the enterprise. Wen believed so and fought fiercely with his former employer by filing an administrative petition and court suit because he felt that he had been short-changed in the pension contributions which the enterprise was supposed to make. Other interviewees too did not attribute their difficult financial situations to their own personal failings or those of any other individual; rather, they blamed larger forces, particularly social injustice. After all, the SOE restructuring was a state policy, so they simply saw themselves as victims of social transformation, but wondered 'why me?' They were angry at the fall in social status of workers in general and questioned the rapidly increasing economic disparity in China. In this context, those receiving the *dibao* perceived the programme as the minimum means of compensating them for their loss of job security. Some also had a sense of their rights as citizens, justifying their entitlement to *dibao* by distinguishing themselves from the former prison inmates whom they considered 'shameless'.

Regardless of what they perceived the causes of poverty to be, interviewees frequently alluded to the need to strive for the best. Their agency was demonstrated by their descriptions of what gave them pleasure and hope. Yin said that, compared with friends of his age, he was the healthiest, as others had health problems of many kinds. Li enjoyed embroidery, and Ren spent much time fishing, although he had to find ways to do it for free, because fishing could be very expensive due to the cost of a rod, transportation, and the admission fees at some places.

Hope was attributed to both material and non-material causes. Several interviewees said that they hoped to be able to improve their housing conditions if the area they lived in underwent redevelopment. Other interviewees had alternative aspirations, such as purchasing a computer for school-aged children, or travelling to other parts of the country or even around the world. Perhaps an inevitable consequence of the single-child policy in China which has been practiced over the past three decades, was the central concern of the needs of children in any family. Child-related expenses were said to exhaust a large portion of the households' income, and interviewees spoke of how they were willing to make any sacrifice needed for the well-being of their child. Parents repeatedly admitted to resting their own hopes and aspirations on the future 'success' of their children and, as higher education is no longer only for the elite, all parents expected their children to do well in school, to finish their college education, and go on to secure a professional job. This, they saw as the trajectory towards upward mobility, and they constantly told their children that they did not want them to take the path that they themselves had taken.

The interviewees, especially the middle-aged ones, hoped for a better life in retirement. The retirement age in urban China, for those engaged in manual labour, is set at 60 for men and 50 for women. However, those who have been exposed to hazardous conditions for a lengthy period of time, for example factory workers, are able to retire five years earlier. The pension they received upon retirement was usually higher than both their current wages and the MSLS and so would contribute significantly to their financial stability in the long term.

Conclusions

This chapter has outlined first-hand experiences of poverty and shame through the voices of a sample of interviewees living in urban China. Their experiences are located in the context of drastic social change; specifically the restructuring of the SOEs and the reform of welfare provision. The low-income groups interviewed suffered from poverty, both absolute and relative, which was due mainly to reasons of unemployment, job insecurity, or health-related issues. They experienced material shortages such as a lack of basic necessities and difficulties in the areas of housing, medical care, and education, which could all be seen as both causes and effects of poverty. Many had been faced with significant reductions in their socio-economic status, often referring to a subsequent loss of identity as they moved from being part of a highly regarded working class to becoming labourers in the financially insecure service sector.

Chapter 5, which offers an analysis of selected Chinese literature, indicates evidence of poverty without shame in particularly harsh circumstances, where those living in poverty were forced to engage in a struggle merely to survive. Similarly, the current research revealed that for those facing penury, the top priority was to make ends meet by whatever means possible. The interviewees accepted their situation and felt that strong support was provided by family, relatives, and friends and so no sense of shame or shaming was necessary. In fact, whether or not people were prone to feelings of shame appeared to have something to do with what they perceived to be the causes of poverty; when it was felt that their situations were beyond their personal control, interviewees tended to be more accepting of their struggles instead of feeling shame.

In a number of cases, however, shame related to poverty was clearly identified. Those living in poverty may experience shame resulting from material shortages or their inability to fulfil certain recreational or social aspirations. Shame is strongly felt by the former SOE workers who had to seek re-employment in the job market, where their age, seniority, and accumulated skills became disadvantages. Shame was equally experienced by some receiving assistance from family and friends, or from formal institutions such as those coordinating *dibao*. In many of these cases, shame was present without evidence of external 'shaming'; in other words, as was found in the analysis of literature, shame was felt internally, with no clear person or agency identified as intentionally causing it.

In terms of the reactions of those in poverty to shame, similar to the examples emerging from the analysis of literary works, instances were found in this phase of the research to support agency, counter-shaming, spiritual victory, and withdrawal. It is also interesting to note the differences among groups in terms of how they experienced and expressed feelings of shame. Although the interviewees were all adult men and women, it appeared evident from their responses that they felt that the older people were not as susceptible to shame as them, due to the relatively good pension provision which granted them financial stability. Similarly, the one-child policy, it was claimed, meant that parents tended to always prioritize the needs of the young. This finding was not consistent with the indications emerging from the literature analysis, which suggested that the old and young were particularly vulnerable to poverty and shame. With regard to gender differences, more female than male respondents referred to instances in which they had experienced shame or embarrassment, but this may be because women were better able and more willing to articulate these sentiments.

Overall, shame clearly has some impact on the lives and psychology of people living in poverty in China. It takes various forms, including emotional pain and embarrassment, loss of face, anger, and low self-esteem. Yet, as discussed earlier, the impact of shame for some is mitigated by certain attitudes towards poverty, such as the belief in fate, taking pleasure in other aspects of life than the financial, and having hopes for oneself or one's children.

References

Mei, S. (2010) *Beijing Economic Development Report, 2009–2010*, Beijing: Sheke wenxian Press.

World Bank (2009) *From poor areas to poor people: China's evolving poverty reduction agenda: An assessment of poverty and inequality in China.* Report No. 48058, March. Washington, DC: World Bank.

Yan, M. (2013) 'New Urban Poverty and New Welfare Provision: China's *Dibao* system', in Gubrium, E., Pellissery, S., and Lødemel, I. (eds) *The Shame Of It: Global Perspectives On Anti-Poverty Policies*, Bristol: Policy Press.

13

The 'Shame' of Shame

Experiences of People Living in Poverty in Britain

Elaine Chase and Robert Walker

Introduction

British film-makers and writers, as reported in Chapter 6, document the psychological costs that they see arising from poverty: poor self-image; an intrinsic sense of inferiority; social isolation, be it chosen or enforced; and, potentially, a gradual disintegration of the core self that can even result in suicide. To the extent that these characteristics are true, they were recognized by novelists and film-makers earlier than they were generally acknowledged to be important by sociologists and social policy scholars. The goal in this chapter is to explore how well these characterizations of the consequences of poverty correlate with the experiences of families experiencing poverty in Britain today.

Qualitative in-depth interviews were conducted with a total of forty-two adults (eleven men and thirty-one women) resident in localities defined as being among the two most materially deprived deciles in England. Participants were selected as eligible to take part in the research if they lived within the defined geographical area and fulfilled the criteria of a) having dependent children; and b) having ever been in receipt of one or more benefits (including Jobseeker's Allowance [JSA], Income Support [IS], Employment and Support Allowance [ESA], or tax credits). Adult participants had between one and seven (with an average of two) dependent children. In addition, twenty-two children and young people between the ages of 5 and 19 years and known to be living in low-income families were interviewed, identified via adult participants or through local children and youth services within the same localities.

Interviews were structured in such a way as to allow research participants to lead the discussion in relation to a range of key topics, beginning with a broad question such as 'Tell me a bit about your current situation?' Using a series of subsequent prompts, adult participants were asked about their perceptions of: their current financial situation; the types of difficulties (if any) that they were facing; the types of strategies they employed to mitigate economic hardship; the sources and types of support (if any) they felt they had access to; the extent to which those not facing economic hardship understood the difficulties they faced; how the circumstances of people on low incomes were presented in the media and in policy discourses; and what could be done to better support people facing economic hardship in Britain. Interviews with children and young people were similarly open-ended and tailored, age appropriately, to focus on their daily lives and whether and how they perceived their economic circumstances to affect their interactions with others.

Facing Daily Hardship

The constant challenges of running a home and supporting a family were frequently denoted by phrases such as 'struggling', nightmare', 'going round and round in circles', 'struggling to keep head above water', 'scuppered', 'stuck in a rut', 'scrimp, save, borrow, beg and steal', 'robbing Peter to pay Paul', 'battering your head against the wall'.

Almost all adults interviewed described regularly facing difficult decisions over whether to pay bills or provide food and clothing for children; having to rely on food banks, family, or friends for food or money; or having to compromise the quality of food they bought. Several lived in overcrowded conditions, described periods of temporary homelessness, or were forced to occupy poor-quality housing which had a detrimental impact on their own health and that of their children.

A number of participants spoke of how major life events such as divorce, separation, redundancy, bereavement, or domestic violence had significantly affected their economic well-being. Tina described fleeing domestic violence with a two-year-old son while pregnant with her second child. After spending 19 months in sheltered housing, she was struggling to adjust financially to bringing up two young children on her own in rented accommodation. And Mike spoke of how, following the death of his wife, he was forced to give up the job he had held for seven years working in a local factory to care for his severely disabled one-year-old daughter, with the result that he was 'getting deeper and deeper in debt', something he had never experienced before.

Feeling but Not Naming 'Shame'

So as not to impose or assume a direct connection between 'poverty' and 'shame', these words were deliberately not introduced during interviews with people on low incomes. Importantly, people repeatedly described their reactions and responses to the circumstances that they faced in terms which implied that they were acutely aware of and subjected to feelings of shame on a daily basis, yet they rarely used the word 'shame' or its associated terms, indicative of what Scheff (2000; 2003) has identified as the 'taboo' surrounding shame. Instead, when people were asked about how the hardships they had described made them 'feel', they frequently spoke of feeling 'ashamed', 'awkward', 'embarrassed', 'guilty', 'rotten', 'degraded', 'crap', 'useless', 'worthless', 'a failure', 'uncomfortable', 'funny', and 'dirty', in certain social and bureaucratic interactions, terms that are elsewhere referred to as the 'colloquialisms of shame' (Chase and Walker, 2013). For children and young people, shame was similarly insinuated but not named, although there appeared for some young people interviewed to be a greater degree of, or at least vocalized, resistance to succumbing to feelings of inadequacy due to economic circumstances.

The Contexts of Feeling Shame

Whether internally felt or imposed by others, there were multiple contexts within which adults and young people alike described feelings denoting 'shame'. However, there were clear linguistic cues denoting whether it was internally felt or externally imposed—the two processes frequently combining to construct shame in complex ways. The settings within which people felt internally 'awkward' or 'embarrassed' at one end of the spectrum, and 'worthless', 'a failure', and 'crap' at the other were multiple. Similarly these same settings were frequently arenas within which others generated, or attempted to generate, feelings of inadequacy and insignificance through their perceived actions such as, 'looking down on', 'turning their nose up', 'judging', 'thinking we're all the same', 'don't get to know you', 'treating you like shit', 'looking at you like crap', or 'preying on people like us'.

Family

Family support was frequently described as crucial in helping people to get through the week with the limited resources they had. Christine, for example, commented, 'two or three times a week sometimes I have to see if mum can actually feed me and the kids because I haven't got what you would call a decent meal to give them'. This said, various people spoke of a heightened discomfort associated with having to resort to family help. This 'awkwardness' for Hilda, for example, stemmed from the fact that, 'I am a mum now myself and I should be able to do it myself and not have to go to my mum all the time just for a pint of milk or a loaf of bread'; and for Tina because, 'it's all to do with admitting the fact that you can't cope. Obviously it was my choice to have the children, and probably not being able to afford them is a horrible feeling'.

Others described 'feeling horrible', 'embarrassed', or 'dreadful' about having to accept help from others or not managing to provide for their families. For Greg, this stemmed from the expectations he had of himself as a man. His dependence on his partner for 'the food in my belly', he said, made him feel 'like shit... I'm the man of this relationship. I am meant to be the man... to take care of the missus and my kids. And I don't, and I hate feeling like I do with myself because of it'.

All interviewees had children to care for and responses of 'feeling guilty', 'feeling rotten', 'awkward', 'useless', 'letting myself down', or 'ashamed' were common in relation to how they viewed their inability to provide for children, sentiments that children and young people were also acutely aware of. Jake, aged 16, observed that he thought his mother 'feels a bit ashamed' at not being able to provide everything he needed, an emotion he tried hard to counter by making it clear to her that he did not need particular things that she thought she should provide for him.

Indeed, most parents interviewed felt conscious of the level of awareness, sometimes from a very young age, that their children had about the degree of hardship that they were facing. Tina, for example, spoke of her 'guilty feeling' when her four-year-old son, on realizing how worried she was about the amount of debt she was in, offered to sell his new Nintendo DS, bought as a birthday present, to help out. Similarly, Jenny described her 'guilt' at having to empty her son's savings account to pay off debts when 'I had the bailiffs threatening'. Children recounted refraining from asking for things that they wanted, such as an ice cream or Easter egg, or resisting asking for toys that others had, to show empathy with parents about the difficulties they were facing. And while such sensitivity was appreciated by parents, at the same time it often exacerbated their sense of failure. Having to watch all the other children in the neighbourhood eat ice cream and not be able to buy one for your own children, not being able to go on holiday, or having to apply for a hardship fund to pay for a child's school trip were all examples given of their failure to provide being publicly exhibited.

School

Children and young people, like adults, spoke of how they strove to be accepted by those around them. School in particular was a space in which many children felt constantly compared with others, where differences in income soon emerged, and where they were more likely to be judged by others or treated unfairly. Anticipating that he would be reprimanded for not having the correct school uniform, Jacob, aged 14, spoke of how he avoided going into school: 'I haven't got any school trousers at this minute in time, I'm not going to come in (to school) until I get them. What they're not understanding is that I can't always go out and buy new things that I need . . . I think it's really cruel'. In a similar vein, Paul, also aged 14, commented that school was a place where he was chided for being a recipient of free school meals. While he felt able to ignore what he perceived as 'teasing', he described others saying, 'oh you're poor . . . benefit bum . . . and stuff like that'.

Jake, aged 16, spoke of how the ability to buy the latest phones, computers, and other electronic equipment was seen as a means of gauging how well-off you were compared to others, and how such gadgets became part of the image that you were expected to project, everyone being 'in competition with everyone else'. Similarly, Billy, aged 10, cited an incident at school where he had felt deeply 'embarrassed' when he brought in a new toy to show his friends and 'then the next day somebody else brings something even bigger and better in and they like show you up, like "look what I've got"'. Hamish, also aged 10, said that when people boasted at school about what they had or asked him if he had certain things, it was just easier for him to say that he had them rather than explain why he didn't.

The social space between school and home was also complex for some young people, who avoided showing or telling others where they lived. Eloise, aged 18, reflected on how at school she was always too embarrassed about inviting friends home because she would have to explain that her mother slept in the front room so that they could let out her bedroom to make ends meet.

On the whole, however, young people interviewed tended to be more likely than adults to vocalize resilience to their circumstances and spoke with optimism about the future. Harry, at the age of 12, had set his sights on becoming a professional sportsman, a profession that would enable him to 'give mum everything she needs'. Billy, aged 10, intended to join the army or become a spy, his ultimate aim to travel and see the world. Although Ella, aged 16, described a constant struggle, since she was very young, of caring and providing for her grandmother and younger siblings, she was adamant that poverty only existed in 'Africa'. Her aspiration, she said, was to have 'a nice house, know that I can settle down, go home and have no arrears to pay . . . have like perfect council tax and that [not owing any]' and not 'worry about being able to put food on the table for my child'. Moreover, she felt strongly that submitting to the notion of being 'poor' implied defeat when in her view, economic hardship was a temporary setback and one which you could overcome with determination and resilience. The idea that admitting to being 'poor' could undermine the self was reiterated by 13-year-old Patrick, who declared, 'you shouldn't call yourself poor'. When asked why he thought this, he replied 'it lowers your self-esteem', a belief which, he claimed, his mother had firmly instilled in him. And other young people too played down the significance of money. Charlie, aged 15, commented, 'Money doesn't make you happy', and Joe, aged 16, reasoned that if his peers couldn't accept him for who he was, then they weren't worth counting as friends.

Institutions

A number of interviewees referred to how they had felt particularly judged by other people in positions of authority and control. Jenny, for instance, recounted an interaction with the head teacher of her son's primary school and how she was cumulatively judged for being a single mother, being on benefits, living on a particular street, and because her son had some behavioural issues. She concluded, 'and so when I go to that meeting, she's there thinking, "oh my God, it's just another one of those mothers", and she couldn't give two monkeys about what I'm saying'. And Susie told of a meeting with a prospective landlord and his candid views that people receiving benefits should be willing to accept poor standard and damp housing.

Equally, feeling degraded, looked down on, judged, and not listened to were ubiquitous in people's accounts of interactions with social security institutions. With a few exceptions, these encounters were typically frustrating and soul destroying and indicative of a perceived institutionalized shaming and stigma. Increasingly stringent eligibility criteria for benefits, as well as unfair conditions and sanctions, were repeatedly mentioned as evidence of this. Some people described being forced to participate in obligatory back-to-work courses which were perceived as a 'waste of time', impractical (for example, when they had small children to take care of), and which served no apparently practical purpose in terms of helping them find work. The threatened sanction for not attending such courses, however, was reportedly a cut in benefits such as JSA, which several people interviewed had borne the brunt of. Equally, there had been cutbacks in provisions that had previously eased the transition into work, such as money to subsidize new work clothes or housing costs during the first month's work.

Being treated as a member of a group rather than an individual, or 'just a number', having to explain circumstances over and over again to different people, having to constantly complete forms, being made to feel small, and the indifference of benefits officers towards them as people were repeatedly cited as examples of the dehumanizing nature of the process of claiming benefits. Sonia, for example, believing that her previous work record had gone unacknowledged, commented about what she was thinking, but had not dared to vocalize in a meeting with an official at the job centre, 'if you checked that, you wouldn't make me feel so bad about sitting here'. Debbie believed that the people working at the employment office 'look at you like you're crap', but also said that she resented the personal restrictions on her when she entered the office, such as having to turn her phone off, not being allowed to wear a 'hoodie', or sanctions for being five minutes late when she was caring for a small baby. And many people alluded to the awkwardness and stigma attached to the process of accessing benefits more generally. Greg commented, 'I feel like I'm sponging', Tina resented the label of 'scrounger', which, she said, was meted out to all people receiving benefits, while Trevor, who had recently had his entitlement to disability living allowance (DLA) contested, observed that he felt as though others thought of him as just trying to work the system, 'You know . . . like I can't get enough money on the dole so I'll go on the sick! It's a stigma; it makes you feel like you're scrounging.'

Even support provided through voluntary or charitable organizations had its drawbacks and negatively impacted on people's sense of self-worth. The number of times that people could access food banks within a certain time period, for example, was limited, irrespective of need, and the impact of being categorized as 'needy' was significant. Susie explained why she refused to go to a food bank: 'Have you ever been to a food bank?', she asked, 'Your name goes down on a piece of paper . . . I don't like the thought of me being [it being recorded] on pieces of paper that I'm hard up.'

Borrowing Money

A further source of shaming was associated with the accumulation of debt, a significant difficulty for the majority of people interviewed. Owing money to banks, to the Social Fund, credit card companies, mail order catalogue services, and personal loan companies were all common. So too was being in arrears with electricity, gas, and water bills or being behind with payments for council tax and rent. Having a poor credit rating, no regular income, and limited wider family resources to draw on, people described having little or no choice but to turn to private loan companies for money. Whereas interviewees felt that they were constantly being judged as profligate, on the contrary, they described a multitude of different circumstances which had culminated in them losing control of their finances and drifting into debt.

Indebtedness and the pressure exerted by money lenders, bailiffs, and loan companies through repeated phone calls, reminder letters, and final demands provoked a great deal of anxiety. George arrived at the interview for this research with a final demand letter for a debt of £1,500 in his back pocket, something that caused him extreme anxiety. For others too, feeling 'swamped' by debt and having to 'fob off' or hide from debt collectors were common concerns. Some people had been evicted from homes, while others had suc-cumbed to declaring bankruptcy. Tony spoke of how he could not even get together the £90 required for a debt relief order which would enable him to wipe out £10,000 worth of debt and relieve him from the constant stress of 'bailiffs knocking on the door..., people I owe money for bills and things phoning me up five times a day, even on a Sunday.'

The impact of debt and its associated anxieties and stress were pervasive across families, and children were sometimes acutely aware of its ramifica-tions. While discussing some of the financial difficulties he had witnessed, Harry, aged 12, described an occasion when his mother anticipated a visit from the bailiffs:

> There was one time I remember that, um, that I'm not sure what they're called... people that come... oh, bailiffs I think, they were meant to come round our house and take all of our stuff. But the bailiffs didn't come thankfully, but my mum was just sat on the sofa, you could see it on her face that she was just worried.

Society

Yet it was perhaps the day-to-day struggles to cope with real or anticipated social judgements that people found most difficult to put up with. Tony, for instance was most anxious about his inability to pay for a haircut, which had a profound impact on his self-esteem, 'I can't even afford to get my hair cut... I feel like a frazzle—that's half the reason for my lack of self-confidence. I mean, if I look in the mirror and see crap, I feel crap'.

And several other people spoke of how they were treated differently once it was realized that they had no money. Debbie referred to the silent disapproval people had of her once she started receiving benefits: 'they never say anything but it's the way they stop asking you out and the way they don't visit you like they used to'; Deva similarly spoke of how someone he had considered a close friend stopped visiting him once he was struggling financially, not even to acknowledge the birth of his new son.

There was also a spatial dimension to how some people felt they were perceived and viewed by others. Certain 'estates' or 'areas' were said to be associated with social or moral deficiencies, being deemed places of high unemployment, high rates of young motherhood, crime, or drug use. Gary, aged 19, who had lived in the same neighbourhood all his life, commented, 'a few of my friends won't even come to where I live because where I live has been given a bad reputation by certain people that live here. That kind of blankets the whole estate really'. Similarly Karen noted that people, 'class X and Y [names of places] as benefits estates, you know?...full of down-and-outs. And I'm like, "I'm no down and out and I'm living there"'. These stereotypical portrayals of housing estate residents, it was said, were driven by the prevailing discourses perpetuated in media representations of such estates, which closely associated them with criminality, dysfunction, and indolence. Mike, for example, remarked that 'there's a stigma isn't there?...about living on a council estate, being on benefits...it's like the image portrayed in the media and stuff—you're this kind of asbo-hoodie'.[1]

Consequences of and Responses to Shame

People interviewed recounted a number of consequences of the shame imposed on them by their economic circumstances and the different ways in which they responded to such shame, with varying degrees of success in mitigating its impact.

Grappling with Pride

Even though participants rarely named 'shame', they frequently vocalized the importance of 'pride' and the significance of maintaining it. Pride often prevented interviewees from asking for help or assistance, no matter how hard things became. Susie spoke of how she worked as a support worker in a children's centre on a low wage, alongside health visitors and other professionals who were earning a lot more than her. She felt that if she let others know how much she was struggling, this would place her in a category alongside others who were 'hard up', those people she was supposed to be helping.

For many, a sense of pride was derived from paid work, hence, circumstances that prevented people from working further exacerbated a sense of inadequacy. Moreover, a number drew a sense of pride from having worked in the past and, as illustrated earlier, were frustrated when this was not acknowledged by others. One of the most valued non-monetary gains associated with work was that you were accorded dignity and respect not granted to those who

---

[1] Someone wearing a sweatshirt with a hood believed to want to conceal deviant behaviour and considered likely to behave in a way which results in a civil court order, an anti-social behaviour order (ASBO).

169

were unemployed. Gary, aged 19 and unable to find work himself, described how hard he had tried to dissuade a close friend from quitting his low-paid job, emphasizing to his friend how 'horrible' it was to be without work, how he had been experiencing a lack of confidence since leaving college which got 'worse every day', and that it was 'also about the perception that other people have of you which changes from being unemployed to being in a job'.

Yet for many, jeopardizing pride to a greater or lesser extent became an inevitable part of getting by. Pride thus became something that you had to 'swallow', 'lose', or 'bury' in order to survive or maintain a family. Stuart, reflecting on his experience of asking for help from the local food bank, commented, 'if you can't swallow your pride, then forget it'. He went on to say that he felt deeply embarrassed about asking for help and was constantly haunted by the principle instilled into him by his own father—that if you didn't have the money to do or have something, then you should go without.

Withdrawing and Pretence

Limited resources were commonly described as a reason for consciously withdrawing from certain social situations. Not having money to buy anything to wear to a wedding or to afford a gift; not having enough money to buy a round of drinks in the pub; or having nothing smart to wear to go out on a date with a new partner or indeed to finance a new relationship were all described as obstacles to engaging socially. People interviewed spoke of how they were constantly having to make up excuses as to why they could not attend various events or outings. This disincentive to engage in social situations imposed significant constraints on those affected. In the words of Geoff, 'it kind of pulls your life in a bit tighter'.

Similar dilemmas were faced by young people when they regularly lacked the resources to join friends on outings to the cinema, shopping in town, or similar activities. Paul, aged 16, for example, said that, on the whole, friends who were generally better-off than he was, were 'quite understanding' when he said he had no money. It became slightly more difficult, however, when he repeatedly had to say that he was unable to join in with them due to lack of funds. This culminated, he said, in a feeling of being 'left out'.

Equally, people described being ground down by the constant struggle to make ends meet, leaving them feeling that they didn't want to socialize anyway since, as Sonia commented, there was nothing to talk about except that 'you feel a bit depressed, you haven't got enough money to pay that bill or eat that day'. Similarly, Tony spoke of how, despite the best efforts of his friends to empathize with his situation when he felt bad, he wanted to 'turn the phone off, shut the curtains and just hide away'.

Several people talked about the strategies they used to mask the reality of their circumstances. Rosemary described how she stoically always gave the impression that everything was fine, even when she was really struggling. Both Gary and Teresa explained how they concealed information about where they lived, anticipating that certain negative assumptions would be made about them if they didn't do so. A number of others admitted that, in order to avoid the anticipated negative judgements of others, they told others that they were working rather than admitting that they were in receipt of benefits.

Reduced Well-Being

Poor physical health emerged as a significant issue for a number of participants and their children, in particular respiratory infections and conditions linked to damp or inadequately heated housing. Even more common, however, than the physical ill-health long associated with poverty, were references to mental health problems. And while it is difficult to draw a direct correlation between poverty-related shame and its negative impact on mental health, the damaging psychological consequences of shame itself have nonetheless been previously established (Tangney and Dearing, 2003; Furukawa et al., 2012).

The psychological impact of economic hardship was suggested by a whole range of different expressions; 'depressing', 'makes you very low', 'gets really down on us', 'pulls your life in a bit tighter', 'plays on the mind', were all terms used. The consequences of money 'worries' were frequently linked to physical or psychological symptoms: Karen said that anxieties about money had made her physically sick; Jessica attributed her hair loss and psoriasis in large part to the financial stresses she was under; and Deva felt that the same anxiety about money had been a contributing factor to his recent heart attack.

And such stresses and anxieties were constant. Trevor commented, 'you lie awake at night thinking "shit, I've got that bill coming in next week"... I mean I've got X [name of water company] on my back at the moment... I phoned them up because they were going to send the bailiffs'. Tony too, spoke of the impact of economic strife on his mental health: 'I don't manage. I just get very depressed...very depressed, you know? That's not managing...[I] just stay in bed all day or watch the TV, its soul destroying'. Several people spoke of how they had contemplated or attempted suicide as a result of not being able to see a way out of their current circumstances. Jessica explained, 'I was going to give my life up because of the debt and stuff', and Julie, reflecting on her attempted suicide, said, 'I got so depressed and couldn't cope with the situation and money and everything else that was going on...it was just too much'.

In somewhat more subtle ways, and less openly vocalized, economic circumstances were seen to be taking a toll on young people too. Boys and young men in particular commonly spoke of how they grappled with a nagging sense of anger. The extent to which such anger was attributable to economic hardship or its related difficulties was hard to determine and there was an evident reticence about making this association. Freddy and Dominic, for example, both aged 12, claimed that money was not a major problem in either of their households yet they both equally cited not having the money to do or have things that others did as frequent sources of anger. Freddy hinted that in certain situations, in order to save face, he pretended he had more money than he actually had, 'so you don't look stupid'.

A testament to the negative impact of financial circumstances on mental health was the fact that some people described the stark contrast evident in their self-image when they had more resources. Geoff, for example, described how previously having some disposable income meant that, 'you could blend in a bit more 'cos you had that little bit of money'. And Susie described how her sense of self was broadened once she had fewer money worries, 'I found a part of myself that I didn't even know existed'.

Distancing Oneself from the Constructed 'Other'

Each of the participants in this study had arrived at their particular circumstances through different routes, events having conspired to make it increasingly difficult for them to provide for themselves and their families. Yet despite these different trajectories, the majority of people felt an acute sense of being treated and judged the same—they intensely resented the dehumanizing ways in which they felt they were viewed and treated by the media, the general public, by politicians, and policymakers as a homogenous category of people who were 'not bothered', 'spongers', 'scroungers', or 'benefit bums'.

A common response to such stereotyping was for people to distance themselves from the socially constructed archetypal 'scroungers', others who they 'knew' or had heard of who really did meet the stereotypes portrayed by the media. Such 'othering' (Lister, 2004) was intensely powerful and, as argued elsewhere, typified the ways in which shame can become detrimental to social cohesion, impeding any sense of collective action by those in similar circumstances and instead acting as a powerful mechanism for further atomizing society (Chase and Walker, 2013).

Conclusion

The review of literature and film corpuses described in Chapter 6 established a robust and durable link between poverty and shame that was deeply embedded in the culturally constructed experience of poverty. The empirical

evidence drawn from interviews with adults and young people facing economic hardship in Britain substantiates that link. Similar to the literary works
and the films that were examined, in real life there is a consistent narrative
that poverty entails a profound sense of inadequacy and unworthiness to
which people risk exposure in multiple social and institutional arenas.

The triggers for these emotions are both internal and external. They are
borne out of a sense of inability to meet the expectations that individuals
place on themselves to progress along certain trajectories; providing or caring
for others; or remaining independent of institutionalized welfare support.
Equally such emotions are generated by dominant cultural norms and values
within contemporary British society which vehemently label and stigmatize
people as 'welfare dependent', 'work shy', 'scroungers', or whom 'can't be
bothered', a theme we turn to in Chapter 20.

These findings are consistent with earlier studies of the lived experiences of
people on low incomes dating back through the work of Tess Ridge (2002),
Sue Middleton and colleagues (1994), Elaine Kempson and colleagues (1994),
and back to Joseph Rowntree (1901; 1941; Rowntree and Lavers, 1951) and
Charles Booth (1892), the latter contemporaries of the Victorian novelists.
The current study in Britain has, however, focused a somewhat different lens
on the experience of poverty, and in doing so, has illuminated the pervasive-
ness of its associated shame, previously hidden, it could be said, by a plethora
of less stigmatizing synonyms which have tended to mask its existence and
power.

References

Booth, C. (1892) *Life and Labour of the People in London* (1889–1903), London:
    Macmillan.
Chase, E. and Walker, R. (2013) 'The co-construction of shame in the context of
    poverty: beyond a threat to the social bond', *Sociology*, 47(4): 739–54.
Furukawa, E., Tangney, J., and Higashibara, F. (2012) 'Cross-cultural Continuities and
    Discontinuities in Shame, Guilt and Pride: A Study of Children Residing in Japan,
    Korea and the USA', *Self and Identity*, 11(1): 90–113.
Kempson, E., Bryson A., and Rowlington, K. (1994) *Hard Times? How poor families make
    ends meet*, London: Policy Studies Institute.
Lister, R. (2004) *Poverty*, Cambridge: Polity Press.
Middleton, S., Ashworth, K., and Walker, R. (eds) (1994) *Family Fortunes: Pressures on
    parents and children in the 1990s*, London: CPAG.
Ridge, T. (2002) *Childhood Poverty and Social Exclusion: From a child's perspective*, Bristol:
    The Policy Press.
Rowntree, B. (1901) *Poverty: A study of town life*, London: Macmillan.

Rowntree, B. (1941) *Poverty and Progress: A second social survey of York*, London: Longmans.

Rowntree, B. and Lavers, G. (1951) *Poverty and the Welfare State: A third social survey of York dealing only with economic questions*, London: Longmans.

Scheff, T. (2000) 'Shame and the social bond', *Sociological Theory*, 18: 84–98.

Scheff, T. (2003) 'Shame in self and society', *Symbolic Interaction*, 26(2): 239–62.

Tangney, J. and Dearing, R. (2003) *Shame and Guilt*, New York: Guilford Press.

14

Social Isolation and Poverty in South Korea

A Manifestation of the Poverty–Shame Nexus

Yongmie Nicola Jo and Robert Walker

Contemporary South Korean society is a product of almost miraculous economic growth, initially facilitated by nationalistic, mildly benevolent, authoritarian governments. Shaken by the 1997 Asian fiscal crisis, democratic governments continue to pursue an economic growth strategy. At the same time, however, they are obliged to respond to high levels of unemployment and an increasingly polarized society at a time when familial obligations to care are rapidly being eroded by social change, including a reduced commitment to Confucian values. The analysis of popular films from South Korea, presented in Chapter 7, illustrated how rapid social transformation from widespread poverty two generations ago to rampant individualism and conspicuous consumption today has been culturally perceived. It also suggested that poverty, once thought to be a product of fate and misfortune, is now interpreted as evidence of personal failure and inadequacy.

This chapter investigates the match between personal experience and the celluloid and digital images that ostensibly reflect, but also necessarily influence, the reality that is modern South Korean society. To achieve this, thirty-one participants (twenty-three women and nine men) from two generations (eleven in their 60s and twenty in their 40s) were interviewed in depth. While all respondents were living on low incomes, they were divided into two distinguishable categories in South Korea. Members of the first group, *'Soo-Geup-Ja'*—those living in poverty—were in receipt of the standard South Korean social assistance, the National Basic Living Security Scheme (NBLSS). The circumstances of the second group, *'Cha-Sang-Wee'*—the near poor—meant that they were not eligible for NBLSS but could access other means-tested benefits to support either health, old age, or the costs of raising children, according to their specific circumstances. Both groups were recruited with the help of local welfare officials administering the NBLSS, hence all participants had at some time sought to access social assistance.

Interviews lasted between two and three hours, allowing time for trust to be built between the interviewer and respondent. Sufficient time was spent discussing participants' life histories and their daily lives in order to get a more complete picture and understanding of the psychological and social dimensions of their experiences of poverty. Questions were never asked explicitly about shame attributed to poverty; instead, conversations were led by interviewees, who typically spontaneously introduced shame or shame-related concepts as they reflected on their lives, both past and present.

Poverty as Material Hardship

All the respondents lived in medium-rise residential housing shared by several households or in high-rise apartment buildings in Seoul that were purpose built for public housing and were equipped with electricity and running water. The people living in the medium rise housing were accommodated in the 'half underground' floor of the house. Typical in urban South Korea, these are rented basements converted to housing that are only halfway above the ground, characterized by limited lighting, frequent problems with damp when it rains, and inadequate heating for the winter. Rental costs in Seoul are high and fear of hikes in monthly rents or an inability to afford to continue to pay the rent were major concerns for many of the respondents. Properties were small and generally sufficient only to accommodate a very small size nuclear family of two to three people. Two out of three respondents (twenty-one out of thirty-one) had children of school age and, reflecting the uptake of social assistance in South Korea, over half (nineteen out of thirty-one) of these respondents were lone parents. About half of the respondents were employed, although many worked part-time in temporary menial public sector jobs.

Homes were quite spartan with minimal, often poor quality furniture and floor coverings and secondhand consumer durables, including clothes. Most people had refrigerators, televisions, and basic mobile phones which were subsidized as part of their benefit entitlements. However, apart from references to the damp and cold or to physical health problems, conversations seldom focused on material deprivation other than acknowledging the difficulties in making ends meet with limited resources. Instead, people spoke more about the stress, uncertainty, and fear for the future that they felt and the strong sense of being alone and ignored by relatives and their communities with whom they had little or no interaction.

Having children of school age to care for was a major source of concern. Unlike in some other countries in this study, all the children of participants seemed to be attending school regularly. However, the cultural emphasis on educational attainment meant that parents were always under pressure to spend more on extracurricular learning opportunities, which they were very aware they could not afford. While schooling is ostensibly free for children aged between 7 and 15, for students aged 16 to 18 in high school, tuition fees are charged despite some government funding. Extracurricular activities often incurred additional costs, and supplementary tuition, both for core academic subjects and artistic endeavours, was the norm. Moreover, parents went to inordinate lengths to meet the costs of these activities, scrimping and saving and taking on multiple jobs in order to do so.

Housing was the next most salient form of financial stress for participants since the consequences of defaulting on their rent payments were severe. At the time of interviewing, one in five respondents considered themselves to be in imminent threat of homelessness. When budgets needed to be carefully managed to ensure that outgoings are no more than income, people were particularly vulnerable to rent increases because small percentage changes translated into a significant proportion of the domestic budget. Equally, health care costs are high in South Korea and similarly unpredictable. The National Health Insurance scheme requires persons to pay around one-third of outpatient and 20 per cent of inpatient expenses and, while the Medical Aid Programme is available to people on low incomes, the eligibility criteria for the scheme vary each year.

Older respondents were obviously less likely to have school-aged children than their younger peers, but otherwise their material circumstances were very similar. While they remembered an era when poverty was much more common and affluence was almost the exception, they, like their younger counterparts, often felt poorer than ever before in relative terms. Irrespective of age, most people could recall better, more prosperous times in the past, but few had ever been rich. For the most part, circumstances, whether economic (unemployment, redundancy, and bankruptcy), personal (sickness, pregnancy, relationship breakdown, and advancing years), or a combination of both, had conspired to push them from a position of just sufficient resources to manage to one in which they were invariably struggling.

Poverty as Social-Relational Hardship

While financial stress was real, respondents placed more emphasis on the effect of poverty on their social relationships and how it created a different form of mental stress, often leaving them feeling isolated and unable to socialize with others in the community. A number of participants described how the sense of rejection by other people as a result of their financial hardships combined with overpowering feelings of loneliness, could lead to depression, and even to thoughts of suicide.

Isolation and Neglect

Marital and relationship difficulties as a result of poverty were common, sometimes leading to divorce and circumstances of lone parenthood, which limited capacity for full-time employment. Working hours are very long in South Korea for women (77 per cent work over forty hours a week, well above the OECD average of 49 per cent) as well as for men. Furthermore, the marked gender wage gap together with high childcare and educational costs imposes substantial constraints on the earning power of divorced or single mothers. Married female respondents were also often vocal in criticizing their husbands, some of whom they considered to be addicted to gambling, drinking, and internet gaming, activities that drained household resources and reduced earning capacity. Some women rationalized their partners' behaviour as a response to unemployment and poverty that made them feel unable to fulfil their male roles and duties properly within the Korean family system. This cultural context created an additional mental stress and pressure for both men and women living in poverty but, in terms of social expectations, arguably took a heavier toll on men, who failed to live up to their roles as primary breadwinners.

While respondents tended to speak at length of their partner's absence or inability to support the family, they also frequently reported being neglected by the extended family. This was something that the older cohort of respondents in particular described as a distinct change from their memories of the past. They felt that in earlier times, during the 1960s and 1970s, although living standards were lower, families and communities were more tight-knit and better able to support each other. By contrast, respondents believed that nowadays even close relatives did not spontaneously offer assistance and so were too embarrassed or unable to ask for help. Relatives were said to frequently refuse requests for help, making it even more difficult to ask again, since one not only had to overcome the shame of seeking aid but also risk the humiliation of being turned down or singled out as incompetent. The potential of losing face or feeling shame in asking for assistance was acutely felt, and people often rejected the idea of seeking help from acquaintances, often recounting unsuccessful experiences of soliciting help that left a painful wound in the memory.

> This is a very dry and cold era where even siblings ignore your difficult situation. Unless I die, maybe. I can't be directly asking them how they could help right?

They should respond when I let them know of my situation, but they have no reaction whatsoever.

(male, 71, single-person household)

I have many siblings, but I can confess here and now, that I pulled through my life (and difficulties) alone and have never been helped even a penny from them. Nor have I ever asked even for a penny.... Even if I asked for some help, they are not the ones who would...be understanding and supportive. I actually have once, when my daughter was sick, asked to borrow 8,500 South Korean Won (£5 pounds). Since then, I have never been back to ask again. She is not even a sister. Even until now, those incidents stay in my heart as a wound. How can a big sister ignore you in your utmost lowest of the low...there is no love, should I say.

(female, 42, single-parent household of two)

The neglect by kin, possibly in part due to migration to the city and the increasing barrier of distance, did not seem to be compensated for by vibrant and supportive urban neighbourhoods. Instead, what was reported was an increasingly individualistic culture in which people looked after themselves or else took time out to spread hurtful gossip and rumours that left people feeling threatened and estranged.

I have no friends in this neighbourhood. If I do (make friends), I'll get hurt. It's easier for me to keep my heart closed to myself. I became a fool here. They even sell my name (talk about me).... I became physically very sick because of stress.

(female, 42, single-parent household of two)

The national welfare system in South Korea has strong expectations that family should be the primary provider of support and that accessing such support is a precondition to applying for and becoming a 'deserving' recipient of the social assistance programme. In contexts where people had no direct access to informal support from family, neighbours, or friends, they were completely stuck, unless they could successfully apply to receive the NBLSS.

Depression and Despair

Respondents very commonly and openly talked of times, either currently or in the past, when they felt depressed and some even talked of having contemplated suicide. On occasion, this was linked to people's sense of rejection and social isolation; at other times it reflected the hard choices imposed by the circumstances of poverty itself.

Traditional Korean society, a culture shaped by Confucian values, relied on the network of family relatives to support those in need. It was an assumption strongly built into state policy that drove the economic recovery in the aftermath of the Korean War, a war that had destroyed so much of the

179

country's infrastructure and resulted in mass poverty. Government resources were directed almost entirely towards supporting economic growth, leaving the family to cope with the inevitable casualties of structural change. This proved generally feasible while the economy continued to expand and growth in inequality was constrained, although those families missing out on the benefits of growth were often placed under considerable strain. The imposition of the International Monetary Fund (IMF) structural adjustment programme brought with it prolonged unemployment at the end of the 1990s and an increasing reliance on casual employment. As a result, families—radically reshaped by rapidly falling birth rates in conjunction with a significant increase in the divorce rate—have been much less equipped to support their poorer members. Although social assistance has been put in place to help mitigate the impact of rapid social change and increasingly irregular employment, it is still premised on strong extended families willing or responsible to be the first defence against poverty. When this was not the case, as was particularly common among older respondents who had vivid recollections of strong filial piety promoted by Confucianism, they felt rejected, despairing, and thoroughly humiliated.

> Even my children won't give me a call. I think I know why those people on the news decide to take their own lives. Feeling betrayed, depressed, and so cut off from your own family ties, tired from this kind of life situation. But I'm trying not to go to the suicidal state of mind. I exercise and try and live a healthy long life even if I am very lonely and depressed.
>
> (male, 71, single-person household)

But the depression that so many respondents talked about, sometimes requiring clinical intervention, was not only a product of rejection by family and friends. It arose too from what they described as a sense of personal failure in a society that increasingly prioritizes economic success and attributes it to individual effort and ability. The talk of depression was in part an expression of the frustration that respondents were experiencing deprivation while others in society were enjoying the products of economic growth, as was widely celebrated on television and in advertisements. It also stemmed from seeking to cope with the pressures imposed by consumerism, pressures brought into the family through the expectations of children but equally lodged in the minds of adults as the epitome of a good life. Sometimes, however, adults noted surprise that their children did not complain more, accepting the need to go without or put up with stigmatizing circumstances.

> My daughter has no problem. . . . You know her friends and girls of her age can be quite embarrassed about it, but she just says God feeds us. When some aid comes, she says God did it for me and that she is thankful for it. She is a rare kind, so I'm very thankful. I was worried that her pride will get hurt with such things, but no.
>
> (female, 42, single-parent household of two)

> My first child has a very strong sense of self. So I was worried about [applying for] this [benefit]. But to my surprise, the child said 'why don't you just give it a go?', so I asked 'would you be okay?' And he showed his consent to applying for it. So I applied for it.
>
> (female, 51, two-parent household of four)

Despite such stoicism on the part of their children, parents nevertheless tended to blame themselves and feel guilty for being unable to afford things they needed and wanted.

The social isolation described by participants was both a product of trying to avoid situations in which expenditure or reciprocity was demanded and an explicit retreat from society as a result of feelings of inadequacy to meet the required standard of living similar to the family or neighbourhood community. At times, too, people were forced by circumstances to entertain actions that were humiliating simply in order to survive. One respondent recalled what it was like being thrust into poverty by the breakdown of her marriage, resulting in prostitution and suicide becoming the only options she felt she had at the time:

> There were times of course when I wanted to die. That was when I had just divorced in my late twenties. I was quite seriously conflicted and split between ending my life or working in a bar as a hostess abandoning my body and life.
>
> (female, 42, single-parent household of two)

Coping simultaneously with poverty and the shame, isolation, and depression it provoked was an issue spontaneously raised by several people interviewed. Important for some was the ability to feel independent. Sometimes this independence was facilitated by claiming social assistance, people believing that seeking authorized help demonstrated an effort to cope with financial hardship which did not impose on family ties or generate unnecessary dependence on family. This incentive sometimes prevailed over the stigma of claiming benefits, although it was often the case that being in receipt of social assistance remained undisclosed to others. The assistance provided was just barely enough to avert the need to ask relatives for help and meant not having to reveal to others how little one had to live on.

> I think receiving the government assistance is still better than feeling embarrassed. If you don't let others know of your difficulties, no one knows. Nobody is going to knock on your door for you or understand your problems if you lock yourself up in your room.
>
> (female, 46, two-parent household of three)

For other people, shame was avoided by deliberately retreating from situations in which it might be provoked, such withdrawal often resulting in going without in order to avoid the shame of asking.

> I do not feel weaker to my siblings (who are better-off), and when we fight I fight confidently, because I have never asked or received any help from them. I did it all on my own until today.
>
> (female, 42, single-parent household of two)

One person felt that it was possible to change one's character or personality in order to cope, a strategy more consonant with Confucian than Western culture, which regards character as largely fixed, although such a strategy is not inconsistent with the aims of cognitive behavioural therapy, used widely in the West to manage depression (Walker, 2014; Wiles et al., 2013; Bower et al., 2011).

> You have to keep trying to change your personality. Consciously. Because if I look depressed, it becomes hard to relate with other people. And if I cannot die anyway, I made up my mind to live fun.
>
> (female, 46, two-parent household of three)

> There are too many wounds (in my heart) really.... Even when I think of it again now, it surges up like mad, but that is my loss if I do that.
>
> (female, 42, single-parent household of two)

Dealings with Social Assistance Officialdom

If, for some, claiming social assistance offered respite from the financial dependency on family that poverty creates, for many others, interactions with officialdom ratcheted the sense of shame to a more intense level. This is partly because of attitudes towards social assistance first introduced in 1961 and largely modelled on the residual, strictly regulated charitable provisions that had previously been available as a result of foreign aid in the post-Korean War period, first under American military rule and subsequently under President Lee Seung-Man (Huh, 2009; Kim, 2010). The current system, NBLSS, while couched within a progressive rhetoric of civil rights, remains residual, enforces familial responsibility for extended kin, and operates a workfare system that differentiates between people on the grounds of employability, and discriminates against those who are work-capable by paying them lower benefits (Jo and Walker, 2013).

> It did hurt my pride... It's not that I wanted to receive this kind of help, is it? It was inevitable. It greatly hurt my pride... I always think about graduating, exiting this status soon, but there is no way is there? It hurts my pride and I want to be independent in my living.
>
> (male, 71, single-person household)

The structure and implementation of NBLSS is such that it explicitly replaces dependence on the family with dependence on the state; financial independence is to be acquired through work but such is the mismatch between the circumstances of some NBLSS recipients and the conditions it imposes that work enforced while in receipt of benefits becomes a form of entrapment. Moreover, the means test used applies to spouses, direct family kin, and their spouses, stretching to siblings, grandparents, and grandchildren in the case of families living together. Applicants have to solicit the family members to be means tested, irrespective of the nature and quality of their relationship with the kin in question. As such, applicants for benefit not only have to reveal their own perilous circumstances to kin but also expose their kin to bureaucratic intrusion. They run the risk of being rejected by kin and, even if not, the structure of the means test is such that relatives may have to set aside half or even more of their income to support kin beyond the nuclear family. This makes them explicitly dependent on both kin and state, and the reality is that the financial contributions expected of kin are often not forthcoming, such that NBLSS recipients frequently have to make do with fewer resources than the state legislators anticipated (Yeo, 2005). One respondent was denied access to benefits because of the house owned by her 90-year-old parents, the shame at this failed application compounded by the shame that she felt from being supported by her elderly parents rather than her supporting them.

People capable of work amongst the NBLSS recipients were obliged to participate in public service in order to receive the living expense element of the assistance. This provision creates a distinction between those perceived as 'deserving' applicants, who physically cannot work, and those who are 'undeserving' who must be made to work and who become targets of suspicion and claims of abuse. Public service work undertaken while receiving NBLSS is therefore not an expression of dignity, effort, or commitment but is seen as a government-imposed badge of shame. It further limits the extent to which applicants can search for mainstream employment, which, if acquired and results in monthly income exceeding the NBLSS threshold, results in the loss of the entire benefits attached to the status of recipient the very next month. Hence, work-capable recipients of NBLSS spoke of how they often became trapped in low-paid work that was publicly recognized as not 'proper' employment and which offered few long-term career prospects (Ku, 2006). They consequently remained on benefit, or at risk of needing benefits, for long periods and were subjected to repeated enquiries into their circumstances by the NBLSS authorities.

> Let's say a young woman gave birth to a baby, and say she is in her twenties, then this mother in her twenties has to live for the rest of life being poor! Helping (through government) to escape poverty is a good thing, but it doesn't quite turn out like that. I want to work to better support my daughter, but as soon as I earn

more than the minimum threshold, I lose the status right away. So I'm always here in the situation of looking only at the 700,000 Won (£370 per month) living assistance. They should set a five-year or 10-year plan for us to be supported by the government while we try to seek extra income through work.

(female, 42, single-parent household of two)

Applications for NBLSS were described as so daunting that one respondent, a single parent with five children, withdrew her application in order to avoid the intrusive and what she considered to be thoroughly and unbearably shaming interrogation to which she was being subjected. Ordinarily, family-wide means tests are repeated regularly for as long as benefits are claimed, with recipients being required once or twice a year, depending on the type of benefit, to submit documentary proof substantiating their continuing inability to independently support themselves and evidence of the unwillingness or inability of kin to assist them. The amount of documentation is considerable and the task stressful, since there is always the risk that benefits will be withdrawn, and even if not, recipients are forced to repeatedly demonstrate their financial and personal inadequacy. The evidence suggests that, while NBLSS did sometimes help alleviate the financial stress of poverty, it regularly added to the psychic pain of its recipients. This is arguably, to some extent, purposive, in that the architects of the post-2000 reforms were deeply concerned about the possibility of moral hazard, people choosing to live on benefits rather than working, and therefore prioritized systems designed to deter abuse (Park, 2002).

Coping and Othering

Like people in poverty everywhere, respondents coped by seeking to maximize their income through work, disposing of saleable assets, borrowing, careful money management, and by going without. For the most part, people were resilient and effective in eking out their limited resources. While repeatedly frustrated in their ambitions, they emphatically denied having given up; those who were younger had hopes for the future, while those who were older invested their hopes in children and grandchildren.

However, respondents found it much more difficult to cope with their own sense of failure and especially the opprobrium they encountered from others. One common strategy was what Ruth Lister (2004) calls 'othering'. Not wanting to accept that they were financially or morally at the bottom of Korean society, people occasionally looked for others who were worse-off than they were. Such people served as counterfactuals ('they did what I would not do and are what I am not'), as loci for compassion or contempt, or as scapegoats ('it is their fault'). The bureaucratic distinctions embedded within NBLSS, between the '*Soo-Geup-Ja*'—those receiving benefits—and the '*Cha-Sang-Wee*'—the near poor—and between the work-capable and those unable to work, provided a definite framework for othering. Intonation in the way they spoke indicated a certain pride in not being categorized as 'worse-off' ('*Soo-Geup-Ja*') even if this meant that they received less or near nothing in terms of benefits.

Often respondents distanced themselves from their neighbours in terms of their social standing and behaviour, or else spoke in the third person about matters that were actually of personal concern. They spoke about other people who felt 'really ashamed' and 'servile' by having to receive government assistance, and one respondent described a neighbourhood as full of people who 'were very jealous of one another', who were 'horribly gossipy', and who had 'dropped to the bottom of life' and were 'hanging onto life just before committing suicide':

> This is not a place a human being can live in. I was hurt a lot by people after moving here. So I just mostly stay at home.
>
> (female, 42, single-parent household of two)

Respondents had tales, too, about other people, none of whom they knew personally, but whom they had heard rumours about, who did not deserve their status as '*Soo-Geup-Ja*', having lied and cheated when making their claims for benefit. They were sure that such people existed because other people had told them, and furthermore the media carried numerous stories about the many people, who unlike themselves, were clearly abusing NBLSS. Sometimes such negative understandings of the social assistance system and the stigma attached to it were given as reasons why respondents themselves had not claimed benefits to which they thought they were entitled, illustrated by the words of one single mother of five children who was living in extreme circumstances: 'I don't want to live like that. Like a beggar'.

Another device that respondents used to ameliorate the shame that they felt and to deflect that which they encountered was to detach themselves emotionally from others and the consumerism around them. This, in turn, required a strong sense of self, sometimes aided by religious adherence, and ran the risk of reinforcing the social isolation often imposed by poverty. Rejecting money as a source of happiness was comparatively easy when money was in short supply, but it required more courage to ignore the things that money could bring, especially when those things could be interpreted as aspects of good citizenship or parenting. As already noted, South Korean culture prioritizes education and the expensive extracurricular activities, both public and private, that accompanies schooling. Therefore, to say that such things do not matter, even if they cannot be afforded, is to stand in opposition to powerful social forces.

> When I meet the mothers of my children's friends, they brag about it. 'My kid goes to learn piano, kendo, and painting' [private classes and institutions]. I do not admire those moms. Kids should learn to study on their own and should be playing outside at their age.
>
> (female, 43, single-parent household of six)

Faced with such pressures, some respondents turned to alternative value systems for moral support, while others claimed to rely on their own strength of character and their need to survive.

> If it wasn't for my faith in Jesus, I would have already done something. Either take drugs and kill myself, or kill someone. If it wasn't for my faith, I cannot find any happiness in my life. It gives me confidence too. This is how I live these days, when someone says something [cruel and hurtful], I just ignore it and say, 'whatever'. If I care about it, it's me who gets stressed and falls sick.
>
> (female, 42, single-parent household of two)

Separated by Shame

Despite unparalleled economic success, poverty has not been eradicated in South Korea, and since the Asian financial crisis of 1997, poverty has returned in different guises and on a new scale. However, poverty is viewed as an unsettling blemish on Korea's record book, and the political mantra of economic success built on collective effort leaves little sympathy for individuals who are not financially successful. A system of residual social assistance is in place to prevent destitution, but it is carries a heavy stigma for those who have no choice but to claim it, designed as it is to reinforce the 'work ethic' and to deter abuse.

Material hardship, if not destitution, is certainly evident in South Korea, as reflected in the life experiences of the people interviewed. But more importantly, the interviews revealed that the task of material survival was made much harder by the sense of isolation felt by those experiencing poverty. Socially surrounded by economic success, it was hard for respondents not to view themselves as society's failures or as standing in the least desirable social status. While they were generally willing to face up to the struggles of making ends meet with limited resources, they frequently described their shame at being at the bottom and were often resigned to depression and despair at not being able adequately to do what mattered most to them, provide for their children. Older respondents reflected the changes that they felt the community had undergone, such that it no longer had either the capacity or perhaps the interest to care for those with limited resources. To have to resort to claiming social assistance in effect amounted to being rejected by one's kin and when in receipt of such assistance, to being treated with contempt by officials and peers. If not explicitly rejected, the temptation was nevertheless to withdraw or step back from society in order to avoid embarrassing scenes, negative comments, and stigma through association.

References

Bower, P., Knowles, S., Coventry, P.A., and Rowland, N. (2011) 'Counselling for mental health and psychosocial problems in primary care', *Cochrane Database Systematic Review*, 9, CD001025.

Huh, S. (2009) 'The 10th anniversary of enactment of National Basic Livelihood Security Act: The limits and tasks', *Citizen and World*, 16(12): 274–89.

Jo, Y. and Walker, R. (2013) 'Self-sufficiency, social assistance and the shaming of poverty in South Korea', in Gubrium, E., Pellissery, S., and Lødemel, I. (eds) *The Shame of It: Global perspectives on anti-poverty policies*, Bristol: Policy Press.

Kim, M. (2010) 'A change of public awareness and attitude towards the National Basic Social Security System and its implications', *Health & Welfare Forum*, KiHASA, September, 39–52.

Ku, I. (2006) *Income Inequality and Poverty in Korea—Worsening Income Distribution and the Need for Social Policy Reform*, Seoul: Seoul National University Press.

Lister, R. (2004) *Poverty*, Cambridge: Polity Press.

Park, N. (2002) 'Issues on the National Basic Livelihood Security Program', *Health & Welfare Forum*, KiHASA, May, 5–16.

Walker, R. (2014) *The Shame of Poverty: Global perspectives*, Oxford: Oxford University Press.

Wiles, N., Thomas, L., Abel, A., et al. (2013) 'Cognitive behavioural therapy as an adjunct to pharmacotherapy for primary care based patients with treatment resistant depression: results of the CoBalT randomised controlled trial', *Lancet*, 381: 375–84.

Yeo, Y. (2005) 'National Basic Livelihood Security: Selection criteria, benefits rules, and problems', *Health & Welfare Forum*, KiHASA, March, 67–79.

15

(Relative) Poverty in a Rich, Egalitarian Welfare State

Experiences from Norway

Erika Gubrium and Ivar Lødemel

Introduction

In the past two decades, poverty has become a focal concept for Norwegian welfare activation strategies promoting labour market inclusion of the unemployed living in poverty (Lødemel and Trickey, 2001; Hagen and Lødemel, 2010; Gubrium et al., forthcoming/2014). The Norwegian work approach (*arbeidslinja*) has intensified efforts to make the receipt of social assistance a last resort, to be accessed only when all other employment-seeking efforts have failed. In this sense, work-related activities are intended, in policy terms, to help individuals 'help themselves' (Hvinden, 1994). As described in Chapter 8, those persons officially defined as 'poor' in Norway are, for the most part, those also most likely to be recipients of social assistance (Halvorsen and Stjernø, 2008). It is, therefore, Norwegian social assistance recipients to whom we draw attention in this chapter.

Informed by the discursive themes emerging from the analysis of Norwegian literature and described in Chapter 8 of this volume, we conducted in-depth interviews with twenty-eight recipients of social assistance in Norway, all of whom were either receiving social assistance benefits or participating in a new human capital–oriented work activation programme. Those participating in the activation programme were receiving a higher level of financial support, paid in the form of wages, rather than benefits. Participants were recruited through caseworkers at local labour and welfare offices in three study sites: a small, coastal Norwegian town; a wealthy city suburb; and an industrial city suburb, two of which were located in or near to Oslo.[1] The majority of the respondents were women, with men making up just over one-third of the sample (n = 10). Twelve respondents were 'ethnic Norwegian' (born in Norway), six had immigrated to Norway at a young age, and ten had immigrated to Norway as adults. All 'non-ethnic' Norwegian respondents had migrated from non-Western countries. Twenty respondents had one child or more, and most children were still living at home at the time of interview.

Many of the respondents lived in circumstances that had resulted in joblessness and social marginalization. Our broad working question was 'What does living in economically difficult circumstances mean to you?' The interviews sought to elicit 'thick descriptions' (Geertz, 1973) of participants' everyday experiences of poverty and how they felt about their participation in Norway's anti-poverty programmes. We applied content and discourse analyses to interview transcripts, paying special attention to the ways in which the experiences of poverty were discursively linked to feelings of shame; the perceived underlying social, economic, and cultural causes of these feelings; and the different ways in which participants responded to their circumstances and the emotions they evoked.

How Contexts Shape the Poverty–Shame Experience

Two overriding themes emerged within respondents' descriptions of their current experiences of poverty. They spoke of poverty in relative terms, contrasting their own situation with that of their peers: members of their local community, parents of their children's friends, close relatives, and their own friends. They also contrasted their current circumstances with earlier points in their life when they were better-off. Some described previous times when they were working, while those who had migrated to Norway from other countries frequently reminisced about a life of higher status enjoyed in their former home countries.

Marginal Poverty and a Marginalized Identity

Interviewees often referred to the socio-economic norms of their local communities when describing the shame they attached to their own economic difficulties. Those living in an affluent suburb of Oslo in particular spoke of

---

[1] The three sites where chosen to reflect differences in economic, health, level of social assistance receipt, and demographic profiles. They included two larger towns, in and around Oslo, and one smaller town, enabling a comparative investigation of the experiences of poverty in industrial versus a rural/coastal setting.

feeling strain and shame due to the 'embarrassingly clear differences' between their own economic situations and those of others in the community. Such feelings were most pronounced when respondents described their efforts to avoid the 'evil eye' by making sure that their children could match the standards of both their classmates and their classmates' parents. In contrast, only one respondent living in a less prosperous industrial suburb of Oslo described experiencing this same sort of pressure.

Relative poverty was not, however, only a matter of concern in the wealthier suburbs. It was also a source of shame for many of those living in a small fishing town on the west coast of Norway, where economic difficulties and struggles with drug addiction have become increasingly prominent in recent years. Social assistance recipients within Norway's small towns are perhaps more likely to feel stigmatized due to the increased likelihood of others knowing about their welfare status. As one respondent, a woman in her early thirties who had struggled with drug addiction in the past, put it, 'they *know*, in a way'. Intimate knowledge about people's economic circumstances within small communities may exacerbate both internalized and externally imposed feelings of shame (Solheim, 2010). While respondents from the wealthier Oslo suburb described their struggles in following social norms in material terms, respondents from the coastal area emphasized the challenge of maintaining 'normal' or respectable identities. Any deviation from the norm was more noticeable given the size of the town and the close nature of the social networks within.

The shame of relative poverty was largely framed in terms of one's current circumstances, yet those respondents with children also spoke of their anxiety concerning their ability to ensure that their children would, in the future, be able to fully participate in so-called normal society. Many described what they saw as the intergenerational effects of receiving social assistance benefits. While some engaged in 'othering', by referring to what they considered the poor example set by other parents in their midst; they also spoke of a palpable dread that they themselves might also eventually fall into this cycle. They equally referred to the importance of finding work so as to avoid this cycle and provide a normal balanced life for their children.

Looking Back: A Fall in Status

Interviewees frequently discussed the temporal dimensions of their experiences of poverty, comparing their current circumstances not only with their future prospects but also with their former economic status. Many contrasted past professional working lives with their current unemployment, noting that this fall in standing seemingly contradicted the Norwegian expectation of upward social mobility. Approximately half of the respondents had previous work experience, and those who had been employed continuously for significant lengths of time expressed pride in their former standing as 'good workers' and 'civic participants'.

A corollary to expressing this pride seemed to be the marked shame attached to what respondents described as a decrease in social rank. Many attached shame not only to past mistakes and actions, but also to the dissonance between these former statuses and their current ones. They felt shame over a current lack of material possessions and troubled identities in relation to the normative expectations of their surrounding communities and peers, as well as in relation to their own past expectations as to how their lives would take shape. Several felt so uncomfortable with their changed identities that they attempted to hide their new circumstances, either by avoiding friends or telling friends and family that they were, in fact, employed. One respondent, a man in his early fifties with extensive work experience, said that everyone whom he knew thought he was working because he was so 'ashamed for not having a job' that he had not told them otherwise. Another had told his partner he had work because she might not understand why he did not have work after so many years and he 'didn't understand it either'.

Reduced social standing also emerged as a common experience among those respondents who had moved to Norway from another country. While many noted they had left difficult living conditions in their former countries, they also described the consequences of experiencing a rapid fall in status upon moving to Norway. This change, for the majority, was a source of shame, as it was in direct contrast to earlier expectations of a better life— hopes that many noted were still held by those family members who had remained abroad. As with those focusing on an earlier working life, several also attached shame to a loss of professional status that they had previously enjoyed.

Interviewees from outside Norway also referred to a degree of cultural marginalization, citing difficulties in building the networks necessary to navigate the welfare system or find secure employment. Several also focused on certain miscalculations they felt they had made, either in choosing to move to Norway, or, subsequent to the move, decisions which they felt had worsened rather than improved their economic situation. These individuals attached shame to the idea of returning or reporting back to loved ones in their home country that they had not found the success that they or everyone else hoped for. Some immigrant respondents focused specifically on the shame evoked from the negative impact their reduced circumstances had had on their family members, most notably, their children.

Arenas of Shaming

Respondents described specific mental or physical spaces in which either the negative social consequences of their low incomes were amplified or the threat of being 'outed' as a 'welfare dependant' loomed. Thus welfare institutions, schools, and communal social settings were all arenas within which participants described being made to feel acutely uneasy about their marginal economic circumstances.

Social Assistance Programmes

In keeping with the findings from the analysis of Norwegian literature (see Chapter 8), respondents frequently described how the emphasis on social mobility permeating a strong welfare state translates into a heightened sense of shame arising from their failure to achieve such mobility or even to make ends meet. Respondents both attached shame to and felt publicly shamed by their dependence on public finances. Reflecting findings from the literature analysis, many described the embarrassment they felt—or had felt, if now engaged in a work activation programme—in association with what they phrased as being on the 'lowest rung' of social assistance. They said that society viewed them as 'leeches' and they themselves noted with chagrin that they were unable to enjoy full citizenship because they did not pay taxes or contribute to the pension system.

All of those participating in the research were either currently receiving social assistance benefits or were enrolled in a work activation programme targeted at social assistance recipients. While some had received social assistance only for a short period, approximately half of our respondents were long-term claimants. Those participating in the activation programme, however, received a higher and more constant level of economic support, paid as wages rather than as a benefit cheque. Participants were engaged in activities designed to simulate a regular workday. Programme participants got 'that job feeling' by paying taxes on their economic benefits and by accruing a pension. This new opportunity challenged the situation of marginality that many social assistance recipients had previously faced.

Within the institutional setting, participants remaining on social assistance repeatedly described how caseworkers and society viewed them as especially 'needy', 'lazy', or 'dependent'. Moreover, they felt demeaned by the fact that institutions and specific caseworkers had such low expectations of them, most emphasizing that, as social assistance recipients, they could expect little more than benefit payments from the Norwegian welfare system. Some described a lack of daily structure and positive support or follow-up by caseworkers—resulting in, as one put it, having 'no rhythm'. This had led to an unfortunate cycle of dependency, demotivation, cynicism, and frustration both with the system and with their own inability to transition into better circumstances. One respondent, a man who had been on social assistance for many years, contrasted his goals with the reality of his life on social assistance, noting, 'you want to work' and yet 'you watch the clock, you become lazy ... that's not what I want to be'. Another described the 'shame' she felt from 'year after year after year after year ... being a burden to other people'.

Furthermore, respondents described a lack of continuity and security in their interactions with the welfare system. Social assistance benefits in Norway are, for the most part, discretionary allocations made by individual caseworkers assigned to each claimant—the same caseworkers charged with providing guidance and support. Respondents spoke of frequent changes in their caseworkers and consequent inconsistencies in the range and level of discretionary benefits offered, as well as in the conditions applied to the granting of such benefits and privileges. Thus, caseworker discretion became a site for arbitrary decisions and judgement, a demeaning experience that led to the perception of extreme insecurity for many of our respondents.

Combined with the wearisome interactions with caseworkers, several respondents described feeling frustration and shame at having to 'lower' themselves to accommodate institutional expectations concerning their neediness. One, a man in his early thirties with little work experience, noted that when on social assistance, 'you don't look people in the face'. As another described it: 'The more pitiful you look, the more help you receive'. Unsurprisingly, given Norway's heavy social, cultural, and institutional emphasis on the importance of working (Stjernø and Øverbye, 2012), most respondents immediately referenced their current or potential employment situation when gauging their future circumstances. Expectations concerning work in Norway are even more explicit in contemporary institutional discourses tied to a relatively new, human capital–based work activation programme (Gubrium and Lødemel, 2014). Participants reflected on how they hoped to sooner or later find 'normal' paid work and to experience the security, inclusion, and balance that this status represented. The lack of consistent, individualized support described earlier, however, meant that most felt that successfully finding work was only possible if they were 'active' enough in battling what was otherwise a frustratingly slow and unresponsive system.

Frønes (2001) describes the modern experience of shame as a distinctly individualized phenomenon, associated with the failure to realize individual goals or potential. Our chapter on general public perceptions in Norway concerning poverty (see Chapter 21) similarly demonstrates the overwhelming emphasis placed on individual responsibility. The respondents we spoke with, likewise, stressed the sense of blame they felt that society placed on them, especially (and as the analysis of Norwegian literature suggests) within the context of Norway's generous welfare state provisions. The sense of shame associated with this individual failure was further exacerbated given the presence of the activation programme for those who were not able to engage in work or for those whose work qualifications and skills made them weak candidates in the broader labour market (Gubrium and Lødemel, 2014). These individuals were either left to remain on what was a new bottom tier of social assistance or dreaded re-applying for social assistance when their participation in the activation programme failed to yield waged work.

Our analysis also revealed gender and ethnicity dimensions to the shame associated with the work approach. Since Norway's modern welfare state has been structured to increase the conditions for women's autonomy in the arenas of labour participation and caregiving (Skevik, 2006), it might be expected that there are minimal differences in how women and men experience shame and social shaming in relation to poverty. The literature analysis (see Chapter 8), however, suggested that women might face an increased risk of poverty, social exclusion, and heightened poverty-induced shame. Norway's welfare offerings have, in large part, been predicated upon a 'male breadwinner model', in which many of the country's more generous benefits are tied to the expectation of full-time employment outside the home. The increased autonomy of women does not, however, necessarily eradicate the particular burden of care associated with the social expectations connected to motherhood, nor society's gendered norms concerning the proper roles, behaviours, and sacrifices of being a woman (O'Connor, 2004; Orloff, 2008).

In fact, many of the women we spoke with had either spent years at home caring for children (in Norway or outside Norway) and had turned to social assistance at the point when a stable partnership had broken down or when partners were continuously unable to find or hold down work. Many had had limited work experience in the service sector or no work experience at all. One respondent, who had had a long and frustrating search for work, described the crushing disappointment of realizing that a potential employer 'really just wanted to hire me to have sex'. Another, a woman who had moved to Norway for a marriage that had ended badly spoke of the 'shamefully' low benefit cheque she received in exchange for her work as an on-call weekend aide at a nursing home. Difficulties in finding work also took on ethnic dimensions. Many of the male and some of the female respondents who had immigrated to Norway as adults, despite their accumulated work histories in other countries, were unable to find work after their move. One, a woman who had immigrated to Norway as an adult, contrasted having owned a retail business in her home country with now working 'like a slave . . . each and every day' for a similar sort of business in Norway, lamenting that the business would 'never hire' her, because 'it's free for them'. The interviewees most confident about finding work tended to be Norwegian-born males with some experience in the technology or skilled trades sector. Thus, the sense of shame tied to an identity as an unemployed member of society, and the level to which the human capital work approach may have mitigated shame, must also be understood within the context of labour market possibilities in contemporary Norway and life trajectories more generally. Given the heavy institutional and societal emphasis on work, shame appeared to be heightened for those characterized as being furthest away from the labour market and as a result considered the most 'vulnerable' recipients of social assistance.

School and Social Networks

Those respondents with children emphasized the importance of finding waged work as a means of moving out of a cycle of poverty and providing a normal or balanced life for their family. As parents, the topic of potential shame came up most keenly with reference to their children's experiences at school. The analysis of literature suggested that schools were a primary site of shaming for children from poor households. Respondents supported this notion, frequently referring to their own or their children's difficult school experiences when describing a sense of emotional strain associated with their poverty. Some described school as a space in which the pressure to have material possessions and resources was strongly felt and that this pressure rose as their children grew older and became more materially oriented and more status conscious. The pressure was not merely attached to relatively small cost items such as clothing and accessories, however, but was also clearly felt with respect to where and how one lived. One woman, for example, explained how she had been snubbed by another parent at her daughter's nursery school for driving a rusty old car. Another, a woman in her mid-thirties who had long searched for employment and had minimal work experience, described the feeling of having been revealed to be 'one of *those* poor people' at the birthday party of her daughter's classmate. Another described the strain he felt when his teenage daughter wanted to have her more affluent friends over to their simple apartment because it contrasted so sharply with the large, nice houses that her friends lived in. Similarly, many other respondents spoke of wanting to protect their children from the experience of feeling or understanding the challenging economic situation that they were facing. Some commented that the act of striving to provide for and shield their children from the negative consequences of hardship was their primary motivation to carry on.

As well as the potential shame attached to school, some adults also described feeling shame because they were unable to ensure that their children could fully participate in a range of social activities, including opportunities offered through the school, such as participation in sports teams or activity days, or other events like birthday parties or cinema trips with peers, which inevitably shaped the school experience. Yet others cited activities that involved family members—most notably, trips to family-owned cabins or to destinations south of Norway—that, when vividly recalled in school, helped to establish who one was and how well-off their families were.

The failure to make ends meet or to move ahead does not chime with the widely held Norwegian idea that all residents have a job and are doing well (Gubrium, 2013). Failure to meet these norms may be internalized and may result in loneliness and self-blame (Skårderud, 2001; Underlid, 2001), deepening the links between economic instability and social exclusion. Respondents described the social exclusion they experienced in connection with their economic situation as a chicken-and-egg phenomenon. Many emphasized their inability to partake in social activities with their peers, such as being unable to meet friends for a cup of coffee or being unable to shop in the stores frequented by most in town. Some tied this to economic difficulties, others to the emotional toll they experienced when meeting friends who were doing better financially. Several respondents also suggested that a lack of work-related social networks was what had made it more difficult to maintain a self-confident identity with friends and family. They noted the 'one-way' nature of friendships. One respondent, a single woman in her late fifties with past work experience, described herself as 'pretty social', but noted that 'you don't meet anyone when you've been at home for two years'. Thus, the potential for social exclusion was not only tied to one's material difficulties, but also to one's difficulties in keeping social networks together in the face of 'abnormal' circumstances.

Responses to Feelings of Poverty-Related Shame

Respondents described the various ways in which they sought to cope with feelings of shame or potential shame. Similar to what was found in the literature analysis (Chapter 8), some focused on the future and how they might change their circumstances. Some engaged in narratives of pride rather than shame, particularly in relation to their children and how they managed their roles as parents. Other responses, especially from those not engaged in the work activation programme, were more negative and included casting shame towards others or, having experienced shame head-on time and again and never finding a successful strategy to minimize its effects, resigning themselves to the inevitability of hardship.

'Moving Ahead'

A number of people, although they felt shame in relation to their dependence on state benefits, were able to mitigate these feelings by rationalizing the real difficulties they had faced in entering the labour market and the absolute necessity of public support to help them move forward. Most also noted that they would rather receive public support than be dependent on family or friends. Many engaged in the work activation programme spoke of the new possibility it offered them to eventually improve their circumstances, meet social norms and expectations regarding work, and escape from an internalized sense of blame. Many noted how these new possibilities had translated into an increased sense of motivation and purpose to move ahead on the trajectory back to 'normal'.

Several participants in the work activation programme also noted the increased social networking possibilities presented by the programme compared to general social assistance and how these had enabled them to place less individual blame on themselves for their situation. The programme's constant and higher benefit helped alleviate the insecurity and feeling of having to demean oneself or be demeaned in institutional interactions. Many activation programme participants described being happy not to be 'forgotten' anymore, to be given better guidance in finding the 'right direction' through more structured support, as well as greater economic security.

Pride in Parenting

Taking pride in their roles as parents was for many respondents a source of satisfaction and motivation. Several described how a change in status from single or childless to caregiver and provider had served to generate the 'new possibility' to build a better life. They spoke about their motivation stemming from a wish to shield their children from the direct material and psychological effects of their difficult economic circumstances. These respondents noted that their first priority was to find work or financial help for the benefit of their children and they were willing to sacrifice previous priorities (material goods, reputation, identity, a social life) in order to do so.

In this sense, public support had enabled many respondents to shift their identity from that of being thought of as a burden on family to one of a successful family provider. Interviewees described how the financial support, training, and work experience they received afforded them greater autonomy in sustaining their families. Some also spoke of public support as a means of enabling them to finance the peer-related activities that normalized their children's lives and ensured their social inclusion.

Casting Shame Outward: Blaming and 'Othering'

Respondents frequently blamed and shamed society and their peers both for their difficult circumstances and for failing to understand their plight. Several used the strategy of 'shaming upward'. These individuals spoke bitterly about those peers and family members who were living in better economic and social circumstances and who, they felt, lacked empathy for their situation. Several also directed shame to the welfare system or Norwegian state and described what they felt were misplaced priorities. Most common was the idea that the welfare system gave greatest attention to those individuals who 'screamed the loudest' and that they themselves as a result had not received the attention they deserved. In this way, the shame they experienced as welfare recipients was shifted, rhetorically at least, from an individual problem (about *them*) to a larger structural problem with the system or state.

Many respondents were less likely to attribute shame to belonging in an unfavourable position on the welfare hierarchy than they were to having been inappropriately placed by the system in a category that was *beneath* them. They spoke of their internalized shame at 'feeling categorized' with certain groups of people. Many engaged in 'othering' through their active refusal to identify as a typical social assistance recipient. Here, the *typical* identity, actions, and behaviours of those receiving social assistance were beneath them. Respondents cast disparaging remarks about these individuals, as well as about those engaged in the work activation programme, whom they characterized as overly dependent or demanding, not accountable for their situations, lazy, or unmotivated. One respondent, a woman in her late thirties who was engaged in the work activation programme after years on social assistance, noted that people receiving the same benefit were 'generally those who have some problems, whether it's either alcohol, or drugs, or... some other abuse'. Another, a man in his early forties who had spent several years on social assistance after extended drug addiction and was now engaged in the work activation programme, noted that social assistance recipients tended to be either 'people who... have given up a little, and who don't have any wishes and dreams' or 'people who are totally on a cruise and have a hundred dreams that don't match reality'.

Failing to Cope with Shame: Disillusionment

Several long-term recipients of social assistance, who had failed to find work and continued to face the daily struggle of making ends meet, suggested that they were disillusioned both with the welfare system and possibly with themselves. These respondents spoke of the stress and anxiety that they felt as a result of constant economic pressure, and emphasized that it was not so much a lack of money, but rather long periods of inactivity and lack of daily structure (mostly due to joblessness) that had led to low self-esteem, depression, and the loss of motivation. As one, a man in his late twenties with work experience limited by chronic back pain, put it, 'there's no point any longer'.

Along with long-term difficulties in finding work, many respondents suggested that they had been disappointed time and time again in accessing what they felt was deserved help from the welfare system in order to move forward with their lives. They spoke of a previous hope that was now gone. Their words suggested disillusionment and a resignation that they would not be able to change their lives for the better, as well as an irritation with themselves for having ever dared to hope for more. Most ascribed a sense of shame to their powerlessness to effect change.

Conclusion

Respondents described how the struggle to make ends meet was impacted by the social context of their everyday lives and life histories. They repeatedly contrasted their own economic circumstances with those of others around them. For example, life in well-heeled suburban Oslo offered a high standard to live up to, extreme for even this generally wealthy country, whereas the strain of material comparisons was perhaps less keenly felt in the more urban, industrial setting. Their experiences of hardship were also tempered by how much negative attention they perceived that the rest of society placed on their situation. For example, life in a small town appeared to bring with it a heightened possibility of being viewed negatively by others, and people were more likely to describe feeling shame as a result of their circumstances. Respondents also often recalled times in the past that had contrasted markedly to their current situations in terms of the material possessions they owned and the social networks that they were part of. The relative nature of their poverty mirrored closely the representations of the experiences of poverty found within Norwegian literary works (Chapter 8).

The shame related to difficult economic circumstances was felt most acutely in several arenas. The social assistance office and the label of social assistance recipient positioned people as marginal to the broader Norwegian norms of general well-being, as well as to the welfare state's intention of social mobility for all. While respondents saw social assistance as necessary in order to provide for families or to move beyond difficult times, the low expectations the system had of them and their general inactivity lowered their motivation, their sense of self-worth, and heightened their anxieties and fears about the future, while at the same time exacerbated their feelings of shame. While for many the work activation programme represented a new opportunity to move towards the labour market, for those not taking part, it further accentuated their sense of marginalization and exclusion. For those with children, school and the associated social spaces that it generated were prime settings within which material hardship was easily exposed. Respondents' efforts here focused, as far as possible, on normalizing children's experiences and sheltering them from the potentially negative social and psychological consequences of poverty.

Likewise, adults' own social networks were curtailed owing to both their financial inability to socialize with others and the inherent shame associated with their economic circumstances.

In order to make meaning of and negotiate the shame they experienced, respondents drew upon several broad strategies, some more positive than others. They described their reliance on social assistance as a stepping stone towards 'normal lives', the activation programme in particular offering them important possibilities. Respondents with children tended to describe the pride they felt in being parents and how parenthood had afforded them an identity through which they could move ahead with their lives.

Others, however, projected elsewhere both the internal and externally imposed shame that they felt. Shame was displaced upwards towards the Norwegian welfare system. It was also shifted downwards by 'othering' fellow social assistance recipients, thus distancing themselves from the typified uncaring, unmotivated, dysfunctional, and shameless character of 'most' other recipients. Several respondents described being disillusioned by years of struggle, feeling shamed by their local communities, and neglected by the welfare system that failed to facilitate their entry into work. Ultimately they had run out of ways to explain why they remained on the margins of society, the perpetual cycle of shame and powerlessness having resulted in the decision to 'give up'.

References

Frønes, I. (2001) 'Skam, skyldogæreidetmoderne [Shame, guilt and honor in modern times]', in Wyller, T. (ed.) *Perspektiver på skam, ære og skamløshet i det moderne [Perspectives on Shame, Honour and Shamelessness in Modern Times]*, Bergen: Fagbokforlaget.

Geertz, C. (1973) 'Thick description: Toward an interpretive theory of culture', in Geertz, C. (ed.) *The Interpretation of Cultures: Selected* Essays, 3–30.

Gubrium, E. K. (2013) 'Poverty, Shame and the Class Journey in Public Imagination', *Distinktion: Scandinavian Journal of Social Theory*. doi: 10.1080/1600910X.2013.809370.

Gubrium, E. K. and Lødemel, I. (2014) "Not Good Enough": Social Assistance and Shaming in a Strong Welfare State', in Gubrium, E. K., Pellissery, S., and Lødemel, I. (eds) *The Shame of It: Global Perspectives on Anti-poverty Policies*, Bristol: Policy Press.

Gubrium, E. K., Lødemel, I., and Harsløf, I. (forthcoming/2014) 'Norwegian activation reform on a wave of wider welfare state change: A critical assessment', in Lødemel, I., and Moreira, A. (eds) *Workfare Revisited.' The Political Economy of Activation Reforms*, Oxford: Oxford University Press.

Hagen, K. and Lødemel, I. (2010) 'Fattigdomstiåret 2000-2010: Parentes eller ny kurs for velferdsstaten?', in Frønes, I. and Kjølsrød, L. (eds) *Det Norske Samfunn*, Oslo: Gylendal Akademisk, pp. 284–307.

Halvorsen, K. and Stjernø, S. (2008) *Work, Oil and Welfare*, Oslo: Universitetsforlaget.

Hvinden, B. (1994) *Divided Against Itself: A Study of Integration in Welfare Bureaucracy*, Oslo: Universitetsforlaget.

Lødemel, I. and Trickey, H. (2001) *An Offer You Can't Refuse: Workfare in International Perspective*, Bristol: Policy Press.

O'Connor, J. S. (2004) 'Gender, citizenship, and welfare state regimes', in Kennett, P. (ed.) *A Handbook of Comparative Social Policy*, Cheltenham, UK, Edward Elgar, pp. 180–200.

Orloff, A. S. (2008) 'Feminism for a post-maternalist era: Gender equality projects in Europe and America', 'Challenging Boundaries' Social Policy Association Conference, Edinburgh, Scotland, 23 June 2008.

Skårderud, F. (2001) 'Tapte ansikter. Introduksjon til en skampsykologi [Lost faces. Introduction to a shamepsychology]', in Wyller, T. (ed.) *Perspektiver på skam, ære og skamløshet i det moderne [Perspectivesonshame, honor and shamelessness in modern times]*, Bergen: Fagbokforlaget.

Skevik, A. (2006) 'Working their way out of poverty? Lone mothers in policies and labour markets', in Bradshaw, J. and A. Hatland (eds) *Social Policy, Employment and Family Change in Comparative Perspective*, Cheltenham, UK: Edward Elgar, pp. 221–36.

Solheim, I. J. (2010) 'Sosialklient i liten kommune: mest på godt? [The social assistance client in the small municipality: mostly good?]', *Fontene Forskning [FO Tidsskrift]*, 1: 17–28.

Stjernø, S. and Øverbye, E. (2012) *Arbeidslinja: Arbeidsmotivasjonen og velferdsstaten*, Oslo: Universitetsforlaget.

Underlid, K. (2001) *Fattigdommens psykologi* [Poverty'sPsychology], Oslo: Det Norske Samlaget.

Section III
The Role of Media and Society in the Construction of Poverty-Related Shame

Preface

The final section of this volume turns our attention to the ways in which society in general generates and sustains discourses surrounding poverty and how these are implicated in the construction of poverty-related shame. With the exception of South Korea, focus group discussions were carried out with people not currently living in poverty in each of the study countries. In addition, in Uganda, India, China, Britain, and Norway a thematic analysis was conducted of a sample of newspaper articles to examine the language, associations, norms, and values projected in the print media about poverty and those most likely to experience it in each of the given contexts. The following chapters provide details of these analyses and what they reveal about how poverty is conceptualized and discussed by society in general.

The external dimensions of shame emerge starkly from the chapters, although in subtly different ways. Important insights emerge concerning the relative weight given to individual and structural causes of poverty, which in turn influence the nature of the debate in each of the different countries. In Uganda and Britain media discourses and representations of people living in poverty focus primarily on individual failings, the structural causes largely muted save for in Britain where the structure of the welfare state is implicated in the generation of 'laziness' and 'dependency'. In both these countries the media discourse is stark and often spiteful, the tone and language often derogatory and accusatory towards people experiencing poverty. Public opinion tended to mirror these dominant media discourses quite closely, although the tone of views appears less strident in Britain than in Uganda.

Importantly, this same synergy was found in Norway, where the debate about poverty primarily focused on individuals who failed to make the most of opportunities in a widely egalitarian society. Although the language and tone of the media was more subtle and less derogatory than in Uganda or Britain, a clear division was drawn between the 'deserving' and 'undeserving' poor. In Pakistan, where focus group discussions were held with adults and children currently not living in poverty, as well as with members of the national Parliament and elite civil society, once again the focus was on individual inabilities and lack of personal motivation or aspiration to improve one's circumstances. By contrast, evidence from India and China suggests some important distinctions between how poverty was portrayed in the media and the views expressed about it by the general public.

The chapters on the whole substantiate the views of people in poverty, detailed in the previous section, that those who were wealthier looked down on and criticized them. They also go a long way towards explaining the common feelings they described as a result of being among the lowest strata of each of the societies studied. As such, the chapters help build the final block in the construction of the poverty–shame nexus and at the same time offer some further clues about how we might begin to deconstruct it.

16

Poverty the Invisible and Inseparable 'Shadow'

Reflections from the Media and the Better-Off in Rural Uganda

Amon Ashaba Mwiine and Grace Bantebya-Kyomuhendo

Introduction

A clear argument is unfolding that poverty-related shame has the potential to bring about social exclusion and reduced social capital and cohesion (Sen, 2000; Chase and Walker, 2012; Walker et al., 2013; Walker, 2014) and that such shame is inherent in the framing, shaping, and delivery of many poverty eradication programmes (Bantebya-Kyomuhendo and Mwiine, 2013; Gubrium et al., 2013). This chapter analyses how, in the Ugandan context, the poverty–shame nexus arises not just from personal feelings of inadequacy and failure but is socially constructed by structures and discourses which impose shame on those living in poverty. It goes on to demonstrate how these processes of shaming can ultimately work to further undermine programmes designed to alleviate poverty. Drawing on the opinions of those not living in poverty gathered through focus group discussions and an analysis of a sample of newspaper coverage, the chapter demonstrates how the general public and the media in Uganda perceive poverty and its causes. It investigates the linguistic and cultural devices used to define poverty and people directly experiencing it, and considers the role that public and media attitudes and opinions about poverty play in the construction of the poverty–shame nexus.

Eight focus group discussions were conducted with men and women in selected local council villages in Western Uganda. Groups were made up of adult men and women from relatively rich households. The criteria for participation included ownership of land, living in a permanent home, possessing livestock (cattle, goats, or poultry), a means of transport (such as a motorbike or car), and having a secure and sustainable source of livelihood such as working in the public service, trading, or commercial farming. Indicators such as types of schools attended by participants' children were also considered. Men and women were organized into separate groups for convenience but also to enable each group to contribute and to share their views freely, as it has been shown that in mixed focus groups, discussions are often characterized by tension arising out of gender differences, and male and female participants do not contribute freely. Overall, sixty-four respondents (thirty-two men and thirty-two women) participated in the discussions.

Media analysis was conducted focusing on five widely read national newspapers in Uganda: *The New Vision*, *The Daily Monitor*, and *The Weekly Observer* are written in English, while *Bukedde* and *Orumuri Rwa Uganda*[1] are produced in the Luganda and Runyankole languages respectively. The article search used terms such as 'shame', 'poverty alleviation', 'exclusion', 'free education', 'UPE (Universal Primary Education), and NAADS (National Agricultural Advisory Services), to find relevant articles on poverty. The analysis covered newspaper articles published in the ten-year period 2001 to 2011 and included a total of 380 articles (*The Daily Monitor*: 120; *The New Vision*: 105; *Bukedde*: 90; *Weekly Observer*: 45; and *Orumuri*: 20).

Understandings of Poverty

Poverty as Material Deprivation

The focus group participants largely described people living in poverty in terms of material deprivation, indicated by their appearance, the type of houses they lived in, their diet, the sorts of household utensils they owned, the quality of their bedding materials and personal effects, the means of transport they were most likely to use, whether or not they had access to safe water and health care, and what sources of production of food they had access to. Physical descriptions of predominantly rural poverty typically conjured images of scarcity, inadequacy, and dirt, illustrated by the following observations expressed by various participants: 'unkempt hair', 'torn old

---

[1] *Bukedde* is a daily Luganda newspaper targeting central Uganda, where the majority of Baganda hail from, while *Orumuri* is a Runyankole/Rukiga newspaper largely targeting Banyankole, Bakiga, Batooro, Banyoro, and many other tribes from Western Uganda.

clothes', 'the children are not well looked after... and when you go to their house it is terrible', 'the courtyard is not swept and they don't have a garden', 'everything is dirty'.

Analysis of the media coverage highlighted the fact that poverty in all regions of Uganda is similarly described in absolute terms. The language of deprivation used defines poverty as a situation in which someone does not have enough money to pay for their basic needs such as food, water, clothing, shelter, health, and education. For example, people are repeatedly described across the media (in topical features, regional news pieces, letters, opinion pieces, and editorials) in terms such as 'economically neglected', 'unable to afford a safety pin to remove jiggers from their feet or to buy soap to wash their clothes or to bathe', or 'dying in misery' (see for example, The Daily Monitor Editorial, 2010; Okuma, 2011). Other discussions about poverty in these newspapers reflected the government's failure to deliver on its promises, the tendency of corrupt government officials to misappropriate resources meant for those in poverty, and the repeated failure of poverty alleviation policies more generally. Interestingly, these failings were frequently referred to as a 'shame' for any country to experience in the twenty-first century (Emojong and Bareebe, 2010).

Both the media analysis and focus group discussions show a common understanding of poverty in terms of what people own or do not own, and what they access in terms of material resources. In general, being 'poor' was not seen as the result of exploitation or oppression by others, or a circumstance of birth or a consequence of unequal access to opportunities but simply caused by a lack of income required to attain a level of consumption seen as acceptable in the community.

Poverty as a Gendered Phenomenon

As well as graphically describing the personal traits, habits, physical appearance, general disposition, and unfulfilled aspirations of their neighbours living in poverty, focus group participants also revealed an important gender dimension to poverty. It was argued in one focus group, for example, that material privation (*obunaku*) is just one type of poverty, while another form of poverty (*enaku*) is directly related to one's gender, especially to being male (*enaku y'ekisaija*). There was unanimity in a men's focus group that in their cultural setting, a man is destined from birth, his wealth or privation notwithstanding, to encounter in his lifetime unique domestic, marital, and relationship challenges that call for assertion of masculine power and a related secure gender identity as a household head and breadwinner. It is failure to meet such expectations, for example by failing to marry and start a family or to provide basics such as shelter and food for the family that typically constitute men's poverty (*enaku y'ekisaija*). Interestingly, and mirroring the analysis of literature and oral traditions in Uganda (Chapter 2), male physiological conditions such as erectile dysfunction, impotence, or male infertility were also highlighted among the key features of masculine poverty. The fact that no focus group participant mentioned feminine poverty (*enaku y'ekikazi*) may be an indicator that in the study area, being a woman is synonymous with living in poverty, and so its gender-specific dimensions go without saying.

The Experience of Poverty within Households

Analysis of findings from the focus group discussions and the media indicate a belief that poverty is experienced differently by children, women, and men within households, not only in terms of privation, but also the likely social consequences of hardship such as shame and stigma.

Children

Participants in focus group discussions frequently spoke of how children living in poor households experienced intolerable circumstances. Children's experiences of neglect, sexual abuse, malnutrition, child labour, and health problems, such as infestation with jiggers, were believed to be manifestations of the insidious evil of poverty. Findings from the focus group discussions indicated that children from poor families were considered to lack the basic necessities of life such as education, medical care, balanced nutrition necessary for proper growth, and adequate clothing. In cases in which children lack educational materials in schools, it was believed that they tended to compare themselves with others, leading to a sense of 'feeling small', causing them to withdraw socially and in some cases even to stop going to school. Discussions consistently associated children from poor families with hardships, shyness, and low self-esteem, especially when they spent time with children from better-off families. Participants acknowledged that these children were likely to be despised by their more affluent peers and sometimes treated badly because they belong to poor households. Some young people were said to be driven to adopt coping mechanisms that further alienated them. For example, one participant commented, 'young girls get pregnant at an early age because they want things that they cannot afford so they fall prey to older men and they drop out of school'.

Participants believed that the hardships experienced by these children were a direct consequence of their parents' preoccupation with attempting to deal with family privations. For instance, some children were said to be denied access by their parents to anti-poverty programmes like UPE, USE (Universal

Primary/Secondary Education), and free childhood immunizations, for a multitude of reasons. A participant in one of the men's focus groups commented, for example:

> Some babies from poor households are not taken for immunization because they have nothing to wear. Their parents feel ashamed to leave the house and go to the health centre.

In effect, parents living in poverty, through their efforts to alleviate immediate financial difficulties, were described as damaging their children's future and ultimately perpetuating their poverty, deprivation, and hopelessness. The children's lack of access to basic needs such as adequate nutrition, decent shelter, clothing, sanitation, and health care was believed to inevitably translate into shame, stigma, and feelings of inferiority and hopelessness that undermine their capabilities to effectively participate in their communities, now and in the future as social beings.

Women

When focus group participants talked about women, the emphasis was on women as wives. What emerged prominently is that acute poverty, especially a deficiency of basic material resources, impacts negatively on a wife's capacity to perform her expected productive and reproductive roles and responsibilities, which in turn undermines her agency and power in the household. In rural households in our study setting, where patriarchal values prevail and are much adhered to, the roles and responsibilities of a married woman are diverse and are culturally constituted as certain fundamental aspirations or dreams which every unmarried woman strives to attain at one time or another in her marriage. These same aspirations are reflected in the newspapers, particularly in articles featuring the failure of women and men to attain such aspirations.

Focus group participants stated that women in poor families are often compelled by chronic hardship into 'undignified' activities such as doing odd jobs outside the home, distilling and selling illicit gin, and engaging in illegal activities such as stealing and prostitution in an attempt to make ends meet. The media also portrayed women in situations of extreme poverty being forced into 'shameful' coping mechanisms. Several newspapers repeatedly linked women in poverty to prostitution, while *Mafaranga* (2011) noted that poverty is the leading cause of immorality among communities. This latter article cited a Catholic archbishop decrying the link between poverty and 'social evils' such as theft, poor health, illiteracy, homosexuality, and prostitution, among others. According to the archbishop, some of the clients 'smell like rats, while others are drunkards but poverty drives these girls to do it'.

The article adds that such 'immoral acts' lead to the 'shame' of those engaged in these acts.

Men

Information from the focus group discussions and media analysis suggests that men as husbands and family heads are confronted with unique and diverse challenges as a result of being poor. It emerged, for instance, that for a man, poverty does not only mean material hardship and substandard levels of consumption (*obunaku*), it also includes challenges associated with being male per se (*enaku y'ekisaija*). In the local language newspapers, poverty is predominantly portrayed as men's failure to provide the material things needed to sustain a marital relationship, with examples of women divorcing their husbands as a consequence (*Bukedde*, April 2002, May 2002, May 2003).

These pressures on men stem from the traditional expectations in patriarchal settings in Uganda, reflected in the communities in which the research was conducted as well as in media discourses. The research areas comprised communities from the Nyoro culture, which determines that men should marry, and adequately provide for their wives, children, and even extended family. Men have gender-specific practical duties within and outside the home. They are expected to construct houses and engage in income-generating productive activities such as growing cash crops, trading, cattle herding, fishing, or taking up government employment. Men are also expected to own and control all the productive assets such as land, movable assets, and all the income accruing from any commercial activity within and outside the home. Moreover, they are the key decision-makers, and must at all times assert themselves, both within the home and in the wider community. Among the Baganda in central Uganda, from where some of the newspaper articles were drawn, marriage is one of those social expectations that must be fulfilled. While all young girls are socialized right from childhood to cherish the institution of marriage, a man neglecting his social obligation of marrying and looking after his children and wife is unheard of. Any man who for one reason or another, including limited financial and material resources, deviates from these social patterns, is labelled 'poor', both in terms of material deprivation and his inadequacies as a male.

Given this broader conceptualization of male poverty, the psycho-social consequences of an inability to meet traditional patriarchal expectations, especially in a rural setting where traditional social norms, morals, and values are still much adhered to, can be severe. Indicators of these consequences become the substance of many media stories, illustrated in the sample headlines in Table 16.1.

Table 16.1. Sample of newspaper headlines focusing on inadequacies of men (Uganda)

Date	*Bukedde* Newspaper (Headlines in local language)	English translation
9 March 2002	*Abako baabammye omukazi lwa mitwalo 20 (80$)*	In-laws who had gone for an introduction ceremony[2] were denied the bride for failing to pay two hundred thousand Uganda Shillings (200,000 Ug. Shs equivalent to 80 USD) as a penalty fine for arriving late
17 April 2002	*Omufumbo eyakwatiddwa mu loogi ayogedde; 'Nkooye okunsuza ku kafaliso ka yinchi emu'*	A married woman caught in the lodge with another man speaks out: 'I am tired of sleeping on a one-inch mattress'
6 May 2002	*Obuwuulu bweyongedde lwa mbeera ya nfuna—bakugu: 'Abako abaavu babagobye'*	Bachelorhood has increased because of poverty, experts have revealed. Poor in-laws chased from an introduction ceremony for failing to pay bride price
1 December 2002	*Sifumbirwa mwavu—Bba bweyagobeddwa ku mulimu, n'asiba ebintu by'awaka byonna, nanoba*	I cannot be married to a poor man. When her husband was chased from his job, she packed all her household belongings and went back to her father's home
5 May 2003	*Eyabbye busuuti agitwale ku buko yasuze mu kaduukulu*	Man who stole a traditional dress and shoes to take to his fiancé for introduction is arrested and taken into police custody

In the focus group discussions, men in poverty were frequently described in terms such as 'too demoralized', 'desperate', 'alcoholic', 'frustrated', 'always reminded by the wife that he is not man enough', 'always insecure', 'always feeling disrespected by his wife'. Ultimately, being unable to meet the social obligations attributed to men was widely considered by participants to be detrimental, likely to lead to a sense of hopelessness, and loss of any power and agency.

Causes of Poverty

The Poor Responsible for their Own Poverty

Those taking part in focus group discussions had clear ideas regarding the causes of poverty. They spoke with conviction about the reasons why some of their neighbours were impoverished. Some intimated that they were talking from the personal experience of having previously faced poverty and hardship

---

[2] In Uganda, most of the tribal communities practice traditional marriage which is commonly known as "Kwanjula" meaning (introduction ceremony). However the Kwanjula ceremony is mostly practiced by the Buganda ethnic community. Among the Buganda "kwanjula" (introduction) ceremony takes place when an intending husband to be is introduced to the future in-laws and the community at large. The ceremony is taken as the official marriage and after the suitor is accepted, he can take his bride home with him as a wife. The ceremony requires the man to go with material things (bride price) to the girls home.

themselves. Newspaper articles, including editorials, features on anti-poverty programmes, and opinions pieces also elaborated on why people continued to live in poverty. Some of the causes of poverty were attributed to structural factors relating to circumstances beyond people's control, such as unequal access to public goods and services like education, health care, employment; as well as the government's failure to stabilize commodity prices. Other causes, however, were largely understood in terms of the unique behavioural and attitudinal differences of individuals. Character traits cited include a lack of focus in life; sheer laziness; a tendency to avoid regular employment; reckless living and spending, especially on alcohol, tobacco, and illicit sex. Another trait described as a cause of poverty was a tendency to internalize poverty as an unavoidable fate caused by supernatural factors including curses and inherent bad luck (*ekisirani*) that were perceived as being beyond the realms of individual control.

People living in poverty were strongly castigated, particularly in the media, for becoming lazy as a result of free government programmes such as the removal of graduated tax and access to free education. They were described in terms such as, 'ancient', 'traditional', and 'rigid', or unwilling to embrace change (Muzaale, 2010). It was stated that 'they want to get rich quick' and therefore opted for petty business ventures rather than engaging in agriculture. These views were expressed in the media in language that was heavily influenced by concepts of blaming and shaming, but also the 'othering' of those in poverty, such that a clear distinction was drawn between 'them' and 'us'. Similarly, focus group participants frequently referred to people facing economic hardship as 'them' or 'they', making claims such as, 'they have to change their attitudes to work'. Responding to prompts about how they interacted with people living in poverty, focus group participants made comments such as, 'we are conscious of them', and 'beware when you are dealing with them'.

In Chapter 9, we described how people living in poverty internalized their situation, perceiving themselves as less valuable than their more affluent peers, and as a result holding back from social interactions. Accordingly, participants in focus group discussions confirmed that they believed that people living in poverty occupied a position of inferiority. This intentional distancing by those who are better-off financially has the potential to socially isolate people living in poverty, provoking their withdrawal, not only from social settings but also from the programmes intended to alleviate their situation.

The responses of focus group participants combined with representations in the media suggest that poverty is essentially caused by factors operating and determined at the level of the individual and that those in poverty are largely to blame for their circumstances. Hence, most of the causes of poverty are seen as superficial, easily rectified by behaviour and attitudinal changes by those experiencing it. Tingatsiga (2002) pointed out in one newspaper article that Ugandans are to blame for being poor because, 'with the fertile soils, good climate, abundant natural resources and cheap labour, Ugandans need not to be poor'. In another article Bahikaho (2008) quoted a presidential adviser on poverty alleviation, Joan Kakwenzire, who blamed those in poverty for refusing to adjust to modern ways of doing things, emphasizing that the government will 'work with those who are quick to implement its policies'.

Deserving and Undeserving of Social Support

There was unanimity that government anti-poverty programmes are poten-tially valuable responses to the plight of people in poverty. Universal access to primary and secondary education through the UPE and USE programmes, for instance, were hailed as having the potential to reduce or even eradicate illiteracy among children belonging to poor families. Similar accounts of allegedly successful anti-poverty programmes were also cited in the media. In one of the *New Vision* articles, Olupot (2008) reported that the Ugandan president Yoweri Museveni was happy that people had finally begun to engage in commercial agriculture:

> I have seen the projects and I have instructed NAADS to construct dams in places where these projects are so that you can do some irrigation during the dry seasons . . . the philosophy of Movement (ruling Political Party in Uganda) is not prosperity for some, but prosperity for all. It was a shame that Uganda used to import powdered milk from Denmark yet the Banyankole and Iteso had been keeping cattle for the last 7,000 years.

However, while the success of anti-poverty programmes such as UPE in widening access to education for all was recognized both in the focus groups and in the media coverage, there was consensus that the quality of educa-tional provision left much to be desired. A *New Vision* editorial (August 2011) and *Bukedde* (January 2002) determined that UPE/USE schools were 'meant for the poor', yet they faced enormous challenges such as overcrowded classes, a high drop-out rate, poor-quality teaching and learning activities, and ultim-ately poor literacy and numeracy skills of the UPE graduates. These constraints made UPE schools another arena for the stigma and shame associated with being a child living in poverty. *The Monitor* (2009) quoted a Resident District Commissioner (RDC) urging rich people to send their children to private schools in order to free up places in UPE schools for the children from poor families. He pointed out how UPE schools in the area were overburdened by pupils, too numerous to be effectively looked after. Although his comments may have been intended to improve UPE as a programme to benefit those most in need, the language used is likely to make UPE beneficiaries derided by other children and parents in non-UPE schools. Some focus group participants in fact asserted that both UPE and USE programmes promote illiteracy for the children who attend such schools.

The other anti-poverty programmes, NAADS and the Savings and Credit Cooperative Organisations (SACCOs), were also seen as having failed in their poverty reduction aims (Muhindo, 2011). NAADS is a presidential agricultural initiative designed to benefit peasant farmers by providing them with subsidized inputs such as certified seeds, improved crop varieties, and hybrid livestock; along with support such as training. The emergent view was that this much-hyped programme, its substantial financial and political backing notwithstanding, is fundamentally flawed both in design and implementation, and lacks the capacity to address the needs of those in poverty. Highlighting the inadequacies of this targeted intervention, a *New Vision* editorial (October, 2009) advised that the success of anti-poverty projects was contingent on them being designed in ways compatible with the high level of illiteracy and a low level of school completion in rural areas.

There was consensus among focus group participants that, despite the formidable presence of NAADS in low-income communities, it merely paid lip service to poverty reduction without having any impact. Better-off focus group participants also expressed the view that NAADS was creating a rift between them and their poorer neighbours who seemed to think that they (the rich) had actually benefited the most from NAADS. Though it was acknowledged that rich individuals have sometimes accessed NAADS benefits at the expense of those in poverty, it was believed that this had been in a few isolated cases which did not warrant the type of generalizations that had been made about this issue across the media.

On the whole, media reporting and discussions in focus groups indicated a perception that the design and implementation of anti-poverty programmes remained flawed, usually devoid of systematic analysis to determine who should be the beneficiaries and what their needs were (Bantebya-Kyomuhendo and Mwiine, 2013). All the anti-poverty programmes were introduced, it was said, without needs assessments or baseline surveys, and therefore there was a lack of understanding of the priorities of those in poverty and of the psychological and social dimensions of poverty such as shame and/or stigma. As a result, those living in poverty, it was felt, had only experienced marginal benefits from such programmes.

Moreover, there was evidence of the view that anti-poverty policies had in fact exacerbated economic hardship by undermining people's independence and motivation. An article in *The Daily Monitor* by Gulumaire (2010) referred to poverty programmes as aggravating poverty, blaming increasing levels of poverty on free education and the scrapping of graduated tax by the government. Gulumaire cited a retired Anglican bishop who claimed that 'the scrapping of graduated tax by the government in 2006 and the introduction of universal education over a decade ago has created laziness in rural areas'. He suggested that, instead of people saving money to pay the tax and school fees, they are engaged in unproductive ventures because they are assured the basics of life, and concluded, 'What we have now is a wasted labour force engaged in gossip, politicking and booze'.

Poverty as Personal Failure

This analysis suggests that the relatively rich in Uganda perceive poverty primarily in terms of deficiencies in the material standards of living acceptable in their society, and that such deficiencies are shaped by what they see as the personal traits, habits, physical appearance, general disposition, and unfulfilled aspirations of those living in poverty.

These findings also indicate that the media plays a significant role in shaping and reinforcing ideas about poverty and in generating its related shame. The perceptions about people facing daily economic hardship are presented in the media, and, in turn, the same language of blaming, shaming, and othering was in turn reflected in the discussions with relatively affluent people. It can be seen that the media not only influences but appears to draw on communities' perceptions and understandings about poverty. The analysis further suggests that the shaming of people in poverty through media discourses impacts on the delivery and take-up of government anti-poverty strategies, especially when shame pushes people in poverty further into social and economic isolation.

The idea that poverty, as one respondent put it, 'cannot be hidden, that it's like a shadow that always trails the poor', remained central to the findings of this study. Participants overtly indicated that, when interacting with someone in poverty, you should be aware of their invisible but inseparable 'shadow'. This notion of the 'shadow' captures the ways in which the relatively rich and those living in poverty view themselves in relation to the other. These societal beliefs, as we have seen in earlier chapters, can have disastrous consequences for those living in poverty and, in turn, impact on social cohesion more broadly. Such perceptions exacerbate feelings of inferiority and inadequacy, leading to social exclusion, self-withdrawal, retreat, and, in the extreme, to suicidal tendencies. The analysis presented in this chapter adds further weight to the evidence that shame experienced as a result of poverty has external as well as internal dimensions, the likes of which are patently evident in the Ugandan context.

References

Bahikaho, C. (2008) 'Government to inject 1billion shillings into model villages', *The New Vision*, 16 November.

Bantebya-Kyomuhendo, G. and Mwiine, A. (2013) ' "Food that cannot be eaten": The shame of Uganda's anti-poverty policies', in Gubrium, E., Pellissery, S., and Lødemel, I. (eds) *The Shame of It: Global perspectives on anti-poverty policies*, Bristol: Policy Press.

Chase, E. and Walker, R. (2012) 'The co-construction of shame in the context of poverty: beyond a threat to the social bond', *Sociology*, 47(4): 739–54.

Emojong, J. A. and Bareebe, G. (2010) 'Museveni has set record of jiggers – Besigye', *The Daily Monitor*, 9 December.

Gubrium, E., Pellissery, S., and Lødemel, I. (eds) (2013) *The Shame of It: Global perspectives on anti-poverty policies*, Bristol: Policy Press.

Gulumaire, A. (2010) 'Bishop blames laziness on free education', *The Daily Monitor*, 30 April.

Kasalabecca, B. (2003) 'Eyabbye busuuti agitwale ku buko yasuze mu kaduukulu: Nfudde', *Bukedde*, 5 May.

Mafaranga, H. (2011) 'Immorality linked to poverty', *The New Vision*, 21 July.

Muhindo, G. (2011) 'What happened to the original Bonna-Bagaggawale programme?', *The Daily Monitor*, Monday, 29 August.

Muwambi, K (2002) 'Obuwuulu bweyongedde lwa mbeera ya nfuna – bakugu', *Bukedde*, 6 May 6.

Muzaale, F. (2010) 'Mukono Bishop blames food insecurity on laziness', *The Daily Monitor*, Thursday, 28 July.

Ndagire, S. (2002) 'Ssemaka adduse n'aleka abaana mu nju. Afumbiddwa nnakyeyombekedde', *Bukedde*, 21 May.

Okuma, D. (2011) 'Lessons to learn from the jiggers pandemic', *The Daily Monitor*, 17 January.

Olupot, M. (2008) 'Museveni happy with poverty campaign', *The New Vision*, 23 August.

Sen, A. (2000) 'Social Exclusion: Concept, Application, and Scrutiny', Social Development Papers No. 1, Manila: Asian Development Bank.

Ssemakula, R. (2002) 'Omufumbo eyakwatiddwa mu loogi ayogedde; "Nkooye okunsuza ku kafaliso ka yinchi emu" ', *Bukedde*, 17 April.

The Daily Monitor Editorial (2010) 'Jiggers are a big shame to Uganda', *The Daily Monitor*, October.

The New Vision (2011) 'Editorial: Too many students straining USE', *The New Vision*, 8 August.

Tingatsiga (2002) 'New Year Eve and why the poor like Sheraton', *The New Vision*, 28 December.

Walker, R., Bantebya-Kyomuhendo, G., Chase, E., et al. (2013) 'Poverty in Global Perspective: Is Shame a Common Denominator?', *Journal of Social Policy*, 42(2): 215–33.

Walker, R. (2014) *The Shame of Poverty*, Oxford: Oxford University Press.

17

How Best to Shame Those in Poverty

Perspectives from Pakistan

Sohail Anwar Choudhry

Introduction

Focus group discussions with people not currently living in poverty in Pakistan offered an additional perspective on the poverty–shame nexus, building on the findings emerging from (1) the analysis of native Pakistani literature to elicit social mores regarding poverty (Chapter 3) and (2) semi-structured interviews with low-income respondents to learn about their experience of poverty-induced shame (Chapter 10).

In total, five focus groups were conducted: three comprising members of the general public, one made up of members of the national Parliament, and one which included representatives from elite civil society. The three general public groups were derived from randomly selected people living in economically stable circumstances and counted among 51 per cent of Pakistan's population living above the multidimensional poverty line (OPHI, 2011). Two of these groups comprised adult male and female participants, aged between 17 and 70, while the third one consisted of children aged between 10 and 16 years. The final two groups included people from influential segments of society, those in a position to initiate public debates or policy action for reform. One of these groups consisted exclusively of nine Members of Parliament (in January 2013) while the other comprised a mix of eleven people from diverse civil service, media, civil society, and social intellectual backgrounds. On average, the focus groups lasted one-and-a-half hours, the discussions were conducted in Urdu, and, with the prior consent of participants, were tape recorded for their later transcription and translation into English.

Understandably, the diversity in the composition of the groups generated a multiplicity of viewpoints on themes surrounding poverty and those facing it. There was evident discord within and between groups concerning the causes of poverty and what were considered to be appropriate policy responses to enhance the social and psychological well-being of people on low incomes. While most relatively well-off members of the general public began by expressing a sympathetic view towards those living in poverty, they swung between extreme opinions when discussing specific issues related to the behaviour of those facing disadvantage, the choices they made, the level of effort they made, and whether or not they demonstrated the right work ethic.

The parliamentarians found themselves confronted with the demand for humane social provision on the one hand and the constraints of their political ideologies regarding work, compensation, and activation on the other. The civil society activists concentrated on the legitimacy of the right to dignity while the civil servants struggled with a way to optimally operationalize the vague concept of dignity in welfare provision. Although this resulted in a vast body of diverse views, it nevertheless provided mutually comparable thematic categories complementing the findings of the first two components of the research, which contributed to a holistic picture of dominant social perceptions about people on low incomes.

Understandings of the Meaning of Poverty

Although the views of the participants tended to shift and develop through the course of discussion, most of them began with certain preconceived notions about the nature, causality, and experience of poverty and usually returned to their original stance towards the end of the dialogue. Many participants reported drawing their knowledge about poverty primarily from their long-term observations and interactions with people on low incomes, including domestic workers, extended family members, or past friends and neighbours. Others were more likely to refer to religious, intellectual, and cultural perspectives on wealth, social responsibility, and accountability. Others still, such as civil servants and legislators, drew on their understandings from training or experience in a poverty-related field, while a minority of the participants mentioned their personal experiences of poverty in the past.

Perceptions concerning who was most likely to experience poverty varied greatly among the groups according to participants' individual, cultural, or professional understanding of concepts such as needs, wants, hardship, and deprivation. For example, while a construction company owner considered labourers 'as the class truly representing real poverty', a college teacher considered that the economic challenges facing 'white collar government officials' most warranted public attention. While understandings of poverty ranged from hunger to multidimensional deprivation, they shared a common element of 'unmet need'. Parliamentarians and policymakers in particular struggled with the idea of how to conceptualize anti-poverty legislation for a single target group. One female parliamentarian, for example, commented that the elected representatives seldom used formal definitions or thresholds of poverty at the time of introducing legislation. They rather initiated such laws on the basis of their personal observations and interactions with people.

Perceived Causes of Poverty

Structural Causes

Most focus group participants attributed poverty primarily to structural causes, although some cited individual and cultural causal factors. This dominant view is significant in the context of this research, since structural explanations for poverty attribute responsibility not to the affected individual but to systemic factors, which would suggest that those living in poverty should experience less externally imposed shame. Specific structural causes identified included the current high level of inflation, which had escalated the prices of basic commodities so much so that people who had never previously considered themselves as being on low incomes were struggling financially. It was widely observed that the prices of essential staple foods such as wheat, rice, pulses, and vegetables had rapidly increased during the previous three to four years, largely as a result of a rapid rise in transport costs in line with sharp inflation in the price of diesel and petrol. Some middle-class participants acknowledged that, because of such inflation, they could easily relate to the plight of people on low incomes. Civil society activists felt that the state was failing to respond to this new widespread poverty. Government was criticized for maintaining its net social assistance expenditure at less than 0.5 per cent of the GDP, not targeting anti-poverty measures effectively, and for not addressing the religious component of contributions and eligibility requirements, which excluded religious minorities from the *Zakat* programme.

Most children showed a basic understanding of the structural causes of poverty by referring to the high cost of urban living and the prevailing inflation. On account of that, they tended, initially at least, to not blame low-income people for their adverse circumstances. A 15-year-old girl, for example, asserted that the government was primarily responsible for the poverty of low-income people and therefore had a responsibility to alleviate their situations.

Drawing upon their personal interactions with those living in their political constituencies, parliamentarians sounded especially concerned about the current energy crisis, which had led to the closure of companies and mass unemployment, causing more people to carry the shame of unemployment. Many participants cited other causes of the failure to address poverty, including the effect on stagflation and political instability of the current law and order situation, the war on terror draining a large chunk of development resources, and incompetence and corruption on the part of civil servants. One parliamentarian noted that corruption 'started at the top and trickled all the way down to the lowest levels of administration'. Widespread corruption was thought to have drastically reduced the budget for welfare spending, driven away investment and charitable contributions, diminished trust in the government, and enhanced anxiety and insecurity amongst 'ordinary state subjects'. Participants also believed that recent and unexpected natural calamities had worsened the effects of poverty and created a new wave of social problems. One elected representative described how the crime rate rose significantly in his village following recent floods.

However, participants also cited individual and community factors which they considered coincided with and aggravated the structural causes of poverty outlined above. People on low incomes in rural areas, they believed, were poorly educated and as a result tended to pay no attention to advance warnings of weather and disease. They were also considered ignorant of new agricultural innovations such as better seed varieties, appropriate fertilizers, and mechanization and, as a result, failed to integrate such know-how into their farming practices. In addition, low literacy and lack of infrastructural development meant they were forced to sell crops such as cotton in their rawest, unprocessed form and at cheap prices, allowing the purchasers to take the largest share of the profit margin. Limited opportunities in rural areas meant that people increasingly migrated towards what they believed would be a better life in urban areas, where they unwittingly became part of a larger population of people facing severe disadvantage and unemployment. A civil servant highlighted the challenges emanating from the unusually high proportion of the population below the age of twenty five in Pakistan (some 60 per cent).[1] Most of these young people, he said, found it immensely difficult to enter a shrinking labour market and, with low education and skills, appeared to have little awareness of their rights and responsibilities, a deficit which exacerbated the risks of poverty.

---

[1] Verified by Pakistan Bureau of Statistics, percentage distribution of population by age, sex, and areas, available at: <www.pbs.gov.pk/sites/default/files/Labour%20Force/publications/lfs2008_09/t01.pdf>.

Individual and Cultural Causes

Despite attributing poverty largely to structural causes, some participants were more inclined than others to emphasize the personal inadequacies of those facing hardship. As one man put it, 'only the idle and lazy drown in acute poverty; the rest manage to keep their heads above troubled waters'. These participants argued that for people who were unwilling to work, the structural causes only provided a convenient excuse for their predisposition for sloth and indolence. They either chose not to work at all, 'staying home blaming the government and the rich', or sought jobs which require the least physical and mental effort.

A parliamentarian spoke of how he found it difficult to respect low-income graduates who came to him seeking employment in the public sector, readily agreeing to work as office boys, but refusing to acquire technical skills for improving their typing or shorthand skills for better openings. A number of participants also criticized the tendency of some men on low incomes to depend on their female family members for financial support. It was pointed out that, given the large family sizes promoted by individual and cultural preferences, such women struggled under the mental and physical pressures of economic and family responsibilities.

Some of the participants thought that technology and changing patterns of need and want had swayed many low-income people to irrationally spend beyond their means. This was evidenced by rapid increases in borrowing from private money lenders, and failure to service the loans. A female elected representative who had been instrumental in the enactment of the Punjab Prohibition of Private Money Lending Act 2007, discussed how inflation had extended the boundaries of vulnerability to the lower-middle classes by compelling them to borrow from private money lenders, thereby exposing themselves to 'a series of financial, emotional and mental miseries . . . culminating in the poverty trap and humiliation'. And while participants acknowledged that many low-income people fell into the trap of unmanageable debt by virtue of social obligations, they felt little sympathy for their current misery, which in their opinion was attributable to their 'irresponsible behaviour and choices'.

The Language and Labelling of Poverty

Focus group participants generally acknowledged that, like all other social groups, the attributes of low-income people varied greatly on account of their individual social and demographic circumstances. Accordingly, the views of participants concerning those in poverty ranged from praising them as 'extremely honourable' to labelling them 'shameless scavengers'. Most participants tended to speak highly of the working low-income people who did not try to cheat the system or give in to the temptation of dependency on benefits. Conversely, the harshest verbal treatment was reserved for 'beggars', who seldom won any words of sympathy from the members of the groups. More than anything else, the issue of employment set the tone and manner of how people on low incomes were described.

While the participants generally referred to people living in poverty who worked in low-paid jobs in a respectful way, they further categorized them into two groups: those who did not claim any supplementary public or private income support and those who did. The former group was considered to be the most tenacious, hard-working, and worthy of respect. A comment by one parliamentarian, for example, typifies this view: 'I know extremely honourable individuals who would rather be street-hawkers, selling vegetables than asking anyone for help. They genuinely have a right to demand respect'. Hence, hard work was regarded as a legitimate basis from which to command social respect and recognition. By implication, therefore, many participants believed that according respect to unemployed low-income people undermined its rightful claim by those who worked, since it blurred the distinction between idleness on the one hand and effort and responsibility on the other.

The second category of working people on low incomes emerged as those who, despite being employed, sought additional state or private help from their employers and other sources. Participants in the focus groups appeared to choose their words carefully when describing them, using phrases such as 'better than the non-working', 'at least trying', or 'halfway there'. Despite appreciating their efforts to work, some of the focus group participants criticized their low-income acquaintances who, they said, could not be 'trusted with their exaggerated appeals for extra help every now and then'. A few participants thought it paradoxical that the domestic workers who, they said, were always looking for small cash or in-kind financial favours, were still conscious of their self-respect and tended to react negatively to any harsh comments levelled at them. In essence, some participants considered it impossible that asking for favours and maintaining self-worth could go hand-in-hand.

As for those people living in poverty who were not working, and including those looking for work, focus group participants by and large used unsympathetic language to define and label them. This seemingly harsh attitude even towards job-seekers was due to participants' firm belief that there were enough job opportunities for those willing to work and who were not too 'unreasonable' or 'choosy' about what work they did. The most heavily criticized group, however, were those who were not working and who, it was said, expected their successful acquaintances to 'magically' lift them out of poverty, without themselves making any 'befitting effort'. Most participants believed that any claim to self-respect on the part of those not working was sheer 'vanity' or 'false pride'. Some of them regarded such expectations as 'deceitful' and 'shameless'.

As expected, participants reserved the most derogatory language for those who they defined as 'professional beggars'. Among other labels, they were referred to as 'detestable', 'parasites', 'lewd', and 'repulsive'. Such outright condemnation was justified on the basis that, far from being the result of sheer and desperate necessity, begging had become a 'wicked profession with a corporate-style planning and execution'. It was stated that often entire families of beggars maintained exclusive 'begging rights' over certain affluent commercial centres in the major cities where adults and children indulged in what one participant described as, 'shameless pauperism through various physical and psychological techniques'.

Other participants suggested that it was important to draw moral distinctions between different groups of people, not on the basis of the degree of poverty they faced but on their behaviour. This is illustrated by the view of one woman participating in a focus group: 'I saw a young man of 20 to 25 years of age begging in a marketplace the other day. Just next to him was an old man of 60 to 65 selling dusters. ... Whom should I respect? We need to disrespect certain people, not on account of their poverty but their bad social behaviour'.

Perceptions of the 'Deserving'

While generally speaking participants showed little sympathy for people who were not working, some of them agreed that it was unjust to categorize all low-income people as 'undeserving' of public sympathy and policy action, without considering the individual characteristics of each of these groups. One participant thought that it was a 'miracle' that despite huge socio-economic stratification, corruption, stagflation, and policy ineffectiveness, the 'delinquent and anti-social low-income people were still a negligible minority'. This view seems perfectly aligned with the moral rights argument propounded by David Lyons (1994: 4), which suggests that for those who are wronged and not compensated, 'resentment or indignation will be all the more appropriate'. Many focus group participants felt that they were not surprised that some extreme manifestations of this indignation were evident in actions of anti-social behaviour and crime and in attitudes which they felt reflected pauperism and state dependency.

Some participants pursued the 'deservingness' argument on account of what they thought was insufficient access to intellectual, social, and moral awareness-raising opportunities for those living in poverty. Not only did impoverished people face inadequate state access to general education, they also benefited less from the age-long tradition of religious education, which was increasingly shrinking in influence due to higher operational costs and diminishing state support. The regular schools, they believed, were pursuing a market-driven curriculum, with fewer hours reserved for moral and social guidance. A mother of four children argued that one of the major sources of idleness and anti-social behaviour was a decline in the inculcation of traditional family values amongst the younger generation. She believed that the contemporary economic requirements of a low-income family left parents working longer hours and having very little time for the civic and moral training of their children. One man participating in the same group believed that while traditionally a retired grandparent might have ample time to provide emotional support to an insecure grandchild, the breakdown of families had even rendered this possibility less likely than before and had instead created even more insecurity, loneliness, and depression for those living in poverty.

A parallel social cohesion argument of deservingness was tabled by one elected representative, who believed that, despite the 'serious individual laxities' of some low-income people, their exclusion from state patronage and support would not only be 'against the spirit of collective good but would also lead to social unrest, inter-class hatred, and political chaos'. Developing this argument, some other members quoted references from religious sources supporting the need to take the 'weak, meek, and oppressed along' on the journey for prosperity and 'share fruits of communal living' with them. They also supported their arguments by referring to the structural causes of poverty.

Others, however, were certain that it was a difference in individual behaviour which accounted for the varying outcomes of people in poverty. They thought that perpetuation of the poverty cycle was the result of either a 'flawed ideology [on the part of those facing hardship], incomprehension of the situation, or an unwillingness to work'. Any suggestion that such people were deserving of support was dismissed as a 'crude joke which disregarded merit'. Moreover, defining such people as deserving would imply political and policy action, which would, one male participant asserted, come at a sizable cost to the economy, 'more taxes, realignment of welfare priorities, and excessively wasteful expenditure'. Despite some strongly conflicting views, there was a general agreement among participants across all five focus groups concerning a progressive concept of eligibility which ensures equitable appreciation of individual effort and optimal use of scarce resources. While the right to dignity was supported by a majority of the participants, some strong outlying voices expressed specific reservations about a 'blanket cover of dignity', asserting that it was a right that should be earned. Similarly, children and young people generally believed that an individual's eligibility for state assistance should be judged on the basis of their respective circumstances and attitudes. One 12-year-old boy said, 'those capable of doing jobs but don't bother to apply are irresponsible', while a 14-year-old maintained that 'the government should help people with more jobs and schooling rather than just money'.

Shame and Social Exclusion

The analysis of the focus group discussions suggests that, because of the essentially negative perceptions of people living in poverty, the affluent generally prefer to maintain a distance from them. Participants noted that this aloofness on the part of those who were relatively wealthy meant that there was minimal interaction and dialogue between people living in very different economic circumstances from each other. One participant remarked, 'Just observe how the rich come out of Mosque stern and uptight after the prayers, lest any needy person dares to come up to them with a request for help'. A businessman felt that the 'demands of modern-day fast lane life' were such that people did not have the time to meet or socialize with anyone unless they had an economic or emotional interest in them. He stressed that he himself did not want to socialize with those who were richer than himself and with whom he had no obvious reason to mix. Given this logic, the relatively rich saw their low-income counterparts as the least desirable people to socialize with, since they were the least likely to benefit them economically or emotionally.

Some participants acknowledged that they only really interacted with people living in poverty when they expected to reap some practical or material benefit, such interaction usually limited to their private and household employees. And despite some of them claiming to have a close relationship with their domestic workers, none of the focus group members thought it appropriate to let their domestic workers share meals with them at their dining table or use their utensils, cutlery, or crockery. Similarly, participants thought it justifiable to maintain a distance between their children and those of low-income people. As one participant explained, 'How can we allow that... there are immense differences in their language, mannerism, and etiquette. We do not want our children to pick those up, their children are generally devoid of good manners'.

As though echoing the views of adults, children and young people themselves referred to their interactions with their peers facing economic hardship in similar ways, frequently indicating that such young people behaved inappropriately or were inferior to them in some way. A 12-year-old boy, for example, said that, while he mixed with the children from the lower social classes, he considered it difficult to be friends with them: 'I think they would make me uncomfortable by their language and manners... if I hang out with them, it will reflect on me as well and I shall form a poor impression on other people'.

Some participants argued that maintaining this social distance and stratification between the two groups was also in the interest of people living in poverty, in the sense that their ignorance about the lifestyles of the rich would cause them less frustration than if they had to be close witnesses of these differences. On the whole, there was unanimity that interaction between the two groups was unlikely to be productive or beneficial for either.

Nonetheless, some participants did acknowledge that sustaining this social distance and segregation between the two income groups could result in implicit shaming of people on low incomes at the individual and collective level. A civil society participant spoke of having come across amazing poets, artists, and folk historians in rural Sindh, who had never travelled to an urban centre in their lives because they had 'no shoes to wear and no clothing to present themselves publicly ... their talent being wasted for lack of exposure'.

One man noted how some high-income communities, social groups, and castes used to frequently refer to their superior origin, lineage, or other demographic traits. An echo of such views in the society, it was noted, had the potential to shame those groups who did not possess those attributes, making them feel inferior. While acknowledging these passive forms of shaming, very few participants admitted to ever having personally been involved in actively shaming others. However, some thought that, since people in poverty tended to exaggerate their misfortunes and make undue claims regarding their rights, there were some grounds to assert the true state of affairs. Some participants admitted that they felt it wholly justifiable to remind people on low incomes how they had failed to take advantage of the state and voluntary sector skill-building opportunities, and thus were indirectly responsible for perpetuating their own cycle of dependency. One participant justified such shaming in the following way, 'You frequently come across paupers ... you offer them employment, they instead ask you for money ... someone who does nothing productive during 40 to 50 years of his adult life does not deserve respect and equality'. In a similar vein, several participants remarked that it was not only 'acceptable but desirable to shame the shameless'.

Denying Shame, Denying Dignity

As noted elsewhere in this volume, the socio-psychological literature strongly suggests that shame causes a painfully negative self-evaluation (Tangney, 1991) leading to a sense of exposure (Lindsay-Hertz, 1984) and an urge to withdraw from the social environment (Lewis, 1992). Even in the absence of active shaming, social psychologists describe the human tendency of viewing oneself through the eyes of others, based on wider social norms and expectations (Cooley, 1922; Mead, 1934; Goffman, 1959). In turn, this shame limits the actions that can be undertaken or avoided by a shamed individual (Lynd, 1958) and may lead to their alienation or withdrawal from the wider society (Oravecz et al., 2004; De Hooge et al., 2010). The above views expressed by focus group participants suggest that poverty-related shame in Pakistan and its associated social isolation, described earlier in Chapter 10 through the voices of those directly experiencing it, are not just derived from their own internalized senses of inadequacy but equally have their roots in the external social environment. There were numerous accounts of shaming, ranging from subtle indifference to the lives of people living in poverty to obvious and active humiliation of them by those living in relative wealth.

The focus group discussions provided a new set of insights into the social picture of poverty in Pakistan by offering reflections on its nature, its causes, and its social outcomes from the perspectives of those who hold relatively privileged positions in society. The research has shown that, despite very varied individual opinions, as a result of economic and social inequalities, a psychological and social divide exists between people who are relatively well-off and those who live in poverty, even though they may live in close proximity to each other. This distance is primarily generated and sustained by the wealthy and is reflected in their perceptions of failure and personal inadequacies as the underlying causes of economic hardship; their low opinion of the ability and efforts of people on low and subsistence incomes; the fact that they see no potential benefit from associating with such people; and a perceived incompatibility of ideas, language, and manners. Overall, people in poverty are viewed as a semi-dysfunctional group in society, largely responsible for their own circumstances and difficulties. While there is some recognition of the overarching structural factors of poverty—the law and order situation, the power crisis, systematic exclusions from welfare, and natural calamities—people on low incomes are still partially blamed for their presumed inadequate efforts compared to their better-off counterparts who have managed to escape poverty.

While these differences cause a general segregation of the relatively well-off and those facing day-to-day hardship, some affluent people are particularly vehement in their criticism and blaming of people living in poverty, actively dismissing the idea that they should expect to receive any respect from others. Set against the narratives of people on low incomes solicited in the earlier phase of this research, it transpires that the sorts of attitudes and behaviours emerging from the focus group discussions undoubtedly cause permanent emotional damage for those subjected to them, often resulting in diminished self-esteem, agency, and reduced social participation. While shame is known to reduce human agency (Walker et al., 2013), there appeared little recognition of this fact on the part of affluent people participating in the current research. None of them thought that their implied or explicit shaming could in any way discourage low-income people from active social and economic participation or that it might in fact be counterproductive or responsible for instilling and perpetuating feelings of lethargy and fatalism.

The focus groups discussions revealed a hierarchy of shaming. So while participants acknowledged some appreciation for people on low incomes who were working, those who were economically inactive were the ones viewed most unsympathetically. The harshest verbal treatment was, however, reserved for 'beggars', who were described as brazen and shameless. While a tendency to favour those who are working and condemn those not working has a certain logic to it in economic and to some extent social terms, it inevitably also serves to perpetuate the status quo. This 'everyone for himself' mentality keeps the rich where they are and sustains the inequalities which permeate society and perpetuate widespread poverty. From this perspective, those who are working receive a modicum of social recognition because they do not demand any change, while the 'beggars' get the worst treatment because they publicly dare to ask for help from others who are wealthier. In a country where less than one per cent of people pay any taxes, it seems more convenient for the wealthy to ignore demands for redistribution and, instead, to take shelter in ideological moral arguments based on notions of efforts and rewards.

Many participants in the focus groups believed that, in the race for survival of the fittest, it was not only counterintuitive but also counterproductive to carry the emotional burden of those who proved themselves unworthy of social and economic participation despite, they believed, having had the same opportunities as them. While several participants contradicted this stance with varying degrees of conviction, very few disputed the idea that respect to those on low incomes should be accorded on the basis of discretional merit, rather than on the grounds of an inalienable right. Following the logic of Jeremy Bentham, as discussed by Lyons (1994), if an individual or group does not accept an obligation to discharge a duty, another individual or group may be denied a right. The right to dignity for people living in poverty in Pakistan is evidently contingent upon the willingness of the higher-income groups to extend it to them as their duty, something which they seemed overwhelming hesitant to do.

References

Cooley, C. H. (1922) *Human Nature and the Social Order*, New York: Scribner's.

De Hooge, E., Zeelenberg, M., and Breugelmans, S. M. (2010) 'Restore and protect motivations following shame', *Cognition & Emotion*, 24(1): 111–27.

Goffman, E. (1959) *Presentation of Self in Everyday Life*, New York: Anchor.

Lewis, M. (1992) *Shame; The Exposed Self*, New York: The Free Press.

Lynd, H. (1958) *On Shame and the Search for Identity*, New York: Harcourt, Brace.

Lindsay-Hertz, J. (1984) 'Contrasting experiences of shame and guilt', *American Behavioural Scientist*, 27(6): 689–704.

Lyons, D. (1994) *Rights, Welfare, and Mill's Moral Theory*, Oxford: Oxford University Press.

Mead, G. H. (1934) *Mind, Self, and Society*, Chicago: University of Chicago Press.

OPHI (2011) 'Country Briefing: Pakistan. Multidimensional Poverty Index at a Glance', Oxford Poverty and Human Development Initiative, Queen Elizabeth House, Oxford.

Oravecz, R., Hárdi, L., and Lajtai, L. (2004) 'Social transition, exclusion, shame and humiliation', *Torture*, 14(1): 3–15.

Tangney, J. P. (1991) 'Moral affect: The good, the bad, and the ugly', *Journal of Personality and Social Psychology*, 61: 598–607.

Walker, R., Bantebya-Kyomuhendo, G., Chase, E., Choudhry, S., et al. (2013) 'Poverty in Global Perspective: Is Shame a Common Denominator?', *Journal of Social Policy*, 42(2): 215–33.

18

Persistence of Shaming in a Hierarchical Society

The Case of India

Sony Pellissery and Leemamol Mathew

Introduction

Michael Young's (1958) classic satirical essay *The Rise of the Meritocracy 1870–2033* outlines the possibility of a double punishment for people in poverty: In addition to being actually worse-off, they are considered worse-off because of their own acts. Rousseau (1754) saw such meritocracy as the first step towards inequality, believing that ultimately, inegalitarian societies, as part of their structure, engage in constantly shaming and humiliating the poorer sections of society. Such is the danger of Rawlsian liberalism. These theoretical frames developed in Western societies become complicated when transposed to the Indian context, where inequality is arguably more layered. As we have seen in previous chapters, social identity plays a crucial role in creating hierarchies in India. On the one hand, personal failure is circumvented through diffused responsibility to immediate societal actors (family, caste, neighbourhood). On the other hand, societal expectations, legitimized by rituals, norms, and symbols, nurture dependency between hierarchies and thus shaming is supposed to be accepted by those belonging to the lower echelons of the hierarchy. While there may be some social insulation from shame, this does not mean that poverty-induced shame disappears. Rather, it emphasizes the plasticity of the human mind to experience shame in different forms, depending on the context. This means that conceptually, it is important to separate the experience of shame from the intentions behind imposing shame. In Chapter 11 we saw evidence of the first; in this chapter we examine the views of the relatively well-off about people facing economic hardship, thus shedding light on the second.

The empirical data that support the arguments in this chapter are derived primarily from two sources. First, we carried out focus group discussions with non-poor sections of society in two localities where we had previously conducted fieldwork to understand the experience of shame among people living in poverty. The key states of investigation were Kerala and Gujarat in India. We conducted two focus group discussions with school teachers (one group of seven teachers in Kerala and one of nine teachers in Gujarat), two focus group discussions with women (twelve women in Kerala and nine women in Gujarat), and two focus group discussions with adult men (six in Kerala and eight in Gujarat). In addition, a series of activity groups were conducted with children during which they were asked to develop bubble diagrams which were used as the basis for subsequent discussion. This work was supplemented by a content analysis of English newspapers that reported on poverty-related issues to understand whether and in what ways discourses around poverty in the print media carried shame-inducing representations. English newspapers, read by the middle and upper-middle classes in India, tend to represent the views of people who are relatively affluent.

One key issue, worth highlighting in advance and evident throughout the chapter, is the difference of views expressed by those people not living in poverty through focus group discussions, and the views expressed in the English language newspapers. While the media was sympathetic to poor people and consistently blamed the state (both the politicians and bureaucrats) for poverty, those not experiencing poverty squarely blamed people living in poverty for their disadvantaged circumstances and, as will be appreciated, there was little or no sympathy in their language when they spoke about them. This difference requires an explanation before we present the empirical evidence. Indian print media was established and grew rapidly during British colonial times. This meant that any anti-colonial stance taken by the newspaper assumed a nationalist perspective, especially since English dailies were circulated nationally (Sonwalker, 2002). With independence in 1947, 'nationalism' became equated with development, and the print media was one channel through which development was to be delivered. By this time there was a clear path dependency of blaming the state for poverty (accusations which were targeted at elected politicians and apathetic bureaucrats), and the presentation of people in poverty in a positive light became the dominant discourse of national newspapers, to the extent that if people in poverty were blamed for their circumstances, the newspaper was perceived as being anti-developmental. This briefly explains the disconnect evident in our analysis between the views promulgated in English print media and those expressed via focus groups by people not living in poverty in India.

Causes of Poverty: Public Views and Media Representations

Paulo Freire, in his influential work *Pedagogy of the Oppressed* (1969), pointed out how different causations of poverty are perceived, depending on the level of consciousness that people have. Hence, it is the perception or understanding of facts, rather than the facts themselves which assume significance when it comes to taking action to change the situation. Similarly, policy science makes a clear distinction between the causes of a problem, and the representations of these causes, the latter arguably most often providing the basis for the policy response. In the Indian context we observed clear differences between public views about the causes of poverty and the causes which were derived through scientific study of the situations of poverty by academics or planning bodies.

The large majority of people participating in the research who were relatively wealthy believed that people lived in poverty because of their own shortcomings. This was particularly true in Gujarat, which has in recent years experienced rapid industrial transformation. Here participants opined that people living in poverty were destined to remain that way. One focus group participant claimed, *'Yeh nange aise hi rahenge. Tapasya bhi karein tab bhi kuch na hone waala!'* ('they will stay naked like that forever in poverty. Even miracles cannot change their situation'). A similar response was uttered by a participant from a village in Kerala in relation to tribal populations who said, 'They are all the same, like, it is their culture. They will live in the forest and drink; they don't want to live like us'.

The view of many focus group discussion respondents was that after the rise of industrialism a lot of opportunities were available to all villagers. In fact, many of them had become rich, they said, by making the most of these opportunities, while those currently living in poverty drank and gambled their money away. As a result, they believe that those experiencing poverty now should take responsibility for their circumstances and should not blame others. One rich woman in Gujarat made the following comment: *'Na zameen rahi aur na hi makaan ban paya'* ('neither do they have land now, nor have they built a house of their own'). In this statement, she was implying that those in poverty in the village had sold their land to the industries for a good amount of money, which, instead of investing in property, they had wasted on liquor and other unproductive activities, leaving them with nothing. Some of the focus group participants felt that people in poverty did not even have aspirations for their children to have better lives.

However, there were some participants who contested the idea that people in poverty should be blamed for their own deprivation. School teachers in particular pointed out the structural forces behind deprivation and how government policies had failed to alleviate the circumstances of those experiencing it day-to-day. One school teacher, although she pointed out drinking as a common problem for people living on low incomes, also openly blamed the government for their circumstances:

> Lots of the schemes are wasted, but we cannot blame poor people for that. Many of the schemes are mis-utilised by middlemen and therefore do not benefit poor people. So the government has to be blamed for poor implementation. Some parents really take advantage and utilize these schemes to come up in life. I have seen one child whose parents herded cows for us. Today, the child has become *Tahasildar* (a sub-collector). This is purely out of efforts and hard work.

As pointed out in the introduction to this chapter, the views expressed by relatively affluent people in focus groups were not found in the media or reported in newspapers. While the newspapers were seen to celebrate the 'successes' of people in poverty (for example when they achieved excellence in education or established a successful business despite the hardships they faced), evidence of people being blamed for their poor economic circumstances was rare.

Labelling People Living in Poverty

In earlier chapters we have shown how poverty in India is closely associated with the social identity of belonging to a lower caste or tribe. These social groups have historically also been forced to carry out traditional jobs. Very often, instead of calling people by their given names, they are either given the label of the job they perform or referred to by the name of their caste. These forms of labelling were clearly evident in the focus group discussions in which the relatively well-off tended to refer to people in poverty by their occupation rather than by their real names. These same forms of derogatory labelling and stigmatizing were similarly evident in our earlier analysis of literature and films and were observed during interactions between children of different economic backgrounds, in which children from upper-caste families were seen to publicly taunt and suppress the decisions and views of their poorer peers.

Within the focus group discussions, school teachers were most likely to express sympathetic understanding of the situation and circumstances of children living in poverty. One teacher at a government school in Gujarat referred to the children from poorer families as having difficulty in studying but that they were always well mannered and respectful to everyone. She made the point of how hard it was for children to get a good education when their own parents had never studied, referring to these children as 'first generation learners'. The same teacher described the typical situation of a child from a poor family: 'The parents usually work as unskilled labourers, they work in the field and sell their goods at the local markets and shops. They leave for the field early in the morning and come back late at night when they go to sleep early. If they spend time with their children they will have nothing to feed them with'. The last sentence demonstrates not only her empathy towards poor parents but also how she perceives poverty as strongly related to extreme physical work, long working hours, and vulnerability to hunger if parents skip work for even a single day. Another male teacher from Gujarat described children from low-income families as highly sensitive, since they understood their families' economic conditions and limitations and were ashamed of them.

One important development in India to prevent humiliation and shaming of the lower castes through labelling is the Prevention of Atrocities Act (1989). 'Atrocity' is defined as a form of violence (such as murder, rape, dacoity, robbery, verbal abuse) carried out by an upper-caste person on a person from a lower caste. Particularly, this legislation can be applied when people are referred to by their demeaning or humiliating caste name or when atrocities are specifically targeted at members of lower castes.[1] Generally speaking, upper-caste members became more cautious about how they referred to others after this legislation came into effect. Many teachers taking part in focus groups reported that they were conscious and careful not to mention caste names in public. They admitted, however, that they often resorted to referring to a particular child by their caste name when they were talking with another teacher who is not from the caste to which the child belonged. A wealthy participant in one of the Gujarat villages said that these days 'the poor' expected respect and equal treatment from the rich: '*Aaj kal to wo mooh mod lete hain, ghar aana jaana band kar dete hain, agar unhe Namaste na karo to, lekin hum aisa karte nahi*' ('These days if we don't greet poor people, poor people turn their backs on us, they refuse to come to our houses'). This observation was seen to represent a significant shift in attitudes from previous generations, when people living in poverty openly showed a high level of dependency and unquestioning respect towards rich people.

The government programmes and schemes were also said to create certain labels for people living in poverty which were widely used by the public. For instance, Below Poverty Line (BPL) has become a stigmatizing label, as has 'slum dwellers', used to signify people living in poverty in urban areas (Pellissery and Mathew, 2013). Similarly, wherever the government provides houses for those living in poverty, such places come to be known as 'colonies',

---

[1] In the year 2008 alone 11,602 cases were filed under this Act. However, there is evidence that the anti-caste attitudes of the police, judges, political parties, and legal system has resulted in a failure to fully comply with the spirit of the Act (Teltumbde, 2010).

and the people living in government-built houses are labelled as 'residents of colonies'.

Irrespective of the fact that newspaper journalists adopted a predominantly empathetic stance in relation to people living in poverty, unconsciously or otherwise they tended to reproduce stereotypes of deprivation in the print media. The media analysis demonstrated that whenever poverty-related news items were reported, a certain type of image was used in the newspapers to depict conditions of poverty. Discussions with editors of newspapers revealed that they keep archives of 'poverty-related pictures' (such as malnourished children, a tribal hut with thatched roof, a manual labourer, a women wearing a torn sari), and that these pictures are reproduced whenever they wish to illustrate a news story about poverty. Editors were casual about this, since they felt the cost of sending a photographer to a location to take pictures of the actual circumstances of poverty was not worth incurring since the 'pictures were readily available in the archive'.

Constructs of the 'Deserving' and 'Undeserving' Poor

The views expressed by relatively affluent participants in focus group discussions indicated criteria against which people might be judged for their 'moral worthiness' to receive government assistance. On this point there was a degree of concordance between media reports and the views of the general public. The media reporting tended to accuse the government of designing anti-poverty programmes purely as vote-gathering mechanisms. Similarly, focus group participants spoke of how they believed that unless people in poverty learned to save money, then anti-poverty programmes designed for them were futile. A particular statement on this subject was vocalized by one of the richest people in the village during one of the groups: '*Inko sab kuch mil sakta hai, par ye log mehanat nahi karna chahte*' ('They can get everything, but they are not ready to work hard'). One participant from Gujarat pointed to an example of labourers buying posters of film stars, expensive cards each worth Rs25, and special electric lights for the festival of Diwali, even though they could not afford such things. Similarly, focus group participants objected to the use of televisions and drinking of alcohol.

One participant in a discussion held in a village in Gujarat spoke of how he believed that people living in poverty were becoming increasingly dishonest in their economic activities, commenting that,

> Now people want to make quicker money, without sweating, without working, the quick way … the easy quickest way is cheating! So they will come to you and ask for help but actually they want to get money from you and run away. If people

have a genuine health problem, they get help. But poor people...many of them want to cheat. This is not the character of Gujarati people...this is happening because of outsiders who are coming to stay in our villages, people from Bihar.

While such behaviour was believed to be common in areas where migrant people were located, in the villages where caste divisions were deep, this lack of trust was noticed even without migrants present. A common example cited was that, whenever cattle were stolen from a rich household, people living in poor households with limited means were always suspected of committing the crime.

The media analysis revealed an additional aspect of stigma that was not captured by the focus group discussions. This concerned the positive discrimination policies of the government of India. Newspapers with liberal ideologies reported that job quotas, emerging out of positive discrimination policies, contributed to inefficiency. Newspapers leaning towards left-wing ideologies pointed out how job opportunities within these quotas were taken up by the richest (non-deserving) sections within lower castes. However, others have argued that the stigma associated with jobs acquired through the positive discrimination quota has diminished in recent times (Patel, 2008).

Perceptions of the General Public and Social Exclusion

One significant effect of the general public in India calling people by their caste or tribal name, or even addressing them by their traditional occupation, is that people in poverty may internalize an identity of poverty. This process has been institutionalized through a number of practices in government policies as well. For instance, lower-caste family members are asked to produce a 'caste certificate' every time they access a benefit from government which is meant for those who are facing particular hardship. These practices have significant implications for how people identify themselves, and increase the likelihood that they will experience social exclusion. For instance, Hoff and Pandey (2004) used a controlled experiment to understand whether revealing caste identity publicly affected the performance of students. The experiment found that if caste identity was not revealed, the performance between Dalit students and non-Dalit students was not significantly different. Once the caste identity was revealed, the Dalit students' performance fell by 23 per cent.

During our interviews with teachers, this impact on social exclusion was confirmed. One teacher in the school for Tribal Children run by the Integrated Tribal Development Department in Kerala, said, 'I have noticed many of these (poor) children are introverts. There is no problem when they interact among themselves in the school. But when we take these children outside the school

237

for events such as inter-school competitions we have noticed tribal children perform poorly in vivas and on occasions when they have to interact with others'.

Another teacher from a government-aided school in Kerala made the following observations: 'During school hours, these dynamics are not visible, but I was hostel warden in our school and I have noticed how somehow poor children identify themselves and sit in separate groups from rich children'. Apparently, while classrooms might enforce uniformity among children, this vanishes when children enter into their private life and social lives outside of school. These teachers noted therefore how the consciousness of 'being poor' plays an important role in defining the types of acceptable social interaction between those in poverty and those who are not. This experience of social grouping according to social identity has been argued as 'social exclusion' occurring alongside elements of 'social inclusion' (such as attending school). This reconfirms the community-wide experience of shame as different to individually focused shame experienced by individuals living in poverty which was elaborated on in Chapter 11.

Shaming certain communities takes its cruelest form in publicly identifying certain tribes as criminal tribes. Such notions stem from the work of certain theorists, which suggest that there are certain hereditary traits for intelligence (Galton, 1869) as well as criminality (Lombroso, 1864) and that the inclination to commit crimes is hereditary rather than being due to sociological or political conditions (Friedman, 2011). These developments took an important turn in 1869 when the Habitual Criminals Act was passed in England. In British colonies, including India, the Act took different forms. In India, some of the poorest nomadic tribes were identified as habitual criminals. Even though the Act has since been repealed, these tribal groups are still always the first to be suspected by the police when a crime or theft takes place in their locality (Devy, 2006).

Shaping of Public and Media Perceptions of People Living in Poverty

What is important to note about the attitudes towards people living in poverty by the relatively affluent is the transformation that has happened in India during a generation. Poverty levels have been reduced significantly between 1970 and 2000. Thus, respondents from the non-poor sections of society may well have experienced poverty in their own childhoods or witnessed it within their vicinities. Such proximity to poverty inevitably shapes views concerning the reasons for poverty in contemporary Indian society, compared to the sort of widespread poverty which was a historical reality of long past. Those who have escaped poverty often pride themselves on their hard work or wise decisions (such as investing in education or training). They also recall that, when facing economic hardship themselves, they had very few sympathizers and limited systems of support. Larger structural factors that are likely to have helped them to escape poverty are given limited significance in their explanation of their improved circumstances. These perceived histories shape the attitudes of the relatively rich towards the poorer sections of their own societies.

Most of the participants within focus group discussions in Kerala and Gujarat lived in close proximity to people living in poverty. However, the social distance between them was huge. Many richer people had direct contact with people in poverty through business or other professional relationships. The government school teachers in particular reported close interaction with their students from poorer families. The views shared by our respondents were shaped more by this direct exposure to people living in poverty than by media or political ideologies. When one participant in a focus group in Kerala, for example, described 'the poor' as, 'those who earn Rs.300 in a day and spend the next two to three days drinking alcohol', he was referring, he said, directly to his own employees. As a businessman owning a number of petrol pumps, trucks, and hotels, he saw people in poverty in terms of the employer–labourer relationship. He accused people of facing economic hardship as a result of their failure to be efficient workers and to turn up regularly for work.

However, some participants, like one 27-year-old married woman from Kerala, admitted having very little practical or direct contact with poor people throughout her life, even though her father and husband were big farmers and were likely to be employing people on low incomes, and despite the fact that she was highly educated. She did, however, note that poor labourers often used to seek financial help from her father yet never repaid him, and that she had often seen the same thing happening with the people that her husband employed. Nonetheless, this lack of awareness of the circumstances of people facing economic hardship is an important change that has taken place over a single generation. Not that long ago, parents were known to sensitize their children towards those in poverty and advise them not to ridicule people about their situations but instead give them alms and support when they could. Increasingly however, as the middle class began to emerge as the result of rapid economic growth, parents began to encourage children to keep away from those in poverty, who became suspected of compromising the safety and moral virtue of their own children.

While journalists generally adopted a supportive stance in their reporting towards people living in poverty, our media analysis showed that, unconsciously or not, they tended to associate negativity with certain social identities. For instance, when crime (rape or stealing) is reported in the newspapers, if the act is committed by a person from a tribal community, a migrant community, or from a slum locality, it is explicitly stated. On the other hand, if the crime is committed by a person from an upper caste or a rich person, their social identity is not revealed. In this way, the media perpetuates the association between certain groups, poverty, and crime, a stance which also has political backing. For instance, whenever a crime against a woman was reported in the newspapers, most of the political parties demanded stringent punishment for the culprits, who were, in most cases, from circumstances of poverty. But when a self-styled guru was accused of crimes against women, the Hindu fundamentalist party was largely silent about punishing him, and instead spoke out in support of him, an illustration of the double standard evident among the political classes.

Conclusion

In a collectivistic culture like that of India, shaming tends to take place at a communal rather than individual level. Shaming is the process of expressing disapproval or condemning a person or group who may in turn be rendered powerless, helpless, or feel inferior as a result. The interesting fact to note in the case of India is that individual shaming directly points towards the community because the individual is part of a strongly bound community.

The material presented in this chapter and in Chapter 11 outlines the differences in opinion between the people living in poverty themselves and their relatively affluent counterparts about the causes and realities poverty. For instance, those in poverty experienced it as a fire-fighting exercise in which they were constantly taunted by decisions about how best to deal with the most pressing matter (finding money to attend hospital or to get the next square meal). As noted in Chapter 11, they considered themselves to be hardworking, striving to make money to meet their immediate needs, in the process often suffering poor health and malnutrition. Those not living in poverty, on the other hand, defined those facing economic hardship as lazy and having generated their own poverty, largely through laziness, ineptitude, alcoholism, or gambling.

As we have seen in the earlier Chapters 4 and 11, attitudes of the general public towards poverty are supported by religious ideologies. It is far easier, for example, for someone who is relatively affluent to be philosophical about the karma (or fate) principle, and to engage in wishful thinking of better outcomes in the next life than it is for someone who is facing deprivation on a daily basis. Indeed, such religious ideologies arguably help to justify the existing inequalities. Furthermore, in the context of anti-poverty policymaking, experts and elites engage in clear processes of 'othering' through a combination of cognition, values, and norms (Reis and Moore, 2005; Pellissery et al., 2013), in which a double standard for appropriate behaviour is applied, depending upon one's socio-economic status. This same double standard is reflected in general popular opinion concerning poverty and people experiencing it.

In the midst of this generally negative attitude towards those facing poverty, however, the print media is a notable exception in its pro-poor stance. In addition to accusing the state of unfairness and incompetence, newspapers also accuse businesses and the corporate sector of being responsible for accelerating poverty through exploitative processes such as land acquisition or the use of child labour. These conflicting attitudes towards poverty and people living in poverty represent the colliding value frames within which anti-poverty policy has to date been formulated.

Yet, as we have seen in this chapter, although the media has generally taken the side of those facing economic hardship, unconsciously it has also played a critical role in perpetuating the stereotypes of persons belonging to certain castes and tribes of a lower socio-economic order. Liberal as well as left-leaning newspapers do this in different ways. This tendency might be addressed in some part by sensitization interventions which encourage journalists and those working in the media to reassess their own value systems with respect to people living in poverty. However, the bigger picture shows a growing polarization between rich and poor, an emergent middle class, and rising inequality in the context of the rapid economic transformations that have taken place in India over the past few decades. These economic changes have such profound social implications that they require not just greater awareness of the daily struggles of people experiencing poverty but a sustained political and policy response that recognizes the growing social divisions between the haves and the have-nots.

References

Devy, G. (2006) *Nomad Called a Thief*, Delhi: Orient Longman.

Freire, P. (1969) *Pedagogy of the Oppressed*, London: Penguin Books.

Friedman, K. (2011) 'From Thugs to Victims: Dakxin Bajrange Chhara's Cinema of Justice', *Visual Anthropology*, 24(3): 1–34.

Galton, F. (1869) *Hereditary Genius*, London: Macmillan.

Hoff, K. and Pandey, P. (2004) 'Belief Systems and Durable Inequalities: An Experimental Investigation of Indian Caste', Policy Research Working Paper 3351, World Bank: Washington, DC.

Lombroso, C. (1864) *Genio e follia*, Rome: Bocca.

Lewis, Oscar (1969) 'Culture of Poverty', in Moynihan, D. P. (ed.) *On Understanding Poverty: Perspectives from the Social Sciences*, New York: Basic Books, pp. 187–220.

Patel, T. (2008) 'Stigma goes Backstage: Reservation in Jobs and Education', *Sociological Bulletin*, 57(1): 97–114.

Pellissery, S., Lødemel, I., and Gubrium, E. K. (2013) 'Shame and shaming in policy processes', in *The Shame of It: Global Perspectives on Anti-Poverty Policies*, Bristol: Policy Press.

Pellissery, S. and Mathew, L. (2013) 'Thick poverty, thicker society and thin state: Policy spaces for human dignity in India', in *The Shame of It: Global Perspectives on Anti-Poverty Policies*, Bristol: Policy Press.

Reis, E. P. and Moore, M. (2005) *Elite Perceptions of Poverty and Inequality*, London: Zed Books.

Rousseau, J. J. (1754) *Discourse on the origin and basis of inequality among men* (English translation by G. D. H. Cole), available at <http://www.constitution.org/jjr/ineq.htm>.

Sonwalker, P. (2002) 'Murdochization' of the Indian press: from by-line to bottom-line', *Media, Culture and Society*, 24: 821–34.

Teltumbde, A. (2010) *The Persistence of Caste*, Delhi: Navayana.

Young, M. (1958) *The Rise of the Meritocracy 1870–2033: An essay on education and society*, London: Thames and Hudson.

19

Society and Shaming

General Public and Media Perceptions of Poverty in Urban China

Ming Yan

Introduction

This chapter examines poverty and shame from the perspectives of people not living in poverty in urban China. It draws upon findings from two sources; focus group discussions with people considered relatively wealthy and an analysis of media coverage of poverty-related issues in national newspapers. Five focus group discussions were conducted with the goal of eliciting public perceptions and attitudes concerning poverty and shame. In order to capture the diverse experiences and views of the general public, groups were purposively sampled to include participants of different ages, occupations, and socio-economic statuses, each one consisting of between five and eight men and women as follows: (1) recent college graduates with an average age of 24 years, some of whom were working in professional fields and others enrolled in postgraduate study; (2) working-class people, aged 43 to 60, employed in the industrial or service sectors; (3) upper and middle-income entrepreneurs and professionals, aged 47 to 62; (4) retirees from the industrial sector (former factory workers, engineers, and managers), aged 60 to 78; and (5) rural-to-urban migrants, aged 18 to 42, self-employed or working in the service sector. The focus group discussions took place in Beijing, China from November to December 2011, each lasting on average two hours.

A content analysis of selected newspapers in China was undertaken, with material collected from two sets of electronic newspaper databases: *Qinghua Tongfang's China National Knowledge Infrastructure (CNKI)* and *Founder's Apabi.*

The CNKI database was used to access three national newspapers from the beginning of 2000 to 31 March 2012: The *People's Daily,* the leading official organ of the Party-State; the *Workers' Daily,* sponsored by the All China Federation of Trade Unions for its orientation towards industrial workers; and the *Chinese Society News,* sponsored by the Ministry of Civil Affairs with a focus on social policy issues. *Founder's Apabi* was used to access four local Beijing newspapers from between 2005 and 2007 until the end of March 2012: the *Beijing Daily,* the *Beijing Morning Post;* the *Beijing Evening News,* and the *Jinghua Times.* The *Beijing Daily* represents the official organ of the Beijing municipal government while the other three newspapers have extensive coverage of local events and are relatively more accessible to the ordinary reader. Through analysis of national and local newspapers the aim was to identify current media concerns and the social and political salience of poverty, shame, and social assistance in urban China, in particular popular views, official positions, as well as policy debates and practices.

Understandings of Poverty

Poverty was recognized as a social problem both by focus group participants and in the selected media. While journalists appeared to draw on factual information on the scope of deprivation, for example citing statistical evidence of an increase in the numbers of people experiencing poverty in urban China (Chen and Zhang, 2006), the focus group participants shared their understandings of poverty largely based on their personal observations.

When asked about their contact with those living in poverty, almost all the focus-group interviewees said that they had first-hand experiences of poverty. Some had lived in poverty themselves, others had relatives or employees who were poor, and many had seen those in poverty in their neighbourhood or had encountered them on the street. Interestingly, some members of the upper- and middle-income focus group noted their personal involvement in poverty relief. One person, for example, spoke of how he sometimes helped relatives who struggled financially, and a female college professor said that she often gave recyclable items to a neighbour who used the small amount of money they raised to supplement his meagre income. Two wealthy entrepreneurs in this group noted that, as the owners of companies, they were required by government to pay a 'disability tax' used to support people with disabilities. The group composed of college graduates also shared their experiences of interacting with classmates from poorer backgrounds, and of how, if going out to a restaurant, they would not let those classmates pay the bill. People's perceptions of poverty were therefore inevitably shaped by their personal experiences, degree of contact with those in poverty, as well as their current occupational or socio-economic status. It was quite evident that those interviewed were quite aware of their socio-economic status and thus their distance from poverty.

Initially, the working-class group stated that they themselves were poor, but after some deliberation on the meaning of poverty, they agreed that while they did not currently live in poverty, they were nonetheless vulnerable to it. The common factors cited that could lead to their falling into poverty included serious illness affecting themselves or some of their family members. This was also the major concern of the retirees who, understandably, were more likely to experience chronic health problems. Several participants in the group of graduate students also said that they felt poor because they could often not afford things they needed or wanted, although they admitted that these were not among the most vital of necessities. The group composed of participants from the upper- and middle-income classes did not think that they would fall into poverty, although some still feared the possibility of bankruptcy due to investment failure and the resultant poverty due to a fall in their relative socio-economic standing.

Interestingly, all the focus group interviewees had difficulties in determining what constitutes poverty and who should be categorized as living in poverty. This was because they felt that the implications of poverty were vague and standards varied. After some deliberation a consensus was reached that people who had nothing to eat could be considered as living in poverty, yet most participants noted that nowadays such people were rare in China, although perhaps some still existed in the remote rural areas. While some were aware of the official definition of poverty in terms of income levels, others ventured into considerations of relative poverty. The focus group made up of migrants perceived poverty distinctively; to them real poverty only existed in rural areas and not in the city. They cited cases from their hometown or village of people whose work was extremely arduous but who continued to live at the subsistence level. Not having the security of pension schemes like those in urban cities, they were forced to labour in the field even in old age and then became dependent on their adult children. The urban respondents identified families with large medical expenses due to illness or those having to cover children's education costs as the most likely to fall into poverty.

Focus group participants agreed that poverty could impact on people's lives in numerous ways and that those experiencing it tended to have lower self-esteem, a form of shame, which might affect their social interaction with others. One obvious example cited was old classmates' reunions, common events which are held throughout urban China. It was believed that the better-off and more successful were more likely to be actively involved in such events, whereas those who struggled financially were more reluctant to participate, an indication of feeling shamed. Furthermore, such reunions were widely recognized as a way of strengthening existing networks for the advancement of personal, professional, or business interests and therefore those with limited economic or social capital would not be made to feel welcome. Equally, participants identified the social demands in rural areas which took other forms; in the close-knit village life, for example, there are high expectations that those invited to special occasions such as weddings or funerals will make monetary contributions. Since failing to attend is not an option, families living in poverty, they recognized, were often forced to borrow money in order to fulfil their social obligations, and were likely to experience shame as a result.

Perceptions Concerning the Causes of Poverty

With regard to the causes of poverty, the media tended to focus mainly on the wider structural factors which accounted for the problems encountered by those living in poverty such as: unemployment, difficulties experienced by college graduates in seeking employment, and economic burdens caused by excessive medical expenses or school costs (Chen et al., 2006; Zhang, 2006). Poverty was also understood in the context of widespread industrial restructuring across urban China, resulting in large-scale unemployment combined with inadequate social security, and causing some groups to suffer from a dramatic decline in living standards, which cannot be attributed entirely to personal reasons (Mo, 2003). In addition to the marketization and privatization of state-owned enterprises (SOEs), the increased international competition resulting from China joining the World Trade Organisation (WTO) in 2001 (Commentator, 2001) was seen as contributing to the closure of some enterprises. Several journalists also acknowledged that the existence of these disadvantaged groups was indicative of the early stage of China's socio-economic development and demonstrated the need to strengthen public policy in order to mitigate the negative effects of economic growth (Qu, 2010). More broadly, it was stressed in the media that urban poverty could be viewed as an inevitable social problem in any country that was going through dramatic social transition with relatively low levels of production and so China, with a population of 1.3 billion people, was even less likely to be able to circumvent it (Commentator, 2003).

Participants within focus group discussions held different views on the causes of poverty, views clearly shaped by the personal experiences of the respondents. The focus group consisting of industrial workers saw unemployment as the main cause of poverty, and blamed the restructuring of SOEs that had taken place over the past two decades. The group comprising migrants, however, did not think that unemployment was the principal factor in creating poverty as they felt that all of those who wanted to work could get jobs of some kind. All the focus groups identified individual and social factors contributing to poverty as understood by the interviewees. Individual factors included personal health, level of education and skills, and life chances; while the wider structural or social factors included governmental policy, limited redistributive mechanisms, socio-economic inequality, and possession or a lack of 'connections'.

Importantly, interviewees often perceived social or structural factors accounting for poverty as individual ones. A person's birth place, for instance, was seen as an important determinant of his or her financial situation and instead of viewing this as a structural factor, the interviewees thought of this as personal 'luck'. Similarly, participants did not believe that the causes of poverty were consistent. While they believed that some residents lived in poverty due to the restructuring of SOEs, other Beijing residents, they felt, lived in poverty because they were too lazy to work or were too concerned about 'losing face' when taking up 'dirty work'. Such people, it was believed would rather stay at home and collect money from the *dibao* than work in low-status manual jobs.

All groups recognized and agreed that the rapid growth in economic disparity created the conditions within which poverty emerged and became a significant issue. This was vocalized by some group members through comments such as, 'those with money are really rich, and those without money are terribly poor' and, 'the rich get richer, and the poor get poorer'. It was by and large recognized that 'connections' played a significant role, either in finding good jobs or opening up a business. The migrant group particularly noted the privileges that Beijingers enjoyed such as access to education and health care. The working-class group, which consisted of current or former SOE employees, emphasized the structural factors such as the closure of SOEs as causing many to fall into poverty. In contrast, the upper- and middle-income group stressed personal abilities and efforts as the most important factors in determining whether or not people succumbed to poverty. One large business owner stated that the government made efforts to control the income of the rich through taxation which was then used for investment, which in turn led to increased employment opportunities, to the benefit of those living in poverty.

Another entrepreneur also felt that individual factors, such as ability and educational attainment, played the major role in deciding people's economic fortunes since the 'larger environment' was the same for everyone. He further elaborated that, for college graduates competing on the job market, it was their abilities and efforts that dictated their career prospects. In addition, this group noted that poverty did exist during the planned economy period but that it had been hidden from view, whereas poverty during the period of marketization was more visible. The group comprising young people focused on education as the main and, for some, the only path to upward mobility. Overall, while the youth and upper- and middle-income groups stressed that opportunities and hard work would lead to the accumulation of wealth, the working-class group expressed less optimism. By comparison, as a general rule the media recognized the severe consequences of poverty at both individual and societal levels, and called for strong policy interventions to mitigate its effects (Sheng, 2002).

Language and Labelling Used in Relation to Poverty

With respect to the types of language and terminology used in relation to poverty, focus-group interviewees tended to be largely neutral in the words and phrases they employed. On the whole, they showed sympathy towards those in poverty, although quite a number of them did not approve of certain *dibao* claimants who were seen to have taken advantage of the policy's 'generosity' and were deemed, 'too lazy to work'.

The rhetoric used by the media in relation to poverty is worth noting; although the term, 'the poor' was occasionally used to refer to those living in poverty, the more commonly used terms were 'disadvantaged groups' (*ruoshi qunti*), 'groups living in difficulties' (*kunnan qunti*), and 'groups living in poverty and difficulties' (*pinkun qunti*). Although no explicit explanation has been found for such choices of words, it is clear that 'the poor' contains a somewhat negative connotation, while the use of the other terms shows relatively more empathy.

When referring to those in poverty, or attitudes or actions towards those in poverty, words and phrases such as 'care' or 'with a caring heart'(*guanxin*), 'sympathy' (*tongqing*), 'attention' (*guanzhu*), and 'giving warmth' (*song wennuan*) are frequently used. It was reported in the media that the poor were in unfortunate and difficult situations and so were in need of help and support, which would be provided by the government through its policies. All members of society should pay 'attention' to the conditions of those in poverty, especially the rich and various social organizations and companies which were reportedly involved in 'giving warmth' through charitable activities. Those in poverty, on the other hand, were reported as having a strong sense of gratitude (Li, 2003). It was recognized by the media that for low-income families, although concerned with issues such as budgeting, children's schooling, possible illness, and economic ruin, above all, their greatest difficulty was in remaining hopeful that their lives could change. They expected to live good lives as much as everybody else, and so it was important to encourage them to work hard to improve their own lives (Bai, 2010).

According to the media, it was issues of shame that caused some laid-off workers to reject *dibao* at the beginning of its implementation. Three main reasons were cited for this: receiving *dibao* was viewed as an indication of incompetence and uselessness; concerns that their children might face discrimination or get bullied at school; and concerns that once they received *dibao*, they might experience difficulty finding employment as they noticed that some employers were reluctant to hire those on social assistance who would possibly bring economic or other burdens to the enterprise or organization. The media widely advocated for the economic and social rights of the unemployed, specifically those laid off due to the restructuring of SOEs (Liu, 2001). However, as *dibao* gained increasing publicity, pieces appeared in the media raising concerns about its abuse.

Construction of the 'Deserving' and 'Undeserving'

The distinction between those experiencing economic hardship who could be considered 'deserving' and those who were conversely 'undeserving' emerged within the groups in relation to discussions about various social assistance programmes such as *dibao*, financial aid in colleges for the youth group, and poverty alleviation programmes targeted at the rural areas for the migrant group. Even though interviewees agreed about the necessity of the existing social assistance provision, strong opinions were expressed concerning the distinction between those who were 'deserving' of support and those who were not. The 'deserving' included those with disabilities or illness who were not able to work and hence should be entitled to social assistance. The 'undeserving', on the other hand, included those of working age who 'chose' not to work. These people, it was believed, should not be entitled to social assistance and they were categorized into at least three different groups. Firstly, those who were able-bodied but too lazy to work and who stayed at home playing *majiang* (a popular game), although some of them were believed to have other sources of income such as rent from properties which they owned. The second group were former prison inmates who were said to receive *dibao* as soon as they are released from prison. This group divided opinion, with some focus group participants commenting that the fact that they received *dibao* upon being released from prison sent the wrong moral message to the public in that *dibao* could be viewed as a reward for their crimes. Others, however, pointed out that the allocation of *dibao* could in fact benefit social stability by reducing the likelihood that ex-prisoners would commit new crimes since their basic necessities were taken care of. The final group identified were professional beggars who, it was believed, might use the money they were given to get rich rather than for survival; these views were apparently influenced by recent newspaper coverage. Overall, these various opinions expressed by focus group participants implied a degree of prejudice or shaming which was embedded within the larger society.

Interviewees from different social backgrounds noted different aspects of 'undeservingness'; the retirees' group, for example, voiced their disapproval about adult children living off their elderly parents' pensions, while the migrant group felt that even the poorest people in Beijing, those receiving *dibao*, lived a much better life than peasants in rural areas materially due to the fact that they could enjoy many privileges.

The media definitions of 'deserving' and 'undeserving' differed somewhat to those expressed by focus group participants. As stated earlier, media journalists mainly attributed poverty to structural factors, and so it is logical that, for the most part, they positioned themselves on the side of those experiencing poverty, proposing goals and measures to alleviate its effects. They stressed the right of those in poverty to equality and to the basic living guarantee, one article stating, 'We cannot guarantee work for everyone, however, it is our bounded responsibility to guarantee that everyone has meals' (Sheng, 2002). The underlying message here clearly signified a shift in ideology: from the rhetoric of guaranteed work during the planned economy to the notion of residual welfare provision in the post-reform period. The priority now was seen to be dealing with the challenges of how to help disadvantaged groups survive through difficult periods (Zhao et al., 2002), such as the economic transition, and how they should be sheltered by a 'protective umbrella' such as through the *dibao* (Ministry of Labour and Social Security, 2007). Nonetheless, there was limited media coverage indicating concerns about so-called *dibao* 'dependency'. In one article, for example, it was reported that some *dibao* recipients had had their payments stopped because although they were capable of working they refused to participate in community organized workfare programmes (Ke, 2002).

The Media's Role in Influencing Public Opinion on Poverty-Related Issues

As discussed previously, the coverage of poverty by the media included descriptions of characteristics of poverty, such as living conditions, as well as reports on specific issues such as the rapidly growing economic disparity reflected in the increased Gini Co-efficient (Ji, 2011). However, although the media viewed itself as responsible for advocating for the interests of disadvantaged groups (Qu, 2010), the media does not assume a neutral position in the system since its primary role is to serve as the official organ of the Party-State. And so, while the Chinese government assumes primary responsibility for poverty alleviation and social assistance, the media channels the official viewpoint to the public. The media, therefore, fulfils two main functions: policy dissemination and reporting on poverty alleviation programmes.

During the time period covered by this analysis (2000 to 2012), a large number of media articles appeared relating to *dibao*, covering such issues as regulations and procedures in the formation and implementation of this social protection programme. According to Chinese Communist tradition, speeches made by top government officials usually signal a change in policy direction or action and so these are invariably covered by the media. In 2003, for instance, Zhu Rongji, then Premier of China, promised in his state of the union address to 'strengthen the *dibao* and ensure that all eligible urban residents in poverty would receive it' (Wang and Long, 2002). In the same report, it was pointed out that some local governments set the *dibao* standard according to their financial capability instead of using the proper procedures. This article therefore gave a clear message that the *dibao* would be expanded with the strong support of central government. It was through the media that the public could learn about the availability and targeting of various social assistance programmes. In addition to statutory social protection provisions, a large part of poverty alleviation in China has been achieved through the efforts of the non-statutory sector (e.g., Zheng, 2003), as well as various charitable activities (Anon, 2007; Anon, 2011; Jia, 2011). The media, therefore, also frequently covered the activities of various organizations and charities that were concerned with poverty alleviation initiatives, such as those of the All China Federation of Trade Unions and local union branches (e.g., Pan, 2003).

It is interesting to note how the media coverage cycle corresponds with the political/policy and charity cycles, media reports relating to poverty and social assistance issues typically peaking at two times of the year. One of the peaks occurs during national holidays, especially the traditional Chinese New Year. This coincides with the winter season and so the media provides intense coverage of disaster relief initiatives and specifically charitable events such as donations of winter clothes and bedding (*People's Daily* Editorial, 2005). The other peak period usually happens prior to, and during, the annual National Convention of the People's Congress in March, when issues covered include topics such as bills proposed by representatives concerning urban poverty or economic disparity. Examples of such media coverage include representatives proposing to increase employment opportunities for the unemployed and to strengthen social security measures (Wang and Long, 2002); and proposals for basic medical care to be provided to those living in poverty in urban cities (Jia, 2006). In addition, poverty, or those living in poverty, tend to receive media attention during special occasions such as during the preparation for the 2008 Beijing Olympics when it was reported that donations of *fuwa* (official 2008

Olympic mascots) were organized for children in low-income families (Du, 2007).

A feeling of optimism around the goals of achieving social equality and justice through poverty alleviation is generated by the media. Even though urban poverty was normally portrayed as being unavoidable and challenging, it was argued that it could be reduced through a series of measures such as the increase of state input along with economic growth; raising the level of *dibao* and minimum wages; improving social insurance measures; the provision of affordable housing; increasing the progressive taxation level and introducing inheritance tax (Ji, 2011); redistribution of income and wealth; and universal public service provision (Bai, 2010).

The significant role that the print media plays in China was clearly acknowledged by the focus-group participants, who all referred to it as an important source of information. For instance, due to a recent high-profile scandal relating to the Red Cross Society of China, which had been uncovered by the media, some interviewees expressed their concern about the corruption of charitable organizations and their reservations as a result about donating to them in future. There was, however, a clear consensus that the media was highly controlled by the Chinese government and obviously used as a function of propaganda, and so did not present an objective reflection of reality. They felt, therefore, that the media provided positive but superficial and limited coverage of issues relating to poverty, mainly focusing on disaster relief or poverty alleviation initiatives instigated by the state. Participants did, however, point out that the media was becoming more diverse in its coverage and that the level of governmental control varied across its different formats. Television news was seen as the media source which presented the strongest 'ideological flavour' and local newspapers were perceived as less controlled than those operated by the central government. The internet was considered to be even less controlled than the conventional media, and it was the internet that the youth group relied on for much of their information, particularly micro-blogs. While interviewees implied the limitations of the media in covering social issues such as poverty, those in poverty, as noted by the upper- and middle-income group, had little power to have their voice heard in society.

Conclusions

The general public, as represented by participants taking part in focus group discussions within this research, appear to have a rather realistic idea concerning poverty and the difficulties those living in poverty face, such as unemployment; financial struggles in the areas of medical care, education, and housing;

as well as issues relating to social interaction. These perceptions are consistent with those presented in Chapter 12 in this volume, which reported the views and experiences of people living in poverty in China.

As for the perceived causes of poverty, while factors at both individual and structural levels were recognized by those not living in poverty, it is interesting to note the differences in opinions as to the causes of poverty between the general public and the media, as well as the variation in the views expressed across the five focus groups. Overall the media put more emphasis on the wider contextual factors such as the restructuring of SOEs, changes in the provision of social protections, China's joining of the WTO, and China's early stage of economic development. The focus-group participants pointed out the roughly equal importance of individual abilities and efforts, and attributed varying weight to the wider social factors. These different perceptions of the causes of poverty were related to the varied personal backgrounds, occupations, and socio-economic statuses of the respondents: at one end of the two extremes stood the working-class group who argued about structural changes, and at the other the upper- and middle-income professionals and entrepreneurs who tended to prioritize the importance of individual initiative and abilities, perhaps based on their own rather 'successful' experiences by societal standards.

Among focus group participants, the distance they felt from those in poverty and the perceived risk of falling into poverty themselves varied. Importantly, all respondents seemed to have had some contact with those in poverty, and a few of them had faced economic hardship themselves. It was not surprising to discover that the working-class group and the retiree group felt the closest to poverty and the most likely to fall into poverty, whereas the upper- and middle-income group did not really think that they faced the same risk, although they always considered the possibility of business failure which could fundamentally change their social and economic standing.

In terms of language used in relation to poverty, the focus-group participants overall tended towards sympathy for those in poverty. While the Chinese media occasionally used the term 'the poor' to refer to those living in poverty, on the whole they employed less demeaning terms including, 'disadvantaged groups', 'those living in difficult situations', and 'those living in poor and difficulty situations'; and words such as 'care', 'with a caring heart', 'sympathy', 'attention' as indications of what were deemed to be appropriate responses towards those in poverty.

However, constructs of 'deserving' and 'undeserving' did appear in coverage concerning poverty when it came to the question of social assistance provisions. In general, the media placed greater emphasis on the function of social assistance programmes such as *dibao*, and only occasionally reported on cases of abuse of the system. Focus-group participants, however, made a much clearer distinction between the 'deserving' and 'undeserving' poor, based on their ability to work and on a range of other moral judgements about their behaviour and priorities.

Finally, the media was viewed as an important source of information through which policy implementation and social assistance programmes are disseminated. At the same time, however, the media was perceived as serving the state's propaganda, so its representation of reality was not seen as being entirely objective.

References

Anonymous (2007) 'Aimu Company launched 'sunshine girls' educational fund', *Beijing Morning Post*, 31 Aug., 34.

Anonymous (2011) 'Tongrentang's sprout children care action', *Beijing Morning Post*, 7 Sep., D04.

Bai, T. (2010) 'Poverty should not be the reason for poverty', *People's Daily*, 18 Nov., 17.

Chen, H., Zhu, X., and Wei, Y. (2006) 'Beijing built two new affordable hospitals', *Beijing Daily*, 21 Feb., 5.

Chen, J. and Zhang, Y. (2006) 'How to view the topical issues concerning population', *Beijing Daily*, 8 May, 18.

Commentator (2001) 'Ensuring the basic rights of the groups in poverty according to the law', *People's Daily*, 18 Nov., 1.

Commentator (2003) 'Weaving the social safety net by government', *Workers Daily*, 28 Jan., 1.

Du, X. (2007) '290 thousand Olympic Mascots donated to poor children', *Beijing Evening News*, 17 Aug., 1.

Editorial (2005) 'Sending the warmth to those in difficulty', *People's Daily*, 13 Dec., 1.

Ji, B. (2011) 'Two key factors in resolving the income gap', *Beijing Daily*, 13 Mar., 17.

Jia, X. (2006) 'Views of the representatives', *Beijing Evening News*, 8 Mar., 2.

Jia, X. (2011) 'Sixteen children with congenital heart diseases recovered', *Beijing Evening News*, 20 Sep., 20.

Ke, S. (2002) 'No dependency on *dibao* in Harbin', *Workers Daily*, 3 Dec., 8.

Li, J. (2003) '*dibao* gave me courage', *Workers Daily*, 28 Jan., 1.

Liu, X. (2001) 'Laid-off workers refused *dibao*', *Workers Daily*, 29 Oct., 8.

Ministry of Labour and Social Security (2007) 'Holding the protective umbrella of the citizens with the *dibao*', *People's Daily*, 9 Oct., 9.

Mo, R. (2003) 'Resolve urban poverty problems', *People's Daily*, 27 Jan., 13.

Pan, Y. (2003) 'Sending warmth project warms heart', *People's Daily*, 11 Mar., 11.

Qu, Z. (2010) 'Who are the disadvantaged groups?', *People's Daily*, 11 Nov., 17.

Sheng, M. (2002) 'Paying attention to the disadvantaged groups means paying attention to the nation's future', *Workers Daily*, 8 Jan., 3.

Wang, Y. and Long, F. (2002) 'Three questions to *dibao*. Workers Daily'*, 23 Mar., 1.

Zhang, Z. (2006) 'Educational costs as the op reason causing poverty for urban and rural residents', *Beijing Evening News*, 8 Feb., 32.

Zhao, Y., Cheng, L., and Wang, J., (2002) 'To hold correct attitude toward poverty', *Workers Daily*, 7 Mar., 1.

Zheng, Y. (2003) 'Shenyang: Paying attention to the 0.35% *dibao* recipient families', *People's Daily*, 1 Jul., 4.

20

Constructing Reality?

The 'Discursive Truth' of Poverty in Britain and How It Frames the Experience of Shame

Elaine Chase and Robert Walker

Introduction

This chapter illustrates how accepted or 'discursive truths' (Foucault, 1980) surrounding poverty are formed and simultaneously reified via media, public, and political debates. The result is that people living in poverty are subjected to a series of uncritical labelling and attributions according to two polarized 'deserving' and 'undeserving' camps. These discourses in turn become regulative as they not only work to inform and determine the general public's responses to those in poverty, but provide the justification for the treatment of people facing hardship, typified for instance by increased conditionality in social protection provisions. Understanding how such discursive truths surrounding poverty are generated and sustained offers insights into how and why policy responses to poverty in Britain have been steered in a particular and increasingly convergent direction, ultimately one which is and arguably always has been inherently shaming (Walker and Chase, 2013).

Discourse analysis entails an examination of the interactional order of communication (how people use language to engage in social life); its psychological order (how a shared understanding of a particular phenomenon is generated); and its historical or institutional order (how meaning making takes on different institutional forms over time) (Taylor and Yates, 2001; Wetherell et al., 2001). Goffman (1967) has theorized how the work of all institutions is shaped by the rules of their interaction order and, in a similar vein, Foucault (1980) claimed that knowledge is created in any society through the mechanism of 'discursive truths', in which certain ideas are prioritized and promulgated over others and then continue to be imposed via statements of morality, regulations, conditions, and forms of administration. Hence Goffman, Foucault and others point to discourse as an institution bound by particular cultural norms and values which ultimately limits the scope and breadth of how we conceptualize and respond to certain social phenomena (Hall, 2001); ideas which have particular resonance in relation to how poverty is socially constructed in Britain.

Data were derived from a combination of a random selection of media coverage and focus group discussions with relatively affluent adults. A total of twenty-one adults (eight men and thirteen women) not currently living in poverty, selected via street recruitment and sift questionnaires, participated in eight focus group discussions of varying sizes. Using the Nexis database (a system providing electronic access to more than 20,000 global news sources), a thematic analysis of samples of all national (UK) newspaper coverage of 'poverty' and 'welfare' was completed for a twelve-week period spanning just over five years. A stratified random sample of weeks was selected between 1st and 7th December 2006 and 1st and 7th January 2012, ensuring that it incorporated all months of the year, a selection of the four weeks over any one month and all seven days of the week. Articles were subdivided into editorial, comment, and news features and the material interrogated with respect to two broad questions: (1) What key themes are reflected in the media with respect to poverty and welfare in Britain over the selected time period?; and (2) In what ways (if at all) do these themes reflect the poverty–shame nexus explored within the wider research project?

Generating 'Truths'—the Actors

The analysis revealed that the dominant 'truths' about poverty in Britain are generated and sustained by a range of privileged actors who hold firmly entrenched views about what does and does not constitute poverty and why people experience it. Such observers include the full spectrum of the media which carefully chooses words so as to propagate particular 'truths' about poverty according to the political and moral stance of its readership; members of society who enjoy relative wealth and who are unlikely to face the daily struggles described, for example, by people in Chapter 13 of this volume; and politicians who not only rhetorically help shape such 'truths' but who are charged to deliver policy on the back of them.

The national print media in Britain comprises a range of daily publications which sit across the political spectrum. Yet it is the popular or commonly described 'tabloid' press, originally established for the non-elite working classes, which today commands by far the largest readership (Audit Bureau of Circulations, 2013). Of the four national tabloids with the highest circulation, three of these (the *Sun*, the *Daily Mail*, and the *Daily Star*) represent a political stance right of centre and one (the *Daily Mirror*) tends to have political allegiance to the left. The broadsheet *Daily Telegraph* and the tabloid *Daily Express* are next in rank in terms of readership, both traditionally supporting the Conservative party; while the broadsheet *The Times* has tended to shift its political allegiance overtime. The *Guardian* and *Independent* broadsheets tend to attract a left of centre and predominantly middle-class readership. Collectively, the print media, as will be seen in the remainder of the chapter, is crucial in shaping contemporary poverty discourses and, by the force of its readership, the tabloid press is particularly influential.

The 'Truth' about the Existence and Causes of Poverty

The nature of poverty and its causes were important themes generated through focus group discussions, and people had firm views about what constituted the 'truth' on these matters in the context of Britain. Group participants frequently alluded to how the media, combined with their own life experiences, had informed and shaped their opinions about the absolute or relative existence of poverty and whether its causes were broadly structural or individualistic.

Absolute or Relative

Participants within focus groups differed in their views of what constituted poverty but essentially the debate centred on ideas of '*absolute*' compared to '*relative*' poverty. While 'absolute' poverty was perceived as something that could easily be identified (and in fact had been seen first-hand by a number of people) in Africa, in countries of South America, or in Asia, it was not readily identified as a phenomenon in Britain. To an extent, people were often stuck with certain images such as famine and squalor as the blueprint of poverty and from there struggled to grasp the relevance of such a definition for Britain.

Some people saw the difference between relative and absolute poverty in terms such as, 'food on the table but no digital TV' (relative poverty) and 'you can't afford to feed yourself' (abject poverty). Yet, others argued that relative poverty meant that 'you can't engage in normal society' which in practice meant being able to 'send kids to school in clean clothes', 'take the bus', or 'take the kids swimming'. And people became quickly absorbed in the debate over whether being without a computer, a mobile phone, or certain 'white goods' constituted poverty, usually concluding that it did not. One man commented that people in Britain might be considered as being in a 'hard time zone', rather than a 'poverty zone'. The most commonly expressed defining line between being in poverty or not, however, was whether or not you could afford to feed and house yourself and your family. Nonetheless, some participants, typified by the following quote, squarely rejected the appropriateness of the word 'poverty' in Britain,

> The reality is, when I hear people talk about poverty to me it just gets a little bit under my skin because I just, you know, I've worked with people who are allegedly within the bracket of poverty and as you say, you know, I kind of think well I don't have the gadgets they have...the word poverty really grated with me...when I hear media talk about poverty within Britain, you know, I can understand there are certain areas which are very deprived etc....but generally, I don't like the word poverty where Britain is concerned.

Participants in groups were presented with a series of vignettes drawn from interviews with people living in poverty conducted in an earlier phase of the research. Interestingly, people who, prior to reading the vignettes, rejected the notion of 'poverty' within the British context, conceded that the situations portrayed in the vignettes did amount to descriptions of 'poverty'. When asked about this inconsistency with their earlier views, they variously reflected that, perhaps they 'lived in a bubble', cushioned from these sorts of difficulties or that the vignettes had dealt with the nuances and details of actual poverty, something which society and the media would not normally take into consideration, as one woman put it, 'Unfortunately society doesn't have time generally to really understand the detail because it's too difficult...it's too complex'. Importantly, at the end of the focus groups, several people reflected that they felt unsettled or 'unnerved' having aired and reflected on some of the ideas they held as truths.

Structural or Individual Causes

Most participants in focus group discussions began by identifying macroeconomic causes of poverty in Britain, including the global recession, the current austerity measures employed by the coalition government, high unemployment, the lack of training and apprenticeship programmes, and the mismatch between a growing service economy and the skill-set of those looking for work. These wider factors played out at the level of individual households, where rising food, fuel, and commodity prices were affecting everyone yet hitting hardest those on the lowest incomes. Almost all participants also made reference to what they saw as growing inequalities in Britain and the growing gap between 'rich and poor'. A number of participants began by criticizing the stance of what they termed the 'gutter press', which tended to vilify people

259

living in poverty and label those in receipt of welfare provisions as 'benefit bums' and 'scroungers'—terms that they strongly objected to. However, only in rare cases did these initial opinions hold firm throughout the course of discussions, most participants tending to oscillate in their views about people on low incomes depending on the examples they referenced, either from their own experience or from the vignettes they were presented with drawn from an earlier phase of the research.

On the other hand, the notion that structural inequalities caused and perpetuated poverty received limited attention across large sections of the media; a theme really only addressed by the *Guardian* and the *Independent* (and occasionally by *The Times*) and couched more succinctly as 'gexploita-tion' by journalists writing in the *Morning Star*. All these publications, for example, responded in May 2008 to a report by the TUC-sponsored Commission on Vulnerable Employment exposing evidence of exploitation affecting some two million workers. A commentary piece in the Guardian (5 May 2008)[1] suggested that 'low-paid, insecure employment has flourished like some rapacious mould'. The piece acknowledged the gains that Gordon Brown and the Labour party had made with respect to child poverty but reported that the extent of working poverty had been largely obscured, leaving some 1.4 million children living in poverty in working households, exactly the same figure as in 1997. These were described as 'hard working' families 'scrabbling to make ends meet'. Amelia Hill (at that time social affairs correspondent) for the *Observer* summarized the report as revealing 'a hidden Britain where those providing the services on which society and the economy rely are trapped in a cycle of poverty and injustice'. In 2009 *The Times*, (24 April 2009) reported on an OECD report predicting that by 2020 some two-thirds of the world's population would be employed without contracts or social protection as the global recession increasingly forced people into low-paid work.

The 'Truth' about People in Poverty

Although most focus group participants began by alluding to the wider inequalities and social injustices underpinning poverty in Britain, they quickly shifted to discussing what they considered to be the individual shortcomings of those living in poverty. An unwillingness to work, a lack of 'work ethic', limited capabilities, dysfunction, and limited aspirations—what one

---

[1] All newspaper articles cited in this chapter can be searched for using the *NexisUK* database accessed via an institution) using the key word, cited newspaper, and date (provided) in the search options.

person described as 'a poverty of aspiration', all emerged as prominent 'truths' firmly embedded in people's understandings about why others faced economic hardships.

They Are Shirkers Not Workers

The notion of a sound work ethic as a route out of poverty was strong, as was the idea that while some people, like some of the focus group participants themselves, seemed able to '*embrace*' opportunities, others lacked the moral fibre to make the most of them. One man explained,

> I've come from humble beginnings and I've worked very, very, very hard, you know, to turn things around. I'm in a very lucky position now, but that's a combination of luck and work. So it's about being dependable, hard working, always smiling. People who don't have a positive attitude to work or helping others, I'm sorry I have less sympathy for them, and that's just my own prejudice I guess.

Importantly, all focus group participants drew an apparently inevitable link between not working and poverty, rarely alluding to the idea of in-work poverty. Within this frame of understanding, several people did acknowledged how quickly people could 'slide into poverty' as a result of circumstances beyond their control, one or two of them having had to face sudden redundancy with no 'big pay off' in the past. And others too recognized illness and incapacity or mental health issues as reasons for not being able to take up employment which may result in poverty. Similarly, they understood, they said, the difficulty in making the transition to work from benefits, and the fact that, all things considered, there may be no or few financial incentives initially to (re)enter the work place.

That said, participants were quick to draw a distinction between people they knew personally who were working, even though they might be 'better off' claiming benefits, and those who 'chose' not to work. The former, they said, continued to work for reasons of 'pride', 'responsibility', or 'wanting to develop a career'. They were held in stark contrast to others who were seen as 'choosing' to remain on benefits. Some people expressed their concerns about the emergence over the past two or three decades of a collective social acceptance of living on benefits; the welfare system that was 'too easy' to access, and the lifestyle it generated, had become, they believed, ingrained as the norm and collectively produced whole 'estates' where it had become 'easier to conform to the norm than to be different'.

The mantra of the unemployed 'not wanting to work' was repeatedly echoed in the media. Newspaper articles were replete with what we coin stereo-stories, used notably by the tabloid press to produce archetypes, epitomizing the antithesis of the political, social, or moral position assumed by the publication or its intended audience. People receiving benefits frequently became the protagonists of these stereo-stories; a *Daily Star* column (15 October 2008), for example, dubbed Tracy and Harry Crompton, reportedly unemployed for fifteen years, 'scroungers who would need to be earning around £70,000 to live like this if they had jobs'. The piece concluded with 'our welfare system is a joke'.

They Make the Wrong Choices

The assumption that people had ended up in poverty because of having made the 'wrong choices' was generally held even when there was a modicum of sympathy that some people faced difficult choices, though it was rarely acknowledged that people may, in reality, have no such choices at all. One woman, for example, spoke of how she worked in a local primary school and found herself teaching children of previous pupils. She spoke of how these girls who had now become young mothers were 'suffering hardship because of that choice'. This 'breeding of single parents' who have 'no aspirations to get out of that rut' was, she considered, a major cause of poverty. Such women were, she felt, perpetuating the 'vicious circle'.

The words and phrases used by people in focus groups were repeatedly echoed across the media and vice versa. People on benefits were defined either individually or collectively as 'a social burden'—particularly if they had children. Such people lived on 'sink estates', defined by one participant as 'a place where the desire to do better is crushed out of you as an individual'. They were similarly categorized using terms such as 'deserving' and 'genuine' on the one hand and 'undeserving' or 'working the system' on the other. Choosing to go down the 'state-supporting route' rather than the 'self-supporting route' was another distinction made. The notion of people 'choosing to live in poverty' was voiced by a number of participants; others defining some people as being 'happy being on benefits' and part of a 'culture of dependency'. Equally, they were considered responsible, at least in part, for a 'vicious circle' of poverty and disadvantage in which the inevitability of poverty in the next generation was often rhetorically linked to the 'lifestyle choices' made by adults now. People who were consistently poor had become what one participant termed, 'impoverished'—lacking things that gave them fulfilment in life and a condition which kept people where they were. Such attributes were also closely associated with what were described as 'disjointed families' and 'fragmented families' and the consequent hardship that was said to trail in the wake of such family disintegration.

They are Dysfunctional

Certain news stories were seemingly framed to point towards presumed individual inadequacies and failings, columnists frequently producing copy which took a particularly negative and derogatory stance towards people living on benefits. An opinion in the *Daily Telegraph* (29 August 2010) piece by Janet Daley, for example, illustrates the ways in which people in poverty were typically represented. Calling for a fundamental rethink of how we assist 'the poor' and responding to a recently published report by the Institute for Fiscal Studies (IFS) which detailed the unfair impact of the budget on those on lower incomes, she commented,

> I realize that there are people whose life circumstances, through no or little fault of their own, have been so calamitous that they will require a great deal of help and charity (in the best sense of the word) to improve their condition. But that is all the more reason why dependence must not be treated as a lifestyle choice worthy of 'protection'; the genuine hard cases need to be identified and dealt with as a matter of urgency, not simply absorbed into a more general undifferentiated underclass, where their severe social dysfunction will be exacerbated and will help to contribute to a wider malaise. (Robust, self-respecting working-class communities used to be able to deal with the odd delinquent youth or disruptive adult in a way that depressed underclass neighbourhoods cannot)

The conflation between unemployment, dependence, lifestyle choice, the underclass, and dysfunction was echoed in much of the right-wing press across the time analysed. In the week of 3–8 September 2009, the case of two brothers aged 10 and 12 attacking a 9- and 11-year-old in Edlington, Doncaster, dominated the media with front page news stories, features, letters, and analysis pieces appearing. The focus was primarily on the horror of the crimes meted out by children so young to other children, the inadequacies of social services provision, and the failure to remove children from their dysfunctional home at an early enough age. But although the media attention initially focused on the events surrounding the particular family in question, the debate descended into insinuations over the links between attributes of their family and wider social problems. Such depravity evidenced in the case led commentators, via an apparently faultless thread, to all those in receipt of welfare and particularly single parents—the 'them' who, according to a piece by Melanie Philips in her column (*Daily Mail*, 7 September 2009) denied their children the opportunity to develop into 'normally functioning human beings'.

Philips went on to declare that welfare and family policy, particularly under the Labour government, had undermined the 'traditional family' and 'incentivised family breakdown by handing out welfare benefits with no conditions attached'. Philips then went on to suggest that 'a more humane response to unmarried motherhood is to treat it for what it is—a potential disaster for both mother and baby' and that 'turning off the benefits spigot...would remove financial incentives that have made such disaster common place'. She ended by stating her opinion that while 'well-heeled intelligentsia' set out to make unmarried motherhood 'normal', they in fact were financially 'cushioned against the worst damage that the removal of such constraints on behaviour inflicted on the poor'.

They Are Not Like Us

Conboy (2002) has described the complex relationship that emerges from the popular press having come to represent the 'ordinary people', or in fact an 'idealised version of the ordinary people', (Conboy, 2002: 2). Over time tabloids have created a mythical 'national community of readers' with a shared identity and sense of national belonging (Conboy, 2006: 94). The strength of this imagined national community is reinforced by constant reference to the outsiders who are seen to threaten such community and who are considered the 'other'. This binarism is used to determine clear categories of desirable and undesirable members of 'the national community' defined by characteristics of 'social responsibility', 'moral worth', and 'a distinctive wholesomeness' (Conboy, 2006: 122); similarly referred to by Anderson (2013: 4) as the 'community of value'.

Whether in news articles, editorials, or commentary, collectively the media reflected these same ideas. Newspapers tended to pitch certain groups in poverty against others who by implication were firmly embedded within the 'the national community': the person receiving benefits versus the tax payer; the family unit versus the 'single mother'; British citizen versus the 'asylum seeker' or 'illegal immigrant'. Right of centre newspapers, for example, repeatedly contrasted the virtues of marriage with single parent families, and especially single mothers, who were repeatedly criticized for having children outside of marriage and the 'poor' life choices they made. Jill Kirby in a piece in the *Daily Telegraph* (9 February 2011) entitled 'Marriage makes us all richer—not poorer', for example, praised Iain Duncan Smith (Secretary of State for Work and Pensions) for his efforts to halt the decline of marriage through promoting relationship education and 'tackling the couple penalty in the welfare system' (that ostensibly makes it financially disadvantageous to be married or cohabiting).

Occasionally, certain newspapers sought to champion the causes of certain groups of people facing hardship, extolling the virtues of some who were struggling but not, by implication, those 'others' who were responsible for their own plight. News and commentary, for instance, covering the circumstances of older people living in poverty, ex-servicemen and women, children, and, sometimes, those who, though working, were unfairly treated in the labour market, tended to collude with the idea that certain people were 'deserving' of support, and by implication that others were 'undeserving', an illustration of the binarism (Conboy, 2002; 2006) which tends to split the 'national community'.

Reflecting the binarism of the media, 'they' was used as a linguistic tool repeatedly in the focus group discussions to indicate others who were different to or in a different category to 'us'—the people participating in the groups. While a number of group participants expressed their horror of the use of terms in the media such as 'scroungers' and 'benefit bums', they nevertheless very often employed similar terms which insinuated that people were living in poverty because by their very nature, values, attitudes, and behaviours they were different to 'us'.

Discursive 'Truths' and Policy

The same constructions of people living in poverty were evident in media debates about politics, with government opponents citing welfare policy as evidence of political incompetence or a product of misplaced values, such that persons in receipt of benefits frequently became pawns in political crossfire. Ignoring a history of welfare provision in Britain dating to the sixteenth century, the idea of the Labour government having created welfare machinery responsible for entrapping people into lives of dependency and economic insecurity was repeatedly aired in the media and alluded to throughout the focus group discussions. The home affairs editor in the *Daily Telegraph*, Philip Johnston (7 December 2006) in 2006, for example, accused the government of creating a 'client nation of supplicants who . . . find it more attractive to stay at home rather than go to work'.

Importantly, the negative portrayals of those in receipt of welfare payments in the media tended to spike to coincide with particular political processes such as welfare reform, budgetary decisions, electioneering, or anti-fraud initiatives (Baumberg et al., 2012). The week of 17–23 November 2007, for example, saw the first revelations concerning new Work Capability Assessments to be introduced in October 2008 in response to what had become dubbed a 'sick note culture' in Britain. This generated similar responses across the media. A letter in the *Sun* (22 November 2007), for example, under the strapline, 'fit as a fiddler', heralded the tests as an 'excellent idea', with one reader stating, 'at last the sick note scroungers are to get a kick up the butt'. *The Times* (20 November 2007) published a news item stating that some 2,000 claims had been made by people 'too fat to work', while in the *Daily Mail*, Kirsty Walker's piece on 'spot the malingerer' derided the welfare system for having provided 'millions of pounds to those too fat, tired or spotty to work'. The main section of the *Daily Mail* (17 November 2007) had a full-page spread entitled 'Make life tough for the idle', praising David Cameron's alleged plans to introduce a Wisconsin-style, subcontracted, payment-by-results system for managing welfare in Britain.

The week of the 3–9 September 2009 heralded the start of political campaigning in the ten-month run up to the 2010 General Election. With a backdrop of recession, the media debate inevitably turned to cuts in public spending and the positioning of the two main political contestants. Two articles in the news section of the *Daily Telegraph* (9 September 2009) were typical of how the media drew attention to the need for the Conservative party to reconsider its budgetary plans by pointing a finger at people in receipt of benefits as responsible for the collective financial plight. George Osborne (Shadow Chancellor), stated the *Daily Telegraph*, was in a position to make cuts where Labour could not and to instigate a 'root and branch' reform of the welfare state. In a similar vein, the leader column in the *Daily Express* on the same day took up the mantle to get Britain back to gainful employment, referring to the 'millions of habitual welfare claimants' who must be taken off the 'intravenous drip of tax payer support and made to earn their keep'.

Stories of 'benefit cheats' allegedly scamming the system appeared intermittently over the period of five years of media coverage examined, although Baumberg and colleagues (2012) have noted that the number of newspaper articles on alleged benefit 'fraud' has remained relatively stable compared to a steady increase in stories implicating people as 'scroungers' or 'poor parents'. Nonetheless, the typical stereo-story used across the print media was, for example, that of benefit recipient Terrence Read seen 'jiving energetically', despite supposedly having received £20,000 in disability allowances over six years (8 July 2010). In February 2011, a report allegedly showing that two-thirds of people currently claiming disability living allowance or employment and support allowance were in fact able to work or could return to work with minimum training and support made the front page of several newspapers. The employment minister Chris Grayling claimed this as proof of the need to reassess incapacity benefit claimants and declared the welfare state 'no longer fit for purpose'. This led to a wave of support in the right of centre press: 'Britain's bloated benefits culture' (the *Daily Telegraph*, 2 February 2011); '1.8 million on sickness benefits are perfectly fit to work' (claimed Emma Boon in the *Daily Mail*, 11 February 2011). Sarah O'Grady in a news column in the *Express* (14 February 2011) extended the argument away from disability benefits to claim that millions of pounds worth of emergency welfare funds were 'squandered on holidays and nights out' and called for an end to 'hole in the wall benefit loans'.

These examples are indicative of the dynamic interaction between media, political, and public discourse in Britain and add weight to how society in general comes to impose shame on people who struggle on the margins of the economy.

Shameful Behaviour

The concept of poverty in Britain is generated within a particular discursive frame which fundamentally regulates how it is understood and responded to by contemporary British society. Moreover, of all the discursive truths employed, it is the idea that poverty is caused by failure to work that fundamentally polarizes the poverty debate in Britain. Hence, a seamless connection is frequently drawn between those living in poverty and those in receipt of welfare benefits. This connection is so strong that most political debate and analysis centres on the solution to poverty through the adjustments to the welfare state and measures to 'reduce dependency'. The emphasis on individual failings rather than structural causes accounting for poverty generates a symbiotic cycle of media furore and political rhetoric, rhetoric that has seen growing convergence irrespective of the ideological allegiance of its orators.

By inculcating the idea that people living in poverty, particularly those receiving benefits, exemplify the 'other' and pose a threat to the 'national community', the 'popular press' plays a central role in generating and perpetuating the discursive 'truths' surrounding poverty, the tabloid media often emerging as the most venomous in its attacks on people facing hardship. These popularized truths invoked by the 'tabloid' media are frequently reiterated in the broadsheet press, even though the analysis, language, terms, and framing used may, on the surface at least, appear more nuanced.

Other studies have demonstrated that the media in Britain has played a key role in demonizing those who are not working and in receipt of benefits, but who are still broadly referred to as the 'working class' (Golding and Middleton, 1992; Lister, 2004; McKendrick et al., 2008; Jones, 2012). Owen Jones (2012), for example, in his exposé of how the 'working class' are vilified around the construction of 'chavs', highlights how journalism mediates public sympathy and/or hatred towards certain social groups via a process of class stratification and labelling. Our analysis confirms previous analysis that media coverage of people in poverty is often vitriolic and destructive, (Mooney, 2009; Armstrong, 2012; Baumberg et al., 2012). Sometimes the media explicitly names and shames specific individuals; more often it targets benefit recipients and people in poverty as a class. Presumably it does so either in the hope that this will, counter to all the evidence (Walker, 2014), help them to help themselves out of poverty or else as a form of gratuitous abuse that amounts to indiscriminate violence against some of society's most vulnerable members (Penny, 2012).

Our analysis suggests that these asserted 'truths' about poverty are equally firmly embedded in the views and perceptions of more affluent members of society. Focus group participants provided sample evidence of the ways in which society in general collectively makes itself blind to the suffering within it and individuals absolve themselves of any personal liability. While the voices heard exhibit varying degrees of empathy with those facing hardship, they at once employ a range of rhetorical devices through which they actively build and reinforce boundaries around their own privilege, distance them-selves from the deficient 'other', and find ways of assuaging guilt by ultimately displacing the responsibility for poverty squarely onto the shoulders of those who bear its daily brunt.

From a political perspective too, sequential discursive truths employed in policy debates tend to reinforce the political claims of the median voter and those more affluent, while vilifying and silencing those left behind. Politicians are thus derided or praised for the various positions they take within the shared policy frame of managing the size of the welfare state and its presumed negative consequences. The rhetoric of dependency; the seamless connection between poverty and welfare; the denigration of people failing to pull them-selves up by their bootstraps—obliterates any historical engagement with an alternative 'truth'.

Certain media outlets, such as the *Guardian* and the *Morning Star*, may remind their readers of the social change and social engineering by govern-ments that have penalized working-class communities—the demise of the mining and steel industries, the sale of social housing—but the policy momentum follows cries from across the political spectrum for the need to end the 'culture of dependency'. The media is a powerful conduit for generat-ing, sustaining, and broadcasting certain 'truths', albeit objectively false, about poverty and its causes that provide a substantive basis for the formula-tion of society's views and opinions. It prioritizes and parrots the ideological stance of politicians most likely to attract the widest readership and panders to the interests of those who are better-off by justifying their privileged positions and according them the moral high ground.

While discourses change over time, there has been considerable path dependency concerning how poverty is constructed and responded to in policy terms in Britain over centuries (Walker and Chase, 2013). Hence, despite changing terminology, the constructed stereotype of 'the work shy', 'the benefit bum', the 'scrounger', are deeply entrenched and widely dissem-inated in public and social discourse. What we have dubbed as stereo-stories repeatedly explain poverty with reference to lifestyles and behaviour that are portrayed as shameful, immoral, depraved, irresponsible, and indolent. Ideas generated by these stories not only fuel public debate but permeate political discourse—hence the stereotype becomes the target of the political response and feeds the rhetorical debates that ensue across the political spectrum. Shame is an integral component of the discursive 'truths' governing how we perceive and respond to poverty in Britain and hence has to be the key to how we reconstruct the so-called 'truth' about poverty.

References

Anderson, B. (2013) *Us and Them*, Oxford: Oxford University Press.

Armstrong, S. (2012) *The Road to Wigan Pier Revisited*, London: Constable and Robinson Ltd.

Baumberg, B., Bell, K., and Gaffney, D. (2012) *Benefits Stigma in Britain*, London: Turn2Us.

Conboy, M. (2002) *The Press and Popular Culture*, London: Routledge.

Conboy, M. (2006) *Constructing a Community through Language*, London: Routledge.

Foucault, M. (1980) *Power/Knowledge*, Brighton: Harvester.

Goffman, E. (1967) *Interaction Ritual*, New York: Anchor.

Golding, P. and Middleton, S. (1992) *Images of Welfare: Press and Public Attitudes to Poverty*, Oxford: Martin Robertson.

Hall, S. (2001) 'Foucault: Power, Knowledge and Discourse', in Wetherell, M., Taylor, S., and Yates, S. (2001) *Discourse Theory and Practice: A Reader*, London: Sage Publications Ltd.

Jones, O. (2012) *CHAVS: The Demonization of the working class*, London: Verso.

Lister, R. (2004) *Poverty: Key Concepts*, Cambridge: Polity.

McKendrick, J., Sinclair, S., Irwin, A., et al. (2008) *The Media, Poverty and Public Opinion in Britain*, London: Joseph Rowntree Foundation.

Mooney, G. (2009) 'The "Broken Society" Election: Class Hatred and the Politics of Poverty and Place in Glasgow East', *Social Policy and Society*, 8(4): 437–50.

Penny, L. (2012) 'Shame has become our stick for beating the poor', *The Independent*, 1 June.

Taylor, S. and Yates, S. (2001) *Discourse Theory and Practice: A Reader*, London: Sage Publications Ltd.

Walker, R. and Chase, E. (2013) 'Separating the sheep from the goats: Tackling poverty in Britain for over four centuries', in Gubrium, E., Pellissery, S., and Lodemel, I. (eds) *The Shame of It: Global perspectives on anti-poverty policies*, Bristol: Policy Press.

Walker, R. (2014) *The Shame of Poverty*, Oxford: Oxford University Press.

Wetherell, M., Taylor, S., and Yates, S. (2001) *Discourse Theory and Practice: A Reader*, London: Sage Publications Ltd.

21

'No One Should Be Poor'

Social Shaming in Norway

Erika Gubrium

Introduction

From the late 1970s until the late 1990s, the term 'poverty' was hardly used in Norway's general public debate and media discourse (Bay and Stang, 2009) and its mention in coverage of the welfare state reached a record low in 1999 (Bay and Saglie, 2003). Poverty re-entered public consciousness during deliberations over whether or not Norway should join the European Union (EU), when it became tied to debates on how to best address it (Bay and Stang, 2009; Hagen and Lødemel, 2010). Following the EU debate (Pedersen, 2006) strategies to address poverty were included in the manifestos of parties across the political spectrum throughout the 2000s, albeit with rather different foci. A 'moral panic' in the early to mid-2000s revolved around the welfare state rather than around those individuals living in poverty (Hagen and Lødemel, 2010). While references to poverty in public and media discourses spiked in the 2000s (Bay and Stang, 2009), it has received less coverage since 2010, perhaps due to an overriding concern with the provision of more universally targeted benefits.

Conceptually, over time poverty has taken on many different meanings in Norway, varying according to the aims of particular political agendas and predicated upon the use of differing indicators (Townsend, 1979; Murray, 1984; Walker, 1995; Wacquant, 1996; Room, 1999; Hagen and Lødemel, 2010). In an everyday sense, its meaning extends to identity. We establish who and what we are through social interaction (Mead, 1934/1967). Who we are draws from, and reflects in complex ways, where we are in social life—we reflexively construct our experiences and ourselves in relationship to available and prevalent social identities (Blumer, 1969; Rose, 1997).

In Chapter 15 we explored poverty and shame from the perspectives of those directly experiencing it. The evidence supports scholarship from the realm of social psychology that has demonstrated the social nature of shame (Becker, 1963; Goffman, 1963; Adler and Adler, 1993). The respondents we spoke with who were struggling to make ends meet spoke vividly of the ways in which the impact of their economic difficulties was felt, not only in an individual, internal sense, but as individuals living within a broader framework of particular social norms and expectations. This chapter shifts the focus to the public frame, exploring the broader perceptions of wider society towards those living in poverty in Norway. Data for this analysis were drawn from two sources: a review of newspapers over a five-year period and six focus group discussions comprising members of the 'general public'.

Our analysis included a random sample of 200 news articles covering poverty-related issues in four Norwegian newspapers with a national readership—*Aftenposten, Dagbladet, VG,* and *Dagsavisen*—over a period of five years (2007 to 2011). The analysis focused on the key themes identified through the literature analysis and through interviews with social assistance recipients. News articles were coded according to the aspect of poverty reported; the discourses and language used to report these events; and whether and in what ways (if at all) shame or shamefulness were associated with poverty-related themes.

The sites of recruitment for our focus groups paralleled the three study locations used during our interviews with social assistance recipients. Discussions were also informed by the discursive themes emerging from earlier analyses. The six groups each had an average of four adult participants between the ages of 18 and 67. All were employed full-time and were not, at the time of the research, in receipt of social assistance or sickness/disability allowances. The broad working question in the focus group discussions was 'What does it mean to be poor in today's Norway?' Discussions focused on participants' understandings of the causes of poverty, on who was defined as 'poor', on the economic and social difficulties likely to be faced by individuals living in poverty, and on whether and in what ways participants interacted with people in poverty.

Findings

Previous chapters have demonstrated the strong norms of egalitarianism and full employment that have arisen in Norway's strong welfare state setting. It is perhaps not surprising in this country, where everyone is presumed to be doing well and where there is a strong sense of equality, that focus groups participants were generally reluctant to use pejorative terms when describing groups of individuals. Mirroring this tendency, a relatively low share of news articles offered a strongly negative view of individuals or groups living in (absolute or relative) poverty. Our analysis begins with a look at who it was that the public described as fitting within the definition of 'poor'. It then considers where participants in focus group discussions and the media reporting placed responsibility for poverty. It continues with a discussion of the distinctions made in Norwegian public discourse concerning deservingness and how this is tied to varying experiences of shame. The chapter then examines the ways in which social exclusion, deprivation, and shame appear to be linked within broader public debates concerning poverty. It ends with a brief discussion of the sources of information focus group participants reportedly drew on to establish their views and opinions about poverty.

Does Poverty Exist?

Several focus group participants grappled with the idea that, given the strong (and generous) Norwegian welfare state, the notion of absolute and visible poverty did not fit with everyday reality in Norway. Some refuted the idea that poverty even existed in the country. Rather than referring to poverty per se, participants tended to describe 'visible' poverty in terms of the circumstances and behaviour of those individuals who they had seen as clearly struggling. There were references to drug 'addicts', 'living in shit' on the streets, and standing in 'incredible contrast to the rest of society'. These individuals were portrayed as engaging in distasteful activities via a recurring image of their 'sitting and smoking'. Along with drug users, there was also some focus on other visibly marginalized groups, among them individuals with ongoing physical and mental health issues. Similarly, news coverage focused most particularly on drug addiction when discussing poverty in terms of explicit economic and social marginalization.

Some participants acknowledged the presence of a more widespread relative and contextual poverty in Norway. Reflecting in many ways the descriptions from our interviews with individuals struggling to make ends meet (see Chapter 15), they suggested that the impact of economic status and circumstances on one's life depended to a large part on where one lived. It was 'easy' for individuals living and struggling in wealthy areas 'to *feel* poor', an idea most strongly held by those participants who themselves lived in such settings.

Certain individuals and groups, such as single-parent families, low-status or low-paid workers, immigrant families, asylum seekers, and single immigrant workers, were identified as facing economic difficulties, yet were not necessarily considered completely marginalized. Unlike references made to the 'visible' poor, these groups of people did not stand out immediately as living in poverty, the discussion surrounding them tending to concentrate less on the material aspects of their circumstances and more on the social-psychological dimensions associated with the impact of them not fully fitting into society's dominant norms. The relational nature of such poverty was suggested in the connections made during group discussions between social expectations, social/peer pressure, status pressure, and economic challenges. Befitting the connection between the social-psychological and the economic, these individuals were said to struggle as they tried to 'hide their poverty'. Reflecting our findings in earlier chapters, focus group participants noted that these individuals strove hard to keep their children from being 'stigmatized in school', yet often children from these families could 'fall out a little' (of mainstream school culture). The positive connotations attached to these groups were typically used to contrast rather ascetic living standards of the 'deserving' poor against those individuals 'choosing' or generating their poverty via excessive consumption or general life mismanagement, a point we return to later on in this chapter.

The views expressed by focus group participants concerning the relatively poor did not, however, closely reflect those found in the media coverage. While news articles, on the whole, portrayed single parents in positive or neutral terms, they tended more frequently to present immigrant families or immigrant workers as a 'problem' or social 'challenge' to be addressed through social policy and tighter regulations. Finally, Norway's street dwelling Roma population[1] was cited within the context of poverty, but their inclusion as 'the real poor' was frequently called to question. While the randomized selection of news articles did not yield specific examples of reporting on Norway's urban Roma population, it is important to note that they have received mixed coverage since the end of the 2000s. Some newspapers have been particularly negative in their portrayal, using terms such as 'begging gangs', 'criminal henchmen', or 'trash'. Others, however, have offered a more critical, in-depth and measured coverage of the Roma population in Norway (Engebrigtsen, 2012). This population was considered by focus group participants to be so far outside the norm of Norwegian society, in both a material sense and in terms of social status, that participants appeared reluctant to include them within the category of 'our poor'.

---

[1] Norway has two distinct Roma populations—(1) the *sigoynere* Roma, many of whom have been in Norway for decades, originally of northern Indian descent, with permanent addresses and housing typically in the countryside and (2) the *reisende* (travelling) Roma, many of whom live on Oslo's streets and have since the early 1990s moved from Romania to Norway on short-term, three-month tourist visas and who constitute Norway's poorest group of people (Engebrigtsen, 2012).

Why Is There Still Poverty?

The findings presented in Chapter 15 showed how individuals experiencing economic hardship were more likely to blame themselves for their circumstances than identify wider structural causes for their poverty. Within the focus group discussions, the sentiment was also overwhelmingly focused on individual responsibility for economic difficulties, with participants primarily identifying individual causes. Poverty was described as the result of one's cultural position (one's ethnicity, generation, or location) and the negative influence that one's networks and culture might have had on one's ability and motivation to tackle a difficult situation. Participants spoke of a generational cycle of poverty, noting that a 'tradition' of poverty was often 'inherited' or reproduced via one's local environment—through 'inheritance and milieu'. They suggested that individuals who struggled economically found it hard to change behavioural patterns reflecting certain 'values' which were detrimental in economic and social terms, instead continuing to do what they 'liked to do'.

Participants also generally described poverty as an individual choice in so far as it was the result of bad decisions. Individuals struggled to make ends meet when they 'prioritized beer drinking . . . and football' over one's own children, or when they chose to live 'centrally in the world's richest country'. Poverty was the result of choosing to spend money 'on the wrong things' or of spending 'too much of [the little money] you have'. Many of the discussions revolving around poverty and choice described alternate actions that were possible. Within this context, a single mother could choose to be 'resourceful enough to cook good food and give her children clothing', one could choose to live 'just outside the city where it's much less expensive', and one could have the wherewithal to 'create a value system' that was less focused on material possessions. This preoccupation with choice squarely placed the cause of poverty in the hands of those individuals experiencing difficult circumstances.

Participants within focus group discussions also commonly contrasted Norway with other countries which they identified as having strong 'class differences' and 'a segmented system'. They referred to Norway's exceptional egalitarian and strong welfare state when they spoke of why they were hesitant to attach structural explanations to poverty. As one participant noted, 'in Norway or Scandinavia, one really doesn't need to be poor . . . there really *are* opportunities'. Structural explanations were reserved almost exclusively for immigrants who might be new to the Norwegian welfare state. Participants in half of the focus groups described a labour market and welfare system in which immigrants were 'stigmatized' and automatically moved onto a social assistance system that pushed them into marginalized 'ghettos'. While most of the news articles analysed did not broadly denounce 'the poor' or seek to find blame in a class-laden 'culture of poverty', negative portrayals of poverty were, however, often connected with dependency on the welfare system or upon one's ethnic background.

Participants described a cycle of poverty in which the cause and effects of poverty were intermixed and were linked to the extent to which those living in poverty were motivated to improve their circumstances. They described a back and forth effect between bad situations and lowered self-esteem, which reduced people's capacity to ameliorate their situations. Poverty was a 'chicken and egg' phenomenon in which individuals had lost motivation to 'get up in the morning', were not able to 'manage', and felt 'unworthy' and 'ashamed' due to their low social status. Participants noted how mental and physical health problems further aggravated economic challenges, leaving those struggling to make ends meet with 'little possibility to change their own economic situation'.

Several people also discussed a generational difference in values and attitudes attached to work and poverty over time in Norway. Reflecting findings from the literature analysis (see Chapter 8), participants noted that younger generations had benefited from the struggles their parents had made. Given the 'enormous expectations of what would come to them', young people were said to have fallen into a culture of dependence in which 'they could easily receive support' through a welfare state that failed to 'set requirements for all people'.

News articles, on the other hand, tended to focus at least minimally on the structural issues that exacerbated poverty. More often than not, it seemed, such articles were a guise for politically motivated campaigning, whereby blame was placed with a faulty welfare system or with misplaced government policy. News articles from 2007 onwards, for example, highlighted troubles with the newly merged Norwegian labour and welfare system and challenged both its generosity and its demeaning process of categorization. Norway's parliamentary elections were held in mid-September, 2009 and the Socialist Left, a member of the reigning 'red–green' coalition government, became the target of criticism because of its stated promise during the 2005 parliamentary election to remove poverty ('with the stroke of a pen'). The reigning administration had, however, failed to fulfil this promise and instead poverty had reportedly increased nationwide. The dissonance between political promise and failure to deliver became a central theme of the election campaign, used by parties to shame each other for either not doing enough to alleviate poverty or for threatening to do even less. From the left of the political spectrum, blame was cast towards a social assistance system that provided 'so little' economic support that most recipients found themselves 'nearly below the hunger line' (Aasheim, 2009). From the right came claims that overly generous policies had both generated 'passivity' (Clemet, 2009) and encouraged people to take 'the victim role and take a piece of others' work earnings... out of laziness' (Stocke-Nicolaisen, 2009).

Across the political continuum, in the news media and in most of the focus group discussions, the issue of poverty was tied to a lack of will or ability to work. In this sense, Norway's work approach formed the basis of both explanation for and solution to poverty. Focus group participants generally adhered to the assumed inherent link between poverty and not working and to its more general individualized rational choice calculus. Most suggested it was necessary to carefully balance incentives and disincentives in order to motivate individuals back into the workforce. These same ideas were widely reflected within the printed media with many articles focusing on entry into the labour force as the way out of poverty. When describing the work approach, the bulk of articles presumed that responsibility for economic difficulties lay overwhelmingly with the individual. Little attention was paid to the possible obstacles generated by discrimination, a difficult job market, or other structural challenges. The primary goal of the work approach was succinctly described in one guest editorial as minimizing the chance that an individual might fall into a 'poverty spiral where it doesn't pay to replace economic support with a single income' (Fløtten, 2009).

The focus group theme of non-Western immigrants being excluded from the labour market was also picked up in the media coverage. Journalists wrote about the necessity to aim the work approach towards non-Western immigrants, thus promoting their 'inclusion' in the economy. While this same goal was echoed across the political parties, the strategy for reaching such inclusion differed. While voices from the left spoke of the need to 'lower the threshold for those excluded to enter work life' (Karlsen, 2009), those on the right proposed the use of 'temporary positions' in order to more quickly provide 'help to those falling outside the labour market' (Jonassen Nordby, 2009). Among the leading parties, the Socialist Left was the lone (and mostly muted) voice of opposition to the strict work approach widely extolled in most news articles. Leaders from this party tended to advocate for the eradication of poverty more broadly, rather than moving individuals into the workplace (Tjernshaugen, 2009), cautioning that 'those on disability hadn't chosen their degree of disability' (Jordheim Larsen and Strøyer Aalborg, 2011).

Deservingness: the Welfare Hierarchy and Self-Reliance

A pervasive distinction between those who were deserving of assistance and those who were not permeated the news articles and the public discourse reflected within the focus group discussions. Participants frequently used the notion of choice to distinguish between those who were 'really' poor and those whose poverty was described as merely the result of bad choices and decisions. They questioned whether it was accurate to define people as 'poor' if they faced difficult circumstances because they were 'lazy' or 'too good to work'. Within the welfare system, those who were on disability benefits and in need of support due to unavoidable health issues were defined as more 'normal', and thus deserving, than social assistant claimants. News articles similarly presented a hierarchy of deservingness within the welfare system. Individuals receiving elderly care services and benefits (minimum pensions) as well as recipients of universally provided welfare benefits and services—education and health care—were placed at the top, whereas those individuals lower down on the hierarchy (social assistance and disability benefit recipients) were described in stigmatizing terms and as a 'challenge' to the system (Solberg, 2010). Rather than viewing claimants as individuals, many newspaper articles described receipt of social assistance as a category or identity to be avoided and certainly one that was at the bottom of the welfare system hierarchy.

Within this hierarchy of the deserving ('real') and less deserving ('fake' or 'by choice'), two groups—families with school-age children and non-Western immigrant families—were highlighted by focus group participants as those for which economic difficulties were quite real. Mirroring what our low-income respondents had described (see Chapter 15), participants noted that low-income parents with school-age children experienced 'greater social pressures', especially within the school setting. Immigrant families, especially, were the 'deserving poor', who were thought to be most likely to feel the shaming effects of their situation, due to loss of status and systematic discrimination. Newly arrived immigrants were seen as an exception to the general expectation of full employment and social participation that emerged from the literature analysis (see Chapter 8). Several focus group participants, in fact, used the image of the hardworking, resourceful immigrant to draw a contrast with 'other' ethnic Norwegians living in poverty.

While there were examples of newspaper articles portraying non-Western immigrant families as deserving of assistance, most media coverage of non-Western immigrants was much less positive than the views expressed during the focus group discussions. During 2008 and early 2009, economies worldwide slowed, as credit tightened and international trade declined. While the global financial crisis was experienced less severely in Norway than in many other OECD countries, there was a significant rise in unemployment and the threat of unemployment risks were tied to heighted global insecurity (OECD, 2010). News articles from winter 2008 and spring 2009 reflected the sense of threat to the Norwegian welfare system and broader economy. Articles focused on the non-Western immigrant burden to Norway's welfare system and engaged in the naming and shaming of certain groups considered to constitute a 'challenge' to the welfare state. In particular, immigrants from Somalia, but also Iraq, Pakistan, and Afghanistan were presented as a problem that had specifically beset the capital city of Oslo. One opinion columnist described non-Western immigrant groups as 'losers' who didn't 'play by society's rules' (Herland, 2007). Another article described a 'vicious cycle' in which young Somalis were rendered 'passive' by an ineffective 'Norwegian welfare system' (Olsen, 2007). A series of articles in 2008 and 2009 focused on statistical studies of immigrants' contribution to, versus use of, the welfare system, claiming to have identified varying degrees of 'self-reliance' according to specific groups (Johansen, 2009). Finally, various news articles engaged in negative portrayals of irresponsible immigrant parents and their misfortunate children. The immigrant family was frequently described as a 'challenge' to a demographically changing Oslo and questions were repeatedly raised concerning the extent to which immigrant mothers were willing to facilitate the integration of their children—and of themselves—into Norwegian society.

At the bottom of the hierarchy of deservingness generated by focus group participants were those who were described as 'shameless' or who 'didn't care'. Here there was a clear separation between 'our poor' 'drug addicts', who some personally knew, and the Roma, who might be said to represent Norway's only example of absolute poverty. Those Roma engaged in begging on the street were described as being part of a larger, corrupt network and as 'being placed' strategically to 'play' the roles of being disabled or poor. Hence there was a clear distinction drawn between 'us' (Norwegians) and 'them' (outsiders) when it came to notions of deservingness.

Social Exclusion by Choice?

Focus group participants described poverty as a phenomenon that was more than economic in nature. It was also shaped according to social, cultural, and economic expectations and norms. Participants recognized the marginality of those on low incomes, describing poverty in Norway as a phenomenon that was characterized by social exclusion as much as by economic difficulties. Poverty was described as 'complicated', 'confusing', and the result of a bad cycle of a difficult situation wherein one's 'self-image grows worse'. In this complex interplay between cause and effect, the cause of one's poverty was often considered 'worse and more stigmatizing than exactly how much money one had'. Social marginalization was also associated with being 'outside work life'.

Despite recognizing this complexity, many focus group participants still placed blame with those individuals, who were described as socially excluded due to their economic struggles. Many suggested that poverty and social exclusion merely reflected 'choices' made by those affected. Participants noted that individuals living in poverty appeared unmotivated to take part in worthwhile activities, such as prioritizing children, working, or participating in the broader activities that made one a social citizen. In response to a vignette drawn from interviews with people experiencing poverty that described the shame felt by a women who was struggling financially, focus group respondents suggested that she had merely 'defined herself as *other*' and had chosen to 'take herself out' of society as a result of the shame she felt because of her situation. Social marginalization was the result of a self-inflicted cycle in which an individual 'went around feeling . . . poor' and consequently life 'became very difficult'.

Participants spoke of the caveat of non-Western immigrants, who many felt were actively socially excluded due in large part to circumstances beyond their control, a phenomenon which was also reflected in the news coverage. Many articles drew attention, for example, to the large socio-economic differences that divided Oslo East and Oslo West. These were associated to a large extent with population demographics between the two areas, with the West side representing a higher percentage of 'ethnic' Norwegians and the East side home to a much larger share of first and second generation non-Western immigrant families. Particularly interesting in this coverage was the strategic use of the East–West division by parties on both right and left of the political spectrum to further their particular political agenda. From the left came the claim that such divisions made the city 'worse for everyone to live in', making it 'unsafe' and threatening diversity (Gerhardsen, 2010). From the right came the charge that the left was further stigmatizing those on the East side as living in 'misery' (Hauglie, 2010).

Informing Perceptions

The tenor of focus group discussions was distinctly shaped by the composition of each group. Participants drew heavily from their own personal experiences and observations when discussing poverty and those individuals living in poverty. The tendency to refer to individual responsibility and explicitly blame individuals for their economic challenges was more pronounced for those participants who had no direct or indirect interaction with poverty. Participants who 'didn't know anyone really poor' were more critical of those individuals claiming to have economic difficulties and were more likely to claim that poverty was a choice in today's Norway. People's views tended to

279

alternate from more critical statements concerning identifiable groups living in poverty to less critical comments when, for example, a participant mentioned a personal story of his or her own past struggles or those of others they knew. These sympathies were countered, however, by the broader Norwegian story of social mobility enabled by generous welfare state provisions (see Chapters 8 and 15). One participant referred to her own transition from a difficult childhood to professional success, proof, she felt, of Norway's egalitarian society and that the 'class journey was possible'. Echoed by others, this view supported the claim that to be poor within the strong welfare state setting of Norway today was effectively a matter of individual choice.

Some participants, such as teachers and social workers, for example, drew on professional experiences which brought them into close contact with individuals and families who were struggling financially. Many participants also described how their understanding of poverty was shaped via media reports and features, not necessarily by casting negative aspersions on those living in poverty, but through the media's roles in reinforcing a social hierarchy of deservingness and extolling the financial successes of the wealthy— 'positioning the rich as wonderful, as if they had ... good morals'. They also described how the limited negative media focus on those experiencing poverty was targeted either at the Roma or on those claiming benefits and the allegedly cynical 'calculations' they made in order to benefit from the state.

Conclusion

The public tendency to emphasize what is seen as the individual rather than structural causes of poverty is perhaps not surprising given the context of Norway, where a strong welfare state has ostensibly succeeded in broadly ensuring economic and social equality and opportunity (see Chapter 8). While social recognition of strong class divisions and social hierarchies in some contexts may provide a framework through which to 'connect and collectivise' rationales concerning one's difficulties (Skeggs and Loveday, 2012), such an overt framework may be lacking within Norway's generous welfare setting (Gubrium, 2013).

Furthermore, Lødemel (1997) notes that Norwegian law has had a long tradition of distinguishing between the deserving and undeserving poor and, while an explicit distinction was taken out of the law in the mid-twentieth century and replaced with a paragraph noting that the 'cause of need was irrelevant', this distinction is nevertheless still voiced by many. Indeed, attitudes in most of the focus group discussions pointed towards a stratification of individuals struggling economically into categories of more and less 'deserving'. The placement of immigrants into a category of 'deserving' is perhaps not surprising given the dominant narrative in which Norway's people are able to benefit from the securities of the welfare state in ways in which others are not.

Earlier chapters outline a broader Norwegian storyline that adheres to the idea of a generous welfare state ensuring not just economic security but also social mobility for the country's residents. Those who struggle to make ends meet, therefore, present a perplexing anomaly in a public Norwegian understanding of egalitarianism. The marginality of those who are struggling to make ends meet and the resulting sense of shame is documented in Chapter 15 of this volume. The public discussions presented in the current chapter largely confirm why those facing economic hardship may indeed experience such marginalization, and offer an explanation, at least in part, of how the recrimination and shame aimed at those who have not fared so well comes about.

References

Aasheim, A. (2009) 'Usle kommuner', *Dagbladet*, 27 Aug.

Adler, P. A. and Adler, P. (1993) *Constructions of Deviance. Social Power, Context, and Interaction*, California: Wadsworth Publishing Co.

Bay, A.-H. and Saglie, J. (2003) *I verdens rikeste land: Pressens dekning av velferdsstaten 1969–99*. Report 25/03, Oslo: NOVA.

Bay, A.-H. and Stang, E. (2009) 'Politisk svikt eller individuelt ansvar? Pressens portrettering av fattigdom', in Bay, A.-H. et al. (eds) *Når velferd blir politikk*, Oslo: Abstrakt forlag AS, Chapter 6.

Becker, H. (1963) *Outsiders*, New York: Free Press.

Blumer, H. (1969) *Symbolic Interactionism; Perspective and Method*, Englewood Cliffs, NJ: Prentice-Hall.

Clemet, K. (2009) 'Uføreeksplosjonen', *Dagbladet*, 29 Aug.

Engebrigtsen, A. I. (2012) *Tiggerbander og kriminelle bakmenn eller fattige EU-borgere? Myter og realiteter om utenlandske tiggere i Oslo*, NOVA notat 2/12.

Fløtten, T. (2009) 'Den norske fattigdommen kan ikke fjernes uten å ta valg som svir', *Dagbladet*, 28 Aug.

Gerhardsen, R. (2010) 'Vi ønsker å ha ett Oslo, ikke en delt by', *Aftenposten*, 22 April.

Goffman, E. (1963) *Stigma: Notes on the Management of Spoiled Identity*, New York: Simon & Schuster.

Gubrium, E. (2013) 'Poverty, shame and the class journey in public imagination', *Distinktion: Scandinavian Journal of Social Theory*. DOI: 10.1080/1600910X.2013.809370.

Hagen, K. and Lødemel, I. (2010) 'Fattigdomstiåret 2000-2010: Parentes eller ny kurs for velferdsstaten?', in Frønes, I. and Kjølsrød, L. (eds) *Det Norske Samfunn*, Oslo: Gylendal Akademisk, 284–307.

Hauglie, A. (2010) 'En mangfoldig by', *Dagsavisen*, 21 April.

Herland, H. N. (2007) 'Unødig sutring om Norge', *Aftenposten*, 7 June.

Johansen, P. A. (2009) 'Knapt 55 prosent selvhjulpene', *Aftenposten*, 26 Aug.

Jonassen Nordby, K. (2009) '"Regjeringen har sviktet"', *Aftenposten*, 24 Aug.

Jordheim Larsen, C. and Strøyer Aalborg, B. (2011) 'Krangler om uføre', *Aftenposten*, 2 May.

Karlsen, K. (2009) 'Slik vil Jens løfte Norge', *Dagbladet*, 30 Aug.

Lødemel, I. (1997) *The Welfare Paradox*, Oslo: Scandinavian University Press.

Mead, G. H. [1934] (1967) *Mind, Self & Society. From the Standpoint of a Social Behaviourist*, Chicago: The University of Chicago Press.

Murray, C. (1984) *Losing Ground*, Chicago: Basic Books.

OECD (2010) 'Economic Survey of Norway: Policy Brief March 2010'.

Olsen, T. (2007) 'Slår alarm om khat', *Aftenposten*, 7 June.

Pedersen, A. W. (2006) 'Velfærdsreformer I oljerike Norge: takt og utakt', *Samfundsøkonomen*, 1: 26–8.

Room, G. J. (1999) 'Social Exclusion, Solidarity and the Challenge of Globalization', *International Journal of Social Welfare*, 8: 166–74.

Rose, N. (1997) *Inventing Ourselves: Psychology, Power, and Personhood*, Cambridge: Cambridge University Press.

Skeggs, B. and Loveday, V. (2012) 'Struggles for value: value practices, injustice, judgment, affect and the idea of class', *British Journal of Sociology*, 63(3): 472–90.

Solberg, E. (2010) 'Vilje til velferd', *Dagsavisen*, 9 July.

Stocke-Nicolaisen, P. T. (2009) 'Den gode grådigheten', *Aftenposten*, 27 Aug.

Tjernshaugen, K. (2009) 'Rødgrønt til lilla', *Dagsavisen*, 28 Aug.

Townsend, P. (1979) *Poverty in the United Kingdom*, Berkeley, CA: University of California Press.

Wacquant, L. (1996) 'The rise of advanced marginality: Notes on its nature and implications', *Acta Sociologica*, 39(2): 121–39.

Walker, R. (1995) 'The dynamics of poverty and social exclusion', in Room, G. (ed.) *Beyond the Threshold*, Bristol: Policy Press, 102–26.

22

Poverty and Shame

The Future

Elaine Chase and Grace Bantebya-Kyomuhendo

In the scientific world, poverty has predominantly been thought of as a lack of income in relation to needs or material deprivation resulting from such lack of income. Arguably, however, there has always been an, albeit minority, group of social scientists who have attempted to emphasize the social dimensions of poverty and their importance with respect to material deprivations. Adam Smith noted back in 1776 how membership of society was contingent on the ability to own those things that were symbolic of such membership, at that time 'a linen shirt and leather shoes' (Smith, 2009 1776). While others have pointed to the association between disadvantage and its role in eroding people's ability to function or be included in society (Townsend, 1979; Jones and Novack, 1999; Lister, 2004, 2008; Tomlinson et al., 2008), Amartya Sen was probably the first academic to illuminate the centrality of 'shame' and how efforts to alleviate poverty needed to enhance the 'capability to go about without shame' (Sen, 1983). In fact it was Sen who pointed to the logic in incorporating 'shame' as a component into any poverty measure:

> The poverty line may be defined to represent the level at which a person can not only meet nutritional requirements, etc., but also achieve adequate participation in communal activities and be free from public shame from failure to satisfy conventions (Sen, 1983: 342).

This volume reflects a collective journey by academics from seven countries across the global North and South to explore the intersection between poverty and shame. In order to do this, they examined evidence from a vast corpus of sources to understand how the poverty–shame nexus is socially and culturally constructed and the impact that is has in very different societies. The corpus comprised more than 500 fictional works including novels, plays, and short stories spanning the Victorian era through to contemporary works and written in more than a dozen languages; proverbs in more than ten languages from India and Uganda; some 3,600 poems from Pakistan; 100 films from India, South Korea, and Britain made between the 1950s and 2012; interviews with over 300 adults and children living in poverty; analysis of samples of media coverage in five countries; and discussions with more than 200 people living in relative prosperity in six of these countries. The work presented here is complemented by a collection of deeper theoretical insights into the evolution of shame in the context of poverty (Walker, 2014) and an analysis of samples of anti-poverty policies from each of the seven countries to determine their role in the poverty–shame nexus (Gubrium et al., 2013).

In the introduction to this volume we suggested that four key contrasts have emerged from this collective body of work which polarize conceptions and understandings of poverty and constitute the basis of the poverty–shame nexus in real life: the distinction between absolute and relative poverty; whether it is measured according only to income or other dimensions; how individuals or groups are judged to be 'deserving' or 'undeserving' of support; and whether poverty is conceptualized as something which is caused by individual failings and inadequacies or by structural inequalities. The chapters in the volume have testified that, though culturally nuanced and determined to varying degrees by history and tradition, these same dichotomies appear to resonate across very diverse global contexts.

This research had the explicit intention to release the debate on poverty from orthodox deliberations about less or more income and its absolute or relative definitions. Instead, the aim was to refocus attention on the psychological and social dimensions of poverty and its impact on people's day-to-day lives. The overriding finding is that shame does indeed appear to permeate the experience of poverty and that it has two fundamental dimensions which interact in complex and dynamic ways: put simply, shame is internally felt and externally imposed—it is co-constructed (Chase and Walker, 2013).

Feeling Shame

Sen (1983) makes a distinction between 'capabilities'—the potential that people have to lead fulfilled and engaging lives—and 'functionings', the facilities and resources necessary to enable people to achieve those capabilities. In material terms we have seen how the poverty suffered by landless farmers in Gujarat, Kerala, Pakistan, and Uganda was radically different from that experienced in urban Beijing, South Korea, or Britain and different again from that faced by new immigrants in an outwardly prosperous Western Oslo or ethnic Norwegians living in a small coastal town.

The diverse experiences of respondents across the seven national sites emphasize the relative nature of poverty in two respects. First, in material terms, the lives lived by adults and children in Pakistan, Uganda, and India compared to those in Norway were vastly different. While all described intense financial pressures, decisions that result in starvation or going without a meal on the one hand and whether one can afford to eat out rather than in on the other, are by no means analogous. Secondly, the expectations on adults and children in India, Uganda, and Pakistan, particularly for those living in closely knit rural communities arguably governed more tightly by traditional social mores and values, also differed greatly from those encountered by people living in more individualized societies such as Norway and Britain.

However, measured against local expectations, the pressures on people to provide the best that they could for their children, their families, and themselves, poverty was much more comparable. As became increasingly apparent throughout this work, the failure to live up to those different expectations took a surprisingly similar toll on the personal psychological and social well-being of people in each of the research settings. And it is this reality about poverty which lays the basis for a global discourse that transcends conceptions of poverty based purely on material shortages.

Across the different cultural divides, people interviewed had very similar concerns: having enough and the right kind of food primarily for the family and then for oneself, having adequate clothing and shelter, having access to health care, being able to live up to one's own and others social expectations, and having a degree of financial independence, including being free from indebtedness to others.

Yet each of these dimensions of life also created space for shame to emerge when resources to meet such needs were inadequate or substandard. Children were worried that others would see the inferior contents of their lunch boxes at school and those in Britain and Norway were as likely as children in India to speak about the stigma of being labelled as recipients of free school meals. The inability to attend a feast or other collective gathering because one had nothing to contribute or to wear, were experiences as likely to be recounted in Britain and Norway as they were in South Korea or in India, Pakistan or Uganda. Similarly, children in Britain, Uganda, and India spoke of refusing to bring friends from school to their homes because they were too embarrassed to show where they lived, a response by children similarly observed in Norway; while adults spoke of only speaking to visitors in the exterior courtyard, knowing that inviting people through the front door would expose the penury of their circumstances. In rural India, Pakistan, and Uganda where homes were typically built of timber and mud, respondents spoke of the overcrowding, of disturbed nights, of lack of privacy and the indignity and, additionally for women, the dangers of having to urinate and defecate in fields and open spaces.

The incapacity to meet these social needs (Clark, 2006) of family and ritual in each of the countries was frequently described as painful. Close-knit families and communities are bound by mutual reciprocities, and these pressures were particularly evident in India, China, and Uganda, where status was directly linked to the visible performance of roles. Whether it was the inability to match the quality of gifts given by others in India or the failure to afford the 'small red packages' for children in China at New Year, or having to turn down an invitation for your child to attend a birthday party in Norway or Britain because you could not afford a gift, the impact was the same—a sense of acute failure to be part of the community. And while kith and kin might provide some immediate cushion from the worst effects of poverty (for example, by offering short-term loans or providing food), at the same time, the need to ask for such support placed individuals in all countries in the invidious position of feeling beholden to others, looked down on for their failure to provide or being tied to family debts which they were unable to honour.

From the interviews it was very clear that the vast majority of respondents in every cultural setting had felt ashamed on account of their poverty at one time or another and that, for many, the shame lingered and permeated their existence. Internalized shame has two components: the sense of failure in not living up to one's own expectations, and the belief that as a consequence of this failure one is not valued as a person by other people. Ugandan respondents spoke of shame, humiliation, and stigma and expressed feelings of worthlessness, low self-esteem, self-pity, disillusionment, and hopelessness. Likewise, in Britain, people used a wide range of terms such as 'awkward', 'embarrassed', 'uncomfortable', 'useless', or 'a failure', which alluded to feelings of shame even if they rarely used the word itself (Chase and Walker, 2013). In India, too, there was the same tendency to refer to 'shame' without actually naming it, instead describing feelings of 'sadness', 'worthlessness',' dejection', or 'rejection'.

Being Shamed

Yet as much as embarrassment, shame, and indignity arose from a sense of internal inadequacy, it was equally imposed by a whole host of individuals, social norms, systems, and structures with which people in poverty interacted. The possible evidence for this conjecture emerged from the analysis of cultural media in each country. Its actual existence was verified by people recounting their experiences of poverty and how they were made to 'feel'; but also through the voices of people not living in poverty, representatives of general society, and, to varying extents, by how people in poverty were portrayed via the media.

Cultural Representations

Across the different cultural media, people were shown to be treated badly, exploited, labelled, publicly shamed, and humiliated by society in general and those in authority in particular. Yet the analysis across the different contexts suggested not only important cultural nuances but also some notable shifts over time in how poverty has been conceptualized in the past and how it is understood culturally and politically in contemporary societies. This was particularly the case in cultures which are defined as collectivist, such as China, South Korea, India, Pakistan, and Uganda. Here, it has been suggested that the salience of shame may be greater than in the more individualistic Norway and Britain. There were repeated hints from the insights of these more collectivist cultures that individual hurt caused by shame must be offset against the greater goal of its positive social benefits such as ensuring conformity and reinforcing social and cultural obligations. So, for instance, shaming the individual was presented as being entirely appropriate in cases in which individual behaviour risked undermining the standing of the family, clan, community, or caste, by bringing on it shame that would be experienced by all members of the social group.

On the other hand, while the experience of shame in Norway and Britain is shaped by the perceived views of relevant others, it is more individualistic in its incidence and in the effects. Most Western scientific literature treats the consequences of shame as being largely deleterious to the person who is shamed. Equally, this research suggests that sections of the general public and some politicians appear to see naming and shaming as positive and valid mechanisms to meet the goal of integrating people back into society and in particular into the labour force.

What emerged from the analysis of cultural conceptions of poverty and shame (through film, literature, poetry, and oral traditions) was an apparent reduction over time in the salience of structural explanations of poverty, often linked to culture and tradition, which became progressively superseded by individualized accounts. In early literature, and in more modern work adopting an historical perspective, poverty tends to be understood as an inevitable part of the natural order of things but also has clear political, ideological, and cultural dimensions. During the Maoist period in China, for example, the belief that poverty was the product of exploitation by the rich displaced Confucian and Daoist acceptance of the status quo which had prevailed before the Communist revolution. In contemporary China, perceptions of poverty have once again shifted from a shared and valued common experience, indicative of solidarity against the 'rich', to one increasingly denoting personal failure in a context where economic growth is now accorded greater importance than ever. In the same vein, in South Korea, the portrayal of poverty in film from the mid-1970s through to the 2000s reveals a definite conceptual move away from poverty seen as primarily the result of exploitation by the wealthy classes towards its construction as a consequence of individual failure to make the most of new opportunities created by rapid economic transformation. Equally, Norwegian literature struggles to explain the perpetuation of poverty in an allegedly egalitarian state founded on notions of equal opportunity and so tends to focus increasingly on flaws in individual character.

Real Life Experiences

In real life, people spoke of being exploited, of being 'preyed' upon, or of being made to feel powerless by others with authority and status. While these feelings are not strictly synonymous with 'shame' they nonetheless had the same effect of evoking feelings of inferiority and inadequacy. Such power to make people in poverty feel this way infiltrated all their social and bureaucratic interactions. Landlords and landowners held positions of enormous authority and control and were as likely to threaten eviction for non-payment of rent, albeit mediated by different bureaucratic processes, in a housing estate in Britain as they were on an informal settlement in Lahore or among the overcrowded semi-underground homes of Seoul in South Korea. Landlords often showed little concern for the quality of the housing they forced people to live in and could largely act with impunity, knowing that tenants were unlikely to complain or faced limited recourse to the law when they did.

The Workplace

Equally, workplaces and the bureaucracies where people looked for work were repeatedly described as arenas which heralded the prospect of being acutely exposed to shame. Being forced to stand in job queues in India and Pakistan, or having job applications repeatedly rejected in Britain, Norway, and China, and having to publicly admit to such rejection in order to sustain access to welfare benefits in South Korea, were common experiences. In countries such as Pakistan and India where opportunities within the labour market were inextricably linked to the caste system, people from the lowest caste structures such as those within the Dalit communities were forced to take on the lowest paid and lowest status jobs such as cleaning toilets or sweeping roads.

A large number of interviewees from China had previously been employees of state-owned enterprises, enjoying high social status and economic security before their fortunes were completely reversed by the rapid privatization and marketization of the economy from the mid-1990s. Not having received training and lacking the skills demanded by this new economy, they related how they had been forced into low-paid, insecure jobs and were looked down on by society rather than respected as they had been before. In Norway, irrespective of their levels of skills and qualifications within their countries of origin, new migrants were met with responses from employers that their professional status was not transferable to Norway or that they lacked proficiency in Norwegian to be able to carry out such work. In order to work, therefore, they were forced to take on any job, lost all status and recognition, and felt unable to do anything about their circumstances. Those people who were forced to beg on the streets were constantly humiliated for it; those in casual labour were faced with having to constantly negotiate pay and conditions, akin to begging for work, with the employer having the power to employ or not to employ and to impose instant sanctions such as dismissal or non-re-employment.

Officialdom

People interviewed frequently reflected on how their interactions with officialdom repeatedly served to reinforce their sense of shame. Many spoke of the very public ways in which they had to admit to poverty in order to access assistance, processes which left them feeling that they had failed miserably to fulfil their roles as providers. In South Korea, people described having to prove to officials that other family members were unable or unwilling to provide assistance before they were eligible for the minimum social assistance support. People from China at regular intervals had to complete lengthy bureaucratic paper work in order to access *dibao,* requiring men to return to their wives' villages to prove that there were no family assets such as land or property to which they had access. In Uganda, people spoke of how they rejected and despised the degrading labels of 'the poor' and 'the needy', used widely in bureaucratic processes and policy discourse. This was so much so that many avoided anti-poverty programmes since, as one respondent put it, it was not worth losing your dignity even if the resources provided meant that you could access the requirements to support the family. In the same vein, respondents in Norway spoke of how being a recipient of social assistance (NAV) rather than the more prestigious activation programme carried the stigma of being considered to be particularly lazy or unsuccessful by Norwegian standards. The associated bureaucratic processes of the NAV meant that they were categorized into a six-step pathway towards work, through which they had to start at 'the bottom', ranked as being the most needy and dependent.

In Britain, people repeatedly referred to ongoing reforms in the welfare system, and the so-called 'crackdown', instigated under a new Conservative–Liberal Democrat coalition government. They referred to increased conditionality, checks, and controls around their receipt of benefits, which left them feeling blamed for their circumstances and mistrusted, as though they were constantly trying to scam the system. With few exceptions, interviewees spoke of how they constantly felt looked down upon, judged as inferior or 'just a number' by the bureaucracies responsible for social assistance. The one exception to this stigma of welfare receipt was in India, where corruption concerning access to benefits was said to translate into a certain pride associated with managing to successfully be included within eligibility criteria. The access point to various government-run support schemes in India is the 'Below the Poverty Line' (BPL) list, which is drawn up every five years. Reported widespread abuse of the list has meant that finding ways to be included is associated with resourcefulness and indicative of social networks and know-how. Having ones name included alongside names of wealthy landowners indicates a certain social status and level of influence with village heads who are primarily the gatekeepers of the BPL.

School

At school, children were exposed to others from more privileged backgrounds and were often the butt of jokes and spitefulness, particularly in situations in which differences between themselves and others were accentuated, such as in the school dinner queue. In South Korea and China, where as much importance is given to participation in extra-curricular activities (such as music and dance lessons) as attendance and achievement at school, parents interviewed were acutely aware of their inability to provide the same opportunities for their children as the wealthier families within their communities.

With all the inherent social pressures that came with education, unsurprisingly children and adults tended to try to avoid situations in which they might be subject to sanction or disapproval. Hence, avoiding school was a tactic cited by a number of children from different countries which, while providing a means of escape from immediate public humiliation, nevertheless contributed to their own isolation. While children were not interviewed in China, Chinese people not living in poverty believed that children from poor families might get bullied at school since, they claimed, children do not hide their prejudices. However, there was also evidence from Uganda which suggested that shame among children may have been more self-inflicted or anticipated than externally imposed. This was possibly partly explained by the alleged impact of government attempts to give universal access to schooling in Uganda, which had had the unintended consequence that universal schools were almost exclusively used by children living in poverty, their more affluent peers having been placed by their parents in the more select private establishments. Arguably, therefore, the space for shaming in universal primary and secondary schools on the basis of family income and circumstances had been reduced.

Nevertheless, school represented an arena within which shame was acutely felt. Running in parallel to the current study, some important pioneering work which has begun to examine the association between poverty and shame and its actual impact on children's learning attests to the salience of shame in learning environments. As part of the Young Lives Study, Dornan and Portela (2013) explored the effects of poverty-related shame on the educational outcomes of children in India, Ethiopia, Peru, and Vietnam. Questions used to elicit experiences of shame interrogated the extent to which children from the age of 12 years old felt embarrassment or shame because of the state of their clothing or lack of possessions. In all countries, except Ethiopia, reported feelings of shame correlated closely with declining household income. Moreover, children's achievements in reading, mathematics, and use of vocabulary were all negatively associated with shame after controlling for other factors such as household income and expenditure. At age 15, these achievement markers remained lower than among other children, particularly in India and Vietnam, where associations between learning outcomes and shame were highly statistically significant. This study nudges us closer towards a hypothesis that poverty-related shame may contribute to intergenerational poverty by inhibiting the acquisition of human capital, though this hypothesis evidently requires further investigation and analysis.

Money Lenders

Resources were invariably scarce for all respondents in the research, and being resourceful in order to sustain precarious livelihoods was an integral part of the experience of poverty everywhere. Yet inevitably there were times when shortages were such that people were forced to borrow money or other goods, a process through which they became indebted to others. Borrowing foodstuffs from neighbours and friends was ubiquitous, as, in rural areas, was the borrowing of tools and equipment. Relatives and sometimes friends were generally preferred sources for borrowing money but employers were also commonly relied on by domestic workers, notably among respondents in Pakistan. Few respondents could access bank loans to ease their financial circumstances, and so money lenders featured in the lives of many respondents across all countries.

People typically intensely disliked the need to borrow and feared its repercussions. They were necessarily under pressure to pay off their debts, which took priority in domestic budgets and reduced flexibility. Being in debt put lives in the hands of other people; respondents were in fear of the final demand, the landlord, the employer, money lender, or bailiff, and the sanctions that might be imposed, legitimate or criminal. People lost their reputations and their respectability. While many people admitted to indebtedness (in India, Pakistan, and Britain almost all respondents had outstanding debts), almost all regretted being in debt, not only for the pressures it caused, the loss of control over their lives, but for what they felt that it said about their ability to cope as people.

In all countries, imposed social sanctions were acutely felt by people whose circumstances were disadvantaged compared to others. Similarly common were the experiences of being overlooked, not being invited to events, and being publicly humiliated, be it in words or labels, or the non-verbal signals of distaste, disgust, or distant pity which were part of the direct experience of many.

The work across the different countries demonstrated how the experience of shame in relation to poverty is layered and complex. Poverty is experienced in real time as material deprivation but within multiple social strata which can either alleviate or, more commonly, exacerbate the experience, or in many cases simultaneously do both. A good example is the young woman in Britain who spoke of how she felt she had no voice in decisions about her children's education because she was a single mother, lived on a disreputable street, was in receipt of benefits, and had a son who displayed behavioural problems. Elsewhere too, the shame attributable to poverty was often merged and sometimes not clearly distinguishable from that linked to other sources of shame that in turn reflected or, indeed, contributed to poverty: class, caste, gender, desertion, widowhood, failure to produce a son, or impotency more generally were all sources of shame imposed by societies in different ways and which frequently coincided with and exacerbated the shame associated with poverty.

Classified Deserving or Undeserving

In all the societies studied interviews with people not living in poverty at the time of the research revealed that society drew clear distinctions between those who were perceived to conform to certain social, economic, and cultural norms or those whose identities were perceived to render them worthy of support (children, older people, people with disabilities, etc.) and those 'others' who were largely blamed for their impoverished circumstances. Hence, to lesser and greater extents, desert was meted out via a series of categorizations according to either individual or group characteristics, which were contrasted with the self and one's own ideas, attitudes, and behaviour.

No 'Work Ethic'

The importance of working and 'the work ethic' emerged as highly salient to the debate across different cultures. Inequalities are judged in terms of the work ethic, affluence is interpreted as being a product of ability and hard work, poverty the result of personal failings. Evidence from Britain repeatedly demonstrated the almost unquestioned yet mythical idea that poverty is inherently linked to not working and the consequent 'dependence' on benefits; the lack of work ethic therefore constituted the undeniable cause of such poverty. And while respondents in focus groups were keen to distance themselves from the language of the 'gutter press', which attributed labels to people in receipt of benefits such as 'scrounger' or 'benefit bum', they nevertheless used similar phrases to imply that they believed that certain people had become a burden on society, notably those, especially single women, who had large families, who lived on housing 'estates' in which everyone came to 'lack aspiration' and to gradually, like everyone else, get sucked in to the 'culture of dependency'. The idea that such 'dependency' had its roots in structural causes centred on the notion that the benefits system was too generous and so generated a 'lifestyle' of recipients typified by an unwillingness to work, having too many children at a young age, and a propensity to demand 'rights' but be unwilling to accept 'responsibility', a discourse that was highly prominent in the media analysis.

Yet arguably it is in Norway, a country bolstered by a relatively buoyant economy that is widely seen as being replete with employment opportunities, that the 'work ethic' concept is most prominent. Here, failure to thrive in such fertile economic conditions is perceived as tantamount to significant personal inadequacies and dysfunction. Such public criticisms, however, were used more sparingly than in other countries and were largely reserved for Roma people who were quite often characterized as 'sitting around', smoking or begging and being bound to 'their cultural traditions'. In China, where the language used to denote people in poverty was less derogatory than in other settings, shame was nevertheless similarly targeted at specific groups including professional beggars, former prisoners receiving social assistance, and able-bodied persons 'too lazy to work'.

'Lazy and Good for Nothing'

There were repeated assertions by the general public, the media, and politicians that those in poverty were lazy, ignorant, and profligate. Adult respondents in focus groups in India, for example, used abusive terms to describe people in poverty and talked extensively about their refusal to work or their immediate spending of everything earned on alcohol. In Pakistan, while there was recognition to some extent of the structural causes of poverty, focus group participants were still inclined to emphasize the personal inadequacies of those facing hardship, suggesting that the structural causes often provided convenient excuses for their 'lazy' predispositions; it was, after all easy to 'blame the government and the rich' for their circumstances. Likewise, the focus groups in Uganda often generated a tirade of abuse. Men suffering from poverty were not only thought to be lazy, drunkards, and unwilling to work, they were described as being 'arrogant, unprepared to listen to good advice', 'breeding every other year like vermin', and either impotent or promiscuous.

All Undeserving

In India, like Uganda, all people living in poverty were considered pretty much the same and broadly considered undeserving of state support; as such, those in poverty were not categorized according to any binary of deservingness in quite the same way as in other countries. It was, however, considered wholly appropriate that limited state support accorded to those in hardship should be inferior and of low quality. State education, for example, was widely perceived as substandard and served as a potent symbol to distinguish children from poor families. Furthermore, in Uganda many of the anti-poverty programmes, especially those directed at agricultural improvement, did not directly benefit the poorest families but were taken up by people who had land and therefore were in a position to gain from state subsidies and investment.

In India, there was clear resentment by the relatively wealthy about state-allocated subsidies to those in poverty, such as employment guarantees or hardship grants and subsidies, for example, those provided in the aftermath of the 2001 earthquake affecting Gujarat. These allocations were criticized for encouraging laziness and rendering those in poverty increasingly choosy about what work they agreed to take on. For those dependent on the labour of domestic workers and land labourers, they believed that these subsidies directly affected their ability to find workers and the nature of their contractual relationship with their employees. A view commonly expressed was that it had made labour more difficult to acquire, since people now had an alternative, and had eroded the hierarchy of respect, since they now had to persuade low-status people to work for them. Moreover, in both countries, those not living in poverty alluded repeatedly to the possibilities of economic growth and, in the case of Uganda, the recent discovery of oil. Unlike themselves, the more affluent argued, people in poverty were too lazy to fully exploit these opportunities and as a result were destined to remain in poverty.

The research was therefore replete with evidence of society categorizing individuals and, in some cases, groups of people, into those who have and do not have legitimate claims to sympathy and support. Such categorizations defined who was inside and who was outside of social constructions such as 'the community of value' (Anderson, 2013), the 'national community' (Conboy, 2006) and what has been referred to as 'the moral economy'; an indeterminate system which nevertheless dictates the relative legitimacy of claims that people make on society (Watters, 2007). Across the study societies, judgements were repeatedly made which pitched individuals against each other—legitimating or dismissing claims for assistance according to subjective assessments of moral worth. Moreover, the evidence suggests that such categorization and judgement are becoming increasingly a feature of collectivist societies such as China and India as they undergo unprecedented economic and social transformations.

Responses to Shame

All interviewees, no matter where they lived in the world, had aspirations for a 'better life'. They frequently saw the odds of achieving this goal to be irrevocably stacked against them, creating the sense of helplessness that so many respondents reported. The exceptions to this were children, who in India, Pakistan, South Korea, Uganda, and Britain all tended to show greater optimism about the future than their parents. Further research is required to understand these dynamics and how and until what age children and young people may experience some degree of insulation from poverty-related shame; or greater resilience to it.

Feeling Inadequate

On the whole, adults tended to be burdened with an internalized belief that they were responsible for, and somehow therefore the cause of, the predicament in which they found themselves, feelings which were rarely assuaged by persons and institutions with whom they interacted on a daily basis. We have noted how respondents in Uganda, for example, were acutely aware of how other people accused them of laziness, dishonesty, lack of focus, and unreliability. Similarly, in Britain, interviewees living in poverty spoke of how they were constituted in the media as a dysfunctional homogenous mass, considered lazy, liable to be criminals, 'dependent' on benefits, and prolific drug and alcohol users. Similar associations were made in Norway, where poverty in public and media discourse was said to be presented as synonymous with receipt of social assistance, unemployment, drug use, and being an immigrant. Even though respondents recognized these images and assertions as stereotypical and unfounded, they nonetheless contributed to internalized feelings of inadequacy, unworthiness, and failure.

Keeping Up Appearances

Faced with circumstances they had no control over and intensely aware of how they were perceived by others, people spoke repeatedly of the strategies they employed essentially to save face and to avoid the full impact of the imposition of shame. Many participants described their struggles to make the best of their situation by drawing on whatever practical solutions were available to get by, even 'swallowing pride' in order to go to the food bank, as one respondent in Britain described it, so that at least it saved the complete shame of not being able to adequately feed one's children.

As well as striving to make ends meet, keeping up appearances and appearing 'normal' at whatever cost were key preoccupations for people taking part in the research, even when this required them to pretend so that they could maintain a modicum of public respectability. This need is typified by the example of the young man from Uganda who felt compelled to pledge a sum that he could not afford in a community fundraising function in order to gain social kudos. When people did begin to pretend that things were better than they appeared, that they were coping and on top of life, they constantly feared having the reality of their circumstances revealed to others.

Anger

Respondents frequently talked of feelings of frustration and anger about their circumstances. Anger for the most part was generalized and frequently directed at the unfairness of systems and structure, at governments and politicians who were ignorant of the realities of poverty, and at the wealthy, who were seen as exploitative and uncaring. In China, people previously employed in state-owned enterprises were angry not only because their position and status had been eroded but because of the growing economic disparities emerging within the country, something which they had never previously experienced within Communist China. In Norway and in Britain, people felt angry about the unfairness of social assistance systems and, in Britain in particular, frustration was targeted directly at the Prime Minister David Cameron, who was deemed largely responsible for an increasingly punitive and degrading system.

Children were also prone to occasional angry outbursts when, for example, they were told that there was no money to buy them what they wanted or needed. But it was just as likely to be repressed and internalized as resentment, examples of which emerged directly from children and young people's accounts in Pakistan, Britain, India, and Uganda. Here children repeatedly alluded to the fact that they were deeply ashamed about their circumstances and even blamed their parents, even though they were aware how hard their mothers and fathers were working to do the best for them. Children and young people interviewed in Britain, especially teenage boys, often spoke about generalized and persistent feelings of anger, though found it hard to articulate its cause.

The academic literature suggests that anger is another manifestation of shame triggered by perceived lack of agency and the resultant frustration at not being able to live up to expectations (Stuewig and Tangney, 2007). Such anger might account for the uncontrollable rage and violence frequently depicted in many British social realist and modern Korean films. Yet, while the film and literature corpuses provided examples of anger being channelled into collective action there was very little evidence of this among the people interviewed. Instead, a sense of resignation was much more common, with respondents feeling that the forces against them were too great to be meaningfully challenged and that mere survival, or the attainment of decency, required all the energy that they had at their disposal.

Withdrawal and Depression

It was when people described the extent of their social withdrawal and self-imposed isolation that the insidious nature of poverty and its impact really began to emerge. Respondents in all seven national settings described stopping going out with friends or inviting people home to eat. Likewise, many began declining invitations to weddings, community receptions, and the like, since they were unable to afford to participate in such activities. And people also withdrew from family, like the woman in Pakistan who longed to visit her daughter but lacked the wherewithal necessary to buy the customary gifts that she should offer. Hiding, withdrawal, and what might be considered adverse coping mechanisms appeared in a range of guises, including alleged 'heavy' drinking of alcohol in India and Uganda, often bringing with it the toll of violence at home.

Accounts of 'depression' and 'low self-esteem' emerged as strong shared experiences, particularly in Britain and Norway, where they were named as such, but also in other countries, where there were clear accounts of retreat, social withdrawal, self-imposed isolation, and feeling 'sad', even if the language of depression was not applied. Just as film and literature often presented suicide as the ultimate retreat and escape from the shame of poverty, it was certainly a reality for a number of participants, particularly in Britain and India, where the association between poverty and suicide is increasingly recognized (Mathew, 2013).

Generating the 'Them' and 'Us' Binary

There were striking similarities across the countries of an acute need to create and sustain social distance, either by those who were being pushed away from the community of value and who were made to feel inadequate and inferior, or by the relatively wealthy who feared being contaminated by those in poverty. Hence the 'them' and 'us' distinction was powerful, though more so in some contexts than in others. People across the different countries knew about their own circumstances and how hard they tried to make ends meet, to provide for their families, and to maintain a modicum of respect within their communities. Acutely aware of the negative judgements that, it appears, are increasingly applied in contemporary societies to people living in poverty, they strived desperately to distance themselves from the pervasive associations of immorality, laziness, inadequacy, and criminality. Since people knew that their own circumstances were not from want of trying to make things better, they sought to deflect accusations made about themselves on to others who they believed were less hard-working or who abused welfare and support systems.

Many of the respondents receiving social assistance in Norway, for example, contrasted their commitment to finding work with the casual attitudes of others, such as 'immigrants' who were considered to not have the same moral fibre or attitudes as themselves. In Britain, there seemed to be a hierarchy of social acceptability based on work, work history, benefit receipt, family size, and migration or 'citizen' status. People who had worked in the past felt morally superior to those who had not; those who received benefits and considered themselves 'deserving' of support drew a distinction between themselves and those 'benefit cheats' that were frequently alluded to in the media and by politicians. And when all else failed, people pointed the finger at the 'immigrants', who were said to get priority housing over others and usurped them in the job market. Similarly in Uganda, house owners perceived themselves to be superior to squatters and to 'transients'. Other Ugandan respondents sought to demonstrate that they were upstanding citizens who coped in the face of adversity by comparing themselves to others whom they believed behaved badly, for example, by begging on the streets, not sending their children to school, or by being 'drunkards' and 'promiscuous'. Likewise, in South Korea, respondents were equally keen to distance themselves from those 'others' who behaved badly or who, unlike them, were classified as the 'worse-off' (the bottom of the hierarchy) in the social assistance programme.

Responding to the Poverty–Shame Nexus

The chapters in this volume attest to the fact that people defined as being poor according to local norms felt similarly about themselves and their circumstances irrespective of objective living standards. The volume as a whole points to the logic of embedding and continuing a debate about poverty which has global relevance. Currently, dominant measures and conceptions of poverty which focus solely on material deprivation tend to draw often irreconcilable lines across this global discourse between North and South. However, if we refocus attention on poverty's psychological and social consequences then, as we have seen, the commonality in the experience of poverty and its impact begin to emerge.

The research bore witness to the fact that poverty-related shame is internally felt but externally imposed, through dealings with others and officialdom and through public discourse, for example, that evident in the print news media. It suggested, too, that the shame attaching to poverty, structural in its origins, supports existing power structures and patterns of inequality. The research differentiated between shame, sometimes thought to promote social cohesion, and stigma, although it showed how both impose psychic pain and rarely achieve beneficial behavioural change. Indeed, a viable model emerges, consistent with the evidence collected, that the shame associated with poverty, reinforced by stigmatizing policies, has the potential to perpetuate poverty through its erosion of human agency as a result of lowered self-esteem and reduced social capital. This is captured in Figure 22.1.

Social psychologists suggest that shame is one of the most harmful of emotions because it has the power to sap people of any agency and leave them feeling unable to change their circumstances. It is especially potent because, unlike guilt, the feeling of shame is not easily allayed since there is often nothing that the person experiencing it can do to make things better. If social psychologists are correct, the poverty–shame nexus might help to explain the persistence of poverty. But perhaps more importantly, such a hypothesis suggests that policies which intentionally or otherwise exacerbate feelings of shame experienced by those facing daily hardship, rather than alleviate their situations, are more likely to make things worse by eroding any personal sense of control over their lives. What is more, if poverty is everywhere associated with shame, then shame, and its possible antonym dignity, might better facilitate a more comprehensive global discourse on poverty than one which is limited to relative and absolute measures of poverty.

The analysis indicates that shame is a recognizable social emotion across the seven national cultures with similar physiological and psychological

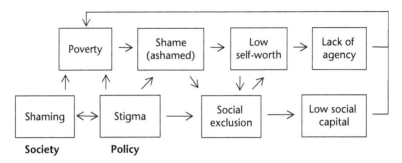

Figure 22.1. Model of the poverty–shame nexus.

Source: Walker (2014: 66)

manifestations. It looks and feels similar to the writers and film-makers that portray it from their different positions across the globe; is similarly endured by those who experience it in real life and real time; and there is a strong coherence between the accounts of those not living in poverty and what they feel about 'the poor' and the experiences recounted by the latter throughout the course of this research.

The evidence of the existence of shame in relation to poverty is compelling, we would argue. Irrespective of the level of deprivation that people endure on a day-to-day basis, their standing and 'face' in society, for most, appears to hold as much if not greater value than how much money is coming in to the household; therefore, much more is at stake when their social standing is jeopardized. However, if we accept this conclusion as the basis on which to promote appropriate policies and responses, then it raises a further set of questions and dilemmas.

If, as our work shows, the maintenance of dignity and self-respect are as important as material security in enabling people fully to participate in society, governments and others responsible for alleviating poverty must accept additional responsibilities in this regard. It is both morally wrong and likely, in policy terms, to be ineffectual to adopt the mantra that 'we have to put food into their mouths, no matter how'. It is, equally, inappropriate to believe that the polite delivery of inadequate benefit by development agencies is sufficient, as is the belief simply that the task is to persuade the public to accept people in poverty as equal citizens. Policymakers need simultaneously to have regard for the material, social, and psychological well-being of people facing economic and social hardship if they are to deliver effective and efficient anti-poverty programmes.

Importantly, in reflecting on the negative impact that such programmes can have on those in poverty—'the direct costs and losses involved in feeling—and being—stigmatised'—Sen himself (1992: 13) has pointed to John Rawls's

(1971) assertion that the maintenance of 'self-respect' lies at the heart of any laudable theory of social justice.

Thankfully, from the taxpayer's perspective, the financial cost of shame-proofing policies so that they enhance rather than undermine self-respect is likely to be negligible, although the challenge of persuading the public that people in poverty should be properly supported may well require political leadership of the highest quality. Welfare systems and programmes that continue to point to individual failure rather than addressing the underlying structures which keep people where they are can only be counterproductive. But perhaps even more importantly, we argue that there is a fundamental economic argument in appreciating the psychological and social consequences of poverty. If people's sense of self and dignity are eroded away by the daily barrage of criticism, vilification, and belittlement, then they have no option but to retreat into social and economic exile and, in so doing, may risk an existence of poverty in perpetuation.

References

Anderson, B. (2013) *Us and Them? The dangerous politics of immigration control*, Oxford: Oxford University Press.

Chase, E. and Walker, R. (2013) 'The co-construction of shame in the context of poverty: beyond a threat to the social bond', *Sociology*, 47(4): 739–54.

Clark, D. (2006) 'Capability Approach', in Clark, D. (ed.) *The Elgar Companion to Development Studies*, Cheltenham: Edward Elgar.

Conboy, M. (2006) *Constructing a Community through Language* London: Routledge.

Dornan, P. and Portela, M. (2013) *Childhood Experience of Shame and Human Capital*, Oxford: Young Lives Study, Mimeo.

Gubrium, E., Pellissery, S., and Lødemel, I. (eds) (2013) *The Shame of It: Global perspectives on anti-poverty policies*, Bristol: Policy Press.

Jones, C. and Novak, T. (1999) *Poverty, Welfare and the Disciplinary State*, London/New York: Routledge.

Lister, R. (2004) *Poverty*, Cambridge: Polity Press.

Lister, R. (2008) 'A Human Rights Conceptualisation of Poverty', International Conference on 'Exclusion, a Challenge to Democracy. How relevant is Joseph Wresinski's Thinking?', 19 December, Paris Institute of Political Studies, Paris.

Mathews, L. (2013) 'Coping with shame of poverty, analysis of farmers in distress', *Psychology and Developing Societies*, 22(2): 385–407.

Rawls, J. (1971) *A Theory of Justice*, Cambridge, Mass.: Harvard University Press.

Sen, A. (1983) 'Poor, relatively speaking', *Oxford Economic Papers*, 35: 153–69.

Sen, A. (1992) *The Political Economy of Targeting*, Annual Bank Conference on Development Economics, World Bank. Available at: <http://scholar.harvard.edu/sen/publications/political-economy-targeting>. Accessed 04/03/2014>.

Smith, A. (2009) *An Enquiry into the Nature and Causes of the Wealth of Nations* [1776], Lawrence, KS: Digireads.com.

Stuewig, J. and Tangney, J. (2007) 'Shame and Guilt in Antisocial and Risky Behaviors', in Tracy, J., Robins, R., and Tangney, J. (eds) *The Self-Conscious Emotions. Theory and research*, The Guilford Press: New York, London, 371–88.

Tomlinson, M., Walker, R., and Williams, G. (2008) 'Measuring Poverty in Britain as a Multi-dimensional Concept, 1991 to 2003', *Journal of Social Policy*, 37(4): 597–620.

Townsend, P. (1979) *Poverty in the United Kingdom*, Harmondsworth: Penguin.

Walker, R. (2014) *The Shame of Poverty*, Oxford: Oxford University Press.

Watters, C. (2007) 'Refugees at Europe's Borders: The Moral Economy of Care', *Trans-cultural Psychiatry*, 44: 394–417.

Index